Amazons, Savages, and Machiavels

Amazons, Savages, and Machiavels

TRAVEL AND COLONIAL WRITING IN ENGLISH, 1550–1630: AN ANTHOLOGY

EDITED BY

ANDREW HADFIELD

OXFORD
UNIVERSITY PRESS

OXFORD
UNIVERSITY PRESS

Great Clarendon Street, Oxford OX2 6DP

Oxford University Press is a department of the University of Oxford.
It furthers the University's objective of excellence in research, scholarship,
and education by publishing worldwide in

Oxford New York

Athens Auckland Bangkok Bogotá Buenos Aires Cape Town
Chennai Dar es Salaam Delhi Florence Hong Kong Istanbul Karachi
Kolkata Kuala Lumpur Madrid Melbourne Mexico City Mumbai Nairobi
Paris São Paulo Shanghai Singapore Taipei Tokyo Toronto Warsaw

and associated companies in Berlin Ibadan

Oxford is a registered trade mark of Oxford University Press
in the UK and in certain other countries

Published in the United States
By Oxford University Press Inc., New York

British Library Cataloguing in Publication Data

Data available

Library of Congress Cataloging in Publication Data
Amazons, savages, and machiavels: travel and colonial writing in English, 1550–1630:
an anthology / edited by Andrew Hadfield.
p. cm.
Includes bibliographical references and index.

1. Travelers' writings, English.   2. English literature—Early modern, 1500–1700.
3. British—Foreign countries—Literary collections.   4. Great Britian—Colonies—Literary
collections. I. Hadfield, Andrew.
PR1309.T73 A5 2001   810.8'0355—dc21   2001021697
ISBN 0–19–871187–5
ISBN 0–19–871186–7 (pbk.)

1 3 5 7 9 10 8 6 4 2

Typeset by Kolam Information Services Pvt. Ltd,
Pondicherry, India
Printed in Great Britain
on acid-free paper by
Biddles Ltd, Guildford and King's Lynn

In Memory of David Yarnold,
Exeter College Oxford, 1951–4

PREFACE

THIS book is dedicated to the memory of my father-in-law, David Yarnold, who died in the summer of 1999, after a long struggle with motor neurone disease. David was an exceptionally generous and kind man. He encouraged my interest in travel writing by supplying me with a large number of obscure and rare books that he regularly hunted out in the most unlikely places. I am sorry that he is unable to see something he helped to create finally appear. All profits from this book which would have accrued to the editor will be given directly to the Motor Neurone Society.

I would like to thank Jason Freeman for suggesting the project to me; Sophie Goldsworthy for being a patient and understanding editor, especially when a number of deadlines rather embarrassingly passed; Michael Brennan for a number of favours and invaluable advice; Telferin Pritchard for advice on the Latin translations; the anonymous readers at Oxford University Press who were constructive and helpful in their criticisms of the original proposal; The Leeds Philosophical and Literary Society for permission to reproduce the extract from *The Travel Diary (1611–1612) of an English Catholic Sir Charles Somerset*, ed. Michael Brennan; David Higham Associates for permission to reproduce material from the Hakluyt Society; The University of North Carolina Press for permission to reproduce material from *The Complete Works of Captain John Smith (1580–1631)*; The Irish Manuscripts Commission for permission to reproduce material from *The Irish Sections of Fynes Moryson's Unpublished* Itinerary; The British Library for permission to reproduce the illustrations.

CONTENTS

Contents

LIST OF FIGURES

All illustrations are reproduced by permission of the British Library, London, with the exception of nos. 10 and 11 which are by permission of the Bodleian Library, University of Oxford.

ABBREVIATIONS

ABES	*Annotated Bibliography of English Studies* (Lisse: Swets and Zeitlinger, 1994–)
DNB	*The Dictionary of National Biography*
ELR	*English Literary Renaissance*
HLQ	*Huntington Library Quarterly*
HMC	*Historical Manuscripts Commission*
MP	*Modern Philology*
PMLA	*Publications of the Modern Language Society of America*
SCen	*The Seventeenth Century*
SP	*Studies in Philology*
WMQ	*William and Mary Quarterly*

CHRONOLOGY

NOTE ON THE TEXTS

I HAVE silently modernized i/j, u/v, and long s, in accordance with standard practice, and I have also removed ligatures. I have tried to preserve sections of text wherever possible, but where passages of the text are omitted, the symbols [...] are used. I have generally included marginal notes and original footnotes; in the few places where these have been omitted, a note is included in the headnote.

GENERAL INTRODUCTION

STUDIES of travel writing, colonialism, and post-colonialism have moved from a virtually invisible periphery to the very centre of the humanities in recent years. Scholars, historians, and critics are vitally concerned with the questions of 'otherness' and 'difference', and the ways in which one culture perceives another. So much so, in effect, that the words in quotation marks in the last sentence have become self-parodic clichés. Some of the most vital contemporary debates have resulted from arguments among scholars of travel and colonial writing. Edward Said's books *Orientalism* (1978) and *Culture and Imperialism* (1993), have made a powerful case that Western thought and writing since the late eighteenth century have been predicated upon the conception of the stable and unchanging barbarism of the Orient.[1] Said has been criticized, sympathetically and not unreasonably, for his rather static conception of cultural interaction, with a hegemonic, active West imposing an idea upon a subordinate, passive East.[2] And, as James G. Carrier has argued, cultures of the East are just as adept at constructing images of the West.[3] There can never be a simple case of one-way traffic. Cultures interact, interrelate, and change, however powerful one might be.

This is, arguably, the central point in the writings of one of the most influential of post-colonial critics, Homi K. Bhabha. For Bhabha, colonial discourse is always invariably split. The colonizer's attempt to impose his or (rarely) her will on the colonized invariably results in the images and representations that the colonizer holds dear becoming transmuted and out of control, available for the colonized to write back. Power can never be monolithic.[4] But Bhabha has in turn been criticized for underplaying the gap between the powerful and the powerless and ignoring the Manichaean gap between the haves and the have-nots.[5] Indeed, many exchanges have

[1] Edward Said, *Orientalism* (London: Routledge, 1978); *Culture and Imperialism* (London: Chatto and Windus, 1993).

[2] Dennis Porter, 'Orientalism and its Problems', in Francis Barker *et al.* (eds.), *The Politics of Theory* (Colchester: Univ. of Essex, 1982).

[3] James G. Carrier (ed.), *Occidentalism: Images of the West* (Oxford: Clarendon Press, 1995).

[4] Homi K. Bhabha, *The Location of Culture* (London: Routledge, 1994).

[5] Abdul R. JanMohamed, 'The Economy of Manichean Allegory: The Function of Racial Difference in Colonialist Literature', in Henry Louis Gates, Jr. (ed.), *'Race', Writing and Difference* (Chicago:

centred around the question of whether two distinct cultures, however much one accepts that they might interact and transform each other through forms of contact, are, in the end, mutually exclusive, a notable example being the clash between Henry Louis Gates, Jr. and Tzvetan Todorov.[6] For Syed Manzurul Islam the process of travelling often leads to 'the performative enactment of "becoming other"'.[7]

Other debates and conceptual ideas have been introduced directly through the study of travel writing. Mary Louise Pratt introduced the term 'contact zone' in her analysis of Victorian expansion into Africa and South America. The 'contact zone' refers to 'the space of colonial encounters, the space in which peoples geographically and historically separated come into contact with each other and establish ongoing relations, usually involving conditions of coercion, radical inequality, and intractable conflict'.[8] Pratt's coinage is useful and helps to vindicate the arguments of scholars such as Karen Kupperman, who argues that English settlers in early colonial Virginia had a much more positive conception of the native Americans through an understanding of their lives and culture, than those who wrote about the Americas from the distance and safety of England.[9] Pratt also argued that women travellers tended to be less hostile towards the natives they encountered in the 'contact zone' and keen to question the ethics of conquest.[10]

Some of these questions and problems are more appropriate for the body of sixteenth- and seventeenth-century travel and colonial writing than others. There are, so far as I know, virtually no records of women travellers. Sir Thomas Palmer, in his *An essay of the meanes how to make our travailes*

Univ. of Chicago Press, 1985), 78–106. Useful commentary is to be found in Bart Moore-Gilbert, *Postcolonial Theory: Contexts, Practices, Politics* (London: Verso, 1997), ch. 4; Robert Young, *White Mythologies: Writing History and the West* (London: Routledge, 1990), ch. 8.

[6] See Tzvetan Todorov, '"Race", Writing, and Culture', and Henry Louis Gates, Jr., 'Talkin' that Talk', in Gates (ed.), *'Race', Writing and Difference*, 370–80, 402–9. See also Gayatri Spivak, 'Subaltern Studies: Deconstructing History', in *In Other Worlds: Essays in Cultural Politics* (London: Routledge, 1988), 197–221.

[7] Syed Manzurul Islam, *The Ethics of Travel: From Marco Polo to Kafka* (Manchester: Manchester Univ. Press, 1996).

[8] Mary Louise Pratt, *Imperial Eyes: Travel Writing and Transculturation* (London: Routledge, 1992), 6.

[9] Karen Ordhal Kupperman, *Settling with the Indians: The Meeting of English and Indian Cultures in America, 1580–1640* (New Jersey: Rowman and Allanheld, 1980).

[10] Pratt, *Imperial Eyes*, ch. 5. See also Sara Mills, *Discourses of Difference: An Analysis of Women's Travel Writing and Colonialism* (London: Routledge, 1991); Saundra Hybels, 'Travelling the World: Does Gender Make a Difference?', in Santiago Henríquez (ed.), *Travel Essentials: Collected Essays on Travel Writing* (Las Palmas de Gran Canaria: Chandlon Inn Press, 1998), 99–109.

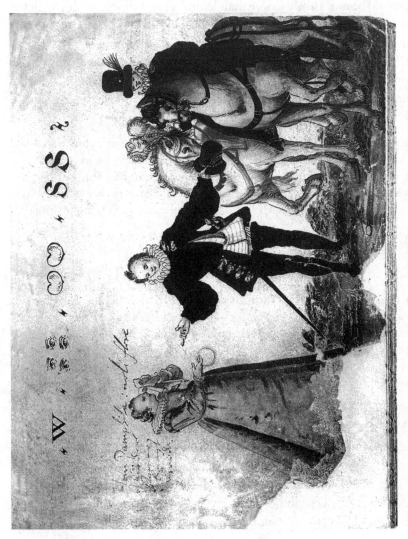

FIG. 1. 'The Departure of a Traveller' (MS Egerton 1222, fo. 44, British Library)

more profitable (1606), expressly forbids women to travel, arguing that they would be better to remain at home. Palmer's strictures are probably based on the assumption that women should not venture into the public realm unless special circumstances arose, and a fear that women, being the weaker sex, would be more likely to lose their identities and choose to remain in the counties they had visited (a constant fear of Palmer's treatise).[11] In fact, what tiny amount of evidence there is, would seem to controvert Pratt's conclusion that women were more sympathetic in their relationships with other cultures than men. The most frequently cited comment by a woman on another culture is Elizabeth I's complaint that friction between England and Spain had led to an influx of unwelcome immigrants:

Whereas the Queen's Majesty is discontented at the great number of 'negars and blackamores' which are crept into the realm since the troubles between her High- ness and the King of Spain, and are fostered here to the annoyance of her own people...In order to discharge them out of this country, her Majesty hath appointed Caspar Van Zeuden, merchant of Lubeck, for their transportation.[12]

Any writer sensitive to the subject of racial prejudice would clearly find examples in the 'contact zone' of home.

Edward Said has claimed that

The Orient was almost a European invention...[it] is not only adjacent to Europe; it is also the place of Europe's greatest and richest and oldest colonies, the source of its civilizations and languages, its cultural contestant, and one of its deepest and most recurring images of the Other. In addition, the Orient has helped to define Europe (or the West) as its contrasting image, idea, personality, experience.[13]

Said's study does not analyse the late Middle Ages or early modern period, but his comments can easily be applied to earlier travel and colonial writing. First, there is the case of Marco Polo, whose tales of the fabulous wealth of the court of the Great Khan had such a decisive influence on medieval and Renaissance travellers and helped establish a desirable goal in the minds of explorers, traders, and adventurers journeying both East and West (see below, p. 189). A similar conception of the Great Khan also

[11] On Renaissance perceptions of women, see Ian MacLean, *The Renaissance Notion of Woman: A Study in the Fortunes of Scholasticism and Medical Science in European Intellectual Life* (Cambridge: Cambridge Univ. Press, 1980), ch. 4.

[12] HMC, Hatfield House, part XI (1601) (1906), 569, cited in William Shakespeare, *Othello*, ed. R. A. Foakes (Walton-on-Thames: Nelson, 1997), 29.

[13] Said, *Orientalism*, 1–2.

appeared in *The Travels of Sir John Mandeville*, the other late medieval travel book which was to have significant impact on the Renaissance conception of the world.[14] Second, the descriptions of the Turks, Chinese, Japanese, and Indians, all fit Said's characterization of Western views of the Orient. They are barbaric peoples. Not savage and uncivilized like the Irish, most native Americans, or the South Sea Islanders, but cruel, pagan, and frightened of change, a pointed and instructive contrast to the enlightened, Christian, and dynamic West, keen to expand geographically and intellectually. Such representations are partly based, of course, on the West's own fears of powerful rivals, especially given the trade disputes over the Spice Islands (see below, pp. 208–18) and conflict with the mighty Ottoman Empire (see below, pp. 166–78).

Homi Bhabha's conceptions of the hybrid culture of the 'colonial space' can also be seen to operate in works written much earlier than those his study examines. The discourses of early modern travel and colonial writing are saturated with the fear of degeneration, miscegenation, and with the traveller refusing to return. Roger Ascham's vociferous attack on the Italianate Englishman is rooted in exactly such anxieties, and there was ample precedent for the religious and cultural transformation he described.[15] There was a related fear much nearer to home, and the problem of 'degeneration' was discussed in virtually all late sixteenth-century English treatises on Ireland.[16] Not all of the evidence is as straightforward. It is arguable that the hostility shown to the Turks and peoples of the Ottoman Empire stems as much from an awareness that cultural traffic was generally from Christianity to Islam as a simple desire to denigrate the enemy (see below, pp. 118–20).

It was also the case that many English colonists in the Americas merged into native society, either through choice or the necessity of moving from an agriculturally incompetent society to one in which people had a chance of survival (see below, pp. 266–78).[17] The discovery of the New World inaugurated a whole series of debates in Europe, principally in Spain, but continued in England, concerning the exact status of the natives. Were

[14] *The Travels of Sir John Mandeville*, ed. C. W. R. D. Moseley (Harmondsworth: Penguin, 1983), chs. 23–5.

[15] Felix Raab, *The English Face of Machiavelli: A Changing Interpretation, 1500–1700* (London: Routledge, 1964), ch. 2.

[16] See Andrew Hadfield, 'English Colonialism and National Identity in Early Modern Ireland', *Eire/Ireland*, 28 i (Spring, 1993), 69–86.

[17] Kupperman, *Settling with the Indians, passim.*

they, as some argued, the 'natural slaves' of whom Aristotle had written; primitive and lacking proper religion and civilization because they were an inferior people who could be exploited as the West required and desired? Or were they actually representatives of pure, innocent humanity which had become tainted by the fall elsewhere in the world, and so had much to teach the old, corrupt world of Europe?[18] Clearly this issue of 'natural man' is central to Montaigne's essay 'Of the Canniballes' (see below, pp. 286–95). It is also relevant to Thomas Harriot's *Briefe and True Report of the New Found Land of Virginia*, which included as an appendix a series of illustrations of the Picts and Britons, inviting the reader to consider the relationship between the ancient inhabitants of Britain and the peoples of the New World (see below, p. 266).[19] Obviously, we can connect such debates to contemporary discussions of race and racism, especially the arguments between Bhabha and Jan Mohamed, and Gates and Todorov mentioned above, even if we might need to be cautious about early modern conceptions of 'race'.[20]

But if numerous connections can be made between contemporary debates and forms of writing, and those produced four hundred years ago, we should also acknowledge stubborn and significant differences in some of their forms, functions, and purposes. We still have a conception of the 'Grand Tour', but it is no longer confined to the aristocracy or to European boundaries. Millions of young people travel abroad as part of their education, whether to see important cultural monuments, learn languages, or simply to experience the diversity of the world. However, as will be clear to the reader, it would be stretching a point rather too much to see the enterprise as straightforwardly comparable to Francis Bacon's notion of travel, or Thomas Coryat's explanation of the reasons for his expedition (see below, pp. 28–32, 33–5).

More significant are the specific historical situations which need to be taken into account when reading many of the narratives reproduced here. Sir Robert Dallington's description of France certainly makes a lot more

[18] See Anthony Pagden, *The Fall of Natural Man: The American Indian and the Origins of Comparative Ethnology* (Cambridge: Cambridge Univ. Press, 1982), for full details of the debates in Spain.

[19] Andrew Hadfield, *Literature, Travel and Colonial Writing in the English Renaissance, 1545–1625* (Oxford: Clarendon Press, 1998), 112–26.

[20] Colin Kidd, *British Identities Before Nationalism: Ethnicity and Nationhood in the Atlantic World, 1600–1800* (Cambridge: Cambridge Univ. Press, 1999), pt. 1. More generally, see Margaret T. Hogden, *Early Anthropology in the Sixteenth and Seventeenth Centuries* (Philadelphia: Univ. of Pennsylvania Press, 1971).

sense for us if we know of the brutal sectarian conflict in late sixteenth-century France and English fears that these could easily be reproduced in England (see below, pp. 46–51). Sir Charles Somerset, William Lithgow, and Fynes Moryson show that European society was invariably read in terms of such religious conflict (see below, pp. 64–97, 106–15). Sir Walter Raleigh's account of Guiana, his emphasis on the sexual restraint of his men, and his description of the mythical Amazonian warrior women needs to be read in terms of his relationship with Queen Elizabeth and anxiety about his won status (see below, p. 279). Thomas Harriot's account of Virginia requires careful decoding. On the one hand, the *Report* is a scientific, ethnographic account of a newly discovered people; on the other, it is a desperate, propagandist enterprise, designed to counter the negative reports of disgruntled colonists who had returned to Britain (see below, pp. 266–78).

As often as not, the observers tell us as much about themselves as they do about those they observed. The most striking example is probably Captain John Smith's account of his rescue by Pocahontas, which has become a foundational American myth (see below, pp. 303–8). Smith seems to realize that he does not understand the Algonkian society he has encountered, and consciously attempts to make sense of it in his own terms. The story can be read as a hopeful exchange between sympathetic humans able to make the effort to cross boundaries; or, as has been more common recently, as the tragic encounter of alien cultures.

This book makes no claims to be a comprehensive survey of English travel writing in the English Renaissance. There is, as there always is, far too much material to cover. Overall, my aim has been to present the reader with the representations of various areas, peoples, and countries which were available to contemporary readers. I have not attempted to include any material on the ways and means of travel in the Renaissance, except in so far as it is included in the first chapter on reasons for travel. Readers interested in such questions should turn to the works of John Stoye, Edward Chaney, John Parker, and Karen Kupperman cited in the 'Guide to Further Reading' for more information on such subjects (or, for an earlier period, Norbert Ohler). I have tried to include material which was in print and hence widely available, so I have included a number of translations—Richard Eden's influential version of Peter Martyr D'Anghera, material from Richard Hakluyt and Samuel Purchas—and not concentrated simply on English travellers abroad. There are, of course, some exceptions, and I have included extracts from Peter Mundy's observations of India because, although they were not published in the author's lifetime, they appear to have been designed for a wider readership and reveal more about Jacobean perceptions of India than many more limited accounts more firmly in the public domain.

Of course, there are a number of regretful exclusions, which I shall draw attention to as a means of forestalling criticism and in the hope of encouraging some intrepid readers to seek out the works in question. I had hoped to include extracts from Pierre D'Avity's large encyclopaedia, *The Estates, Empires and Principalities of the World*, trans. Edward Grimestone (1615). The work was clearly important, is unjustly neglected—Grimestone was a busy and important translator—and shows that a comprehensive collection of geographical knowledge was within the reach of many readers.[21] I also regret that I have been unable to include passages from Richard Knolles's *Generall Historie of the Turkes* (1603), which would have served as a nice companion piece to Leo Africanus's *Historie of Africa*.[22] Considerations of space dictated that only one substantial account of the Turks could be included and I opted for the colourful comments of Fynes Moryson. The same has been the case with William Thomas's influential *Historie of Italie* (1549), as there is quite a lot of material on Italy in the anthology.

I should also confess that I had originally intended to provide a broad sweep of the hundred years between 1550 and 1650 when I started out on the project. Again, considerations of space necessitated the choice of 1630 as a *terminus ad quem*. This means that I have had to omit planned extracts from John Evelyn's travel diary, John Milton's account of his formative tour of Italy, and less celebrated works such as William Brereton's comments on his tour of the Netherlands. There is never a cast iron reason why an anthology should start and finish where it does and whatever I claim here will be open to certain objections. I have started the anthology in the 1550s, because English consciousness of the extent of Spanish imperial and trading ambitions first began to take hold at that point with the marriage of Mary and Philip, stimulating a political and religious rivalry which was to define English relations with the wider world until well into the seventeenth century. I have finished the anthology at about 1630, soon after the

---

[21] For some comment on d'Avity and Grimestone, see Hadfield, *Literature, Travel and Colonial Writing*, 105–11.

[22] Both works, incidentally, sources for *Othello*. See Virginia Mason Vaughan, *Othello: A Contextual History* (Cambridge: Cambridge Univ. Press, 1994), 3.

death of James I (1625) and the publication of Samuel Purchas's expanded collection, *Purchas His Pilgrimes* (1625), the most frequently consulted source of information on travel and other cultures in the seventeenth century.[23]

Another problematic choice an editor has to make is how to organize the material selected. I have chosen to produce five chapters divided up into a preliminary study of 'Motives for Travel and Instructions to Travellers', followed by four geographically based selections: 'Europe', 'Africa and the Near East', 'The Far East', and 'The Americas'. There is a good reason for dividing the anthology up in this manner. These areas do reflect the practical Elizabethan and Jacobean perceptions of the world. The trading companies established at the turn of the seventeenth century, the Levant Company, the East India Company, and the Virginia Company, all correspond with the areas I have outlined in this anthology. I have attempted to balance the material as fairly as possible so that countries such as Italy, to take the most obvious example, are represented more frequently than countries and cultures that were less central to the English imagination in the early modern period.

This seemed to me to create fewer problems than producing an anthology based on chronology. However, given that I have only occasionally been able to include more than one piece on any one region or people—Italy, Japan, the Jews—it does mean that accounts of one region produced in, say, 1560, appear alongside accounts of another produced in, say, 1630. This is by no means an insurmountable problem, as perceptions and stereotypes often remain the same in the short to medium term. Nevertheless, I have produced a series of headnotes to outline the specific circumstances of each extract included so that readers can comprehend that travel writing does not exist in a vacuum outside the contingencies of history. One should not lose sight of the fact that England in 1550 was an isolated, second-rate power on the fringes of Europe, having lost ground in France and maintaining a precarious foothold in Ireland. Spain was the dominant force in Europe and when the two nations were briefly united (1554–8), it was hardly on an equal footing. In 1630 England was a major imperial power and had eclipsed Spain. James VI and I had virtually united the British Isles under English suzerainty. Rebellion in Ireland had been suppressed; an empire in America was developing; trade with Asia and the

---

[23] See James P. Helfers, 'The Explorer or the Pilgrim? Modern Critical Opinion and the Editorial Methods of Richard Hakluyt and Samuel Purchas', *SP* 94 (1997), 160–86.

Far East had become increasingly important. If English readers relied mainly on a few translations in the 1550s for their perceptions of other cultures, huge collections provided mainly first-hand accounts for a much wider readership by 1630.

Chapter One

MOTIVES FOR TRAVEL AND
INSTRUCTIONS TO TRAVELLERS

WHY did people decide to travel and how were they encouraged to regard other cultures? The answer to the first part of this question is, of course, that people travelled for a variety of reasons. Many aristocratic young men travelled as part of their education, to observe other cultures, to make contact with influential people at major European courts, to gain confidence in the ways of the world they were to inhabit in their adult life. While it is true that the 'Grand Tour', as it became known in the seventeenth century, assumed a greater importance and more central role in upper-class English life in the later seventeenth and eighteenth centuries, many influential courtiers and statesmen of the sixteenth and eighteenth centuries, many influential courtiers and statesmen of the sixteenth century went on long European tours as young men.[1] Their usual route was to travel through France and Italy towards Rome or Naples, stopping off in Venice and Florence, often returning through Switzerland, Germany, and the Low Countries.[2] From quite early on in Elizabeth's reign guides were available, which aimed to offset any 'perceived perils of travel' and 'turn it as far as possible into a controlled exercise, setting out itineraries and stipulating the conduct and agenda of the cultural

---

[1] See Edward Chaney, *The Evolution of the Grand Tour: Anglo-Italian Cultural Relations since the Renaissance* (London: Frank Cass, 1998), chs. 3–4.

[2] John Stoye, *English Travellers Abroad, 1604–1667: Their Influence in English Society and Politics* (New Haven: Yale Univ. Press, 1989, rev. edn.); Claire Howard, *English Travellers of the Renaissance* (London: John Lane, 1914).

tourist'.[3] The three most influential guides were probably Jerome Turler, *The Traveiler* (1575); William Bourne, *A Treasure for Travelers* (1578), and Justus Lipsius, *A Direction for Travailers* (1592). These were supplemented by translations in later works such as Fynes Moryson's *An Itinerary Containing His Ten Yeeres Travell* (1617), in which volume iii opened with a long 'Discourse of Travelling in generall', containing a series of precepts for travellers, a collection of opinions of old writers, and advice on the fit means to travel.[4] Works such as Thomas Palmer's *An essay of the meanes how to make our travailes more profitable* (1606), contain a series of elaborate charts to help the traveller plan out a route, learn how to observe the correct details, and take useful notes of his experiences. Perhaps the most succinct expression of such advice is Francis Bacon's essay 'Of Travel', which I have included here. As Michael Brennan observes (see below, p. 64), travellers to Europe such as Sir Charles Somerset, appear to have planned their diaries in term of the advice offered by writers like Bacon.

Not everyone was convinced of the benefits of travel. Many suspected that the motives of travellers were rather less pure than simply a search for educational enlightenment. All travellers had to obtain a licence from the monarch or Privy Council (in itself an indication of the desire to regulate travel). The document would note the period of absence granted, amount of money taken, size of entourage (tutors, servants, and travelling companions), and places forbidden to the traveller (most often, Spain).[5] As Felix Raab has pointed out, Henry VIII's close links with Italian courts and policy of encouraging courtiers to travel to Italy in order to increase the sophistication of his own court, led to a number of bitter theological and political disputes, as well as some spectacular defections, especially after the Reformation cut England off from most of the rest of Europe.[6] Moreover, the first serious analysis of Italy, William Thomas's *Historie of Italie* (1549), was produced with the purpose of using Italy to influence and alter English

[3] Anthony Parr (ed.), *Three Renaissance Travel Plays* (Manchester: Manchester Univ. Press, 1995), introd. p. 2.

[4] Fynes Moryson, *An Itinerary Containing His Ten Yeeres Travell through the Twelve Dominions of Germany, Bohmerland, Switzerland, Netherland, Denmarke, Poland, Italy, Turky, France, England, Scotland & Ireland* (1617) (Glasgow: MacLehose, 1907), 4 vols., iii. 349–499.

[5] *The Travel Diary (1611–1612) of an English Catholic Sir Charles Somerset*, ed. Michael Brennan (Leeds: Leeds Philosophical and Literary Society, 1993), introd. p. 14.

[6] Felix Raab, *The English Face of Machiavelli: A Changing Interpretation, 1500–1700* (London: Routledge, 1964), ch. 2.

politics, a project which was encouraged by Edward VI, but met with rather less approval from his successors.[7]

Of course, the question of comparative government was a thorny issue. If some, like William Thomas, showed an especial enthusiasm for states, cities, and constitutions which appeared to be far better run than England, then they ran the risk of treasonably denigrating their own country. Equally however, comparative government obtained through travel taught the negative lessons of how *not* to rule and mistakes to avoid (Thomas's *Historie* is full of such examples, notably in his discussion of Naples). Moreover, as authorities such as Thomas Palmer were at pains to argue, travellers could be made—indeed, should be made—to serve the state. When possible travellers should act as spies, reproducing maps, charts, and plans which would prove useful to their monarch.[8] Palmer is at pains to warn the traveller to police himself constantly, especially against banished subjects who will try to convert the unwary (p. 7). Palmer argues that some people should not be permitted to travel—lawyers and women—and warns travellers of the seductive dangers of Italy (pp. 17, 23, 43).

Attacks on travel were, in fact, relatively frequent, the most celebrated being Roger Ascham's irascible attack on 'Italianate Englishmen' in *The Scholemaster* (1570) (reproduced below). Ascham felt that travel served less to broaden the mind than to corrupt the body and soul, and advised those who really wished to be educated to stay at home and learn about other cultures from the safety of their studies. Ascham's attack was later reproduced by Thomas Nashe in *The Unfortunate Traveller* (1594), a work which relies on the reader's understanding that the hero, Jack Wilton, has a number of terrible experiences that are completely unnecessary, dangerous, and counter-productive. Wilton appears all the more culpable and foolish because he has been forced to travel to Europe and has witnessed horrifying events first-hand, so he should have acquired the knowledge that he is better off at home long before he actually does.[9]

By the early seventeenth century, there were a number of travellers who were neither aristocrats nor courtiers preparing for higher things. Travel had become less a means to an end and more of an end in itself for writers

[7] Andrew Hadfield, *Literature, Travel and Colonial Writing in the English Renaissance, 1545–1625* (Oxford: Clarendon Press, 1998), 24–32. See also Catherine Shrank, 'English Humanism and National identity (1530–1570)' (unpub. Ph.D. thesis, Univ of Cambridge, 1999), ch. 3.

[8] Thomas Palmer, *An essay of the meanes how to make our travailes more profitable* (1606), 20. Subsequent references in parentheses in the text.

[9] Hadfield, *Literature, Travel and Colonial Writing*, 192–6.

such as Fynes Moryson, Thomas Coryat, William Lithgow, George Sandys, and Peter Mundy (all represented below). Ascham's comments clearly
failed to deter them. The problem they all faced was how to publish their
work and make it available for a wide readership. It is clearly no accident
that the first travelogues published in the early seventeenth century (Coryat (1611); Lithgow (1614, 1618, 1632); Sandys (1615); Moryson (1617), are all
voluminous and eccentric works. Included here are extracts from *Coryats
Crudities*, perhaps the oddest of all these works (and, significantly enough,
the first published). It should also be noted that Moryson and Lithgow
both became embittered in later life as a result of their failure to become as
eminent as they felt their experiences and achievements merited. Moryson's feelings were engendered in part by the strenuous efforts he had to
undertake to get his *Itinerary* published. Much of it remained in manuscript.[10]

Intercontinental travel is perhaps easier to deal with as it generally had a
more specific function. The most common reasons were trade, exploration,
the establishment of colonies, and economic warfare (most frequently,
privateering).[11] What is clear from the extract from Richard Eden's lengthy
preface to his translation of Peter Martyr d'Anghera's *Decades of the Newe
Worlde* is how much the English were in awe of the achievements of the
Spanish in the Americas. Eden, writing in the reign of Mary I, argues that
the English need to copy the Spanish with whom they were allied by the
queen's marriage to Philip II of Spain. But if the Spanish served as an
inspiration for writers like Eden, they were later to be counted as Protestant
England's deadly enemies. Religious struggles and European politics were
never far away from debates about trade or expansion.

As has often been pointed out, no English colonies were established
until the early 1600s with the establishment of Jamestown (see below, pp.
239, 296–302).[12] There was a general fear that if British colonies were

[10] For a recent discussion see *The Irish Sections of Fynes Moryson's Unpublished* Itinerary, ed. Graham
Kew (Dublin: Irish Manuscripts Commission, 1998), introd. pp. 6–7 (I owe this reference to Garrett
Fagan).

[11] Two useful works are Lisa Jardine, *Worldly Goods: A New History of the Renaissance* (Basingstoke:
Macmillan, 1996), which explains the significance of various forms of trade in the 16th and 17th cents.;
and K. R. Andrews, *Trade, Plunder and Settlement: Maritime Enterprise and the Genesis of the British
Empire, 1480–1630* (Cambridge: Cambridge Univ. Press, 1984), an overview of the functions of the early
British Empire.

[12] Hadfield, *Literature, Travel and Colonial Writing*, ch. 2; Jeffrey Knapp, *An Empire Nowhere:
England, America, and Literature from* Utopia *to* The Tempest (Berkeley: Univ. of California Press,
1992), introd.

not established in the Americas, then Spain would dominate Europe and eventually crush the Protestant Reformation. Colonies would help to prevent the shipment of gold and other precious metals to Spain by providing privateering bases for English ships.[13] Spain would be unable to dominate Europe economically, or pay for her huge armies.[14] Equally important for other propagandists of colonialism was the conversion of native Americans, helping to enlarge Christ's Protestant empire, as well as the chance to export difficult and recalcitrant social elements.

Probably the key figure who argued this case and who realized the urgent need to establish a British empire in late Elizabethan times was Richard Hakluyt. Included here is an extract from Hakluyt's preface to his vast collection of voyages, *The Principall Navigations* in which he exhorts his fellow-countrymen to explore and colonize the world and so establish themselves as a powerful nation blessed by God.[15] National identity and colonial expansion turn out to be different sides of the same coin. The last extract included is that of Hakluyt's sometime disciple and collaborator, Samuel Purchas. Purchas's collection of voyages, *Purchas His Pilgrimes*, is even vaster than Hakluyt's. As the extract from the preface included here indicates, religion was still a significant factor in organizing and establishing the purpose of the voyage. But for Purchas, writing at a time when the threat from Spain had largely receded, the importance of travel in establishing the nation had disappeared.

[13] K. R. Andrews, *Elizabethan Privateering during the Spanish War, 1585–1603* (Cambridge: Cambridge Univ. Press, 1964).

[14] J. H. Elliott, *Europe Divided, 1559–1598* (London: Fontana, 1968), pt. 4; R. Trevor Davies, *The Golden Century of Spain, 1501–1621* (London: Macmillan, 1967), chs. 9–10.

[15] See also 'Discourse of Western Planting', in E. G. R. Taylor (ed.), *The Original Writings and Correspondence of the Two Richard Hakluyts* (London: Hakluyt Society, 1935), 211–326.

Richard Eden, *The Decades of the Newe Worlde, or West India* (1555), 'The Preface to the Reader'

RICHARD EDEN (1521?–76) was an important translator and civil servant. He became prominent at the court of Edward VI as a promoter of colonial enterprises, encouraging English voyages to the New World, translating Sebastian Münster's *Cosmography* (1553). While many of his circle went into exile with Mary's accession, Eden remained at court and translated Peter Martyr d'Anghera's *Decades of the Newe Worlde* (1555). The latter work is accompanied by a long preface urging the English to imitate and support the efforts of the Spanish in establishing empires in the Americas, inspired by the link between England and Spain through the marriage of Mary and Philip II. Eden translated further works in the reign of Elizabeth, including the posthumously published *The History of Travayle in the East and West Indies* (1577).[1]

The passage included here details Eden's admiration for the achievements of the Spanish and his hope to use the book as a means to spur the English—at this time allied to the Spanish—to follow their enterprise. According to Eden, the Spanish deserve to be compared to the heroes of ancient Greece and Rome, but have gone beyond their achievements in spreading true religion to the unenlightened. This suggests that, even if Eden's comments are cynical propaganda, he expected readers to take his comments seriously and be persuaded to help with the enterprise.[2] The emphasis placed on religion carries a certain irony, as the Americas were to become another battleground in the sectarian war between Protestants and Catholics in Europe. Equally telling is the attempt to refute any suggestion that the Spanish were motivated purely by greed.[3]

---

[1] On Eden's life, see David Gwyn, 'Richard Eden: Cosmographer and Alchemist', *Sixteenth Century Journal*, 15 (1984), 13–34. See also Andrew Hadfield, 'Peter Martyr, Richard Eden and the New World: Reading, Experience, and Translation', *Connotations*, 5 (1995–6), 1–22.

[2] For the argument that imperial expansion was based purely on the profit motive, see K. R. Andrews, *Trade, Plunder, and Settlement: Maritime Enterprise and the Genesis of the British Empire, 1480–1630* (Cambridge: Cambridge Univ. Press, 1984), introd.

[3] Text is from Petrus Martyr Anglerius, *The decades of the newe worlde or west India. Written in Latine and tr. By R. Eden [w. additions from other sources]* (1555), aii*r*–aiii*v*; ciii*v*–civ*r*.

[…] They have therefore deserved more trewe commendation whiche in buyldynge of cities, townes, fortresses, bridges, cundites, havens, shyppes, and suche other, have so joyned magnificence with prosecte, that bothe may remaine for an eternal testimonie of absolute glory, whose perfection extendeth to the gratifyinge of universal mankind as farre as mans mortalitie wyll permit. The whiche thinge whyle I consider, and caule to memorie howe Cicero defineth trewe glory to bee a fame of many and greate desertes eyther towarde owre citizens, owre countrey, or towarde all man kynde, and the same to bee of such excellencie that the owlde poetes for sume effecte fayned it to bee the sweete Ambrosia and Nectar wherwith the goddes are fedde, and that of such force that who so may drynke therof, shal also become a god, (that is to say immortall and happy) mee thynke verely that (yf man maye be a god to men as holy scripture speaketh of Moises and other) the kynges of Spayne of late dayes (if I may speake it without offence of other) may so much the more for theyr just desertes and good fortune be compared to those goddes made of men (whom the antiquitie cauled Heroes and for theyr manyfolde benefites to man kynde honoured theym with divine honoure) as theyr famous factes so farre excell al other, as I dare not speake to such as have not yet harde or redde of the same, least the greatnesse therof shulde at the first brunte so muche astonyshe the reader that he myght geve the lesse credite to the autoure of this booke, who neverthelesse hath moste faythfully wrytten this hystorye of suche thynges wherof he hath seene a greate parte him selfe (as being by the moste catholyke and puissaunt kynge Ferdinando appoynted a commissionarie in the[e]affayres of India) and gathered the residewe partly by information and partly out of the wrytinges of such as have byn (as Vyrgyll wryteth of Eneas, *Et quorum pars magna fui*)[1] that is, doers and parte of such thynges as are conteyned in the hystorie: as Governours, Lieuetenauntes, Capitaynes, Admirals, and Pylottes, who by theyr painefull travayles and prowes, have not onely subdued these landes and seas, but have also with lyke diligence commytted th[e]order therof to wrytinge: And not this onely, but for the better tryall of the trewth herein, have and yet doo in maner dayly sende from thense into Spayne such monumentes as are most certeyne testimonies of theyr doynge, as yow may reade in dyvers places in this boke. This newe worlde is nowe so much frequented, the Ocean nowe so well knowen, and the commodities so greate, that the kynge erected a house in the citie of Sivile (cauled the house of the contractes of India) perteynynge onely to the[e]affayres of the Ocean, to the which al such resorte for

Absolute glory.

What is true glory.

The kynges of Spayne.

Heroes.

The certentie of this hystory.

The house of the contractes of India.

---

[1] 'And in which I played a large part' (Vergil, *Aeneid* 2. 6).

necessaries as attempte anye vyage to this newe worlde, and lykewyse at

theyr returne make theyr accompte to the counsayle for the Indies for the golde and suche other thynges as they brynge from thense. It is therefore

apparent that the heroical factes of the Spaniardes of these days, deserve so greate prayse that th[e]autour of this booke (beinge no Spanyarde) doth woorthely extolle theyr doynge above the famous actes of Hercules and Saturnus and such other which for theyr glorious and vertuous enterpryses

were accoumpted as goddes amonge men. And surely if great Alexander and the Romans which have rather obteyned then deserved immortall fame amonge men for theyr bluddye victories onely for theyr owne glory and amplifyinge theyr empire obteyned by slawghter of innocentes and kepte by violence, have byn magnified for theyr doinges, howe much more then shal we thynke these men woorthy just commendations which in theyr mercy-

full warres ageynst these naked people have so used them selves towarde them in exchaungynge of benefites for victorie, that greater commoditie hath therof ensewed to the vanquisshed then the victourers. They have taken nothynge from them but such as they them selves were wel wyllynge to departe with, and accoumpted as superfluities, as golde, perles, precious

The benefites
that the Indians
have received by
the Spanyardes.

stones and such other: for the which they recompensed theym with suche thynges as they muche more estemed. But sum wyll say, they possesse and inhabyte theyr regions and use theym as bondemen and tributaries, where before they were free. They inhabite theyr regions indeede: Yet so, that by theyr diligence and better manurynge the same, they maye nowe better susteyne both, then one before. Theyr bondage is suche as is much rather to

be desired then theyr former libertie which was to the cruell Canibales rather a horrible licenciousnesse then a libertie, and to the innocent so

terrible a bondage, that in the myddest of theyr ferefull idlenesse, they were ever in daunger to be a pray to those manhuntynge woolves. But nowe thanked be God, by the manhodde and pollicie of the Spanyardes, this develysshe generation is so consumed, partly by the slaughter of suche as coulde by no meanes be brought to civilitie, and partly by reservynge such as were overcome in the warres, and convertynge them to a better mynde,

that the prophecie may herein bee fulfylled that the woolfe and the lambe shall feede together, and the wylde fieldes with the vale of Achor, shalbe the folde of the heard of gods people.

Even so may these barbarians by the only conversation with the Christians, (although they were enforced therto) be brought to such familiaritie with civilitie and vertue, that not onely we maye take greate commoditie thereby, but they may also herewith imbibe trewe religion as a thing accidental although neyther they nor we shulde seeke the same. For lyke as they that goo much in the soonne, are coloured therewith although they go not for that purpose, So may the conversation of the Christians with the gentyles induce theym to owre religion, where there is no greater cause of contrarye to resyste as is in the Juwes and Turkes who are alredy drowned in theyr confirmed erroure. But these simple gentiles lyvinge only after the lawe of nature, may well bee lykened to a smoothe and bare table unpainted, or a white paper unwritten, upon the which yow may at the fyrst paynte or wryte what yow lyste, as yow can not uppon tables alredy paynted, unlesse yow rase or blot owt the fyrste formes. They may also th[e]eslyer bee allured to the Christian fayth, for that it is more agreable to the lawe of nature then eyther the cerimonious lawe of Moises, or portentous fables of Mahometes Alcharon. If we were therfore as desyrous to enlarge the fayth of Chryste as to seeke worldly gooddes, why do we deferre to adventure that wherin we may doo bothe.

The conversion of the gentiles.

The christian faythe.

Roger Ascham, *The Scholemaster* (1570)

ROGER ASCHAM (1515–68) was a prominent teacher and educator, notable particularly for his prose works, *Toxophilis* (1545), a dialogue on the subject of archery, and the posthumously published *The Scholemaster* (1570), which outlines Ascham's educational principles.[1] Ascham is included here as a writer who sought to dissuade aristocrats from sending their sons on educational visits to Europe, principally Italy, as part of an early form of the 'Grand Tour'.[2] Ascham argued that they would acquire more vices than virtues in being exposed to the licentiousness of Italian culture and politics, and the falsehood of its Catholicism. It was more educational to stay at home and read books about Italy. Ascham's views are part of a long-running debate in Tudor and Stuart England and it is likely that the prefaces attached to the works of Coryat and Purchas are designed as responses to his statement.[3]

[1] For details, see Roger Ascham, *English Works*, ed. W. A. Wright (Cambridge: Cambridge Univ. Press, 1904); Lawrence V. Ryan, *Roger Ascham* (Stanford: Stanford Univ. Press, 1963).

[2] For details, see Edward Chaney, *The Evolution of the Grand Tour: Anglo-Italian Cultural Relations since the Renaissance* (London: Frank Cass, 1998).

[3] Text here from Roger Ascham, *The Scholemaster or plaine and perfite way of teachyng children, the Latin tong* (1570), 25–7 29–30.

I know diverse noble personages, and many worthie Gentlemen of England, whom all the *Siren* songes of *Italie*, could never untwyne from the maste of Gods word: nor no inchantment of vanitie, overturne them, from the feare of God, and love of honestie.[1]

But I know as many, or mo, and some, sometyme my deare frendes, for whose sake I hate going into that countrey the more, who, partyng out of England fervent in the love of Christes doctrine, and well furnished with the feare of God, returned out of *Italie* worse transformed, than ever was any in *Circes* Court.[2] I know diverse, that went out of England, men of innocent life, men of excellent learnyng, who returned out of *Italie*, not onely with worse maners, but also with lesse learnyng: neither so willing to live orderly, nor yet so hable to speake learnedlie, as they were at home, before they went abroad. And why? *Plato*, that wise writer, and worthy

[1] See Homer, *The Odyssey*, 12.　　[2] See Homer, *The Odyssey*, 10.

traveler him selfe, telleth the cause why. He went into *Sicilia*, a countrey, no nigher *Italy* by site of place, than *Italie* that is now, is like *Sicilia* that was then, in all corrupt maners and licentiousnesse of life. *Plato* found in *Sicilia*, every Citie full of vanitie, full of factions, even as *Italie* is now. And as *Homere*, like a learned Poete, doth feyne, that *Circes*, by pleasant inchantments, did turne men into beasts, some into Swine, some into Asses, some into Foxes, some into Wolves &c. even so *Plato*, like a wise Philosopher, doth plainlie declare, that pleasure, by licentious vanitie, that sweete and perilous poyson, of all youth, doth ingender in all those that yeld up themselves to her, foure notorious properties.

Plat. ad Dionys. Epist. 3.

1. λήθην
2. δυσμαθίαν
3. ἀφροσύνην
4. ὕβριν[3]

The fruits of vayne pleasure.

The first, forgetfulness of all good thinges learned before: the second, dulnes to receyve either learnyng or honestie ever after: the third, a mynde embracing lightlie the worse opinion, and barren of discretion to make trewe difference betwixt good and ill, betwixt troth, and vanite: the fourth, a proude disdainfulness of other good men, in all honest matters. *Homere* and *Plato*, have both one meanyng, looke both to one end. For, if a man inglutte him selfe with vanitie, or walter in filthiness like a Swyne, all learnyng, all goodness, is sone forgotten. Than, quicklie shall he becum a dull Asse, to understand wither learning or honestie: and yet shall he be as sutle as a Foxe, in breedyng of mischief, in bringyng in misorder, with a busie head, a discoursing tong, and a factious harte, in every private affaire, in all matters of state, with this pretie propertie, always glad to commend the worse partie, and ever ready to defend the falser opinion. And why? For, where will is given from goodness to vanitie, the mynde is sone caryed from right judgement, to any fond opinion, in Religion, in Philosophie, or any other kynde of learning. The fourth fruite of vaine pleasure, by *Homer* and *Platos* judgement, is pride in them selves, contempt of others, the very badge of all those that serve in *Circes* Court. The trewe meenyng of both *Homer* and *Plato*, is plainlie declared in one short sentence of the holy Prophet of God *Hieremie* [Jerome],[4] crying out of the vaine and vicious life of the *Israelities*. This people (sayth he) be fooles and dulheded to all goodness, but sotle, cunning and bolde, in any mischiefe, &c. [...]

Causes, why men returne out of Italie, lesse learned and worse mannered.

Homer and *Plato* joyned and expounded.

A Swyne.

An Asse.

A Foxe.

Hieremias, 4. Cap [v. 22.]

---

[3] 1. Forgetfulness / 2. Slowness to learn / 3. Senselessness / 4. Aggressive arrogance.
[4] Jeremiah 4: 22.

If some yet do not well understand, what is an English man Italianated, I will plainlie tell him. He, that by living, and traveling in *Italie*, bringeth home into England out of *Italie*, the Religion, the learning, the policie, the experience, the maners of *Italie*. That is to say, for Religion, Papistrie or worse: for learnyng, lesse commonly than they carried out with them: for pollicie, a factious hart, a discoursing head, a mynde to medle in all mens matters: for experience, plentie of new mischieves never knowne in England before: for maners, varietie of vanities, and chaunge of filthy lyving. These be the inchantements of *Circes* brought out of *Italie*, to marre mens maners in England: much, by example of ill life, but more by preceptes of fonde bookes, of late translated out of *Italian* into English, sold in every shop in London, commended by honest titles the soner to corrupt honest maners: dedicated over boldlie to vertuous and honorable personages, the easielier to beguile simple and innocent wittes.

1. Religion
2. Learnyng
3. Pollicie
4. Experience
5. Maners

Italian bookes translated into English.

I was once in Italie my selfe: but I thanke God, my abode there, was but ix. dayes: And yet I sawe in that little tyme, in one Citie, more libertie to sinne, than ever I hard tell of in our noble Citie of London in ix. yeare. I sawe, it was there as free to sinne, not onelie without all punishment, but also without any mans marking, as it is free in the Citie of London, to chose, without all blame, whether a man lust to weare Shoo or pantofle.[5] And good cause why: For being unlike in troth of Religion, they must nedes be unlike in honestie of living. For blessed be Christ, in our Citie of London, commonlie the commandments of God, be more diligentlie taught, and the service of God more reverentlie used, and that daylie in many private mens houses, than they be in Italie once a weeke in their common Chirches: where, masking Ceremonies, to delite the eye, and vaine soundes, to please the eare, do quite thrust out of the Chirches, all service of God in spirit and troth. Yea, the Lord Maior of London, being but a Civill officer, is commonlie for his tyme, more diligent, in punishing sinne, the bent enemie against God and good order, than all the bloodie Inquisitors in Italie be in seaven yeare. For their care and charge is, not to punish sinne, not to amend manners, not to purge doctrine, but onelie to watch and oversee that Christes trewe Religion set no sure footing, where the Pope hath any jurisdiction. I learned, when I was at *Venice*, that there it is counted good pollicie, when there be foure or five brethren of one familie,

Venice.

London.

Service of God in England.

Service of God in Italie.

The Lord Maior of London.

The Inquisitors in Italie.

An ungodlie pollicie.

---

[5] Pantofle was a form of fashionable slipper.

one, onelie to marie: and all the rest, to waulter, with as little shame, in open lecherie, as Swyne do here in the common myre. Yea, there be as fayre houses of Religion, as great provision, as diligent officers, to kepe up this misorder, as Bridewell[6] is, and all the Masters there, to kepe downe misorder. And therefore, if the Pope himselfe, do not onelie graunt pardons to furder thies wicked purposes abrode in Italie, but also (although this present Pope, in the beginning, made som shewe of misliking thereof) assigne both meede and merite to the maintenance of stewes and brothel-houses at home in Rome, than let wise men thinke Italie a safe place for holsom doctrine, and godlie manners, and a fitte schole for young gentle-men of England to be brought up in.

Our Italians bring home with them other faultes from Italie, though not so great as this of Religion, yet a great deale greater, than many good men can well beare. For commonlie they cum home, common contemners of mariage and readie persuaders of all other to the same: not that they love virginitie, nor yet because they hate prettie yong virgines, but, being free in Italie, to go whither so ever lust will cary them, they do not like, that lawe and honestie should be soch a barre to their like libertie at home in England. And yet they be, the greatest makers of love, the daylie daliers, with such pleasant wordes, with such smilyng and secret countenances, with such signes, tokens, wagers, purposed to be lost, before they were purposed to be made, with bargaines of wearing colours, floures, and herbes, to breede occasion of ofter meeting of him and her, and bolder talking of this and that &c. And although I have seene some, innocent of all ill, and stayed in all honestie, that have used these thinges without all harme, without all suspicion of harme, yet these knackes were brought first into England by them, that learned them before in *Italie* in *Circes* Court: and how Courtlie curtesses so ever they be counted now, yet, if the meaning and maners of some that do use them were somewhat amended, it were no great hurt, neither to them selves, nor to others.

Contempt of marriage.

---

[6] Workhouses, named after the Palace of Bridewell, Blackfriars, London, given by Edward VI to the City of London to control vagrants and troublesome apprentices.

Richard Hakluyt the younger, Prefatory Material to *The Principall Navigations* (1589, 1598)

RICHARD HAKLUYT the younger (1552–1616) was the first Englishman to collect together the travel writings of the English and publish them in a large series of volumes. The first edition of *The Principall Navigations, Voyages, Traffiques & Discoveries of the English Nation* appeared in 1589 and was dedicated to Sir Francis Walsingham, Elizabeth's Secretary of State for foreign affairs (1568–90), indicating the importance Hakluyt attached to his work and his hope of encouraging his fellow countrymen to explore and colonize the world. A revised and expanded edition appeared in 1598.[1]

Hakluyt's enterprise was carried out for a number of interconnected motives, as the extracts below indicate. Hakluyt was an ordained priest and he hoped to enlarge the Protestant community through encouraging Englishmen to convert natives throughout the world. He, perhaps more than any of his contemporaries, felt that unless Protestant England sought to enlarge its imperial domains, then it risked falling prey to the threat of the Catholic Spanish empire. *The Principall Navigations* was designed to exhort Englishmen to preserve their nation. It achieved this by presenting contemporary readers with a history of England's heroic deeds and so helped to construct a sense of national identity through the past labours of those who observed and conquered other nations and races, a potent reminder that no nation stands alone.[2]

---

[1] For details of Hakluyt's life and influence, see Alison and David Beers Quinn (eds.), *The Hakluyt Handbook*, 2 vols. (London: Hakluyt Society, 1974).

[2] For further comment see Richard Helgerson, *Forms of Nationhood: The Elizabethan Writing of England* (Chicago: Chicago Univ. Press, 1992), ch. 4. Text from Richard Hakluyt, *The Principall Navigations*, 12 vols. (Glasgow: MacLehose, 1903), vol. i, pp. xvii–xix, xxxix–xl.

THE EPISTLE DEDICATORIE IN THE
FIRST EDITION, 1589

To the Right Honorable Sir Francis Walsingham[1] Knight, Principall Secretarie to her Majestie, Chancellor of the Duchie of Lancaster, and one of her Majesties most honourable Privie Councell.

Right Honorable, I do remember that being a youth, and one of her Majesties scholars at Westminster that fruitfull nurserie, it was my happe to visit the chamber of M. Richard Hakluyt my cosin, a Gentleman of the Middle Temple,[2] well knowen unto you, at a time when I found lying open upon his boord certeine bookes of Cosmographie, with an universall Mappe: he seeing me somewhat curious in the view therof, began to instruct my ignorance, by shewing me the division of the earth into three parts after the olde account, and then according to the latter, & better distribution, into more: he pointed with his wand to all the knowen Seas, Gulfs, Bayes, Straights, Capes, Rivers, Empires, Kingdomes, Dukedomes, and Territories of ech part, with declaration also of their speciall commodities, & particular wants, which by the benefit of traffike, & entercourse of merchants, are plentifully supplied. From the Mappe he brought me to the Bible, and turning to the 107 Psalme, directed mee to the 23 & 24 verses, where I read, that they which go downe to the sea in ships, and occupy by the great waters, they see the works of the Lord, and his woonders in the deepe, &c. Which words of the Prophet together with my cousins discourse (things of high and rare delight to my yong nature) tooke in me so deepe an impression, that I constantly resolved, if ever I were preferred to the University, where better time, and more convenient place might be ministred for these studies, I would by Gods assistance prosecute that knowledge and kinde of literature, the doores whereof (after a sort) were so happily opened before me.

According to which my resolution, when, not long after, I was removed to Christ-church in Oxford, my exercises of duety first performed, I fell to my intended course, and by degrees read over whatsoever printed or written discoveries and voyages I found extant either in the Greeke, Latine, Italian, Spanish, Portugall, French, or English languages, and in my publike

[1] Sir Francis Walsingham (1532–90), Secretary of State for foreign affairs, 1568–90, was a noted Protestant who argued strongly for a foreign policy which helped co-religionists throughout Europe.
[2] Richard Hakluyt the elder (d. 1587), lawyer.

lectures was the first, that produced and shewed both the olde imperfectly composed, and the new lately reformed Mappes, Globes, Spheares, and other instruments of this Art for demonstration in the common schooles, to the singular pleasure, and generall contentment of my auditory. In continuance of time, and by reason principally of my insight in this study, I grew familiarly acquainted with the chiefest Captaines at sea, the greatest Merchants, and the best Mariners of our nation: by which meanes having gotten somewhat more then common knowledge, I passed at length the narrow seas into France with sir Edward Stafford, her Majesties carefull and discreet Ligier, where during my five yeeres aboad with him in his dangerous and chargeable residencie in her Highnes service, I both heard in speech, and read in books other nations miraculously extolled for their discoveries and notable enterprises by sea, but the English of all others for their sluggish security, and continuall neglect of the like attempts especially in so long and happy a time of peace, either ignominiously reported, or exceedingly condemned: which singular opportunity, if some other people our neighbors had beene blessed with, their protestations are often and vehement, they would farre otherwise have used. [...] Thus both hearing, and reading the obloquie of our nation, and finding few or none of our owne men able to replie heerin: and further, not seeing any man to have care to recommend to the world, the industrious labors, and painefull travels of our countrey men: for stopping the mouthes of the reprochers, my selfe being the last winter returned from France with the honorable the Lady Sheffield, for her passing good behavior highly esteemed in all the French court, determined notwithstanding all difficulties, to undertake the burden of that worke wherin all others pretended either ignorance, or lacke of leasure, or want of sufficient argument, whereas (to speake truely) the huge toile, and the small profit to insue, were the chiefe causes of the refusall. [...]

THE PREFACE TO THE SECOND EDITION, 1598

A preface to the Reader as touching the principall Voyages
and discourses in this first part.

Having for the benefit and honour of my Countrey zealously bestowed so many yeres, so much traveile and cost, to bring Antiquities smothered and buried in darke silence, to light, and to preserve certaine memorable exploits of late yeeres by our English nation atchieved, from the greedy and devouring jawes of oblivion: to gather likewise, and as it were to incorporate into one body the torne and scattered limmes of our ancient and late Navigations by Sea, our voyages by land, and traffiques of merchandise by both: and having (so much as in me lieth) restored ech particular member, being before displaced, to their true joynts and ligaments; I meane, by the helpe of Geographie and Chronologie (which I may call the Sunne and the Moone, the right eye and the left of all history) referred ech particular relation to the due time and place: I do this second time (friendly Reader, if not to satisfie, yet at least for the present to allay and hold in suspense thine expectation) presume to offer unto thy view this first part of my threefold discourse. For the bringing of which into this homely and rough-hewen shape, which here thou seest; what restlesse nights, what painefull dayes, what heat, what cold I have indured; how many long & chargeable journeys I have traveiled; how many famous libraries I have searched into; what varietie of ancient and moderne writers I have perused; what a number of old records, patents, privileges, letters, &c. I have redeemed from obscuritie and perishing; into how manifold acquaintance I have entred; what expenses I have not spared; and yet what faire opportunities of private gaine, preferment, and ease I have neglected; albeit thy selfe canst hardly imagine, yet I by daily experience do finde & feele, and some of my entier friends can sufficiently testifie. Howbeit (as I told thee at the first) the honour and benefit of this Common weale wherein I live and breathe, hath made all difficulties seeme easie, all paines and industrie pleasant, and all expenses of light value and moment unto me.

For (to conteine my selfe onely within the bounds of this present discourse, and in the midst thereof to begin) wil it not in all posteritie be as great a renowme unto our English nation, to have bene the first discoverers of a Sea beyond the North cape (never certainly knowen before) and of a convenient passage into the huge Empire of Russia by the bay of S. Nicolas and the river of Duina; as for the Portugales to have found a Sea beyond the Cape of Buona Esperanza, and so consequently a passage by Sea into the East Indies; or for the Italians and Spaniards to have discovered unknowen landes so many hundred leagues Westward and South-westward of the streits of Gibraltar, & of the pillers of Hercules? [...]

Thomas Coryat, Prefatory Material to *Coryats Crudities, Hastily gobled up in five monethes travells in France, Savoy, Italy, Rhetia commonly called the Grisons country, Helvetia alias Switzerland, some parts of high Germany and the Netherlands; Newly digested in the hungry aire of Oldcombe in the County of Somerset, and now dispersed to the nourishment of the travelling Members of this Kingdome* (1611)

THOMAS CORYAT (1577–1617), was, like Fynes Moryson and William Lithgow, one of the first British travellers who made strenuous efforts to have their work published and so can be seen as a pioneer of travel writing in English.[1] Like their works, *Coryats Crudities*, as the title indicates, is individual, even eccentric in style. Coryat was the son of a rector from the village of Oldcombe in Somerset and he makes much of his country origins in his work. He had been received at court by Prince Henry in the early 1600s and had a number of influential friends and acquaintances, including Ben Jonson, Thomas Campion, Inigo Jones, and Michael Drayton, many of whom used to meet in London to discuss literary matters. When he had difficulty in publishing his account of his travels, he persuaded many of them to write panegyric verses and eventually convinced Prince Henry to help have the substantial book published in 1611. In 1612 Coryat ventured to the East, travelling to Smyrna and Constantinople, before moving on to Persia, and India, where he died in December 1617. Part of the journal he kept was printed in *Purchas His Pilgrimes*.

Coryat is a problematic writer. He frequently represents himself as a fool, an impression strengthened by the panegyric verses that preface the *Crudities*. All too often he has been taken at face value, but it is clear that an astute intelligence is at work in his writing, although to what end is hard to judge.[2] Did Coryat have a serious political purpose that he was disguising (many radical writers were attracted to Prince Henry's circle at court)?[3]

---

[1] For details of Coryat's life, see Michael Strachan, *The Life and Adventures of Thomas Coryate* (London: Oxford Univ. Press, 1962).

[2] For one, probably overstated, reading, see Andrew Hadfield, *Literature, Travel and Colonial Writing in the English Renaissance, 1545–1625* (Oxford: Clarendon Press, 1998), 58–68.

[3] See Roy Strong, *Henry Prince of Wales and England's Lost Renaissance* (London: Thames and Hudson, 1986).

Was he an experimental author trying out new ways of writing? Was he attempting to make the new genre of travel writing appeal to readers? Or was the whole project a huge joke for the entertainment of his intimate circle? The answer is probably a mixture of the above.

Included here are Coryat's comments from 'The Epistle to the Reader' on the benefits of travel. These were later supplemented by a translation of Hermann Kirchner's 'Oration of Travel'.[4] I have also appended two poems from the vast collection of prefatory verses to give some sense of the eccentric nature of Coryat's work.[5] Scholars do not agree why Coryat's work is presented so individualistically; perhaps Coryat was trying to disguise a more serious purpose; perhaps he simply wanted to gain attention for his book and was conscious of its experimental nature; perhaps he just was eccentric.

[4] Thomas Coryat, *Coryat's Crudities*, 2 vols. (Glasgow: MacLehose, 1905), i. 122–48.
[5] Text from Coryat, *Crudities*, i. 7–9, 19, 41–2.

THE EPISTLE TO THE READER

[. . .] I was plunged in an Ocean of doubts, whether it were best that my Observations gathered in forraine countries should be continually confined within the bounds of my poore studie, and so at length squalere situ, & cum tineis ac blattis rixari;[1] or be presented to the view of my country, being (I confesse) by so much the more doubtfull to evulge the same, by how much the more I am no schollar, but only a superficiall smatterer in learning, and therefore most unwilling to incurre the censure of such severe Aristarches as are wont ὀβελίζειν[2] and with their censorious rods doe use to chastise the lucubrations of most kinde of writers. But at length post varias cogitationum fluctuationes,[3] by the counsell of certaine of my deare friendes I put on a constant resolution, and determined to expose the abortive fruits of my travels to the sight of the world (after they had for the space of two whole yeares lurked in a kinde of Cimmerian darkenesse) which if they cannot endure, but will be dazeled with the least glimpse thereof, I wish the

[1] 'To rot with neglect and to brawl with bookworms and moths'.
[2] 'To place a critical mark'.
[3] 'After manifold vacillations of [my] thoughts'.

same of them that elegant Angelus Politianus did of his Latin translation of
Homer, even that I might aut Thetidi aut Veneris largiri marito.[4]

Since then I have thus farre ventured with them, I will take occasion to
speake a little of the thing which begat and produced these my observations, even of travell into forraine countries, whereby I may the better
encourage Gentlemen and lovers of travell to undertake journeys beyond
the seas. Of all the pleasures in the world travell is (in my opinion) the
sweetest and most delightfull. For what can be more pleasant then to see
passing variety of beautifull Cities, Kings and Princes Courts, gorgeous
Palaces, impregnable Castles and Fortresses, Towers piercing in a manner
up to the cloudes, fertill territories replenished with a very Cornucopia of
all manner of commodities as it were with the horne of Amalthea,[5] tending
both to pleasure and profit, that the heart of man can wish for: flourishing
Universities (whereof only Germany yeeldeth no lesse than three and
twenty) furnished with store of learned men of all faculties, by whose
conversation a learned traveller may much informe and augment his
knowledge. What a singular and incomparable comfort is it to conferre
with those learned men in forraine Universities and noble Cities, whose
excellent workes we read in our private studies at home, as with Isaac
Casaubonus the pearle of Paris: Paulus Aemylius in Padua: Rodolphus
Hospinianus, Gasper Waserus, Henricus Bullingerus in Zurich: Amandus
Polanus, Joannes Jacobus Gryneus in Basil: Janus Gruterus, David Pareus,
Dionysius Gothofredus at Heidelberg: Joannes Piscator at Herborne:
Bonaventura Vulcanius at Leyden? Most of whom it was my good hap
not only to see in my travels, but also to my unspeakable solace to enjoy very
copious and fruitfull discourse with them. Againe, what a contentment is it
to a holy and religious Christian to visit the monuments and tombes of
some of the ancient Saints and Fathers of the primitive Church; as of
S. Augustine in Pavie, S. Ambrose in Milan? &c. Also the ἐρείπια[6] and
ruines of the houses wherein those famous men lived, as Cicero, Varro,
Virgil, Livie, &c. that are to this day shewed in sundry places of Italie,
strike no small impression in the heart of an observative traveller. Likewise
the places wherein divers famous battels have beene fought, so much

---

[4] 'To give a lavish gift either to Thetis or to Venus's husband' [i.e. Vulcan] (to throw into the sea or
the fire).
[5] The horn of plenty, the cornucopia (Zeus gave the horn to the nymph Amalthea, after she had used
a goat to suckle him).
[6] Ruins.

celebrated partly by the ancient Roman historiographers, and partly by other neotericke[7] authors (many of which I exactly observed in my short voyage) when they are survayed by a curious traveller, doe seeme to present to the eyes of his mind a certaine Idea of the bloudy skirmishes themselves. Yea such is the exuberancie and superfluity of these exoticke pleasures, that for my owne part I will most truly affirme, I reaped more entire and sweet comfort in five moneths travels of those seven countries mentioned in the front of my booke, then I did all the dayes of my life before in England, which contayned two and thirty yeares. [...]

To the Right Noble Tom, Tell-Troth, of his Travailes, The Coryate of Odcombe, and his Booke now going to travell.

Ben Jonson's Acrostic on the Author.

   T rie and trust Roger, was the word, but now
   H onest Tom Tell-Troth puts down Roger, How?
   O f travell he discourseth so at large,
   M arry he sets it out at his owne charge;
   A nd therein (which is worth his valour too)
   S hews he dares more then Paules Church-yard durst do.

   C ome forth thou bonnie bouncing booke then, daughter
   O f Tom of Odcombe that odde Joviall Author,
   R ather his sonne I should have cal'd thee, why?
   Y es thou wert borne out of his travelling thigh
   A s well as from his braines, and claimest thereby
   T o be his Bacchus as his Pallas: bee
   E ver his thighes Male then, and his braines Shee.

                                     Ben. Jonson.

To the most peerelesse Poetical Prose-writer, the most Transcendent, Tramontane Traveller, and the most single-soled, single-souled, and single-shirted Observer, the Odcombian Gallo-belgicus.

    Wonder of worlds, that with one fustian case,
    One payre of shoes, hast done Odcombe the grace
    To make her name knowen past the Alpine hils,
    And home return'd hast worne out many quils

---

[7] New, recent, innovative.

In writing faire thy large red-lin'd Rehearsall
Of what thou saw'st with sharpe eyes which did pearce all
Stone Tombes, great gates, and manners of the people,
Besides the height of many a Tower and Steeple,
Snailes, Butterflies, black sheep, black hogs, & Storks
And the neate use of eating meate with forkes:
And, that of stuffe thou might'st leave out no odd piece
To raise thy worke, th' hast writ o' th' Switzers Cod-piece:
Thou saw'st the Venice Donna's, & didst quarrell
With the Dutch Boore, thou saw'st the monstrous barrel:
But O thy temper! seldome wast thou drunke,
Nor hadst but one night's solace with thy punke:
Nor in thy pilgrimage wert much a sinner,
But when thou didst steale bread to save a dinner.
Thou in all sorts of travell hadst thy part,
But most on foote, and sometimes in a cart.
Nor didst thou scorne for all spruce Criticks mockings,
T' accept of gift a Prussians aged stockings.
Thow sawst the field of many a famous battell,
And home thou cam'st well furnisht with quicke cattell;
Yet must I say thy fortune therein was ill,
For thou wentst nak't to wash thy shirt at Basil;
And having seene Cloysters, and many a Monke,
Becam'st thy selfe a Recluse in a trunke.

    But I'le not write thy labours Inventory,
    I'le say but this of thee, and of thy story,
    Thou well describ'st the marvels thou didst see,
    And this thy booke as well describeth thee.

Laurence
Whitaker

Francis Bacon, 'Of Travel' (1612)

FRANCIS BACON (1561–1626) was a politician, writer, and scientist, championing an empirical method based on the observation of natural phenomena and performance of experiments. He had a meteoric rise as a politician, before his career was abruptly ended by a charge of corruption in 1621. Thereafter, he devoted most of his attention to writing.

Bacon's *Essays* were obviously important to their author as three editions were published in his lifetime; the first edition, containing ten essays, appeared in 1587 and was reprinted in 1598 and 1606; the second, containing thirty-eight essays, with many of the originals carefully revised, appeared in 1612, and was reprinted five times subsequently; the third, from which the text included here comes (although the essay was first published in the second edition), was published in 1625, and contained fifty-eight essays, with further revisions. It is significant that Bacon saw fit to include an essay on travel—by which he clearly means European travel—in 1625. This indicates that the 'Grand Tour' was obviously already an established part of the education of many young aristocrats.[1] Bacon clearly expects his readers to enjoy a studious and educational experience, as his suggested itinerary indicates. Also significant are Bacon's comments on the danger of young men changing 'country manners for those of foreign parts', suggesting that Ascham's fears never really went away.[2]

[1] An early date for the 'Grand Tour' is established in Edward Chaney, *The Evolution of the Grand Tour: Anglo-Italian Cultural Relations since the Renaissance* (London: Frank Cass, 1998), chs. 3–4.
[2] Text from Francis Bacon, *Essayes* (1625), 100–4.

Travaile, in the younger Sort, is a Part of Education; In the Elder, a Part of Experience. He that *travaileth* into a Country, before he hath some Entrance into the Language, goeth to *Schoole*, and not to *Travaile*. That Young Men travaile under some Tutor, or grave Servant, I allow well; So that he be such a one, that hath the Language, and hath been in the Country before; whereby he may be able to tell them, what Things are worthy to be seene in the Country where they goe; what Acquaintances they are to seeke; What Exercises or discipline the Place yeeldeth. For else young Men shall goe hooded, and looke abroad little. It is a strange Thing, that in Sea voyages, where there is nothing to be seene, but Sky and Sea,

Men should make Diaries; But in *Land-Travile*, wherin so much is to be observed, for the most part, they omit it; As if Chance, were fitter to be registred, then Observation. Let Diaries, therefore, be brought in use. The Things to be seene and observed are. The Courts of Princes, specially when they give Audience to Ambassadours: The Courts of Justice, while they sit and heare Causes; And so of Consistories Ecclesiasticke: The Churches, and Monasteries, with the Monuments which are therein extant: The Wals and Fortifications of Cities and Townes; And so the Havens & Harbours: Antiquities, and Ruines: Libraries; Colledges, Disputations, and Lectures, where any are: Shipping and Navies: Houses, and Gardens of State, and Pleasure, neare great Cities: Armories: Arsenals: Magazens: Exchanges: Burses; Ware-houses: Exercises of Horseman-ship; Fencing; Trayning of Souldiers; and the like: Comedies; Such wherunto the better Sort of persons doe resort; Treasuries of Jewels, and Robes; Cabinets, and Rarities: And to conclude, whatsoever is memorable in the Places; where they goe. After all which, the Tutors or Servants, ought to make diligent Enquirie. As for Triumphs; Masques; Feasts; Weddings; Funeralls; Capitall Execu-ons; and such Shewes; Men need not to be put in minde of them; Yet are they not to be neglected. If you will have a Young Man, to put his *Travaile*, into a little Roome, and in short time, to gather much, this you must doe. First, as was said, he must have some Entrance into the Language, before he goeth. Then he must have such a Servant, or Tutor, as knoweth the Country, as was likewise said. Let him carry with him also some Card or Booke describing the Country, where he travelleth; which will be a good Key to his Enquiry. Let him keepe also a Diary. Let him not stay long in one Citty, or Towne; More or lesse as the place deserveth, but not long: Nay, when he stayeth in one City or Towne, let him change his Lodging, from one End and Part of the Towne, to another; which is a great Adamant of Acquaintance. Let him sequester himselfe from the Company of his Country men, and diet in such Places, where there is good Company of the Nation, where he travaileth. Let him upon his Removes, from one place to another, procure Recommendation, to some person of Quality, residing in the Place, whither he removeth; that he may use his Favour, in those things, he desireth to see or know. Thus he may abridge his *Travaile*, with much profit. As for the acquaintance, which is to be sought in *Travaile*; That which is most of all profitable, is Acquaintance with the Secretaries, and Employd Men of Ambassadours; For so in *Travailing* in one Country he shall sucke the Experience of many. Let him also see and visit, Eminent

Persons, in all Kindes, which are of great Name abroad; That he may be able to tell, how the Life agreeth with the Fame. For Quarels, they are with Care and Discretion to be avoided: They are, commonly, for Mistresses; Healths; Place; and Words. And let a Man beware, how he keepeth Company, with Cholerick and Quarelsome Persons; for they will engage him into their owne Quarels. When a *Travailer* returneth home, let him not leave the Countries, where he hath *Travailed*, altogether behinde him; But maintaine a Correspondence, by letters, with those of his Acquaintance, which are of most Worth. And let his *Travaile* appeare rather in his Discourse, then in his Apparrell, or Gesture: And in his Discourse, let him be rather advised in his Answers, then forwards to tell Stories: And let it appeare, that he doth not change his Country Manners, for those of Forraigne Parts; But onely, prick in some Flowers, of that he hath Learned abroad, into the Customes of his owne Country.

Samuel Purchas, *Hakluytus Posthumus or Purchas His Pilgrimes Contayning a History of the World in Sea Voyages and Lande Travells by Englishmen and others* (1625), 'Epistle to the Reader'

SAMUEL PURCHAS (*c*.1577–1626) was a divine who took it upon himself to expand Richard Hakluyt's *Principall Navigations*.[1] Purchas has not had a good press. He was not a traveller himself (like Hakluyt); in gathering materials from Hakluyt he managed to fall out spectacularly with his mentor; he has generally been regarded as an inferior scholar to the cautious Hakluyt, taking liberties with texts, clouding a coherent enterprise with his own strange agenda, and expressing his ideas poorly when he had to provide links in the narrative.[2]

Purchas reorganized Hakluyt's work so that it no longer sought to represent and define the glories of a nation (see above, pp. 24–7). He included material describing the activities of explorers from other countries so that the collection was transformed into an encyclopaedia of travel since the world began. The first extract described how King Solomon established a navy, an event which Purchas read in terms of medieval theories of fourfold allegory in the Bible, whereby 'Every Christian man is a ship, a weake vessell, in this Navie of Solomon'.[3] In essence, Purchas sees travel as an allegory of man's fate on earth in line with the long-established Christian tradition of *peregrinatio*, seeing life as a journey towards the final destination of the afterlife.[4] *Purchas His Pilgrimes* set out to be a reference work based on the principle that travel was interesting because it was central to human life, as a reality and an allegory. Included here are extracts from the prefatory letter 'To the Reader', which set out Purchas's ideas and principles. Purchas writes in a style as eccentric as that of Coryat (see above, pp. 28–32), representing his work as simultaneously comprehensive and a collection of curiosities, a *wunderkammer*.[5] Like Ascham (see above,

---

[1] For details of Purchas's life, see *DNB* entry.

[2] A recent, more sympathetic evaluation of Purchas is provided in James P. Helfers, 'The Explorer or the Pilgrim? Modern Critical Opinion and the Editorial Methods of Richard Hakluyt and Samuel Purchas', *SP* 94 (1997), 160–86.

[3] Samuel Purchas, *Hakluytus Posthumous or Purchas His Pilgrimes*, 20 vols. (Glasgow: MacLehose, 1905–7), i. 6.

[4] See C. L. Wrenn, *A Study of Old English Literature* (London: Harrap, 1967), 148.

[5] See Steven Mulaney, 'Strange Things, Gross Terms, Curious Customs: The Rehearsal of Cultures in the Late Renaissance', in Stephen Greenblatt (ed.), *Representing the English Renaissance* (Berkeley: Univ. of California Press, 1988), 65–92.

pp. 20–3), Purchas is well aware of the dangers and temptations of exotic lands, and argues that his work serves as a substitute for travel, a sort of prophylactic or substitute.[6]

[6] Text from Purchas, *Purchas His Pilgrimes*, vol. i, pp. xl–xliv.

[...] What a World of Travellers have by their owne eyes observed in this kinde, is here (for the most part in their owne words transcribed or translated) delivered, not by one professing Methodically to deliver the Historie of Nature according to rules of Art, nor Philosophically to discusse and dispute; but as in way of Discourse, by each Traveller relating what in that kind he hath seene. And as David prepared materials for Salomons Temple; or (if that be too arrogant) as Alex[ander] furnished Aristotle with Huntsmen and Observers of Creatures, to acquaint him with their diversified kinds and natures; or (if that also seeme too ambitious) as Sense by Induction of particulars yeeldeth the premisses to Reasons Syllogisticall arguing; or if we shall be yet more homely, as Pioners are employed by Enginers, and Labourers serve Masons, and Bricklayers, and these the best Surveyers and Architects: so here Purchas and his Pilgrimes minister individuall and sensible materials (as it were with Stones, Brickes and Mortar) to those universall Speculators for their Theoricall structures. And well may the Author be ranked with such Labourers (howsoever here a Master-builder also) for that he hath beene forced as much to the Hod, Barrow and Trowel, as to contemplative survaying: neither in so many Labyrinthian Perambulations thorow, and Circumnavigations about the World in this and his other Workes, was ever enabled to maintaine a Vicarian or Subordinate Scribe, but his own hands to worke, as well as his head to contrive these voluminous Buildings; except in some few Transcriptions or Translations, the most also of them by his sonne S.P. that one and the same name might both father and further the whole. [...]

What kinde of Naturall Historie this is.

I also have beene an Athenian with these Athenians, one delighting to tell, the others to heare some new thing. I have therefore either wholly ommitted or passed dry foot things neere and common; Far fetched and deare bought are the Lettice sutable to our lips. Common and ordinarie plants I remit to the Herbarists. Europaean Rarities (except in the remoter

Regions both from our habitation and knowledge, as Island, Norway, Sueden, Constantinople, the Mediterranean Ilands, &c.) to the Historians peculiar to each Countrey therein. My Genius delights rather in by-wayes then high-wayes, and hath therein by Tracts and Tractates of Travellers made Causies and High-wayes, every where disposing these Pilgrime-Guides, that men without feare may travell to and over the most uncouth Countries of the World: and there be shewed with others Eyes, the Rarities of Nature, and of such things also as are not against Nature, but either above it, as Miracles, or beside the ordinarie course of it, in the extraordinary Wonders, which Gods Providence hath therein effected according to his good and just pleasure. And thus much for the workes of God.

Things humane, are such as Men are, or have, or have done or suffered in the World. Here therefore the various Nations, Persons, Shapes, Colours, Habits, Rites, Religions, Complexions, Conditions, Politike and Oeconomike Customes, Languages, Letters, Arts, Merchandises, Wares, and other remarkeable Varieties of Men and humane Affaires are by Eye-witnesses related more amply and certainly then any Collector ever hath done, or perhaps without these helpes could doe. And thus we have shewed the scope of the Author, and profitable use of the Worke: which could not but be voluminous, having a World for the subject, and a World of Witnesses for the Evidence: and yet (except where the Author or Worke it selfe permitted not) these vast Volumes are contracted, and Epitomised, that the nicer Reader might not be cloyed. Here also both Elephants may swimme in deepe voluminous Seas, and such as want either lust or leisure, may single out, as in a Library of Bookes, what Author or Voyage shall best fit to his profit or pleasure. I might adde that such a Worke may seeme necessarie to these times, wherein not many Scholers are so studious of Geographie, and of Naturall and Universall knowledge in the diversified varieties which the various Seas and Lands in the World produce, seeming as exceptions to Generall Rules, which Aristotle the best Scholer in Natures Schoole and her principall Secretarie could not so punctually and individually see in the Ocean, the Remoter Lands and New Worlds, none of which he ever saw, nor till this last Age were knowne. And for the most part, those which are studious know not either to get, or to read the Authors of this kinde, of which so few speake Latine.

As for Gentlemen, Travell is accounted an excellent Ornament to them; and therefore many of them comming to their Lands sooner then to their Wits, adventure themselves to see the Fashions of other Countries, where their soules and bodies find temptations to a twofold Whoredom, whence they see the World as Adam had knowledge of good and evill, with the losse or lessening of their estate in this English (and perhaps also in the heavenly Paradise) & bring home a few smattering termes, flattering garbes, Apish crings, foppish fancies, foolish guises and disguises, the vanities of Neighbour Nations (I name not Naples) without furthering of their knowledge of God, the World, or themselves. I speake not against Travell, so usefull to usefull men, I honour the industrious of the liberall and ingenuous in arts, bloud, education: and to prevent exorbitancies of the other, which cannot travell farre, or are in danger to travell from God and themselves, at no great charge I offer a World of Travellers to their domestike entertainment, easie to be spared from their Smoke, Cup, or Butter-flie vanities and superfluities, and fit mutually to entertaine them in a better Schoole to better purposes. [...]

Chapter Two

EUROPE

Most English travellers in the sixteenth and seventeenth centuries went, of course, to their nearest neighbours. Contact was frequent in a variety of ways with France, Germany, the Netherlands, Spain, and, most important of all in the English imagination, Italy. England was always keen to be involved in European affairs, whatever reputation it had for seeking isolation and whatever arguments there were for going it alone. Henry VIII was keen to establish extensive contact with both Burgundian courts and culture as well as Italy in order to Europeanize England and make it more sophisticated, in line with the rest of Europe.[1] Numerous intellectuals were sent to study in Italian courts—something which proved to be a considerable problem after the religious divisions inaugurated by the Reformation—and the French and Italian influence on English art, music, and literature is clear throughout the century.[2]

Edward VI, certainly during the Protectorship of Edward Seymour, duke of Somerset (1548–51), was keen to continue Henry's European connections.[3] A significant work published during Edward's reign was William Thomas's *Historie of Italie* (1549). Thomas, who was either Welsh or of Welsh extraction, had lived in Italy since 1544 following a scandal.[4] He

[1] Maria Dowling, *Humanism in the Age of Henry VIII* (London: Croom Helm, 1986); Gordon Kipling, *The Triumph of Honour: Burgundian Origins of the Elizabethan Renaissance* (Leiden: Sir Thomas Browne Institute, 1977).

[2] See Roy Strong, *Artists of the Tudor Court: The Portrait Miniature Rediscovered, 1520–1620* (London: Victoria and Albert Museum, 1983), and *The English Icon: Elizabethan and Jacobean Portraiture* (New York: Pantheon, 1969); John Stevens, *Music and Poetry in the Early Tudor Court* (London: Methuen, 1961); Joel E. Spingarn, *Literary Criticism in the Renaissance* (New York: Harbinger, 1963), pt. 3.

[3] W. K. Jordan, *Edward VI: The Young King* (Cambridge, Mass.: Harvard Univ. Press, 1971).

[4] For details of Thomas's life see *DNB* entry.

returned with considerable enthusiasm for Edward's regime in 1549 and was rewarded with an important position within Edward's household, where he was able to provide political advice. Thomas appears to have been one of a number of intellectuals who were excited by the Edwardian regime's plans for religious and social reform, and the liberal press freedoms granted after the repression of Henry's last years.[5] He clearly made it his aim to make Italy more accessible for an English audience and published the revealingly entitled *Principal Rules of Italian Grammar with Dictionarie for the better understanding of Boccace, Petracha, and Dante* (1550).

Thomas's *Historie* argued that anyone who might hold a position of power ought to read and learn from the book. Furthermore, he urged would-be magistrates and governors to visit Italy so that they could study Italian government and culture. Thomas divided his substantial work up into regions of Italy, with Venice first, followed by Naples, Florence, Genoa, and Milan, with a few pages on Mantua, Ferrara, Piacentia, Parma, and Urbino. Each region provided a series of lessons from which English governors ought to be able to draw obvious conclusions. Genoa, Florence, and Milan provided mixed lessons, some of their political history demonstrating conspicuous success, and other periods, disastrous failure. For example, Florence was generally divided between the rival factions of the Guelfs and the Ghibellines, much to its cost, until united by the foresight of Cosimo de' Medici. Genoa was similarly hobbled by a fierce conflict between commons and nobles, suffering inconstant government as a result. Naples served as an example of dreadful, tyrannical government. In contrast Venice, despite some misfortunes and problems, shows how a carefully elected oligarchy and a well-thought-out constitution could protect and develop the liberty and happiness of its citizens.[6] It is no accident that the Venetian council in Shakespeare's *Othello* (1603/4) is able to sort out prejudice and other political problems with relative ease.[7]

Although there was always a fear of excessive liberty becoming licence, and Venice remained notorious for its prostitutes (see the description of Thomas Coryat's encounter with a Venetian courtesan below, pp. 52–9), Thomas is the first in a long line of English travellers who

---

[5] John King, *English Reformation Literature: The Tudor Origins of the Protestant Tradition* (Princeton: Princeton Univ. Press, 1982); Jordan, *Edward VI*, ch. 4.

[6] See Andrew Hadfield, *Literature, Travel and Colonial Writing in the English Renaissance, 1545–1625* (Oxford: Clarendon Press, 1998) 24–32, for further analysis.

[7] See Hadfield, *Literature, Travel and Colonial Writing*, 217–42.

expressed sincere admiration for the people and politics of Venice. Henry Wotton, the most celebrated English ambassador to Venice, who entertained a variety of English travellers to the city-state, shows how relations between Britain and Venice were more often than not cordial in the sixteenth and seventeenth centuries. This was not true of all Italy, which had an ambivalent reputation in Renaissance England. If Italian culture and sophistication were envied and admired, Italian politics were often thought to be based on duplicity, treachery, and violence; religion on superstition and deceit; and sexual relations on lust and animal passions.[8] Florence was regarded as the centre of the evils of Italian politics, undoubtedly through the figure of Machiavelli, as well as being a great cultural centre (see Moryson's and Somerset's comments below, pp. 72–80, 89–90);[9] Rome, as Fynes Moryson's comments indicate, the centre of Italian religion.

Spain was generally regarded as an equally abhorrent Catholic nation and far fewer Englishmen ventured there. Those who did, like William Lithgow, generally came back with negative reports, although few were as unfortunate as Lithgow to be captured and tortured by the Inquisition. Mary's reign (1553–8) became more and more vilified by the skilful and vociferous propaganda of the exiled Protestants who returned from Germany, Switzerland, and France on the accession of Elizabeth (1558), culminating in John Foxe's *Acts and Monuments of the Christian Church* (1563, 1570). Partly as a result of these factors, any rapprochement with Spain was usually attacked by the large Protestant faction at court as a deal with the devil likely to lead to the dark days of Mary's marriage to Philip II of Spain when an alien Catholic culture had been imposed on a reluctant people. That not everyone followed such a straightforwardly Protestant line can be seen in Sir Charles Somerset's account of his visit to Rome, one which marks a pointed contrast to that of Moryson.[10] The English generally regarded the Spanish as brutal and hypocritical, a representation

---

[8] Convenient overviews are provided in Michele Marrapodi, A. J. Hoenselaars, Marcello Cappuzzo, and L. Falzon Santucci (eds.), *Shakespeare's Italy: Functions of Italian Locations in Renaissance Drama* (Manchester: Manchester Univ. Press, rev. edn., 1997); Jonathan Bate, 'The Elizabethans in Italy', in Jean-Pierre Maquerlot and Michèle Willems (ed.), *Travel and Drama in Shakespeare's Time* (Cambridge: Cambridge Univ. Press, 1996), 55–74.

[9] Felix Raab, *The English Face of Machiavelli: A Changing Interpretation, 1500–1700* (London: Routledge, 1964).

[10] Clearly such an interpretation underestimates the large number of enthusiasts for Catholicism alive in England and exaggerates the triumph of Protestantism. For another view of the Reformation, see Eamon Duffy, *The Stripping of the Altars* (New Haven: Yale Univ. Press, 1993).

enshrined in the 'Black Legend' (see below, p. 250). Throughout Elizabeth's reign Spain was considered, not unreasonably, as Protestant England's main enemy. Indeed, Fynes Moryson's observations of Ireland were the direct result of the fear that a religious alliance between the Irish and the Spanish could lead to the overthrow of English power in Ireland and the establishment of a Catholic base from which to launch another—and much more dangerous—invasion of England than the Armada.[11]

The Irish were usually regarded as a primitive people, horrifying even other Catholics by their ignorant superstition. As Colin Kidd has argued so persuasively, no conception of race or nation was possible without consideration of religion in the early modern period. Kidd suggests that peoples were generally regarded in terms of an 'ethnic theology'; more pristine notions of 'race' only developed in the nineteenth century with the rise of the 'scientific' theories of the nineteenth century.[12] Hence it was quite possible for English writers to signal a pointed contrast between the 'English Christian' and the 'Irish Catholic', the two being mutually exclusive categories.[13] Moryson's aggression towards the Irish undoubtedly stems from his English Protestantism, but he is also a keen observer of Irish social and political practices, despite his manifest hostility.[14]

Elizabeth's conflict with Spain continually threatened to embroil England in a wider European conflict, especially after the revolt of the Netherlands in an attempt to overthrow Spanish domination. Elizabeth had to resist numerous attempts from the more internationally minded Protestants at court under the leadership of Robert Dudley, earl of Leicester, and later, Robert Devereux, earl of Essex, to intervene on the side of the Dutch in the name of a wider Protestant community. Elizabeth eventually sent some limited aid, but made sure that England was not forced to fight what she saw as a potentially ruinous conflict.[15]

[11] R. B. Wernham, *After the Armada: Elizabethan England and the Struggle for Western Europe, 1588–1595* (Oxford: Clarendon Press, 1984); J. J. Silke, *Kinsale: The Spanish Intervention in Ireland at the End of the Elizabethan Wars* (Liverpool: Liverpool Univ. Press, 1970).

[12] Colin Kidd, *British Identities Before Nationalism: Ethnicity and Nationhood in the Atlantic World, 1600–1800* (Cambridge: Cambridge Univ. Press, 1999), ch. 3.

[13] Andrew Hadfield, 'Translating the Reformation: John Bale's Irish *Vocation*', in Brendan Bradshaw, Andrew Hadfield, and Willy Maley (eds.), *Representing Ireland: Literature and the Origins of Conflict, 1534–1660* (Cambridge: Cambridge Univ. Press, 1993), 43–59.

[14] For further contemporary English observations of the Irish, see Andrew Hadfield and John McVeagh (eds.), *Strangers to that Land: British Perceptions of Ireland from the Reformation to the Famine* (Gerard's Cross: Colin Smythe, 1994).

[15] See Charles Wilson, *Queen Elizabeth and the Revolt of the Netherlands* (London: Macmillan, 1970).

One of the key events which shadowed English conceptions of their European neighbours and fed English desires for splendid isolation was the Saint Bartholomew's Day Massacre, 23 August 1572.[16] Some accounts suggest that as many as 50,000 Protestant Huguenots were massacred on the orders of Catherine de' Medici, who was later personally congratulated by the Pope. The Massacre could almost have been invented to magnify fears that were already in place, containing the elements of brutal killings and dismemberment; sudden and unexpected Catholic atrocities; conniving Italian *politiques*; and a bloody civil war to follow. As Sir Robert Dallington's authoritative account for English readers demonstrates, France was regarded as a fractious nation, hopelessly split between violently opposed religious factions: a warning to England of what could happen if excessive religious toleration were ever countenanced. Dallington is writing within a tradition that looks back to writers such as William Thomas, using other countries to provide a political message for readers at home. If Spain and Italy were the true enemies of Protestant England, France serves as an example of what England could become.

In contrast, as Thomas Coryat's account shows, Protestant countries such as Switzerland and regions of Germany, received a much better press. Although the Germans were often criticized for their excessive drinking—a vice they had in common with the Dutch, the English, and the Irish—they were generally regarded as learned and reasonable allies, even if their culture did not inspire the same sense of wonder that Italian art did. Switzerland was also admired for the democratic constitutions of its cities, and its religious zeal in promoting the Reformation. Swiss reformers had a considerable influence on the doctrines and beliefs of many English Protestants, partly though the generation of exiles in the mid-sixteenth century.[17] Such religious tensions were diffused to a certain extent in the early 1600s as James sought to remove any remaining hostilities with Spain, which was declining rapidly as a European power. However, as William Lithgow's account of his imprisonment in Malaga demonstrates, the old religious/national divisions still lived on.

---

[16] Hadfield, *Literature, Travel, and Colonial Writing, passim*; Robert M. Kingdon, *Myths about the Saint Bartholomew's Day Massacres, 1572–1576* (Cambridge, Mass.: Harvard Univ. Press, 1988).

[17] A. G. Dickens, *The English Reformation* (London: Fontana, rev. edn., 1967), *passim*.

Sir Robert Dallington, *The View of France* (1604)

SIR ROBERT DALLINGTON (1561–1637) was a schoolmaster and a Jacobean and Caroline courtier. He travelled to France and Italy in the 1590s and subsequently became secretary to Francis, earl of Rutland. He started to publish works on politics, art, and travel based on his European experiences, partly in his capacity as a servant of Rutland. Dallington was a prominent supporter of Prince Henry at court and later became Master of Charterhouse.[1]

Dallington wrote influential books on Italy, making use of Italian political ideas—notably those of Guicciardini—and Tuscany. His book on France, *The View of France* (1604), was influential enough to be republished in the following year as a general guide for travellers, entitled *A Method for Travell: shewed by taking the view of France as it stood in the yeare of our Lord 1598*. Dallington clearly wants his readers to learn from his observations of the French and their political and social systems. His book is aimed at travellers and those involved in government in England. Dallington sees the English as a sensible balanced medium between the extremes of the French and Italians. But he emphasizes the fear in England that the bitter sectarian religious wars which had erupted in France could easily cross the Channel.[2]

See also:

Thomas Coryat, *Coryat's Crudities*, 2 vols. (Glasgow: MacLehose, 1905), i. 152–226.

The Travel Diary (1611–1612) of an English Catholic, Sir Charles Somerset, ed. Michael G. Brennan (Leeds: Leeds Philosophical and Literary Society, 1993).

Fynes Moryson, *An Itinerary*, 4 vols. (Glasgow: MacLehose, 1907), iv. 131–42.

Shakespeare's Europe, ed. Charles Hughes (London: Sherratt and Hughes, 1903), 170–3, 284.

---

[1] On Dallington's life, see Karl Joseph Höltgen, 'Sir Robert Dallington (1561–1637): Author, Traveller and Pioneer of Taste', *HLQ* 47 (1984), 147–77; Andrew Hadfield, *Literature, Travel and Colonial Writing in the English Renaissance, 1545–1625* (Oxford: Clarendon Press, 1998), 34–44; Edward Chaney, *The Evolution of the Grand Tour: Anglo-Italian Cultural Relations since the Renaissance* (London: Frank Cass, 1998), ch. 5.

[2] Text from Sir Robert Dallington, *The View of France (1604)*, sigs. V4ʳ–Y2ᵛ. I have removed some marginal notes, mainly dealing with sources of references.

It now remaineth I speake of the French nature and humour: which by the *Their nature and* change of his speech, apparrell, building, by his credulity to any tale which *humour.* is told, & by his impatience & haste in matter of deliberation, whereof I shall not omit presently to speake, ye may judge to be very idle, wavering and inconstant. Saith one, [...] As the Frenchmens pronunciation is very fast, so are their wits very wavering. And yee shall reade in *Caesars* Commentaries very often, how hee taxeth them of this legerity and sud-dennesse [...] *Caesar* being enformed of these matters, and fearing the unstablenesse of the *Gaules* (as being sudden and wavering in their reso-lutions, and generally desirous of innovation) he thought fit not to trust them. And in another place [...] *Caesar* understanding, that almost all the *Gaules* were naturally hungry of change, and unconstantly, and suddenly stirred to warre, &c. And againe, [...] As the resolution of the *Gaules* are sudden, and unlooked for, &c.

To conclude, if yee will rightly knowe the nature & humor of the ancient *Gaules*, ye must read the sixt of these Commentaries, and you shal observe how strange it is, that though all other things in the world are subject to change, yet the same *naturel* of lightnesse and inconstancy still remaines in the French. This is aptly shewed by *Haillan*, in his description of *Lewes* the eleventh: [...] If hee had one thing, hee straight casts his affection to another, being violent, busy-headed and impatient.

To this accordeth another of their owne writers, [...]: Such is the condition of France, that if shee have no Warres abroad against powerfull *2. In matter of* neighbours, shee must have broyles at home among her owne Subjects, and *warre.* her working spirits can never remaine long quiet. And therefore *Tacitus* calles them, [...] The most fickle kinde of men; sudden to begin and more sudden to ende, apter to apprehend the action, then comprehend the cause, ready to lay hold, notable to hold fast: as by the making and revoking of so many Edicts, against the *Reformed Religion* in so fewe yeeres, by the winning and losing of *Naples* and *Millaine* in so short time, and by many other their actions appeareth.

For yee must observe of the French, that he entreth a Countrie like thunder, and vanisheth out againe like smoke: hee resembleth the Waspe, who after the first stroke, loseth her sting, and can hurt no more.

He sheweth this his lightnesse and inconstancie, not onely in matters of service and warre, (whereof I have before made mention) but also even in other his actions and carriages: But in nothing more, then in his familiar- *3. In intertayning* itie, with whome a stranger cannot so soone bee off his horse, but he will be *of friendship.*

acquainted; not so soone in his Chamber, but the other like an Ape will bee on his shoulder: and as suddenly and without cause yee shall lose him also. A childish humour, to bee wonne with as little as an Apple, and lost with lesse then a Nut: Quite contrarie to the nature of the *Italian*, of whome yee shall in your travell shortly observe, that he is of too sullen and retired a fashion, & a *loup-garou* (as the French man calles him) wherein I would have you observe the vertue of the English man (for vertue is a mediocrity betweene two extremes) who is neyther so childishly and Apishly familiar, as the French; nor so scornefully and Cynically solitary as the other.

So are we in matter of duell and private quarrell, in a meane, me thinks, betweene these two Nations: for we are neither so devillishly mindfull of revenge, as to tarry seven or ten yeres for an opportunity upon our enemy, as doeth the Italian: nor so inconsideratly hasty, as we must needs eyther fight to day, or be friends to morrow, as doth the French. Hereat *Rablais* scoffingly glanceth, where he telleth a tale of a *Gascoigne*, that having lost his money, would needs in the heat of his choller fight with any man that bore head: and for want of an enemy fell asleepe. By that time he was waking, comes mee another *Rhodomonte*, and upon like cause of losse, would have this fellow by the eares: but then the edge of this other was off. In conclusion (sayth *Rablais*) they went both to the Taverne, and there for want of money which they had lost at Dice, drunke themselves friends upon their swords, without farther mediation, or troubling of others to take up the quarrell.

Of the French carriage and manage of a quarrell, how childish and ridiculous it is, ye have already seene two or three examples, wherein the parties have neyther shewed judgement, to know their owne right, nor valor to revenge their wrong: whereas the English Gentleman, with mature deliberation disputeth how farre his honour is ingaged, by the injury offered, and judiciously determineth his maner of satisfaction, according to the quality of the offence: which done, hee presently embarqueth himselfe into the action, according to the prescription of the olde rule, [...] Wise resolutions should be speedily executed.

I will heere remember you of one other instance more, wherein our Countreymen keepe the golden meane, betweene the two extremes of defect and excesse, and wherein these two Nations of Italy and France are culpable, and heere worthily to be taxed.

We may say of the Italian, who maketh his house his wives prison, as *Plutarch* sayth of the Persians [...] They are by nature strangely and cruelly jealous of their women, not onely of their wives, but also of their slaves and

Concubines, whom they gard so straitly, that they are never seene abroad, but remayne alwayes locked up in their houses: Whereas the French liberty on the other side is too much: for here a man hath many occasions offred upon any small entrance, to come acquainted; and upon every least acquaintance, to enter, where he may come to her house, accompany her arme in arme in the streets, court her in all places, & at all seasons, without imputation. Wherein, me thinks, the French maried man doth as *Plutarch* reports of *Pericles, take away the walles & fences of his orchards & gardens, to th'end every man might freely enter and gather fruit at his pleasure.*

No marvell then, the bridle being left in their owne hands, though sometimes they be saddled, & their husbands know not. You may observe therefore, that in this matter of wedlocke also, the English use is better then either the Italian or French.

It is also naturall to the French, to be a great scoffer; for men of light and unsteadie braines, have commonly sudden and sharpe conceites. Hereto also their language well agreeth, as being currant and full of proverbes; to which purpose I will remember you of two answeres, not long since made by two Frenchmen, with one of which you are well acquainted, wherein also you may observe, how little esteeme they hold of the *Romane* Religion in heart, though they make profession thereof in shew.

The one of these being very sicke, &, as was thought, in danger of death, his ghostly father comes to him with his *Corpus domini*, and tels him, that hearing of the extremitie wherein he was, he had brought him his *Saviour*, to comfort him before his departure. The sicke Gentleman withdrawing the Curtaine, and seeing there the fat lubberly Frier with the *Oast* in his hand, answereth, I know it is our *Saviour*; he comes to me as he went to Jerusalem, *C'est vn asne quile porte*: He is carried by an Asse.

The other Gentleman upon like danger of sicknesse, having the Frier come to him to instruct him in the Faith, and after, to give him the *Oast*, and then the extreme unction (it was on a Friday) tolde him that hee must beleeve, that this *Corpus domini* which he brought, was the very reall flesh, blood and bone of our Saviour. Which after the sicke man had freely confessed, the Frier offered it him to receyve for his comfort. Nay, quoth the other [...] You shall excuse me, for I eate no flesh on Fridayes. So that yee see the French will rather lose his god, then his good jest.

The French humour also (sayth one) [...] cannot away with patience & modesty. And therefore another sayth of him, that he is as shamefast and modest, *comme vn Page de la Cour*: as a Page of the Court. Or as *Hiperbolus*, who, *Plutarch* saith, for his boldnesse and saucy impudency, was the only Subject in his time for all Satyricks and Commedians to worke upon.

He is also such a one, as *Theophrastus* calles, *Duscherès*, i. *immundus*, uncleanly, [...] Who being leprous and scabby, and wearing long unpared nayles, thrusts himselfe into company, and sayes, those diseases come to him by kind; for both his Father and his Grandfather were subject unto them.

Uncleanly.

Hee is *Adolésches*, i. *loquax*, Talkative, [...] Who had rather seeme more chattering then a Swallow, then hold his peace; so willing is hee to make himselfe ridiculous. With which people (it is strange) ye shall talke all day, & yet at night not remember whereof hee hath talked; such multiplicity of words he hath, and so idle is the matter whereof he treateth.

Talkative.

Hee is *Acairos*, i. *intempestinus*, unseasonably troublesome, [...] Who comming to his friend full of businesse, will give him counsell, before he have imparted the matter unto him: And therefore they themselves have here a proverbe, [...] To surprise one after the French fashion, when they take one of a suddaine, comming unlooked for and unsent for. Of which kind of people, *Theophrastus* bids us beware, where he saith: [...] If you will not bee troubled with a fit of Ague, you must run as fast as your legs can carie you from such kind of men: for it is very troublesome living with fellowes, that cannot distinguish the seasons of leysure and affaires.

Troublesome.

He is [...] Proud of trifles [...] Who, if he have sacrificed an Oxe, useth to nayle up the head and hornes at his gate, that all that come to him, may take notice that he hath kild an Oxe. And if he bee to pay fortie shillings, will be sure to pay it in new-coynd money. This is he that comes to the Tennis Court, throwes his Purse full of coyne at the line, which giveth a sound, as if there were no, lesse then thirtie or fourtie Crownes, when as sometimes by mischance, we have discovered that it was nothing, but Paper, and a fewe Sols, and doubles of Brasse, that made it so swell, in all, scarce eighteene pence sterling.

Vainely proude.

He is *Alazòn*. i. *Ostentator*, A Craker: [...] Who comming to such as have great horses to sell, makes them beleeve hee will buy some: And at great Faires, drawing to their shops that sell apparell, cals to see a sute of an hundred pound: and when they are agreed of the price, fals out with his boy, for following him without his purse. Such a one was the gallant, of whome yee told me this other day, who in the middest of his discourse with you and other Gentlemen, suddenly turnes backe to his Lackie, Fetch me, saith he, my *Horologe*, Clocke, it lies in my lodging in such or such a place, neere such or such a Jewell. The *Lalero* returnes with a *nonest inventus*.[1] My French

Boasting of things nothing worth.

---

[1] 'It has not been found'.

gallant streight bethinkes himselfe that it is in his pocket (which hee knew well enough before) which presently he puls out, not so much to shew how the time passeth, (whereof he takes little care) as the curiousnesse of the worke, and the beautie of the case, whereof hee is not a little brag & enamoured. To speake thus particularly of all his severall humours and customes, would be very prolixe, and not much necessarie: I will only referre you to the fourth of *Tullies Rhetorickes*, where he speaketh of a bragging Rhodomonte, and to the first booke of *Horace Satyres*, speaking of an endles & needles prater, a fastidious & irkesome companion, where you shall see the French *naturel*, very lively & admirably well described.

I will onely speake of his impatience and precipitation in deliberations of *Hastie to conclude* Warre or Peace, and such other affayres of greatest importance, and so end. *a Peace.* To this effect *Bodin*[2] saith of him, [...] The French is of so sudden & busy a disposition, that he quickly yeelds to that a man demands, being soone tired with messages to & fro, and other delayes peculiar to the Spanyard. And in another place, [...] The Spanyard had need of a more ready dispatch then he hath, & the French of more moderation in his actions and passions. And whereas *Commines* saith of us, that we be not [...] so crafty in our treaties & *Commines.* agreements, as the French. I thinke, saving the credit of so great an Author, he might better have said, [...] so headstrong and precipitate. But where he saith, that he that will treat & determine matters with us, must have [...] a little patience: I yeeld unto him, he hath good reason so to say; for his Countrymen, the French, can endure no delay; they must propound and conclude all in one day. Whether of these be more praisworthy *Plutarch* thus decideth: *Agatharcus* bragged of his ready and quick hand, & that he painted faster then any other: which *Zeuxes* understanding, And I, quoth he, quite contrary, doe glory in this, that I am long in the doing: for ordinarily such suddennesse and facility can not give eyther a lasting firmnesse, or a perfect beauty to the worke. Therefore saith one very well, *That should bee long in deliberation, that must be resolved but once.* To this agreeth the saying of *Pericles* to *Tolmides, We must tarry the time, which is the wisest Counseller we can have.* [...]

Thus have you a superficiall survey of this Country and People of *France*, of whom we may conclude with *Le Nouë* [...] More then halfe the Noblesse is perished, the people diminished, the Treasure exhausted, the debts increased, good Order overthrown, Religion languished, maners debaucked, Justice corrupted, and the men divided.

---

[2] Jean Bodin (1529/30–96), French political theorist.

Thomas Coryat, *Coryats Crudities* (1611), Observations of Venice, Germany, and Switzerland

FOR details on Coryat, see above, pp. 28–9.

Included here are three extracts. The first contains Coryat's well-known description of the courtesans of Venice and his encounter with one. Coryat is, as usual, entertaining the reader and playing the fool, but also making a serious point about the fine line between liberty and licence, courtesy and prostitution, and the seductive appeal of Venice for English travellers.[1] The second contains an example of his praise of the learning of the Germans, as well as a defence of them against the charge of excessive drinking, and the third, the liberty of the Swiss, illustrated through the story of William Tell.[2]

See also:

William Thomas, *Historie of Italie* (1549), 73–112.

The Commonwealth and Government of Venice. Written by the Cardinall Gaspar Contareno, trans. Lewis Lewkenor (1599).

The Travel Diary (1611–1612) of an English Catholic, Sir Charles Somerset, ed. Michael G. Brennan (Leeds: Leeds Philosophical and Literary Society, 1993), 247–56.

Fynes Moryson, *An Itinerary*, 4 vols. (Glasgow: MacLehose, 1907), i. 160–96; iv. 6–46.

---

[1] See Ann Rosalind Jones, 'Italians and Others: Venice and the Irish in *Coryat's Crudities* and *The White Devil*', *Renaissance Drama*, NS 18 (1987), 101–19.

[2] Text from Thomas Coryat, *Coryat's Crudities*, 2 vols. (Glasgow: MacLehose, 1905), i. 401–8; ii. 174–5, 209–11, 101–3.

The Courtesans. But since I have taken occasion to mention some notable particulars of their women, I will insist farther upon that matter, and make relation of their Cortezans also, as being a thing incident and very proper to this discourse, especially because the name of a Cortezan of Venice is famoused over all Christendome. And I have here inserted a picture of one of their nobler Cortezans, according to her Venetian habites, with my owne neare unto her, made in that forme as we saluted each other. Surely by so much the more willing I am to treat something of them, because I perceive it is so rare a matter to find a description of the Venetian Cortezans in any

Il Signior Tomaso Odcombiano

Margarita Emiliana bella
Cortesana di Venetia

Gu: Hole sculp

FIG. 2. Coryat and a Venetian Courtesan (Thomas Coryat,
Coryats Crudities (1611), p. 263)

Authour, that all the writers that I could ever see, which have described the city, have altogether excluded them out of their writings. Therefore seeing the History of these famous gallants is omitted by all others that have written just Commentaries of the Venetian state, as I know it is not impertinent to this present Discourse to write of them; so I hope it will not be ungratefull to the Reader to reade that of these notable persons, which no Author whatsoever doth impart unto him but my selfe. Onely I feare least I shall expose my selfe to the severe censure and scandalous imputations of many carping Criticks, who I thinke will taxe me for luxury and wantonnesse to insert so lascivious a matter into this Treatise of Venice. Wherefore at the end of this discourse of the Cortezans I will adde some Apologie for my selfe, which I hope will in some sort satisfie them, if they are not too captious.

The woman that professeth this trade is called in the Italian tongue Cortezana, which word is derived from the Italian word cortesia that signifieth courtesie. Because these kinde of women are said to receive courtesies of their favourites. Which word hath some kinde of affinitie with the Greeke word ἑταίρα which signifieth properly a sociable woman, and is by Demosthenes, Athenaeus, and divers other prose writers often *Their number* taken for a woman of a dissolute conversation.[1] As for the number of these *very great.* Venetian Cortezans it is very great. For it is thought there are of them in the whole City and other adjacent places, as Murano, Malomocco, &c. at the least twenty thousand, whereof many are esteemed so loose, that they are said to open their quivers to every arrow. A most ungodly thing without doubt that there should be a tolleration of such licentious wantons in so glorious, so potent, so renowned a city. For me thinks that the Venetians should be daylie affraid least their winking at such uncleannesse should be an occasion to draw down upon them Gods curses and vengeance from heaven, and to consume their city with fire and brimstone, as in times past he did Sodome and Gomorrha. But they not fearing any such thing doe graunt large dispensation and indulgence unto them, and that for these two causes. First, ad vitanda majora mala.[2] For they thinke that the chastity of their wives would be the sooner assaulted, and so consequently they should be capricornified, (which of all the indignities in the world the Venetian cannot patiently endure) were it not for these places of

---

[1] Demosthenes, greatest of Athenian orators, 4th cent. BC; Athenaeus, fl. c.AD 200, wrote on learned men banqueting together.
[2] 'To avoid greater evils'.

evacuation. But I marvaile how that should be true though these Cortezans were utterly rooted out of the City. For the Gentlemen do even coope up their wives alwaies within the walles of their houses for feare of these inconveniences, as much as if there were no Cortezans at all in the City. So that you shall very seldome see a Venetian Gentleman's wife but either at the solemnization of a great marriage, or at the Christning of a Jew, or late in the evening rowing in a Gondola. The second cause is for that the revenues which they pay unto the Senate for their tolleration, doe main- *Great revenues* taine a dozen of their galleys, (as many reported unto me in Venice) and so *paid to the State.* save them a great charge. The consideration of these two things hath moved them to tolerate for the space of these many hundred yeares these kinde of Laides and Thaides,[3] who may as fitly be termed the stales [whores] of Christendome as those were heretofore of Greece. For so infinite are the allurements of these amorous Calypsoes,[4] that the fame of them hath drawn many to Venice from some of the remotest parts of Christendome, to contemplate their beauties, and enjoy their pleasing dalliances. And indeede such is the variety of the delicious objects they minister to their lovers, that they want nothing tending to delight. For when you come into one of their Palaces (as indeed some few of the principallest of them live in very magnificent and portly buildings fit for the entertainement of a great Prince) you seeme to enter into the Paradise of Venus. For their fairest roomes are most glorious and glittering *The Paradise of* to behold. The walles round about being adorned with most sumptuous *Venus.* tapistry and gilt leather, such as I have spoken of in my Treatise of Padua. Besides you may see the picture of the noble Cortezan most exquisitely drawn. As for her selfe shee comes to thee decked like the Queene and Goddesse of love, in so much that thou wilt thinke she made a late transmigration from Paphos, Cnidos, or Cythera, the auncient habitations of Dame Venus. For her face is adorned with the quintessence of beauty. In her cheekes thou shalt see the Lilly and the Rose strive for the suprem- acy, and the silver tramels of her haire displayed in that curious manner besides her two frisled peakes standing up like prety Pyramides, that they give thee the true Cos amoris.[5] But if thou hast an exact judgement, thou maist easily discerne the effects of those famous apothecary drugs here- *Apothecary drugs.* tofore used amongst the Noble Ladies of Rome, even stibium, cerussa, and

---

[3] Famous Greek courtesans, lovers of Diogenes the Cynic and Alexander the Great, respectively.
[4] Goddess who detained Odysseus for 7 years.
[5] Greek island, famous for pictures of Venus painted by Apelles.

purpurissum.[6] For few of the Cortezans are so much beholding to nature, but that they adulterate their faces, and supply her defect with one of these three. A thing so common amongst them, that many of them which have an elegant naturall beauty, doe varnish their faces (the observation whereof made me not a little pitty their vanities) with these kinde of sordid trumperies. Wherein me thinks they seeme ebur atramento candefacere,[7] according to that excellent Proverbe of Plautus; that is, to make ivorie white with inke. Also the ornaments of her body are so rich, that except thou dost even geld thy affections (a thing hardly to be done) or carry with thee Ulysses hearbe called Moly[8] which is mentioned by Homer, that is, some antidote against those Venereous titillations, shee wil very neare benumme and captivate thy senses, and make reason vale bonnet to affection. For thou

Costly gems.   shalt see her decked with many chaines of gold and orient pearle like a second Cleopatra, (but they are very litle) divers gold rings beautified with diamonds and other costly stones, jewels in both her eares of great worth. A gowne of damaske (I speake this of the nobler Cortizans) either decked with a deep gold fringe (according as I have expressed it in the picture of the Cortizan that I have placed about the beginning of this discourse) or laced with five or six gold laces each two inches broade. Her petticoate of red chamlet edged with rich gold fringe, stockings of carnasion silke, her breath and her whole body, the more to enamour thee, most fragrantly perfumed. Though these things will at the first sight seeme unto thee most delectable allurements, yet if thou shalt rightly weigh them in the scales of a mature judgement, thou wilt say with the wise man, and that very truely, that they are like a golden ring in a swines snowt.[9] Moreover shee will endevour to enchaunt thee partly with her melodious notes that she warbles out upon her lute, which shee fingers with as laudable a stroake as many men that are excellent professors in the noble science of Musicke; and partly with that heart-tempting harmony of her voice. Also thou wilt

Good
Rhetoricians.   finde the Venetian Cortezan (if she be a selected woman indeede) a good Rhetorician, and a most elegant discourser, so that if she cannot move thee with all these foresaid delights, shee will assay thy constancy with her Rhetoricall tongue. And to the end shee may minister unto thee the

---

[6] Cosmetics: stibium, used to colour eyebrows; cerussa, white lead to whiten skin; purpurissum, a form of rouge (I owe this note to Dr T. Pritchard).

[7] 'To make ivory white with black pigment' (Plautus, *Mostellaria*, line 259) (I owe this note to Dr T. Pritchard).

[8] *Odyssey* 10. 305.

[9] Proverbs 11: 22.

stronger temptations to come to her lure, shee will shew thee her chamber of recreation, where thou shalt see all manner of pleasing objects, as many faire painted coffers wherewith it is garnished round about, a curious milke-white canopy of needle worke, a silke quilt embrodered with gold: and generally all her bedding sweetly perfumed. And amongst other amiable ornaments shee will shew thee one thing only in her chamber tending to mortification, a matter strange amongst so many irritamenta malorum;[10] even the picture of our Lady by her bedde side, with Christ in her armes, placed within a cristall glasse. But beware notwithstanding all these illecebrae & lenocinia amoris,[11] that thou enter not into termes of private conversation with her. For then thou shalt finde her such a one as Lipsius[12] truly cals her, callidam & calidam Solis filiam, that is, the crafty and hot daughter of the Sunne. Moreover I will tell thee this newes which is most true, that if thou shouldest wantonly converse with her, and not give her that salarium iniquitatis,[13] which thou hast promised her, but perhaps cunningly escape from her company, shee will either cause thy throate to be cut by her Ruffiano, if he can after catch thee in the City, or procure thee to be arrested (if thou art to be found) and clapped up in the prison, where thou shalt remaine till thou hast paid her all thou didst promise her. Therefore for avoiding of those inconveniences, I will give thee the same counsell that Lipsius did to a friend of his that was to travell into Italy, *Lipsius's counsel.* even to furnish thy selfe with a double armour, the one for thine eyes, the other for thine eares. As for thine eyes, shut them and turne them aside from these venereous Venetian objects. For they are the double windowes that conveigh them to thy heart. Also thou must fortifie thine eares against the attractive inchauntments of their plausible speeches. Therefore even as wrestlers were wont heretofore to fence their eares against al exterior annoyances, by putting to them certaine instruments called ἀμφῶτιδες [ear-covers]: so doe thou take unto thy selfe this firme foundation against the amorous woundes of the Venetian Cortezans, to heare none of their wanton toyes; or if thou wilt needes both see and heare them, doe thou only cast thy breath upon them in that manner as we doe upon steele, which is no sooner on but incontinent it falleth off againe: so doe thou only breath a few words upon them, and presently be gone from them: for if thou dost linger with them thou wilt finde their poyson to be more pernicious then that of the scorpion, aspe, or cocatrice. Amongst other things that I heard of these

---

[10] 'Incentives for evil' (Ovid, *Metamorphoses* I. 140).   [11] 'Allurements and charms of love'.
[12] Justus Lipsius, 1547–1606, Latinist and political theorist.   [13] 'Payment for evil'.

A strange end.

kinde of women in Venice, one is this, that when their Cos amoris beginneth to decay, when their youthfull vigor is spent, then they consecrate the dregs of their olde age to God by going into a Nunnery, having before dedicated the flower of their youth to the divell; some of them also having scraped together so much pelfe by their sordid facultie as doth maintaine them well in their old age: For many of them are as rich as ever was Rhodope in Egypt, Flora in Rome, or Lais in Corinth. One example whereof I have before mentioned in Margarita Aemiliana that built a faire Monastery of Augustinian Monkes. There is one most notable thing more to be mentioned concerning these Venetian Cortezans, with the relation whereof I will end this discourse of them. If any of them happen to have any children (as indeede they have but few, for according to the old proverbe the best carpenters make the fewest chips) they are brought up either at their own charge, or in a certaine house of the citie appointed for no other use but onely for the bringing up of the Cortezans bastards, which I saw Eastward above Saint Markes streete neare to the sea side. In the south wall of which building that looketh towards the sea, I observed a certaine yron grate inserted into a hollow peece of the wall, betwixt which grate and a plaine stone beneath it, there is a convenient little space to put in an infant. Hither doth the mother or some body for her bring the child shortly after it is borne into the world; and if the body of it be no greater, but that it may conveniently without any hurt to the infant bee conveighed in at the foresaid space, they put it in there without speaking at all to any body that is in the house to take charge thereof. And from thenceforth the mother is absolutely discharged of her child. But if the child bee growne to that bignesse that they cannot conveigh it through that space, it is carryed backe againe to the mother, who taketh charge of it her selfe, and bringeth it up as well as she can. Those that are brought up in this foresaid house, are removed therehence when they come to yeares of discretion, and many of the male children are employed in the warres, or to serve in the Arsenall, or Galleys at sea, or some other publique service for the Common weale. And many of the females if they bee faire doe matrizare, that is, imitate their mothers in their gainfull facultie, and get their living by prostituting their bodies to their favourites. Thus have I described unto thee the Venetian Cortezans; but because I have related so many particulars of them, as few Englishmen that have lived many years in Venice, can do the like, or at the least if they can, they will not upon their returne into England, I beleeve thou wilt cast an aspersion of

A notable custom.

wantonnesse upon me, and say that I could not know all these matters without mine owne experience. I answere thee, that although I might have knowne them without my experience, yet for my better satisfaction, I went to one of their noble houses (I wil confesse) to see the manner of their life, and observe their behaviour, but not with such an intent as we reade Demosthenes went to Lais, to the end to pay something for repentance; but rather as Panutius did to Thais, of whom we read that when he came to her, and craved a secret roome for his pastime, she should answere him that the same roome where they were together, was secret enough, because no body could see them but onely God; upon which speech the godly man tooke occasion to persuade her to the feare of God and religion, and to the reformation of her licentious life, since God was able to prie into the secretest corners of the world. And so at last converted her by this meanes from a wanton Cortezan to a holy and religious woman. [...]

Neither can I be perswaded that it ought to be esteemed for a staine or blemish to the reputation of an honest and ingenuous man to see a Cortezan in her house, and note her manners and conversation, because according to the old maxime, Cognitio mali non est mala, the knowledge of evill is not evill, but the practice and execution thereof. For I thinke that a virtuous man will be the more confirmed and settled in virtue by the observation of some vices, then if he did not at all know what they were.

The knowledge of evil is not evil.

The first noble carowsing that I saw in Germany was at mine Inne in Basil. Where I saw the Germanes drink helter-skelter very sociably, exempting my selfe from their liquid impositions as well as I could. It is their custome whensoever they drink to another, to see their glasse filled up incontinent, (for therein they most commonly drinke) and then they deliver it into the hand of him to whome they drinke, esteeming him a very curteous man that doth pledge the whole, according to the old verse:

Drinking habits.

Germanus mihi frater eris si pocula siccas.[14]

But on the contrary side, they deeme that man for a very rusticall and unsociable peasant, utterly unworthy of their company, that will not with reciprocal turnes mutually retaliate a health. And they verifie the olde speech ἢ πίθι ἢ ἄπιθι, that is, eyther drinke or be gon. For though they will not offer any villanie or injury unto him that refuseth to pledge him the

---

[14] 'You will be a true full brother to me if you drain the cups' (I owe this translation to Dr T. Pritchard).

whole, (which I have often seene in England to my great griefe) yet they will so little regard him, that they will scarce vouchsafe to converse with him. Truly I have heard Germany much dispraised for drunkennesse before I saw it; but that vice reigneth no more there (that I could perceive) then in other countries. For I saw no man drunke in any place of Germany, though I was in many goodly Cities, and in much notable company. I would God the imputation of that vice could not be almost as truly cast upon mine owne nation as upon Germany. Besides I observed that they impose not such an inevitable necessity of drinking a whole health, especially those of the greater size, as many of our English gallants doe, a custome (in my opinion) most barbarous, and fitter to bee used amongst the rude Scythians and Gothes then civill Christians: yet so frequently practised in England, that I have often most heartily wished it were clean abolished out of our land, as being no small blemish to so renowned and well governed a Kingdome as England is. [...]

The City.

The City [Heidelberg] is strongly walled, and hath foure faire gates in the walles, and one very goodly streete above the rest both for breadth and length. For it is at the least an English mile long: and garnished with many beautifull houses, whereof some have their fronts fairely painted, which doe yeeld an excellent shew. Also it hath sixe Churches. Namely that of the holy Ghost: St. Peters: The Church in the Princes Palace: the French Church: a Church in the suburbes: And the Predicatorie church which belonged once to the Dominican Friers. But the Church of the holy Ghost which adjoyneth to their great market place, is the fairest of all, being beautified with two singular ornaments above the other Churches that doe greatly grace the same: the one the Palatine Librarie, the other the monu-

The Palatine Library.

ments of their Princes. The Palatine Librarie is kept by that most excellent and generall Schollar Mr. Janus Gruterus the Princes Bibliothecarie, of whom I have reason to make a kind and thankeful mention, because I received great favours of him in Heidelberg. For he entertained me very courteously in his house, shewed me the Librarie, and made meanes for my

A scholarly librarian.

admission into the Princes Court. [...] A man that for his exquisite learning hath beene received into the friendship of some of the greatest Schollars of Christendome, especially of Justus Lipsius, betwixt whom divers elegant Epistles have passed that are published to the world. I observed him to be a very sweet and eloquent discourser. For he speaketh a most elegant and true Ciceronian phrase which is graced with a facill & expedite deliverie. [...]

But I will cease to praise my friend Mr. Gruterus, because his owne worth doth more truly commend him then I shall ever be able to doe with my inelegant stile, and so I will returne to that famous Palatine Librarie. It is built over the roofe of the body of the Church. A place most beautifull, and divided into two very large and stately roomes that are singular well furnished with store of bookes of all faculties. Here are so many auncient manuscripts, especially of the Greeke and Latin Fathers of the Church, as no Librarie of all Christendome, no not the Vatican of Rome nor Cardinall Bessarions of Venice can compare with it. Besides there is a great multitude of manuscripts of many other sorts, in so much that Mr. Gruterus told he could shew in this Librarie at the least a hundred more manuscripts then Mr. James the publique Bibliothecarie of Oxford could in his famous Universitie Librarie. [...] *Ancient manuscripts.*

Truly the beauty of this Librarie is such both for the notable magnifi-cence of the building, and the admirable variety of bookes of all sciences and languages, that I beleeve none of those notable Libraries in ancient times so celebrated by many worthy historians, neither that of the royall Ptolomies of Alexandria, burnt by Julius Caesar, not that of King Eumenes at Pergamum in Greece, nor Augustus his Palatine in Rome, nor Trajans Ulpian, nor that of Serenus Sammonicus, which he left to the Emperor Gordianus the yonger, nor any other whatsoever in the whole world before the time of the invention of printing, could compare with this Palatine. *Notable Libraries.*

Also there [Zurich] is shewed another most worthy monument in the same roome, even the sword of William Tell an Helvetian of the towne of Swice, who about some three hundred years since was the first author of the Helveticall confederation which hath been ever since retained in their popular government, by reason of a certaine notable exploit that he atchieved. Therefore I will tell a most memorable history of Will Tell before I proceede any further, being very pertinent to this purpose, which was this, as I both heard it in the Citie, and afterward read it in the third booke of Munsters Cosmography. When as the Germane Emperours being the Lords of the principall Cities of Helvetia constituted forraine Prefects and rulers about three hundred yeares since as their deputies over three townes, especially above the rest, namely Sylvania, otherwise called Underwald, Urania, commonly called Uri, and Swice, it happned that the Prefect of the towne of Swice behaved himselfe very insolently, abusing his *History of William Tell.*

authority by immoderate tyrannizing over the people. For amongst other enormous outrages that he committed, this was one. He commanded one of

Travellers compelled to do reverence to a hat.

his servants to compell all travellers that passed such a way, to doe reverence to his hat that was hanged upon a staffe in the high way. The people unwilling to offend the Magistrate, did their obeysance unto the hat. But one amongst the rest, even this foresaid William Tell, being a man of a stout courage, refused to doe as the rest did. Whereupon he was brought before the Magistrate, who being grievously incensed against him for his contumacie, injoyned him this pennance: that he should shoote an arrow out of a crosse-bow at an apple set upon his sonnes head that was a little child, whom he caused to be tied to a tree for the same purpose, so that if he had fayled to strike the apple, he must needs have shot through his sonne. This he commanded him because this Tell was esteemed a cunning archer: At the first he refused to doe it: But at last because he saw there was an inevitable necessity imposed upon him, he performed the matter greatly against his will, and that with most happy successe. For God himselfe

The apple cunningly shot by Tell.

directing the arrow, he shot him so cunningly, that he strooke off the apple from the childs head without any hurt at all to the child. And whereas he had another arrow left besides that which he shot at his sonne, the Prefect asked him what he meant to do with that arrow: he made him this bould and resolute answere. If I had slaine my child with the first, I would have shot thee through with the second. The magistrate hearing that, commanded him to be apprehended, and carried away in a barke. And when he was come betwixt the towne of Urania, and a certaine village called Brun, having by good fortune escaped out of the boate, he ranne away with all possible expedition over the difficult places of the mountaines, where there was no common way, and so came to a place neere to the which he knew the tyrant would passe, where he lay in ambush in a secret corner of the wood till he came that way, and then shot him through with his other arrow. It hapned that this Tell did weare the foresaid sword about him when he atchieved these worthy actes, in regard whereof the Switzers have ever since that time hanged up the same in their Armory for a most remarkable monument, though me thinks it had beene much better to have reserved the arrow with which he shot through the tyrant, then the sword that he

Tell's exploit the original of the Helvetic confederation.

wore then. This noble exploit was the first originall of the Helveticall confederation. For shortly after these matters were acted, those three foresaid townes of Underwald, Uri, and Swice united themselves together in a league by a solemne forme of oath about the year 1316. to the end to shake off the yoake of those forraine tyrants. And afterward the other Cities of the Province imitated them, so that in the end all the Cities of Helvetia combined themselves together in a league of unity, which though it hath beene often assayed since that time to be dissolved and violated by the forraine forces of mighty men, as by some of the German Emperours, by Leopold, and Fredericke, brothers and Dukes of Austria, by the Earles of Kyburg, &c. yet it hath continued firme and inviolable to this day. As for the name of Switzers it grew upon this foresaid occasion, even because the above mentioned William Tell the first author of this league was borne in the towne of Swice. For before that time all the inhabitants of the country were called Helvetians.

Sir Charles Somerset, *Travel Diary* (1611–12), Observations of Paris and Florence

SIR CHARLES SOMERSET (*c.*1588–1665) was the third son of the earl of Worcester, and from a prominent English Catholic family. He appears to have been a cultured and highly educated young man with a wide range of interests, notably in theology, literature, architecture, philosophy, and travel writing. His journey was considerably less ambitious than those of the older travellers represented here, and was undoubtedly designed as part of his education. He may also have decided to leave England through fear of persecution.[1]

As the diary's editor, Michael Brennan, points out, Somerset appears to have chosen to keep a diary as a private record of his observations, and also to produce a document which could be 'perused by other interested individuals as an informative handbook of intelligence material on such politically charged topics as military and naval fortifications, national and civic administration, and urban design'.[2] It is remarkable how closely Somerset's diary conforms to advice manuals for young gentlemen such as Bacon's essay on travel, or the prefatory remarks to Robert Dallington's *The View of France* (1604), indicating that such works were taken seriously by travellers. Somerset, not surprisingly, comments extensively on churches, monasteries, and other religious institutions and his writing marks an instructive contrast to the heavily Protestant bias of writers such as Fynes Moryson and William Lithgow. Somerset's comments on Rome, for example, could not be more different from those of Moryson. An indication is given of the wide range of an English Catholic tradition as well as how history might have been different if certain English monarchs had had different religious persuasions. Equally, a sense of the varied group of courtiers and intellectuals who surrounded Prince Henry before his premature death in 1612, is given (Thomas Coryat was another traveller whom the prince encouraged).[3]

The extracts included here describe Somerset's impressions of Paris and Florence. Somerset is a perceptive and acute observer, interested in matters

---

[1] Biographical details are contained in *The Travel Diary (1611–1612) of an English Catholic, Sir Charles Somerset*, ed. Michael Brennan (Leeds: Leeds Philosophical and Literary Society, 1993), introd., pp. 9–12, 33–6.

[2] *Travel Diary*, ed. Brennan, p. 2.

[3] *Travel Diary*, ed. Brennan, introd., pp. 29–33; Roy Strong, *Henry Prince of Wales and England's Lost Renaissance* (London: Thames and Hudson, 1986).

of political and military significance, culture (especially buildings and music), and, like most travellers, ordinary human affairs.[4]

See also:

William Thomas, *Historie of Italie* (1549), 137–60.
Sir Robert Dallington, *The Survey of the Great Dukes State of Tuscany* (1605).
Fynes Moryson, *An Itinerary* (Glasgow: MacLehose, 1907), i. 406–19.

[4] Text from *Travel Diary*, ed. Brennan, pp. 70–4, 86–93, 193–200, 211–13. I am grateful to Dr Brennan for permission to adapt the excellent notes to his edition.

PARIS

The 1. of May I went to see Queene Margarets gardins[1] some two leagues out of the towne; they are verie pleasant and only for pleasure, they have store of fountaines and streames, that runne up and downe the gardin of some five or six foote broad.

The 7. of May I saw the *Louvre*[2] the kings house in *Paris*. the *grand' Salle* where the Swissers lye in garde is a fayre roome and also that over it, that roome which they call the Cablinett and other chambers within are prettie roomes, and they have marvelous rich seelings at the toppe, and the Chamber, where the king doth dine, hath a space rayled rounde, wherein the table is, and also where the king his bedchamber is, it hath also a little parte rayled in, where the bed is contayned, for it is in a corner of the chamber, and in that respect doth not encomber the chamber so much as we doe in England, who for the most parte doe so place our beds, that the most of the roome of the chamber is taken up, there is one private chamber[3] fayrely sett forth and well furnished, the others nothing well, where the Queene Regente and the king heretofore did use to sitt in Counsell with some particular men of the State about important affayres belonging unto

[1] Marguerite de Valois (1553–1615). Somerset is perhaps referring to the gardens at the Château de Madrid, her official residence.
[2] François I demolished the medieval fortress, or Château du Louvre, and began plans for his own magnificent palace in 1541. The building was extended by Henri IV and Louis XIII and the quadrangle was completed during the minority of Louis XIV. The buildings were left to decay from 1676 and occupied by squatters until 1754.
[3] La chambre d'état, or la chambre d'audience. Between 1574 and 1585 Henri III had sought more privacy by regulating access to the royal presence at the Louvre.

it. There is one gallerie[4] allreadie finnished, wherein are the kings of France their pictures, beginning at *St. Lewis* until *Henrie* the 3. on the one side, and on the other, their wives over against them, with the Noblemen of the kings side, and the Ladies of the Queenes side, of those times. *Henry* the 4th. his picture, nor his wifes the Queene Regent that now is, were not sett up, only there was roome for them. This gallerie is not furnished with chayres and stooles at all as ours in England are, only there be seates as it were benches or formes fastned unto the walles, couloured and richly donne, answerable unto the seeling, and so it is on both sides for men to sitt, and out of this gallerie, we passe into a gallerie,[5] which for breadth and length the Christian worlde, as it is thought, doth not afforde the like, which is as yet nothing garnished on the inside.

Through this gallerie a man passeth unto the *Tuilleries*,[6] where are manie other statelie and fayre large Chambers, verie richly sett out, with manie excellent peeces of good worke of goulde and coulours and fayre chimney peeces, and *Henry* the 4th. over one chimney peece is cutt out naked in white marble, with some of his mistresses naked with him. In these lodgings it is sayde he kept his mistresses. Here is an excellent fine stayre in the Tuilleries verie cunningly and curiously made, for as farre as a man can discerne, and as the keepers of the lodgings tell us, it standes upon nothing, it is so finely donne, that a man windes rounde to the toppe, and when a man is there, the excellencie of the stayre is, a man may see where he came up, and also may discerne he that is on high a man coming up from the verie first steppe unto the highest. Under the side of these lodgings is the goodlie gardin[7] called the *Tuilleries* of some three score and ten acres of grounde, as the gardiners themselves tolde me, it hath manie fine delicate walkes of that varietie that will afforde great contentment, there is one close walke, the verie length of the gardin, the walkes are made of boxe tree, there is one greate ponde in it, that is filled from the waterworkes at the New-bridge by pipes, besides other fountaines. There is wayes out of this unto the Capucins and unto the

[4] The gallery overlooking the quai du Louvre.
[5] Catherine de' Medici began the Long Gallery flanking the river to connect the Louvre with her new palace at the Tuileries.
[6] The Tuileries, destroyed in 1871, was the principal imperial and royal residence in Paris. It had been begun by Catherine de' Medici in 1564 as a royal retreat from the congested Louvre; Henri IV added the large wing towards the quai.
[7] The gardens of the Tuileries were laid out by Catherine de' Medici between 1564 and 1572. They were remade between 1594 and 1609 by Henri IV after they had been virtually destroyed during his siege of Paris.

Feuillans,[8] for whome the Queene regent that now is hath built a fayre Church and a house, to one of these two Religious houses, the king that now is and the Queene goe to Masse, and she most usually to the *Feuillans*. Of the one side of the *Louvre* the river of *Seyne* runneth, and on the other side *Henry* the 4. meant, and so it shalbe, a gardin[9] in time, and when it is made so and all the buildings finished, and the things that are intended to be donne accomplished, a man may justly say that there cannot be a place of more pleasure then this will be. Under these galleries and lodgings there are roomes, which the king hath bestowed upon those that are trades-men, and that are his servants, of all manner of artificers that are necessarie belonging unto him, and of all kinde of mechanickes, he hath a way out of the Gallerie downe into the Chamber called the Counsell Chamber donne with marble all under foote, all seeled with marble at the toppe and with manie Antikes carved and cutt very curiously, all the sides of the chamber donne also with marble, all over marble in everie parte of the Chamber, and over the Chimney the true effigies of *Diana of Ephesus*,[10] for which the Venetians offered *Henrie* the 4th. millions of Crownes. Out of this chamber the king hath a doore, that bringeth a secrett way to the *Tuilleries*, that when they thought him at counsell there, he meant to be at the *Tuilleries*. Out of this narrowe private passage, the king hath a doore to everie trade-mans house, to see at his pleasure how they goe forwards with his workes, when they have anie of his in hand.

On the 20th. of May I saw the Ceremonie of the Entrance into Religion of a verie fayre Gentlewoman about the age of 17. who was the fift daughter that her mother had and all Nunnes, the Order she was to be of, was the Order of the Carmelines,[11] one of the strictest orders for women that is.

Paris[12] the Capitall Cittie of *France*, and of all *Europe* held to be the greatest and the most populous. It is manie mile compas, being walled[13] and moted

---

[8] The monastery of the Capuchins was situated to the west of the Rue Castiglione. The present Terrasse des Feuillants adjoined the convent of the Feuillant order (reformed Cistercians), which was dissolved in 1791.

[9] The garden of Marie de' Medici, later known as le Jardin de l'Infante, ran eastward from the Petite Galerie between the Louvre and the river.

[10] The famous 'Diana with the Fawn', now in the Louvre.

[11] Either the Carmelite Nuns of the Ancient Observance, introduced into France in the 15th cent., or the Discalced Carmelite Nuns, established in France in 1604 by a noblewoman, Barbe Acane (d. 1618).

[12] Somerset visited Paris at a period of extensive building and redevelopment.

[13] Most of the walls at this period dated from *c*.1560. However, the late 12th-cent. wall of Philip Augustus was still largely intact on the Left Bank. On the Right Bank, the same wall had been extended outwards in the 14th cent. by Charles V.

about, in forme almost rounde, and hath very large suburbes, especially those of *St. Germain*, where manie Noblemen, and most strangers keepe, *St. Honoré*, *St. Jacques* and others. It standeth upon a navigable river, though but shallow hereabouts, called *La Seyne*, yet notwithstanding with great labour and difficultie, the streame running continually very swift without flowing & ebbing there cometh to this towne by means thereof manie good provisions of corne, wine, wood and the like. A speciall benefitt which the towne makes of this river, is, that there be manie milles built upon boates upon it, that serve to grinde their Corne. This river devides Paris into 3. partes, the Cittie, the Universitie, and the Towne, the towne being the greatest and fayrest parte lying on the North side of the river, the next in bignesse is the universitie on the south-side, the least is the Cittie, which is an Iland in midst of the river called *L'Isle du Palais*, where the pallace or olde house[14] of the kings of France is (whence the Iland takes it's name) now serving for law and Justice, as Westminster-hall doth, and also is become the Exchange and common meeting of Marchants. In this Iland stands also the Cathedrall Church *Nostre Dame*[15] a goodlie and fayre building (built, as it is held, by Englishmen) though not so richly adorned within as manie Churches of France are. The steepel is of 2. great towers both of one heighth and workemanshipp. *Paris* hath manie statelie and sumptuous buildings in it, both of Churches, kings pallaces, & Noblemens houses, some reasonable large streetes, most narrowe, yet all well paved, comelie houses for the most parte built upright and uniformally and of a fayre kinde of stone, which they have very necessarie and commodious and neere unto the towne, the fayrest streetes are *la rue St. Honoré* and *la rue St. Antoine*, whereof the one is at one ende of the towne, the other at the other and make the length of *Paris*, as *la rue St. Martin* and *la rue St. Jacques* also 2. verie fayre streetes make the breadth of it. It is no small blemish to this towne, and greate pittie it is so fayre a Cittie should have so fowle a blemish, that the streetes are at all times almost of the yeare verie durtie and mirie,[16] which of long time hath caused so much riding on horse and footecloth in the towne, and of late an incredible number of coches, which were held to surpasse the number of 26. thousand. This *bouë de Paris* (for so the durte is commonly called) comes by reason of the infinite multitude of

[14] L'Île de la Cité was the royal, legal, and ecclesiastical centre of Paris.
[15] The metropolitan cathedral of Paris, founded in 1163 and completed between the 13th and 14th cents., survived largely untouched until 1700.
[16] A common complaint about Paris.

people, that continually is in it, insomuch as manie English travellers holde, that at all times here the towne is as full of people, as *London* is in Tearme-time, there being manie houses, which have 3. or 4. householdes in them a peece. The Churches, which are here in great number (there being 69. parish-churches, besides monasteries, religious houses and Chappells) are for the most parte verie sumptuously built, and richly adorned within with hangings, chappells, altars, pictures, and threasures of great value in shreenes and other cases of relikes, chalices and other sacred vessells and instruments of silver and golde, manie sett with pretious stone, besides the richenesse and great store of Copes, vestements, and other ornaments of the altar. And indeede the Churches of France are generally very remarkable as well for their greatenesse and statelie curious building, as for the aforesayd kinde of treasure. There are also (as I sayd before) manie greate and goodlie monasteries of all sortes of Religious Orders both of men and women, as that of *St. Germain les Prez*,[17] *St. Genoviefve*,[18] *St. Victor*,[19] and diverse goodlie hospitalls, as *l'hostel Dieu*,[20] *les quinzevingts*,[21] a famous hospitall of 300. blinde men, founded by *St. Lewis* king of France in memorie of the suffering of so manie Christians, as the Saracens being maisters of some partes hereabouts, did putt their eyes out. The *Louvre*, which is the kings house, as much as is finished of it according to the first designe, is verie Majesticall, whereof I have spoken more particularly at my first being at *Paris*, but the new building of the Queene Regent[22] (for as yet it hath no other name but *le nouveau bastiment de la Reyne*) in the suburbes of *St. Germain* is farre more compleate both for strength and curious workemanship. When the king is at the *Louvre* or at anie other place, he hath continually his guarde with him, which consisteth of three nations, the Scottish which are next to his bodie, by reason of the greate league, which hath ever bene betweene France & Scottland in the times of the warres, that England held against them both; French, which are the next in place, and the Swissers, which by most princes in Christendome are for

[17] The church of St-Germain-des-Prés (of the mid-11th cent.), the oldest in Paris, was by the 17th cent. the chief house of the reformed Congregation de Saint-Maur (formerly the order of St Benedict).

[18] The abbey of Ste-Geneviève, demolished in 1807, but recalled in name by the present-day Bibliothèque Ste-Geneviève, near the Sorbonne, which originated from the abbey's library.

[19] The abbey of St-Victor, in whose library Rabelais had studied, was dispersed in 1790.

[20] The Hôtel Dieu, the oldest hospital in Paris, was greatly enlarged by Henri IV. It was situated near the place du Parvis Notre-Dame.

[21] The Hôpital des Quinze-Vingts, founded by Louis IX in 1260 for the care of 300 blind men. The original building stood between the Palais Royal and the Louvre.

[22] The Palais du Luxembourg, built between 1615 and 1627 by Salomon de Brosse.

their fidelitie made use of in that kinde of service. The number of the whole guarde is 1500. divided into sundrie companies, whereof eache contayneth 300. which companies watche by turnes, the souldiers, which are the French, setting their watch everie day at 11. of the clock, & marching to the Court in their bright armour, with their coulours, drumme and fife verie bravely.

The *Bastille*[23] (built, as themselves doe affirme, by Englishmen) is a place worth the observation, where I saw 80. peeces of great ordinance, and amongst the rest there was foure peeces of them, which were the finest of all the rest, which the Duke of *Guise* that was slayne by *Henry* the 3. at *Bloys*,[24] wonne in a battayle against the Almans. There are 40. men, which I may tearme Warders, that doe continually watche within the *Bastille*, where the Treasurie of France is kept. The *Bastille* is there in the same manner, as the Tower of *London* is in England. The Arcenal,[25] which the Duke of *Suilly*[26] whilest he was Treasurer made a fayre house with a fayre gardin and walkes belonging unto it; there is hard by it a fayre *Pall malle*[27] seated by the river side. The armorie in this Arcinall is thought able to arme 8000. foote, and 2000. horse. *La Place Royalle*[28] is a most beautiefull place, square and uniformally built. Besides these places *le Palais, la Sainte Chapelle*,[29] hard by it, *l'hostel de la ville*,[30] *Saincts Innocents*,[31] the kings librarie at the *Cordeliers*,[32] and that at *St. Victors*[33] and manie others, are singularities most worthie the curious observation of a Traveller. There goe 5. or 6. bridges over

[23] The original Bastille St-Antoine was redesigned and extended into a fortress with eight towers during the reign of Charles V (1364–80). By the time of Louis XIII, it was regarded primarily as a state prison for political offenders.

[24] Henri, duc de Guise (b. 1550), and his brother Louis (b. 1555), cardinal de Guise, were assassinated on Henri III's orders in the royal chambers of the Château de Blois on 23 Dec. 1588.

[25] A 14th-cent. ammunition store, rebuilt and enlarged by Henri IV. The Bibliothèque de l'Arsenal is housed in the rooms occupied by Sully when master general of the artillery and until his death in 1634.

[26] Maximilien de Béthune, baron de Rosny and duc de Sully (1560–1641), statesman, favourite of Henri IV, and author of the *Mémoires* (first printed in 1638).

[27] The alley in which the game 'pall-mall' was played.

[28] Built between 1606 and 1611 on the site of the garden of the Palais des Tournelles, and now known as the place des Vosges.

[29] Built between 1243 and 1248 as a shrine for various relics owned by St Louis, including a 'Crown of Thorns'.

[30] The Hôtel de Ville. The building of 1533–40, renovated between 1608 and 1610, was burned down by the Communards in 1871.

[31] In the Rue St-Denis, the Cemetery of the Holy Innocents, probably founded in the 11th cent., was only abandoned in 1785. During this period an estimated 1,200,000 corpses were buried there. It was also used as the main burial ground for foreigners in Paris.

[32] The 15th-cent. Couvent des Cordeliers, a Franciscan convent in the Faubourg St-Germain.

[33] The library of the abbey of St-Victor, dispersed in 1790.

la Seyne, the fayrest is *Pont-noeuf* [34] or the New bridge all built of great free stone, without anie houses upon it, because it should not hinder the kings prospect out of the *Louvre* into the towne, & in particular of his statelie late building in the *Isle du Palais*, saving only there standes close by the bridge a waterworke called *la Samaritaine*[35] intended to have had thereby water conveyed into all or most streetes of *Paris*, and by that meanes to have kept the streetes cleane, but it could not hitherto be brought to passe, &, now it serves only some parte of the kings house and *Tuilleries*. This bridge is also become a place of great meeting and walking. From thence you may see a greate parte of the *Louvre*, especially the statelie gallerie, which for a quarter of a mile and more in length runnes along the river. *Pont nostre Dame*[36] when you are upon it, hath so little signe of being a bridge, as you cannot discerne, but that you are walking in one of the fayrest neatest and most beautiefull streetes, the houses being built all of one heighth and forme on both sides, that a man shall lightly see. Such another is also *le Pont au change*[37] where all the goldesmithes dwell, and *le Pont aux oiseaux*, another streete upon the same river, so called, because there is never a house upon it; but hath the signe of one kinde of birde or others. *Petit Pont* [38] is also such another bridge, as being upon it, you can no way discerne it from a streete. The universitie,[39] I cannot greatly commende for anie brave Colledges (which in number both publike and private are some 50.) though I must needes say that the learning of that Universitie hath ever ranked with those of the best reputation, especially that of the *Sorbone*, from whence *St. Thomas of Aquin*, *St. Bonaventure* and manie other greate personages have sprung. This Universitie was founded by that ever renowned Emperour & king *Charlemagne* at the instancie of his maister *Alcuinus* an Englishman, and hath manie great priviledges belonging unto it distinct from the Cittie. I saw at my being in *Paris* the famous procession of the bodie of *St. Genoveva*,[40] patronesse of the towne, the which is never carried in

[34] The oldest existing bridge in Paris, crossing the western extremity of the island, was begun in 1578 and completed *c.*1606. It was the first bridge in Paris to be built without houses.

[35] Originally situated in the Place Dauphine, the Samaritaine was one of the earliest hydraulic pumps, constructed by Lintlaër for Henri IV to supfnply water to the Louvre and Tuileries.

[36] This bridge, on the site of the main Roman bridge into Paris, was rebuilt in 1913.

[37] A wooden bridge, lined with money-changers' and goldsmiths' shops, was replaced by a stone one in the 1640s (and again in 1858–9).

[38] On the site of another Roman bridge, originally defended by the Petit Châtelet.

[39] The university was founded in the early 12th cent., and by the 17th cent. there were over sixty separate colleges.

[40] Ste Geneviève (d. *c.*500), patroness of Paris. Her relics were carried in procession through the city in times of national crisis or local hardship, particularly drought.

procession, but in greate extremitie of drawthe, and it is carried by the Bishop of *Paris* being barefooted, accompanied with all the Clergie of the towne, and likewise with all the Companies of Religious Orders in the towne. And it is ever found, I myself at that time did see it at that time, that although there was a greate drawth before, then it did rayne. I also at my being there saw the feast of *Corpus Christi* day sollemnized with great devotion, as the *Parisians* are very devoute; the streetes were hangd and adorned in as riche manner as might be, with rich hangings and Carpetts; and in manie places of the towne there were altars erected verie riche for plate and Jewells, where the priests did rest with the Blessed Sacrament. Moreover I saw at my being in *Paris* a brave shew made, which is everie yeare in June; they are those Sergeants only, which are of the Presidiall of *Chastelett*[41] and belonging unto it, and also by all the Counsellours, Judges and Advocates, that ridde on horseback in their robes, and that are only belonging unto the Court. These sergeants have this priviledge, that they may arreste anie man in anie place within the territories of the Courte Parlement of *Paris*, and they come once a yeare to presente themselves, unto the Courte, that they may be knowen unto the Judges; if they come not unto this meeting, they forfeite some summes of monie. I saw also a fine shew upon May-day made by the guarde of the towne in their liveries, which were richly embroadered some upon velvett. There was a general assemblie of Jacobins Fryers at *Paris* at that time, and I was at their disputations, and there I heard Cardinall *Peron*[42] moderate, who was carried in his chayre, for he was not able to goe by reason of the gowte had taken away the use of his legs. At my being here Sir Thomas Edmonds[43] was leger embassadour for his Majestie of England. [. . .]

FLORENCE

[It] is a fayre towne; it hath long broade streetes, manie fayre statelie pallaces, the buildings of the towne most of them are of stone; there are

[41] On the place du Châtelet, at the northern side of the Pont au Change, once stood the Grand Châtelet, a fortress gateway to the Cité, formerly the headquarters of the provost of Paris and the guild of notaries. Dating originally from 1130, it was rebuilt several times, notably in 1506 and 1684, and demolished between 1802 and 1810.

[42] Jacques Davy, cardinal Du Perron (1556–1618), formerly a favourite of Gabrielle d'Estrées, and by 1612 a powerful court intriguer. He was also widely admired as a scholar and cultivated patron of letters.

[43] Sir Thomas Edmondes (c.1563–1639) held appointments as English agent at Paris from 1592 to 1594, in 1597, and from 1598 to 1599; and as ambassador from 1610 to 1616, and again in 1617.

also manie goodlie fayre churches, the chiefest is the *Domo*,[44] which hath the fayrest outside of anie church in Christendome; and the finest steeple,[45] insomuch that when *Charles* the 5. came through the towne, he sayde it was too fine to be shewen everie day, and wondered they had not a case for it; it is as curiously wrought with marble of sundrie coulours as it is possible;[46] the Cuppolo[47] of the Church is a marvelous fine peece of architecture, for which the *Italians* exceede all other countries farre; there is also *Santo Spirito*[48] a fayre church that hath a high altar which cost a hundred thousand Crownes built by a gentleman of the towne; it is of *lapis* and aggott and other pretious stones; there is also a fayre altar at *St. Michael*[49] built by a gentle man of the towne in the time of the *Republic*. There is also *St. Laurence* church,[50] where the obsequies of all Catholike princes are, and at my being there I saw the funeralls of the Queene of Spayne very costly performed & of the Emperour *Rodolphus*;[51] there is a librarie by this church of *manuscripts* all, accounted the best librarie of the world in that kinde; amongst others there is *Terence* in *manuscript* written by the Authour himself;[52] I saw also the 7. of February a procession from

[44] The cathedral of Santa Maria del Fiore is dedicated to the Madonna of Florence. It was built mostly during the 14th and 15th cents. on the site of the ancient cathedral of Santa Reparata.

[45] The construction of the campanile, almost 85 m. high, was begun in 1334 by Giotto, continued by Andrea Pisano, and completed in 1359 by Francesco Talenti. It displays the same contrasting marble colours as the Duomo.

[46] The building is characterized by its white marble from Carrara, green from Prato, and red from the Maremma.

[47] The cupola, the largest and highest dome of its time, was erected by Brunelleschi between 1420 and 1426. It has two concentric shells, the outer being thinner than the inner. Brunelleschi died in 1446 and Verrocchio was responsible for placing the hollow bronze ball (capable of holding some ten people inside it) and cross on the summit in the late 1460s.

[48] Santo Spirito, in the Oltrarno district on the south bank of the Arno, was originally a mid-13th-cent. Augustinian foundation. In 1428 Brunelleschi was commissioned to design a new church but building only began in 1444, two years before his death. The elaborate high altar was begun in the early 17th cent. by Giovanni Battista Caccini (1556–*c.*1612).

[49] The Or San Michele. A grain market was erected here *c.*1290 but it burned down in 1304. The present building was used as a market from 1337; and the interior of the hall is now used as a church. The high altar by Andrea Oreagna, set with precious stones in marble over an image of the Virgin, was completed in 1359.

[50] San Lorenzo. The Medicis commissioned Brunelleschi to rebuild the church in 1425. It became the main burial place for the principal members of their family, from Cosimo il Vecchio (1389–1464) to Cosimo III (1642–1723).

[51] Margaret of Austria (b. 1584), queen of Spain, married Philip III in 1598. She died at the Escorial on 3 Oct. 1611. Emperor Rudolph II (b. 1552) died at Prague on 20 Jan. 1612. He had been educated at the royal court at Madrid from 1564 to 1570, as a possible successor to Philip II, who had not yet entered into his fourth marriage which later produced Philip III. Somerset is perhaps referring to masses of remembrance.

[52] The Biblioteca Laurenziana (or Laurentian Library), commissioned from Michelangelo *c.*1524 by Pope Clement VII (Giulio de' Medici) to house the Medici's collections of MSS.

the *Annunciata*[53] unto this church; in which the Duke and the Dutchesse
went in person, the cause of which was when *Ferdinando*[54] this mans father
dyed, whereas there was to have bene bestowed upon the funeralls 40.
thousand Crownes, he altered that before his death and ordained that for
ever as upon that day there should be bestowed everie yeare 4. thousand
Crownes to the marrying of poore maydes and orphanes, and these poore
people are lead by the chiefe gentlewomen of the towne from the *Annunciata* unto *St. Laurence*, and in the *Annunciata* there is a purse tyed about
everie one of their neckes with a tickett of the name of the mayde and her
parents and where she dwelles, and withall that when she is to be married,
she is to repayre to such an Office in the towne of the Dukes, where she
shall receave so manie Crownes truly and surely payde her, as her tickett
maketh mention; but she cannot have it but when she is to marrie; they
have also given them by the Duke all that which they have about them that
day which is all new, they are clothed in blew cloath with white veyles on
their heades. By the Church of the *Annunciata*, which is another fayre
church of the towne, there is a fayre *Piatsa*[55] as they tearme it, a broade
peece of ground, as it were a markett place or a fayre square, in the middle
of which there is *Ferdinando* on horseback in brasse very bravely cutt;[56] and
of one side there is a fayre hospitall[57] erected for no other intent and
purpose then to maintayne some 100. nurses to nurse those children that
their parents will not acknowledge; as if anie maide should be gott with
childe, rather then she should use anie unlawfull meanes to destroye it, she
may cause it to be sent thither anie night she will, and there it shalbe
receaved at a hole without anie farther questions, for there are those for the
purpose to receave them, so that the parents never come to knowe their
childe after, nor never are at anie charge whatsoever; it is called the hospitall
of the Innocents, and over against this hospitall, there is a fayre goodlie
building[58] answerable unto that of the same manner of building, which is

[53] The church of the Santissima Annunziata was founded by the Servite Order in 1250. It was rebuilt
in the 15th cent. and extensively renovated between 1601 and 1615. It contains the chapel of the
Annunziata, built in 1448 at the expense of Pietro de' Medici.

[54] Ferdinando I (1549–1609).

[55] The Piazza Santissima Annunziata was designed by Brunelleschi.

[56] An equestrian statue of Ferdinando I by Giambologna; his last work, cast reputedly from Turkish
cannons by Tacca in 1608.

[57] The Spedale degli Innocenti opened in 1445 as a hospital for foundlings. It is decorated between
the arches with carvings of infants in swaddling clothes. Vincenzo Borghini, a friend of Vasari and
artistic adviser to Cosimo I, was prior from 1552 to 1580.

[58] Probably the Chiostro degli Uomini (1422–45) in the convent which now contains the Museo dello
Spedale degli Innocenti. The Chiostro delle Donne (1438) was reserved for women workers.

for the mayntaining of phisitians to looke unto the hospitall. There is also *Santa Maria Novella*[59] a verie fayre church for building, and there is *Santa Croce*[60] a faire church in the piatsa; before that church there is a place that is rayled in, where the gentlemen of the towne in the time of *Carnevalle* which beginneth at the Epiphane and lasteth till Lent, doe play at a sporte called: *Calce*,[61] which in English is footeball; it is a sporte which they are here much wedded unto, and the Duke himself when he is in towne cometh to it, and at my being in the towne his brother *Francesco*[62] played at it; noe man darres come within the rayles to play, unlesse he be a gentleman; for if he doe, they will buffett him quickly out; and because opportunitie offereth itself, I will here speake of their *Carnevale*, at which time they use all their sportes & triumphes as we in England doe at Christmas. The manner of it is that they putt vizards on their faces and so goe up and downe the towne, some a foote, some a horseback, as they please and as their conceipts are; some goe a masking like Turkes apparrelled, some like one countrie people, some like another, some will ride up and downe in a riding coate & his poste before him, as if he were newly come to the towne; some will goe a masking in coaches, which are made so that they may all uncover it over head, and ride so; some will go a masking and everie one will play upon an instrument and make good musike, and so everie one after his owne capriccho; the better sorte that goe a masking have alwaies fellowes that follow with egs, the meate being taken out and filled with rose-water, and so whome they favour as they go along the streete, they will fling those egs at them they knowe, which is a favour, and at this time a man may fling egs at anie woman in a windowe or riding in her coche; they of the common sorte fill their egs with ordinarie water; a masker is very free at this time; such is the manner of the custome of the Countrie; this is the onlie time that a man may come boldely to his mistrisses windowe, and there tosse egs with them; the women that be honest will tosse egs for sporte; the women

[59] The Dominican church of Santa Maria Novella, generally regarded as the most important Gothic church in Tuscany. It was completed in the mid-14th cent., with further work on its façade and portal (1456–70) by Leon Battista Alberti.

[60] The Franciscan church of Santa Croce was rebuilt in 1294/5 and after many delays consecrated in 1442. The interior was redesigned by Vasari in the 1560s. There is a monument to Machiavelli (d. 1527), who is buried here, and the tomb of Michelangelo Buonarroti (d. 1564) by Vasari.

[61] The Piazza Santa Croce has been used since the 14th cent. for tournaments, festivals, and spectacles. The traditional football game, 'calcio in costume', is still played here once a year with few rules and considerable violence. The teams represent the four quartiere of the city (San Giovanni, Santa Croce, S. M. Novella, S. Spirito).

[62] Cosimo II had three brothers: Carlo, cardinal (d. 1666); Francesco (d. 1614); and Lorenzo (d. 1648).

have that slight to catche the egs and wett him that casteth and he shall seldome wett her. Now may a man thinke that if a man have this libertie to goe in this manner a masking, that there might much mischiefe be donne; for as the Italians are deadlie in their hate, so have they at this time, as a man would imagine, fitt occasion to compasse their designe, by killing those, whome they have anie quarrell unto; true, it seemed unto me at the first time so; untill I was better informed; for though these maskers have this free-dome, yet upon paine of death he dareth not carrie anie kinde of weapon, whatsoever he be; for if he be found with it, he dyeth for it, such is the law; or else there might much harme ensue by this meanes; and here in this piatsa before *Santa Croce* are alwaies all the maskes of the towne; but had it not bene that the Duke mourned at that time for the Queene of Spaine the Dutchesses sister; there had bene braver masking farre then there was. This towne of *Florence* is the best towne of *Italie* to live in for a stranger both in respect of the good language & for the cleanlinesse; for though it rayne never so much, yet in one quarter that it holdes up, a man may goe over the towne drye, and therefore it is called *Firenza la Bella*; there are all Exercises to be had. It is the Capitall towne of *Tuscanie*; it hath in it but 30. parishes that are Cures;[63] but those were too few to serve the towne, but only that there are besides a hundred Churches that belong to monasteries and religious houses, where the people resorte; there are 60. monasteries of women, there are also manie fayre hospitalls of greate *entrada*;[64] there are also manie Companies of lay men, inhabitants of the towne, that meete thrice in a weeke, as wednesdayes, frydaies and sonnedaies, and also holie daies, at the Church or chappell which belongeth unto their Companie, and there they have prayers and a sermon, and upon anie Saints day they reade the life of that Sainte, and after that they discipline themselves, all the candles being taken away, and before the light cometh againe, they make themselves readie and are in their places as when the candles went away, and their devotions doe last for some 2. or 3. howers. There is also a Companie, which they call the Companie of *St. Martin*,[65] which are gentlemen, whose office is to looke unto those that be poore and in want, and least that if they were not supplyed, they might take bad courses, as poore womens children

---

[63] Parishes or other spheres of spiritual ministration.

[64] (Spanish): income or revenue.

[65] The chapel of San Martino del Vescovo, rebuilt in 1479 as the seat of the Compagnia dei Buonomini, a charitable society founded in 1442 by St Antoninus, devoted to assisting the poor and those too ashamed to beg ('poveri vergognosi'). Traditionally, some eighteen members of the nobility undertook the work.

for wante of meanes might become naught; and this Companie is only to take notice of such as stande in wante and to relieve them, that by this meanes such bad courses might be hindred; and for this use and purpose is this Companie erected. The river of *Arno* parteth some parte of the towne from the other; there are foure bridges,[66] and one that hath houses upon it, and there the goldesmithes dwell;[67] the marketts are very well served with provision and great store of it. This towne hath ever carried the name for paynting and sculpture, and here are the best and richest stuffes made of all Italie, and there is a good order for it; for there are certaine men which viewe the stuffes, and if they be not of such a weight, they are forfeyted and lost. The Duke hath a fayre pallace,[68] and had it bene finished as the project was intended, it had bene a very fayre one; and as much as is built, is brave statelie building, and so that a stranger cannot see that ever there was anie farther plott intended, unlesse he be informed of it; he hath as riche furniture for his house, as anie prince in Christendome neede to have, or, as I thinke, hath. I saw his *guarderobe* of his dwelling house,[69] which is most sumptuous and riche, which is only stuffe to furnish his pallace; the verie ordinarie hangings that doe hang chambers for those Cardinalls & Bishops, and princes that come sometimes unto him, are of golde and silver and silke; and besides I saw diverse sutes of hangings, and bed and all things sutable for a chamber that is necessarie, of velvett embroadered with pearle, and diverse sutes also of tissues marvelous rich ones embossed with goulde, and also manie others of riche stuffes as possible can be made in a loome; in the time of the heates the Duke lyeth in the lower roomes of his pallace, which are so commodious that he never feeles anie heate; he hath a secrett way under grounde to go out of his pallace unto the forte upon the toppe of a hill, where greate store of his treasure lyeth; In this forte[70] there are manie

[66] The Ponte alla Carraia (Ponte Nuovo) was the second bridge built after the Ponte Vecchio. Its 14th-cent. structure, extensively repaired in 1559, was blown up in 1944. A similar fate befell the Ponte alla Grazie (Ponte Rubaconte), originally of the 13th cent. with several later rebuildings; and the Ponte a Santa Trinità (1567).

[67] The Ponte Vecchio was lined with houses and shops, some of which had been occupied since the 15th cent. by goldsmiths.

[68] The Palazzo Pitti, built by the merchant, Lucca Pitti (d. 1572), a rival of the Medicis. It was incomplete at the time of his death. In 1549 it was purchased by Eleonora di Toledo, the wife of Cosimo I. It became the official residence of the Medicis after Cosimo I moved here from the Palazzo Vecchio. Building work was resumed c.1560 under the direction of Bartolomeo Ammannati.

[69] Garderobe, a secure chamber for the storage of garments, armour, and stores; and by extension, a private room, a bedchamber.

[70] The Forte di Belvedere was a huge fortress commissioned by Ferdinando I in 1590 and designed by Buontalenti in the shape of a six-pointed star. It was usually entered by means of a secret doorway in the Boboli Gardens behind the Palazzo Pitti.

goodlie peeces of ordinance, and when anie embassadour or anie prince of
Italie cometh unto him as they enter in at the house, the peeces goe all of,
which gives a greate state unto the house as a stranger cometh in; for it is so
finely seated over his pallace and so neere that a man seeth all the peeces goe
of full right before his face. At my being there I saw an embassadour of the
king of *Spayne*, which came to give an accounte of the death of the queene,
and brought a present unto the Great Dutchesse the Queenes sister, which
should have come before; for she was godmother unto one of her children; it
was valued at the least worth 2000[li]. sterling, they were Jewells all of
Orientall Diamonds; his name was *Fernando Burja*,[71] nephew to the
Duke of *Lerma*[72] of the house of *Bourja*, the Duke of *Candie*[73] that made
himselfe a Jesuite was his uncle, that was so holie a man in his life; this
Fernando Bourja is the chiefe of the Order of knighthood in *Spayne* called
Monteta.[74] [. . .]

The making of *rash* is only proper to this towne, for it is called by the name
of *Rashe of Florence*.[75] There is no freedomes of Companies as shomakers &
other trades, as we have in our townes of *England*; for here anie man may
keepe shop though he never was in the towne, nay if he never was in the
countrie, so he pay the Duke his gabelle [tax]. This is a towne so well
governed, that a man may walke safely all howers of the night as safely as in
his owne house; but after the bell that rings at 5. hower in the night, which
is called the bell of Justice, no man can weare a weapon; for there is a watch
that goeth all night long over all the partes of the towne, and if they take
any with anie weapon, to prison they goe without anie farther delay.
Concerning the bad women of the towne, that are connived at, not
tollerated, but as it is better so to doe for to suffer an evill then a mischiefe,
for if it were not so, there would be much blood shed then now is, for they
are a strange people for those matters when it takes them in the head, all
that God hath pleased to withdrawe his grace from, and prostitute themselves to all comers, there is an Office, where all their names are putt, that

[71] Possibly Don Francisco de Borja y Aragon (c.1581–1658), prince of Esquilache, noted diplomat and
poet who was viceroy of Peru from 1615 to 1622.

[72] Francisco de Sandoval y Rojas (1552–1625), duke of Lerma, a leading opponent of England until
1604.

[73] Francis Borgia (1510–72), duke of Gandia (Valencia), chosen as third general of the Jesuits in 1563.
He was canonized in 1671.

[74] *Monteta*: derivation unknown.

[75] A smooth textile fabric made of silk (silk rash) or worsted (cloth rash); from the Italian 'raso', a
silk, satin, or fine serge.

will come into that Companie and societie, and so they pay the Duke so manie Crownes a yeare, and that according to the streetes where they dwell; for the fayrer the streete is the more they pay; and that which is raysed by their illnesse, is converted to a good use, which is for the maintayning of a monasterie, which is called the *Convertites*,[76] where when anie will leave their ill life, they may have entertainement; everie Lente all these bad women come unto the *Domo* the chiefe Church of the Cittie to heare a sermon, and those that be Officers over them come along and bring them thither, and at that sermon manie leave their former bad courses, and the vertuous women of the towne come also thither, and take great paynes in talking with those naughtie woemen, and after their sermon is donne, they carrie them with them in their coches full of them, and so by these meanes manie of them are turned; all these bad women weare a blew ribban in their hatts to be knowen, wheresoever they goe, and darre not go but with it; for there is very good order kept concerning them, that by that meanes there is not that mischiefe donne, which would be. Most of the Duke's revenues are raysed by gabelles; as everie hog that cometh into the towne to be killed, he hath a Crowne, everie beefe 3. Crownes, everie sheepe 3. Julies & a halfe; and in such like things, and those hogs are the onlie meate that commonly they eate; it is excellent sweete flesh, and it cannot be otherwise, for they feede only of chestnutts; They have a custome everie yeare upon midsommer day to have a race of Barbarie horses, to which the Duke comes, and some of the horses are so inured to it, that they will runne as true and as fast, as if a man were on their backes; for some of the horses are so trayned to it, that they know quickly, what they have to doe, when they come to it; for as soone as they starte, he lettes his horse goe loose, and he will runne strayte unto the ende of the course and then he will stoppe. There come horses from *Rome* and other partes unto this race, which is some 3. Italian miles; there is also upon this day a race with coches, the gentlemen will lay a greate deale of monie upon these races, and whereas in England they winne a bell that winne, so here the *pallium* is a peece of cloth of golde of some 10. yardes, which is made into the forme of a flag, and so putt upon the toppe of a high powle at the ende of the race, and he that winnes it, carries it quite away, and brings it not in the next yeare as they doe the bell in England. The *pallium* is a thing that is donne and provided by the bodie of the towne. *St. John Baptist* is the patrone of the towne; this day they make a greate

---

[76] Magdalens.

feaste and triumphe.[77] There lyeth buried in the *Domo* one Sir John Haiewood an Essex gentleman,[78] that did serve the *Florentins* against the state of *Pisa* and did them greate service in the siedge of *Pisa*; The villa's that are neere Florence round about it, will make a towne twice as big as it; this commoditie this cittie hath that all the trades-men and mechanicall men of the towne doe all dwell in streetes togeather, so that all the private gentlemens houses are freed from anie annoyance by them; they use not glasse for windowes here, no more then in anie parte of Italie, because of the reflexion of the sunne; in the time of the heates; the women go marvelous rich in this towne in their apparrell; this towne of *Florence* is not very populous; but all the Duke his state over as a man rideth, is exceeding populous; and in all his state there is an excellent course taken for the mending of the high waies; for everie parish is charged with their parte, and so putt upon the high waies as a man doth travell how farre such a parish boundes extendes and what quantitie of ground in length it is to looke unto; this is carved in stone, and so putt on the high waies. In Florence there are store of Jewes, and everie one that is above 18. yeares of age pay the Duke a tribute yearely of some half a Crowne or there abouts. At my being there, there was 3. of the Duke his slaves, that were Turkes, turned Christians, and were Christened in *St. Johns* Chappell,[79] where all Christenings are, and only there; the Chappell is Mosaicall building, the gates of it are of brasse and most curiously cast that they are thought worth manie thousand Crownes.[80] [. . .]

[77] St John the Baptist traditionally has two feast-days: 7 Jan. (the baptism), and 24 June (his birthday).

[78] In the north aisle of the Duomo is an equestrian memorial to Sir John Hawkwood ('Giovanni Acuto'), who commanded the Florentine army from 1377 to 1394.

[79] The Baptistery of San Giovanni, of the 6th to 9th cents. In the 11th and 12th cents. the exterior was entirely encased in white and green marble from Prato in geometrical designs, at the expense of the Arte di Calimala, the most important guild of the medieval city. The vault and cupola are decorated with a series of outstanding mosaics.

[80] The three sets of gilded bronze doors. The earliest is by Andrea Pisano (1336) and originally acted as the main entrance facing the Duomo but was repositioned in 1424 to make way for two new pairs (1403–24; 1425–52). The earlier 15th-cent. doors were designed by Lorenzo Ghiberti, who won a competition, sponsored by the Arte di Calimala, in the year 1401, regarded as a key moment in the Florentine renaissance.

Fynes Moryson, *An Itinerary Containing His Ten Yeeres Travell through the Twelve Dominions of Germany, Bohmerland, Sweitzerland, Netherland, Denmarke, Poland, Italy, Turky, France, England, Scotland & Ireland* (1617), Observations of Italy and Ireland

FYNES MORYSON (1566–1630) has a good claim to have been the first professional travel writer. His account of his travels is the most comprehensive by an early modern English writer. He was educated at Peterhouse College Cambridge, and became a fellow there. At the age of 23 he persuaded the college to let him travel at its expense and, after studying law at Oxford, he left for Germany on 1 May 1591. Moryson spent the next four years travelling through Germany, the Low Countries, Denmark, Poland, and Austria, before returning to London on 13 May 1595. He then wished to venture further afield, having a particular desire to see 'Jerusalem, the fountaine of Religion, and Constantinople, of old the seat of Christian Emperours, and now the seate of the Turkish Ottoman'. Together with his brother, Henry, he set out from London on 29 November 1595. He travelled overland to Venice before sailing to Joppa and proceeding to Jerusalem. They then travelled to Tripoli, Aleppo, and Antioch where Henry Moryson died of dysentery. Fynes, having recovered from the illness, returned to London via Crete, Constantinople, and Venice, arriving on 10 July 1597.

In 1599 Moryson was employed as secretary to Charles Blount, Lord Mountjoy, the Lord Deputy of Ireland, remaining in his service until 1606. He spent much of the rest of his life trying to find a publisher for the increasingly voluminous account of his travels, eventually persuading John Beale of Aldersgate Street, to produce three huge volumes entitled *An Itinerary* (1617). A fourth volume was licensed in 1626, but remained in manuscript until sections of it were published in the twentieth century.[1] Moryson was clearly frustrated by these problems and vowed that he would give up writing in order to concentrate on theology. Little is known of the last years of his life. He died in 1630.[2]

---

[1] *Shakespeare's Europe: Unpublished Chapters of Fynes Moryson's Itinerary. Being a Survey of the Condition of Europe at the end of the 16th Century*, ed. Charles Hughes (London: Sherratt and Hughes, 1903); *The Irish Sections of Fynes Moryson's Unpublished Itinerary*, ed. Graham Kew (Dublin: Irish Manuscripts Commission, 1998).

[2] This account of Moryson's life is based on Kew (ed.), *Irish Sections*, 6–7; *DNB* entry; Charles Hughes (ed.), *Shakespeare's Europe*, introd.

Moryson, like many other travellers, appears to have used his wide experience to denigrate virtually all the cultures and peoples with which he came into contact. Throughout his travels he preserves his sense of English Protestantism and classically educated gentility. In many ways it is hardly surprising that his book found no ready publisher or audience, given not only his belief that he was writing in a 'Crittick Age' with little respect for true scholarship like his, but also his bigotry and inability to be succinct. The suspicion will always remain that Moryson did not really understand the medium of print or the audiences of printed books. He is not especially flattering about northern Europeans or the French but the Italians, Irish, and Turks arouse his particular ire. The Turks represent the epitome of barbarism (see below, pp. 166–78); the Italians, the forces of evil Catholic Europe; and the Irish, perhaps the worst of all, both tendencies, being superstitious Catholics who refuse to obey the legitimate English sovereign who rules them.

The extracts here give some sense of Moryson's fascination with and contempt for Italy. While he is attracted by the glamour of its riches, architectural beauties, and images—which, as a Protestant, he is duty bound to be suspicious of—he is horrified by the superstitiousness he encounters.[3] Other passages reveal his traveller's taste for anecdotes. The representations of the Irish display Moryson's dark fears and horror that England's civilization and true religion may be overwhelmed by their savage neighbours. The Irish are seen to form a bridge between England and those hostile peoples recently discovered in the New World. Equally, they are the barbarous savages who have always haunted European civilization from the time of Herodotus ($c.490$–425 BC) onwards, and who represent what civilization hopes it has left behind.[4]

See also:

Edmund Spenser, *A View of the State of Ireland*, ed. Andrew Hadfield and Willy Maley (Oxford: Blackwell, 1997).

William Lithgow, *A Totall Discourse of his Rare Adventures* (Glasgow: MacLehose, 1906).

William Brereton, *Travels in Holland, the United Provinces, England, Scotland and Ireland: 1634–5*, ed. E. Hawkins (London: Chetham Society, 1844).[5]

[3] Compare Stephen Greenblatt's comments on Spenser in *Renaissance Self-Fashioning from More to Shakespeare* (Chicago: Chicago Univ. Press, 1980), ch. 4.

[4] See David Beers Quinn, *The Elizabethans and the Irish* (Ithaca, NY: Cornell Univ. Press, 1966); Andrew Hadfield, *Spenser's Irish Experience: Wilde Fruit and Salvage Soyl* (Oxford: Clarendon Press, 1997), ch. 2.

[5] Text from Fynes Moryson, *An Itinerary*, 4 vols. (Glasgow: MacLehose, 1907), i. 213–16, 279–82, 326–7; *Irish Sections of Fynes Moryson's Unpublished* Itinerary, 101–5, 107–10.

Now we were to crosse the bredth of Italy, from the Adriatique to the A.D. 1594. Tyrrhene Sea. The first day in the Morning, we rode fifteene miles to a little Citie, called Madonna di Loretto, through fruitful Mountaines, and passing an high Promontary. By the way was an Altar, with this inscription in Latin; O passenger, goe on merily, &c. Gregorie the thirteenth hath well paved the rest of the way. The like inscription is in the ascent of the Mountaine, upon which the little Citie Loreto stands: for this way (in a fruitful Countrey of corne, and a dirty soile) was paved at the charge of the said Pope.

A certaine chamber hath given beginning to this Citie and the Church *Loreto.* thereof, then which nothing is esteemed more holy among the Papists; and because many gifts of great price use to be given by vow to our Lady of this Church, the City is well fortified against Pirats, who did once spoile the same, and were like againe to be invited by the hope of rich spoiles to the like attempt, if the Towne lay unfortified. It is of little circuit, and lieth in length from East to the West, so narrow; as it hath almost but one streete in the bredth, and all the houses of this streete are Innes, or Shops of them that sell Beades to number prayers. On the East side, after a steepe descent of a Mountaine, lies a valley of two miles, and beyond that the sea. On the North side, towards Ancona, though the sea be very farre distant, yet from this Citie, seated upon a high Mountaine, it may easily be seene. Upon the dores of this Church, famous for mens superstitious worship, these verses *The Church of* are written: *Loreto.*

> Illotus timeat quicunque intrara, Sacellum,
> In terris nullum sanctius orbis habet.

> Enter not here unwasht of any spot,
> For a more holy Church the world hath not.

At the Church dore is a statua of brasse erected to Pope Gregorie the thirteenth. As I walked about the Church, behold in a darke Chappell a Priest, by his Exorcismes casting a divell out of a poore woman: Good *A priest casting* Lord what fencing and truly conjuring words he used! How much more *out divells.* skilfull was he in the divels names? then any ambitious Roman ever was in the names of his Citizens, whom he courted for their voices. If he had eaten a bushell of salt in hell; If he had been an inhabitant thereof, surely this Art could never have been more familiar to him. He often spake to the ignorant woman in the Latin tongue, but nothing lesse then in

8484

Europe

Tullies[1] phrase, and at last the poore wretch, either hired to deceive the people, or (if that be more probable) drawne by familiar practice with the Priest, or at least affrighted with his strange language and cries, confessed her selfe dispossessed by his exorcisme. In the body of the Church, a Table of written hand, in the Greeke, Latin, and many other tongues, was fastened to a Piller, setting downe at large the wonderfull historie of the Chamber in the midst of the Church, which I confesse was lesse curiously observed by me, abhorring from that superstition, & hastening from thence as much as I might; yet give me leave to set down the sum thereof out of the

Let the Reader beleeve as he list. Woe to him that beleeves. Woe to him that beleeves.

itinerary of Villamont a French Gentleman. This Chamber or Chappell (saith he) is the very house, in which the Queene Virgin of Nazaret was borne, brought up, and saluted by the Angell, foretelling her of Christs birth, and in which Christ was conceived, and in which the Virgin dwelt after Christs ascention, accompanied with the holy Apostles, especially with Saint John by Christs commaund, which the Apostles after the Virgins death, for the great mysteries done here, turned into a Chappell, consecrated to the sacrificing of Christ, and dedicated the same, and with their owne hands, made the great Crosse of wood, now set in the window of the Chappell, and in which Saint Luke made with his hand the picture and Image now set above it. Let mee adde: This Chappell from a House became a Chamber, and of a Chamber was made a Chappell, and it is built of bricke, and is thirtie foote long, twelve and a halfe broad. In the chimney (as Villamont saith) as yet remaine the holy ashes, which no man dare take away, and the Altar also, upon which the Masse is sung, was made by the Apostles hand. There is a roome into which you first enter, which is divided from the Chappel by an iron grate, for no man enters the chappell without leave, but must say his prayers in the outter roome; yet leave is given to any that aske it. Villamont addeth, that he found by diligent search, that this Chappell was much reverenced in the primitive Church: but the holy land being subdued by Sarasens, then by Turkes; he saith it hapned in the yeere 1291. that this house was taken up from the founda-

The Chappell miraculously carried to Sclavonia.

tions, by Angels, who in the night miraculously carried it to the Sea shoare of Sclavonia, where it was made knowne to the people by the shining of the Virgines Image, and then by a vision of a religious man, the Virgine her selfe made knowne the History to him. He addeth the Virgins Oration,

---

[1] Marcus Tullius Cicero (106–43 BC), Roman orator and statesman. One of the models of Renaissance prose style.

wherein shee gives her selfe many titles, which in later ages were first invented, and shee doth so extoll her owne praises with her owne mouth, as hee that reades the old song of the blessed Virgin, would cry out with the Latine Poet, onely changing the name. O how is she changed from the Virgin, which so modestly spake of her selfe.

Villamont addeth, that messengers were sent into Palestina, who found this History to be most true: yet this Chappell did not long abide in Slavonia, but the Angels in the yeere 1294. tooke it up againe, and trans- *The Chappell* ported it to this Sea coast of Italy, where againe it was made knowne by the *transported to Italy.* shining of the Image, and many miracles daily done; whereupon the Chappell of the Image was called Madonna at Loreto, that is, our Lady of Loreto. And because theeves lying in the wood, did spoile strangers, who daily came thither for devotion, the Angels (as he saith) the third time tooke it up, and set it downe in a private possession of two brothers, who disagreeing in the division of the profit rising by the concourse of people, the Angels the fourth time tooke it up, and placed it in this firme seat, *This image never* where now it remaineth. After it was often visited by strangers, Pope Paul *rested till it came into the Popes* the second built an other stately Church over it, Pope Leo the tenth having *Territory where it* first fortified the little City against Pirates. Let me adde, that Pope Sixtus *is not more* the fifth, borne in this Marca of Ancona, established a Bishop in this *then profitable to* Towne, and so made it a City. Villamont relating the treasure of this *the Pope and* Church, among the rest, nameth certaine Mapps of Cities, and Moun- *Church men.* taines, and the Images of the twelve Apostles, a great Crucifix, Candle-sticks, and infinite Vessels of silver, Images, Chalices, Crosses, of gold, and many precious stones of huge value, two Crosses made all of precious stones (whereof one was given by the Arch-Duke of Austria), and a Harte of gold set with precious stones (the gift of the Duchesse of Lorayne) and a vessell of huge value [...]

The second day we began the view of Rome with the Popes Pallace, seated *The Popes Pallace.* in the part of the Citie, called Il Borgo; which Pallace Pope Nicholas the third built, and Nicholas the fifth compassed with walles, and the Pallace is of great circuit, and the staires are so easie, that Horses and Mules may goe up to the top of the Mountaine, and with easie ascent and descent beare the Popes carriage.[2] At the enterance there be three galleries one above the

---

[2] Moryson's visit would seem to indicate that the papal buildings were more accessible and less obviously threatening and paranoid fortresses than many contemporary English accounts would indicate.

other, whereof the two first were built by Leo the tenth, and Paul the third, and the third and highest by Sixtus Quintus, and they are all fairely painted and guilded. Upon these lie two large chambers, and beyond them is a vast and long gallery of foure hundred seventie and one walking paces, in *The famous* the middest whereof is the famous Librarie of the Popes In vaticano; and *Librarie.* therein are many inscriptions of the Pope Sixtus Quintus who repaired it, and it is adorned with many faire pictures guilded all over. I did see the severall roomes thereof. The first one hundred fortie and seven walking paces long, had three rowes of Cubbards filled with bookes: the second was thirtie nine paces long; and the third containing the bookes of greatest price locked up, was twentie paces long. Pope Sixtus the fourth built this Librarie, with the Chappell of the Pallace, and the Conclave. The wall of the Chappell shineth like a glasse with precious stones: where the Pope Sixtus Quintus commanded Michael Angelo to paint the day of Judgement, and the common report is, that this Pope promised this famous Painter, that he would not come into the Chappell, till he had finished his worke; yet by some Cardinals perswasions that he broke his promise, and that the Painter thereupon made the pictures of the Pope and the Cardinals in hell amongst the Divels, so lively as every man might know them. Betweene this Chappell and the Conclave, (where they chuse the Popes) lies a Kingly Gallery, not unworthily called vulgarly Sala Regia, (which others call Sala del Conclave). The wall of this Gallery in like sort shineth with pretious stones, and the pavement is of pretious marble, the arched *The Massacre of* roofe all guilded, and at the upper end I wondred to see the Massacre of *Paris painted.* Paris painted upon the wall, with the Popes inscription greatly commending that detestable cruelty.[3] At the same upper end the foresaid Chappell (as you come up) lies on the left hand, and the Conclave on the right hand; in which Conclave the Cardinals meete to chuse the Pope, devided into severall roomes, but meeting at a common table, and when they have chosen him, they leade him into a Chappell at the lower end, and neere the dore of the said Kingly Gallery, and place him there upon a hollow seate of Marble. I know not whether this be the chaire, in which the sex of the Pope is tried, but I am sure it is hollow, with a hole in the bottom. After they put a Banner out of a high window, and there make knowne to the

---

[3] Protestants regarded the Massacre of Saint Bartholomew's Day, 23 Aug. 1572, when the Catholic Guise faction in Paris killed 50,000 Protestant Huguenots, as one of the most significant dates of European history. The evil genius behind the massacre was said to be Catherine de' Medici—who was, of course, Italian. She was congratulated by Pope Gregory XIII.

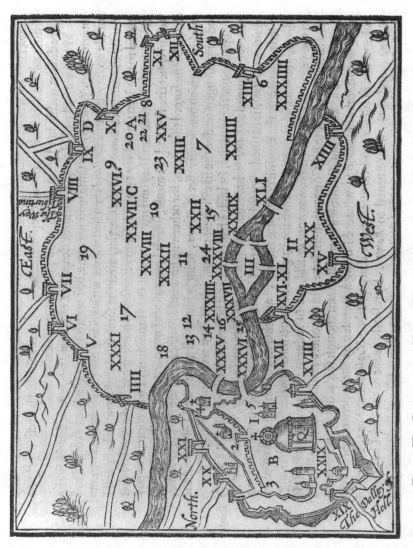

FIG. 3. The Description of Rome (Fynes Moryson, *Itinerary* (1617), I, ii, p. 122)

*The Chappell of
Pope Paul the
third.*
people the name that the Pope hath chosen, and then his armes are hung up
round about. This Chappell at the lower end of the said Gallery, hath the
name of Pope Paul the third, of the Family of Farnese, and it is little, and of
a round forme (as I remember), but it is beautiful beyond imagination. The
images of the Apostles seeme to bee of silver, and Paradice painted upon
the arched roofe, with Angels flying, being the worke of Michael Angelo,
seemed to me admirable. Upon the other side of the said Library is the
private Gallery of the Pope, looking into the Garden (3) Belvedere, which
is seated upon the side of the Mount Vatican, where Pope Innocent the
eight built part of the Pallace, and called it Belvedere, of the faire prospect
of all Rome subject to the eye. And Pope Julius the second placed in this
Garden many very faire statuaes, namely, of the River Nilus, of the River
Tyber, of Romulus and Remus playing with the papps of a shee-Wolfe, all
being placed in the open Garden, and a most faire statua of Apollo, another
admirable statua of Lycaon with his children, another of the boy Antoninus, whom the Emperour Adrian loved, another of Hercules another of
Cupid, another of Venus, another of Cleopatra sleeping with her arme over
her face, and bearing a Serpent, being a wonderfull faire statua. And these
are all locked up, and not to be seene without favour.

*The Castle of
Saint Angelo.*
Hence we went to the Castle (4) of Saint Angelo of old called Moles
Adriani, for it was the Sepulcher of the Emperour Adrian, upon the
top whereof was the Pine apple of brasse, which before I said was since
placed in the open Court-yard of Saint Peters Church. This Sepulcher of
Adrian called Moles (B) was demolished by Belisarius, in the warre of the
Goathes, upon the ruines whereof Pope Boniface the eight built this
Castle, and Pope Alexander the sixth compassed it with walles and ditches,
and placed therein a guard of Souldiers, and built from this Castle to the
Popes Pallace an open and a close gallery, by which upon any tumult, the
Pope may passe safely from his Pallace to the Castle. And after Pope Paul
the third built very faire chambers in this Castle. On the outside is the
*Statuaes of the
Popes.*
statua of Pope Pius the fourth, and within is the statua of Paul the third,
upon which these verses are written of the Emperour Charles the fifth
comming to Rome.

E Lybia venit Romanas victor ad arces
Caesar, & in niveis aureus ivit Equis.
Ille triumphavit, sed tu plus Paule triumphas,
Victor namque tuis oscula dat pedibus.

With victory to Rome from Affrick came
Caesar, on milke white Horses, golden all.
He Triumph'd, Paul thy triumph hath more fame,
This Conquerour to kisse thy feete did fall.

In this Castle they shew the head of Adrian, the statua of Saint Peter, a bunch of Grapes of brasse, the place where the Cardinall Caietan escaped out of prison, and a Trap-doore where prisoners are let downe into a dungeon. The chambers are built in a circle round about the great chamber in the middest, which is called Sala regia, and without is a round Garden within the walles, and upon the top of the Castle, in the place of the said Pine-apple, is the statua of the Angell Michael, of which the Castle hath the name. The medowes of Quintis Cincinates lie neere this Castle.

Upon the wals of the Church S. Croce, is a monument of Arno over-flowing, with this inscription in the Italian tongue: In the yeere 1333. the water of Arno overflowed to this height, and in the yeere 1557. to this, yet higher. In this Church is the sepulcher of Michaele Angelo Bonoritio, a *The Sepulcher of* most famous Engraver, Painter, and Builder, whose bones were brought *Michaele Angelo.* from Rome, at the instance of Duke Cosmo, in the yeere 1570, and laid here.[4] It is most certaine that he was most skilfull in those Arts, and of him the Italians greatly boast, and with all tell much of his fantasticke humours: namely, that when he painted the Popes Chappell, (whereof I spake in discribing the Popes Pallace) that he first obtained the Popes promise, that no man should come in, till the worke were finished; and understanding that the Pope had broken this promise, comming in himselfe with some Cardinals at the backe doore of the vestery, that he being then to paint the last Judgement, did so lively figure the Pope and the Cardinall (that tempted him) amongst the Divels, as every man might easily know them. But that is abhominable, which the Romans of the better sort seriously tell of him, that he being to paint a crucifix for the Pope, when he came to expresse the lively actions of the passion, hired a Porter to be fastned upon a Crosse, and at that very time stabbed him with a penknife, and while he was dying, made a rare peece of worke for the Art, but infamous for the murther: and that hereupon he was banished Rome, and went to the *Michaele Angelo banished.*

---

[4] Further details of Michelangelo's life and career can be found in Vasari's life (see Giorgio Vasari, *Lives of the Artists*, trans. George Bull (Harmondsworth: Penguin, 1965), 325–442. Given that Vasari's text was published in Florence in 1568, it is possible that Moryson saw a copy, although he makes no mention of the book.

Court of the Duke of Urbino, where he was entertained with much honour. And they report also that when he was recalled to Rome with pardon of that fault, the Dutchesse of Urbino being bold upon her former acquaintance, should entreat him at his leasure to paint all the Saints for her: and that he to shew that so great a taske should not be imposed upon a workman of his sort, should satisfie this request, or rather put it off with a rude & uncivill jest, sending her the picture of a mans privy part, most artificially painted, and praying her to take in good part the Father of all the Saints, till he could at leasure send their pictures.

OF IRELAND, TOUCHING NATURE, AND MAMERS, BODYES AND WITTS, MANUALL ARTES SCIENCES, UNIVERSITIES, LANGUAGE, CEREMONYES, PARTICULARLY IN MARYAGES, CHILDBEARINGES, CHRISTNINGES, AND FUNERALLS, AS ALSO OF DIVERS CUSTOMES, OF PASTYMES, EXERCISES, PARTICULARLY OF THEIR *HUNTING HAWKING*, BIRDING FOWLING AND FISHING

{m.n. 12–15. Nature manners Bodies and witts.}
In this Chapter I will [only] speake of the meere Irish. Only I will say for the English Irish that they may be knowne by the discription of our English at home.[5] But as horses Cowes and sheepe transported out of England into Ireland, doe each race and breeding declyne worse and worse, till in fewe yeares they nothing differ from the races and breeds of the Irish horses and Cattle. So the posterities of the English planted in Ireland, doe each discent growe more and more Irish, in nature manners and customes, so as wee founde in the last Rebellion divers of the most ancient English Familyes planted of old in Ireland, to be turned as rude and barbarous as any of the meere Irish lords. Partly because the manners and Customes of the meere Irish give great liberty to all mens lives, and absolute power to

[5] The 'English Irish' are sometimes called the 'Old English' or the 'Anglo-Irish'. They were usually descendants of the Anglo-Normans who came to Ireland in the 12th cent. More recent immigrants were referred to as 'New English'. For a discussion of the terms see T. W. Moody (ed.), *A New History of Ireland*, iii: *Early Modern Ireland, 1534–1691* (Oxford: Clarendon Press, 1976), pp. xlii–xlvii.

great men over the inferiors, both which men naturally affect. Partly because the meere Irish[6] of old overtopped the English Irish in nomber and nothing is more naturall yea necessary, then for the lesse nomber to accommodate it selfe to the greater. And espetially because the English are naturally inclyned to apply themselves to the manners and Customes of any forrayne nations with whome they live and Converse, whereas the meere Irish by nature have singular and obstinate pertinacity in retayning their old manners and Customes, so as they could never be drawne, by the lawes, gentile governnment, and free conversation of the English, to any Civility in manners, or reformation in Religion.

Now to retorne to the meere Irish. The lords or rather cheefes of Countryes (for most of them are not lords from any gramts [grants] of our kings, which English titles indeede they dispise), prefix O or Mac before their names, in token of greatnes, being absolut Tyrants over their people, themselves eating upon them and making them feede their kerne or footemen, and their horsemen.[7] Also they, and gentlemen under them, before their names putt nicknames, given them from the Colour of their haire, from lamenes, stuttering, diseases, or villanous inclinations, which they disdayne not, being otherwise most impatient of Reproch though indeede they take it rather for a grace to be reputed active in any Villany, espetially Cruelty and theft. But it is strange howe Contrary they are to themselves, for in apparrell, meate, Fashions, and Customes, they are most base and abject, yet are they by nature proude and disaynefull of reproch. In fighting they will runne away and turne agayne to fight, because they thincke it no shame to runne away, and to make use of the advantage they have in swift running, yet have they great Corage infighting, and I have seene many of them suffer death with as constant resolution as ever Romans did. To conclude this point they knowe not truely what honor is, but according to their knowledge no men more desyre it. affecting extreamely to be Celebrated by their Poetts or rather Rimers, and fearing more then death to have a Ryme made in their disgrace & infamye. So as these Rymers, pestilent members in that commonwealth, by animating all sortes by their Rymes, to licentious living, to lawlesse and rebellious actions are somuch regarded by them, as they grow very rich, the very wemen, when they are young and new Marryed or

---

[6] The native Irish. 'Mere' is not pejorative in early modern English. Elizabeth I could refer to herself as 'mere English'.

[7] A custom referred to elsewhere as 'coine and livery' and adopted by the English in Ireland too.

brought to bed, for feare of Rymes, giving them the best Apparrell and ornaments the have.

The Irish are by nature very factious, all of a Sept or name living together, and cleeving close [to] one to another in all quarrells and actions whatsoever, in which kynde they willingly suffer great men to eate upon them, and take whatsoever they have, proverbyally saying defende mee and spende Me, but this defence must be in all cawses, Just ot unjust, for they are not content to be protected from wronge, except the may be borne out to doe wronge.

They are by nature extreamely given to Idlenes. The Sea Coasts and harbors abounde with fish, but the fishermen must be beaten out, before they will goe to their Boates. Theft is not infamous but rather commendable among them so as the greatest men affect to have the best theeves to attend upon them, and if any man reprove them, they Answer that they doe as their fathers did, and it is infamy for gentlemen and swordmen to live by labour and manuall trades. yea they will not be perswaded that theft displeaseth God, because he gives the pray into their handes and if he be displeased, they say yet he is mercyfull and will pardon them for using meanes to live. This Idlenes makes them also slovenly and sluttish in their howses and apparrell, so as upon every hill they lye lowsing themselves, as for[m]erly in the discourse of the Commonwealth. I have remembred foure verses, of foure beasts that plague Ireland namely, lyse upon their bodyes, Ratts in theire howses, Wollves in their fieldes and swarmes of Romish Prists tyranising over their Consciences. This Idlenes, also makes them to love liberty a bove all thinges, and likewise naturally to delight in musick, so as the Irish *H*arpers are excelent, and their solemne musicke is much liked of strangers, and the wemen of some partes of mounster, as they weare Turkish heades and are thought to have come first out of those partes, so the have pleasant tunes of Moresco Danses.

They are by nature very Clamorous, upon every small occasion raysing the hobou[8] (that is adolefull outcrye) which they take one from anothers mouthe till they putt the whole towne in tumult. And their complaynts to magistrates are commonly strayned to the higest points of Calamity, sometymes in hyperbolicall tearmes, as many upon small violences offered them, have Petioned to the lord Deputy for Justice against men for murthering them, while they stoode before him sounde and not so much as wounded. [...]

---

[8] Elsewhere called the 'hubub'.

They are by nature superstitious and given to use witchcrafts. The approved Auther by Master Camden Cited in his owne wordes, sayth they salute the newe Moone with bended knee, saying to it. leave us as sounde as thou fyndest us. He adds incantations they use against wolves. Their opinions, that some one shall dye if they fynde a blacke spott upon a bared Mutton bone: and their horses shall live long if they give no fyer out of the howse, and that some ill lucke will fall to their horses if the ryder having eaten eges doe not wash his handes after them, or be not carefull to chuse the eggs of equall bignes. That they are much offended if a man commend their Cattle, except withall he say God save them, or ells spitt upon them. That some mens eyes bewitch their horses, and if they prove lame or ill, old wemen are sought for to say short prayers and use many incantations to recover them. That if a man fall on the grounde, he useth to turne thrise about towards his right hand, and to digg up a sodd of earth with his sword or knife, to prevent ill lucke. That they use many like incantations when they goe to fyght. That wemen divorced bewitch the men putting them away, with disability of generation and many diseases, against which men use the helpe of witches. That when Children be sicke, the Nurses fly to old wemen to helpe them with prayer and incantations. But I will omitt many other superstitions and witchcrafts, which he there relateth.[9]

The wemen generally are not much commended for Chastity Chastty, but the Common voyce was that generally, as kissing goes by favor, so they would rather offende with an Irish horseboy then with the English of better rancke. And the foresayd author sayth that Ireland abounded with Prists bastards, knowne by theire names as Mac Decan, mac phersan, that is the sonne of the Deene, or of the Church, and like names to that purpose, and that [se] these men were the most notorious theeves & Rebells of Ireland.

The same author Relates that the Irish were great swearrers and forswearers, presuming upon Gods mercy, and that to make them keepe Fayth there was no other meanes, but to have them sweare before the Alter, upon a booke opened and layd upon their head, and to sweare by some Saynt, or with kissing of a bell, or to sweare by the head of the lord of their Country,

---

[9] William Camden (1551–1623). Moryson is referring to Camden's topographical and historical survey, *Britannia* (1586), which he uses throughout *An Itinerary*. A convenient translation is that of William Gibson (1695). The reference here is to pp. 1046–7. Moryson's debt is also to Gerald of Wales (*c.* 1145–1223), author of *The History and Topography of Ireland* (1185), which influenced virtually all 16-cent. English commentators on Ireland.

which they most feared, because these lords used to extort Cowes from them for perjuryes as having theirin abused their Names. [...]

Touching Ceremonyes of State or of Civill Actions, the meere Irish being barbarous and loving so to continue, can not be acquainted with them, which they affect not.

For maryage, I will only say of the English Irish, that they keepe it orderly as in England, save that, inrespect of the lawe forbidding them to marrye with the meere Irish, the Cittizens taking wives within there owne walls, were growne to be all of kindred one with another, and so used to mary those of neere kindred. The fore sayde author printed in his owne wordes by master Camden[10] affirmeth, that among meere Irish dwelling in the fieldes, maryage was rare, and when they were maryed divorces were most frequent, and because they were given to Incest many divorces were made upon pretence of Conscience. In our experience, till the ende of the last Rebellion, these divorces Continued frequent among them, nothinge being more ordinary then to take a wife with a Certayne number of Cowes (their Common Portion)[11] and to send her backe to her frendes at the yeares end with some small increase of them, which Divorces the Bre-hounes or barbarous Judges among them esily admitted, upon a brybe of Cowes, and that upon trifeling causes. And it was likewise a common Custome for a woman lying at the point of death, to name the true Father of each of her Children, and for the Children to leave their Father reputed by the lawe, and with the stayne of Basterdy (which they regaurd not) to Followe the Father named by the dying mother, and this Custome caused many tymes disorders, for if the man childe had a lord or gentleman named to be his Father, he would presently be a swordman, living by rapyne or Rebelion, holding nothinge more infamous then to live by his labour. For Ceremonyes of Ring and the like, it will not be expected I shoulde write any thinge, the people being conditioned as the sayde credible Author reports.

Touching Chyldbearing, wemen within two howres after they are deliv-ered many tymes leave their beds to gossop and drincke with wemen comming to visite them, and in our experience a Soldyers wife delivered in the Campe, did the same day and within fewe howres after her delivery march six myles on Foote with the Armye to the next Camping place. Some say that commonly the weomen have litle or no payne in Chyldebearing,

<hr/>

[10] Camden, *Britannia*, 1042.   [11] Dowry.

and attribute the same to a bone broken when [re] the are tender Children, but whatsoever the cause be, no doubt they have easye deliverance, and commonly such strang ability of body presently after it, as I never heard any wemen in the worlde to have the like, and not only the meere Irish, but most of the old English Irish dwelling in the Cittyes, yea the foresayde Author in his owne wordes Printed by m*aste*r Camden affirmeth, that the wemen delivered of Children did after the sixth day admitt theire husbandes to lye w*i*th them,[12] midwives and neighbors come to helpe wemen to be delivered commonly more for fashion then any great neede of them, and here is no talke of a months lying in, or soleme Churching at the end of the month, as w*i*th us in England. They seldome Nurse their owne Children, espetially the Wives of lords, and gentlemen (aswell meere Irish as English Irish) For wemen of good wealth seeke w*i*th great ambition to Nurse them, not for any profitt, rather spending much upon them while they live, and giving them when they dye sometymes more then to their owne Children. But they doe it only to have the Protection and love of the Parents whose Children the Nurse. And old Custome is so turned into a second nature w*i*th them, as they esteeme the Children they nurse more then their owne, and holding it a reproach to nurse their owne Children, yet men will forbeare their wyves beds for the good of the children they Nurse or Foster, but not for nursing their owne. Yea the foster brothers, I meane the Children of the Nurse and strangers that have sucked her milke, love one another better then naturall brothers, and hate them in respect of the other, and by frequent examples wee have seene, many mourne for their foster brothers much more then they would have done for theire Naturall brothers, and some to expose their owne brothers to death, that they might save their forster brothers from danger therof. The worst is, that these Nurses w*i*th this extreame indulgency corrupt the Children they foster, Norishing and hartning the boyes in all villanye, and the girlls in obscenity.

In Christnings and like Rites of Religion, they use generally the Rites of the Roman Church in w*h*ich they persist w*i*th obstinacy, little care having beene taken to instruct them in the Reformed Doctryne. But in all thinges they intermix barbarous Customes, as when the Chylde is caryed to be paptised, they tye a little peece of silver in the Corner of the Cloth wherein the Chylde is wrapped, to begiven to the Priest, and likewise Salt to be putt in the Chyldes mouth. And at Christnings they have plenty of drincke, and

---

[12] Camden, *Britannia*, 1044.

of flesh meates to intertayne the frendes invited. Yea among the very English Irish remayning Papists, the Father intertaynes the guests, though he be a Bachiler and have disvirgined the mother, for it is no shame to be or to begett a Bastard. Banquets of sweete meates are unknowne to the meere Irish, and the Nurses are rather beneficiall to the Children they foster, then receave anything of them or their Frendes (as in the Commenwealth above written I have shewed, in the abuse of fostering Children, both among the meere Irish, and also among the English Irish.

Touching Funeralls, when any be sicke, they never speake to them of making any will, nether care they to have any made, for the wife hath the thirds of goods, and the Children the rest devided among them, and the land, after their lawe of Tanistry, (which they willingly observe rather then the English) is commonly possessed by the most active and powerfull of the Sept and kindred bearing all one Sir name, so as the uncles on the Fathers syde or the Nephewes many tymes invade it, excluding the sonnes. Nether doe they who visite the sicke person speake ought to him of good Counsell for his soules health, which sad discourses they thincke like to increase his sicknes, taking it for a desperate signe of death, if the sicke person desyre to receave the Sacraments But all their speeches tend to mirth and hope of recovery, and the sicke person hath about him many lights and great stoore of Company, as if thereby they could keepe him from death, wherof I remember an English gentleman who seeing a sicke lord of great quality thus invironed with lights and hundreths of men and wemen attending in his owne and the next Chambers sayd merily to a frend, if this man thincke not better of Repentance then he doth, all this light and Company cannot keepe him from the handes of death and the Devill. And when the sicke person draweth to the point of death, the neere frendes and all the Company call and crye out to him, as if they would stay the soule from departing, by remembring the goodnes of the wife or husband and Children, and the welth and frendes to beleft behinde him, reproching him with unkyndnes in forsaking them, and asking whether and to whome he will goe to be in better case then he is with them, When the sicke person is dead, they make a monsterous Cry, with shriking, howling and clampping of hands, and in like sort they followe the dead body, at the buryall, in which outcryes the Norse, the daughters, and the Concubynes, are most vehement. The wenen espetially and Children doe weekely visite the graves of theire dead frendes, casting flowers and Crosses upon them, with weeping and many prayers for the dead. In like sorte with outcryes they

bewayle those that dye in the warr, and in stelthes or taking prayes, though they thincke the death of them more happy then any other. The Septs of one name carye deadly feude towardes the man who kills any of their name, and towardes all that are of the same name or Sept of him who killed him.[13]
[...]

---

[13] Camden, *Britannia*, 1048. See also Barnaby Rich, *A New Description of Ireland* (1610), sig. D3^r.

Sir Henry Wotton, Letter to James I
from Venice (1618)

SIR HENRY WOTTON (1568–1639) was a poet and diplomat. Wotton went on a tour of Europe in 1588, travelling to Austria, Italy, France, and Switzerland, which appears to have lasted for about seven years. He became a secretary of Robert Devereux, second earl of Essex, in 1595, and helped collect foreign intelligence in various European countries. Under James I, he served as the ambassador to Venice, where he lived and worked for nearly twenty years, helping to protect Venice from papal designs and incursions upon its authority. Wotton became a noted figure and entertained a number of English travellers including Thomas Coryat. He was made Provost of Eton, holding the post until his death.[1]

Wotton was a noted correspondent. The letter included here is a good account of the daily business of an important ambassador, dealing with significant and petty matters; petitions from individuals, spying, international affairs, and court life. For those who governed in Britain, observations and accounts like Wotton's were probably the most influential accounts of other European courts and cultures.[2]

[1] Accounts of Wotton's life are provided in Adolphus William Ward, *Sir Henry Wotton: A Biographical Sketch* (London: Constable, 1898); H. H. Asquith, *Sir Henry Wotton, with some general reflections on style in English Poetry* (London: English Association, 1919); *DNB* entry.

[2] Text from *Letters and Dispatches from Sir Henry Wotton to James the First and his Ministers, in the years MDCXVII–XX* (London: William Nicols, 1850), 28–35.

Right Honorable*

I have newly receaved by one Mr Keire a Scottish gentleman youre letters written by his Majesties direction more then two moneths sithence in behalf of Sr Henry Peyton: whereunto before I make my humble answer It shalbe fitt to acquant his Majestie with diverse things bothe touching the state of this Cuntrie, and some other intervenient mater wherein I will beginn first of all with a late accident wch did keepe me some dayes even from congratulating with this new Duke albeit that office had been perfourmed not only by all other publique Ministers heere resident but

* Indorsed 'Sr H. Wotton's last letters dated at Venice 5° Julij 1618.'

L'Ecc.mo Gñale mette à banco le Gallere doue si fa un belliss.mo apparato di Tapez:
zarie et si mette fuori gran quantità di dinari d'oro et argento et in
particolare una Cattenna di Vergle d'oro di valuta d'un Millione. I. franco.
Con prideg.

Fig. 4. Venetian Gentlemen at St Mark's Piazza, Venice (G. Franco,
Habiti d'huomini et donne venetiane (1610–14))

likewise by one extraordinarie Ambassadour expresly sent to that perpose from the Duke of Urbine, and therefore you may imagin that the cause of my forbearance was verie sensible: whereof this is the storie.

I sent my Steward to invite my Lord of Oxforde and my Lord Graye to dine the next day with me: who returning somewhat late home in my Lord of Oxfords Gondola was not farr from the Arsenale stayed by a ruffianlike fellow that cales himself per buffoneria the Conte Piero and was at that tyme Captayne of the watche though otherwise by profession a shipwright, and therein of so singular use to the State that they are now and then contented to wincke at his madd humors. This man accompagned with a sutable Trayne takes my Stewarde then alone and unarmed (after information tayrely given him whose he was and whether he was going) out of my Lord's Gondola, carries him to the Arsenale, handles the mater so that he is kept all night in a filthie roome under guarde as a prisoner, returnes to him agayne in the morning and then besides other contemptuouse usage tels him in verie distinct language *that if he had not the night before sayed that he did belong to the Ambassadour of the King of England he would have lett him goe*: which wordes he repeated three several tymes even after warning to take heede what he sayed. This being of it self intollerable was made much worse by coincidence with a tyme wherein a foreine conspiracie having been so newly detected, and the processe thereof as yet unfinished my mans retention, and the insuing wordes of such pregnant consequence begann to breede some voice that owre nation had a hande in those foule buisinesses, and theare could not want heere fomentors of this conceyte: some for hate of owre religion, some for diversion from others, and some even uppon sportful malice. All which having considered after the dismission of my servant by wiser folkes then those that tooke him, I made my complaynt to the High Councel of Ten: who immediatly gave such order that the felow was snatched up in the open place of St Marcks and thence caried to close prison. After this I demaunded sentence agaynst him proportionable to his offense bothe for violating the immunitie of my familie and espetially for his opprobriouse wordes whereby the Kings honor was touched and Scandal put uppon owre nation. The Councel of Ten considering my complaynt to infolde respect of State, and theire Tribunal to be rather judicatorie did remitt the mater to the Senat: which made me recurr by my Secretarie to the Duke for a speedie and congruouse sentence: protesting that notwithstanding my Masters affection and mine owne particular zeale to this State I could appeare no more in the seate of Ambassadours (which is at the right hand of the Duke) after such an indignitie and violation without some publique judgment to satisfie the world.

To be short. After the hearing of my servants report the felow was condemned to perpetual imprisonment senza luce never to be freed without my assent and desire and then, to make a confession of his fault, and submission of himself at my howse. Heereuppon I did instantly deliver him as not delighting in his miserie, though justly incensed with his error: for in truthe an error it was: having mistaken his commission which (as I afterwardes heard) was to stopp the servants of some other publique person if they should fall within his walke. Thus all parties are satisfyed, The State to whom I have restored an useful man, the Representants of other Princes who were Scandalized with the example, owre nation likewise that might have come into some obloquie, and lastly the fellow himself is perchaunce not the least contented. It remayneth that his Majestie by youre opportune remembrance will be pleased to take notice heereof to the Venetian Ambassadour for the respect which uppon this occasion hath been heere showed towards his sacred name.

I have now visited the Prince who used me with singular kindenesse: whereof he hath the true art, and did his Majestie much right in caling him the most intelligent Prince on the Earthe, and *la vera anchora di questa Republica nelle occasioni turbulente*.[1] Of owre Nation he spake honorably *though from some others* (sayed he) *we have receaved smale* satisfaction. Whether he ment the French or the Fleamish I dare not affirme. Of the late practises his discourse was verie tender: giving me only thus much light that they were well informed of the fountayne, and willing that I should rather conceave it to come from the Spanish side (though the Frenche were the instruments) then he saye so. This was all that I then drewe from him.

To couple Homogenea. Theare is an other satisfaction to be related which hath been heere given me wherein I assure my self his Ma[tie] will take good contentment as I have donn in the discharge of my dutie therein. Some two moneths sithence arrived heere S[r] Thomas Strudder from Bruxelles who since the 23th of January last had closely (I knowe not yeat by what meanes made a contract with this State to serve them at an hundreth Crownes of monethly pension: Heere at his first arrival he followed his owne buisinesse and ends without taking any notice that his

---

[1] 'The true anchor of this republic in dangerous times'.

M^tie had a servant uppon the place, and when he thought himself setled, then he bestowes a visit uppon me. This is the man that in the Arche Dukes Court hath maynly opposed himself to all his Majesties Instruments as Mr Trumbal can well relate: valuing himself with profession of Catholicisme and so recommended hether where he begann presently to insinuat (as I gatt knowledge) with the Popes Nuntio: Whereuppon considering how unseemely it was for this Republique to cherish such an ill affected fugitive (wch they had donn for lack of due information) and waying withall that his aboade heere (where many Englishe haunte) could breede no good effects I made a little civil expostulation with the State about him, and prevayled so farr (his owne presumptuouse behaviour cooperating with me) that he was dismissed, and so betooke himself in a Pilgrimes weede to the Shryne of Loreto and thense to Rome: *quo omnia flagitiosa et pudenda confluunt*[2] as you knowe who sayed of it long sithence even when it was better.

I am now after thease duties at ease to discourse somewhat of the present affayres: which seeme reduced to this question: *Whether since the restitution of Vercelli the King of Spayne intende farther to molest the Venetians eather by Sea or by Land*. In this conjectural subject nothing doeth trouble us more then the caling of the Spanish Ambassadour from hense to Milan, who though he hath left heere his Secretarie and the Kings Armes over his doore (like a returner) yet some construe it for a civil withdrawing of himself before the moment of rupture. But this poynt I will cleere: For certayne it is or at least so beleeved by himself that Don Pedro intended to make him the Instrument of yeilding Vercelli: but the Ambassadour being loath to be imployed in that which the Governor thought his owne disgrace interposed delayes: sending to borrowe the Duke of Mantouaes Barge to carie him up the Po even when he was required to come in post, and so covering apparent dilation with State: In which meane while the Governour being extreamely pressed by the Frenche gave up the place while this Ambassadour was on the waye. whom he yet detayneth theare (as I will thinke till I see farther cause) for a little amuzement of his Neighbours.

It is more considerable in my opinion that Don Pedro (as we are intelligenced) hath yet some 12000 foote and 2300 horse in readinesse, and that he hath given order for a supplie of his Cavallarie, and for a fresh Regiment of Swizzers. It is likewise very probable if Ossuna shall returne into the Gulf (for at the present he hath no armed vessels therein) that then

---

[2] 'To which all scandalous and shameful things together flow' (Tacitus, *Annals* 15. 44). Wotton is clearly quoting from memory (I owe this note to Dr T. Pritchard).

Don Pedro will make head towards owre confines to healp him at least by way of distraction. But being so strong as we are at Sea, eased of contribution to Savoye, neere a conclusion of peace in Friuli, and the motions in Bohemia seconded (as they write from Augusta) by the Austrians and Hungarians why should we fear any more noise in Italie? espetially the Spaniard being well assured that thease Signori in case of ruine and desperation (if they shall neede sharper diversions) will *Acheronta movere*:[3] I meane, turne the Turcke into Calabria among the silke wormes. Yet true it is that besides the late French conspiracie some close and daungerous plotts uppon the frontering Towns of Crema and Brescia are newly come to light, and six persons have been sent hether in fetters two from the one place and foure from the other (among whom a woeman of qualitie) whom Don Pedro had practised: So as we may thinke that without thease seasonable discoveries somewhat had been donn, and the same must have been made good by an armie. Hereuppon among owre Politiques hath been moved a pretie doubt: what foundation in such a case the Venetians might make uppon the Duke of Savoye. And for aught I perceave they all inferr that being so newly setled he would hardly reenter into action for their sakes: espetially having receaved and perchaunce reserved some notable disgust for the peace which theyre Ministers signed in Paris without his participation or inclusion.

I will seale thease discourses with an observation which hath been taken uppon the whole mater by men of grave judgment. That though the King of Spaynes owne intentions be supposed to be quiet yet in a tyme which requireth quick counsayles, and in a Cuntrie more importing him then any other (for if he faynt in Italie he will dissolve in the rest) he hath been forced thorough the seperation of his Estates to leave himself much in the handes of his ministers with some hazard of the publique repose. And thus much of the present condition of the tyme wherein we have not yet perfectam crisim though theare be a kinde of ἀπυρεξία.[4]

Now, Touching his Majesties directions in behalf of Sʳ Henry Peyton so effectually set downe by youre pen.

I must first professe that he is my particular frend and therefore besides my dutie even in privat respect I shalbe glad to presse his advauntage, but having sent me a forme of his Commission and Contracte, I finde it so deficient that I wonder in good faythe so judiciouse a gentleman could love

---

[3] 'To move hell' (*Aeneid* 7. 312).   [4] 'Absence of fever'.

himself so little. I hold that opinion of bargayns with states that Aristotle doeth of Lawes: of which (as you well knowe) those in his judgment are the best that leave least to the Judge. And surely those contracts are likewise the Wisest which leave least to favour: wch I feare this worthie Knight will finde heere: espetially coming when the Cofers peradventure beginn to sounde. Not to trouble you with all particulars theare is in his contract one unfortunate worde *di moneta corrente* [current prices, value] which will irremediably prejudice him at least 8 per 100 in his receyts. This I speake by way of provision that no want be imputed to me if he misse his contentment: which others have not altogether had even when they might chalenge it. And of mine owne endevors for him when he arriveth (of which we wonder not yeat to have heard) I will render the King as you require a particular accoumpt.

Theare doeth remayne for the last part of this dispatche a buisinesse or two of secret and important qualite: which have made me commit it to an honest Marchant, and to impose hast uppon him. For the first. It may please his M^{tie} to understande that theare is in Augusta one Philip Hain-hoffer a Patricius of that smale Communitie. This man holds correspond-ence with diverse Princes, and doeth much desire to have some relation towards the King. In playner language, a pension of aboute one hundred powndes yearly: promising to intertayne his M^{tie} with many curiouse things. I have not with him any acquayntance by sight: but I finde him by his letters and by report easie to be moulded as we list: whereuppon I have lately conceaved a notable use of him for the Kings service. Augusta (his natural seate) is the place where all the letters and pacquets doe weekely concentrat, and theare they be first seavered in the Common Valigia and thense distributed to and fro into sundrie parts. Now, the thing that I would wishe donn is the intercepting of the Jesuites pacquets, and parti-cularly those that passe ultra citraque betweene the English Preests in England and Rome, and the intermediat places of Rhemes, Doway, St Omers and other. This can be donn no where so featly as in Augusta, nor by none so easily as himself who commaunds theare the Master of the Posts and by his correspondence from diverse parts hauntes him weekely. So that he hath great opportunitie to doe this thing: and may transport them continually to his Majestie thorough youre handes under a new Cover. If therefore it may please the King to give me authoritie to handle this buisinesse with him, and to promisse him his graciouse favor uppon such a peece of meritoriouse curiositie I will tentatively propounde it unto him in my returne homewardes that way: and be provided in the meane while by a frend I have in Rome to instruct him under what seales and names those intelligences passe, and with some other circumstances belonging to this mater: Wherewith I was well acquaynted in my first Ambassage when the Jesuites were heere, and heald theire weekely intercourse with Rome. Captayn Henry Bell (who is ere this tyme arrived in England) was sollicited by this man in his late passage by Augusta to represent his devotion to the King: from whom (if it please you) you may take some farther description then I can give of him without any mention of this project which I humbly commit to y^r closest Cabinet; Since the lyfe of it is the secrecie.

The other buisinesse is of greater consequence and worthie of the Kings wise and Christian care: which I have now committed to Mr Isaac Bargrave my late Chapelan with whom I spent much conference aboute it heere. He hath order from me to repayre unto you and I hope well, by y^r favour to be introduced to his M^{tie} when the mater shall first have passed the file of y^r owne judgment. Now, a word touching myself and so I will humbly take my leave.

I besought his M^{tie} by the forenamed Captayn Bell to grawnt mine owne returne unto his comfortable sight towards next winter: Since when I have considered that the Summer spends a pace; and besides I would fayne see a full end of owre noise which being not likely to be before the cold wether I shalbe cast into a very incommodiouse passage. Therefore (Sir) I humbly beseeche you that by y^r favorable intercession I may returne towards the beginning of next Marche and in the meane tyme be furnished with his M^{ties} letters of revocation, and with his farther commaundes aboute the propositions now made

And in all this or any thing else that may healp my poore fortune. I doe hartily begg y^r love as I doe unenviousely wish y^r prosperitie: having been long acquaynted with youre worthinesse. From Venice this 5th of July 1618.

Youre Hon^{rs} with true
devotion

HENRY WOTTON.

William Lithgow, *The Totall Discourse of The Rare Adventures & Painfull Peregrinations of long Nineteene Yeares Travayles from Scotland to the most famous Kingdomes in Europe, Asia and Affrica* (1632), Account of his Imprisonment in Spain

LITHGOW was born in Lanark, Scotland, and appears to have been interested in travel from an early age. He spent nineteen years travelling after he went to Paris in 1609 and claimed to have walked some 36,000 miles (twice the circumference of the earth) in the three journeys that were recounted in his *Totall Discourse of The Rare Adventures*, the full text of which was published in 1632, early accounts having appeared in 1614 and 1615. Lithgow travelled, like Fynes Moryson and George Sandys, around Europe then on to Constantinople, North Africa, Palestine, and Egypt. On his final expedition, Lithgow was imprisoned in Malaga, Spain, by the Inquisition and tortured, before a happy accident enabled him to be released. Lithgow was clearly bitter about his treatment and publicly exhibited his extensive wounds at court, eventually precipitating an unpleasant incident with the Spanish ambassador, Gondomar, after which he was imprisoned. Lithgow later witnessed the sieges of Breda (1637) and Newcastle (1645), writing accounts of these as well as a description of London (1643). He probably died sometime in the mid-1640s.[1]

Lithgow is a remarkably similar writer to Moryson and Coryat. He is eccentric, his style wandering like his travels (although Jerusalem clearly marks the furthest stage of his journey, literally and symbolically (see below, pp. 179–87)). Like Moryson he was a noted Protestant, intolerant of foreigners and their religion, and it is not surprising that he fell foul of the Spanish Inquisition. Lithgow is keen to assert the superiority of the British to other peoples. Two passages are reproduced here. The first gives Lithgow's reflections on the Spanish which are uniformly hostile (but they were written after his imprisonment). The second describes his imprisonment, where he represents himself as a suffering martyr, his body a testament to his faith.[2]

[1] For details of Lithgow's life, see *DNB* entry.
[2] Text from William Lithgow, *The Totall Discourse of The Rare Adventures* (Glasgow, 1906), 388–90, 398–405.

See also:

Lewis Lewkenor, *A Discourse of the Usage of the English Fugitives by the Spaniard* (1595).

It is miserable travelling, lesse profitable, in these ten Provinces, or petty Kingdomes, hard lodging and poore, great scarcity of beds and deare: And no ready drest diet, unlesse you buy it raw; and cause dresse, or dresse it your selfe, buying first in one place your fire, your meate from the Butcher, your bread from the Baker, your Wine from the Taverne, your Fruites, Oyle, and Hearbes from the Botega, carying all to the last place, your bed-lodging: Thus must the weary Stranger toile, or else fast: And in infinite places for Gold nor money can have no victuals; but restrained to a relenting jejunation. The high-minded Spaniard and their high topped mountaines, have an infused contention together. The one through arrogant ambition, would invade the whole earth to inlarge his dominions: The other by a steepe swolne hight, seeme to threaten the Heavens to pull down Jupiter from his throne. And as I take it, the Spaniard being of a low stature, borroweth his high-minded breast from the high topped mountaines, for the one in quality, and the other in quantity, be extraordinarily infounded. *A.D. 1620. It is miserable travelling in Spaine.*

Certaine it is, as the Spaniard in all things standeth mainely upon his reputation (but never to avouch it with single combat) so he vaunteth not a little of his antiquity, deriving his pedegree from Tubal, the Nephew of Noe. But (especially as they draw it) how often hath the Line of Tubal, beene bastarded, degenerated, and quite expelled, by invasions of Phaenicians, oppressions of the Greekes, incursiones of the Carthaginians, the Conquest and planting of Provinces, and Colonies of the Romanes, the general deluge of the Gothes, Hunnes, and Vandales: and lastly, by the long and intollerable Tyranny of the Moores, whose slavish yoake and bondage in 800. yeares, hee could scarcely shake off; his owne Histories beare sufficient testimony and Record. Then it is manifest, that this mixture of Nations, must of necessity make a compounded Nature, such as having affinity with many, have no perfection in any one. *The long captivity of the Spaniards under the Mores.*

Their Manners are conformable to their discent, and their conditionall Vertues semblable to their last and longest Conquerors, of whom they retayne the truest stampe.

The most penurious Peasants in the World be heere, whose Quotidian moanes, might draw teares from stones. Their Villages stand as wast like as the Sabunck, Garamont, or Arabian Pavilleons, wanting Gardens, Hedges, Closses, Barnes, or Backe-sides: This sluggish and idle husbandry, being a natural instinct of their neighbour or paternal Moores.

As for industrious Artes, Inventions, and Vertues, they are as dull there-of, as their late Predecessours: and truely I confesse for the Spanish Nunne, she is more holy then the Italian; the former are onely Reserved to the Friers, and Priests: The latter being more Noble, have most affinity with Gentle-men. The Spaniard is of a spare dyet and temperate, if at his owne cost he spend; but if given Gratis, he hath the longest Tuskes that ever stroke at Table.

After a doubtfull and dangerous departure from Madrid (as Sir Walter Aston his Majesties Ambassador can testifie with his Followers, as some of his people have already here done the same,) being the drift of my owne Country-men, I came to Toledo twelve Leagues distant from thence: This Citty is situate on a ragged Rocke upon the River Tagus, being an Arch-bishops seate, the Primat and Metropolitan Sea of all Spaine: Yet a mis-erably impoverished and deformed place.

Naked ambition conferred upon poore Toledo.
And although the Spaniard, of all Townes in Spaine, braggeth most of Toledo, it is neyther (doubtlesse I know) for beauty, bounds, nor Wealth, if not for the Intrado belongeth to it, amounting yearely (as they affirme) to 200000 Duckats; for there is no other Episcopal Seate, in all Castilia, or Kingdome of Toledo. Giving backe to Toledo, I crossed the crossing Siera de Morada, (which divideth the Kingdome of Grenada, from the Mansha of the new Castilia) and arrived at Grenada, the Capital of Andolusia.

Here had the Moores their last residence in Spaine, and was magnanim-ously recovered, Anno 1499. yeares, by Ferdinando the Castilian King, and his wife Isabella. It standeth at the foote of Siera de Nevada (the Snowy Alpes,) who reserve continually Snow on their tops, and partly inclosed betweene two Snow-melting Rivers. In this Citty is the principall Seate, and Colledge of Justice, of all South Spaine: As Valladoli is for the North of Spaine, the high Court of Madrid having Prerogative over both.

It hath a spacious and strong Castle, which was builded by the Moores, and indeede a Kingly mansion: Where I saw the Hals and Bed-Chambers of the Moorish Kings, most exquisitly, over-siled, and indented with Mosaicall worke; excelling farre any moderne industry whatsoever.

The Emperour Charles the fift, and King of Spaine; after his returne from that misfortunate voyage of Algier, left a monument here, never likely to have beene accomplished, that is, the foundation of an admirable worke advanced two stories high: without it is quadrangled, and within round; having two degrees of incircling promontores, supported by Marble pillars, and Allabaster arches.

[M]y roome was made a darke-drawne Dungeon, my belly the anatomy of mercilesse hunger, my comfortlesse hearing, the receptacle of sounding Bells, my eye wanting light, a loathsome languishing in despaire, and my ground lying body, the woefull mirrour of misfortunes: every houre wishing anothers comming, every day the night, and every night the morning.

And now being every second or third day attended with the twinckling of an eye, and my sustenance agreeable to my attendance, my body grew exceeding debile and infirme; insomuch that the Governour (after his answers receaved from Madrile) made haste to put in execution, his bloody and mercilesse purpose before Christmas Holy-dayes: least ere the expiring of the twelfth day, I should be utterly famished, and unable to undergoe my tryall, without present perishing, yet unknowne to me, save onely in this knowledge, that I was confident to dye a fearefull and unacquainted death: for it is a current custome with the Spaniard, that if a stranger be apprehended upon any suspicion, he is never brought to open tryall, and common Jayle, but clapd up in a Dungeon, and there tortured, impoysoned, or starved to death: Such meritorious deeds, accompany these onely titular Christians: for the Spaniard accounteth it more to be called a Christian, than either to beleeve what hee professeth, or to conforme him selfe to the life of Christianity: yea, I sparingly avouch it, hee is the worst and baddest creature of the Christian name; having no more Religion (and lesse respective to devotion) than an externall presumptuous show; which perfiteth this ancient Proverbe, The Spaniard; est bonus Catholicus, sed malus Christianus. [A good Catholic, but a bad Christian.] *A speedy expedition for a mercilesse mischeife.*

In end, by Gods permission, the scourge of my fiery tryall approaching; upon the forty seventh day after my first imprisonment, and five dayes before Christmas; about two a clocke in the morning, I heard the noyse of a Coach in the fore-street, marvelling much what it might meane.

Within a pretty while I heard the locks of my Prison-doore in opening; whereupon bequeathing my soule to God, I humbly implored his gracious mercie and pardon for my sinnes: for neither in the former night nor this, *My transportation from prison to the fields to be racked.*

could I get any sleepe, such was the force of gnawing hunger, and the portending heavinesse of my presaging soule.

Meanewhile the former nine Sergeants, accompanied with the Scrivan, entered the roome without word speaking, and carrying mee thence, with irons and all, on their armes through the house, to the street, they layd mee on my backe in the Coach: where two of them sat up beside mee, (the rest using great silence) went softly along by the Coach side.

Then Baptista the Coach-man, an Indian Negro droving out at the Sea-gate, the way of the shoare-side, I was brought Westward almost a league from the Towne, to a Vine-presse house, standing alone amongst Vine-yards, where they inclosed mee in a roome till day light, for hither was the Racke brought the night before, and privately placed in the ende of a Trance.

And all this secresie was used, that neyther English, French, or Flem-ings, should see or get any knowledge of my Tryall, my grievous Tortures, and dreadfull dispatch, because of their treacherous and cruel proceedings.

At the breach of day the Governour, Don Francesco, and the Alcalde, came foorth in another Coach: where when arrived, and I invited to their presence, I pleaded for a Trench man, being against their Law, to accuse or condemne a Stranger, without a sufficient Interpreter. The which they absolutely refused, neyther would they suffer or grant mee an Appellation to Madrid.

A stranger ought not to be accused with strangers without an Interpreter.

And now after long and new Examinations, from morning to darke night, they finding my first and second Confession so runne in one, that the Governour swore, I had learned the Arte of Memory: Saying further, is it possible hee can in such distresse, and so long a time, observe so strictly in every manner the poynts of his first Confession, and I so often shifting him too and fro.

Well, the Governours interrogation and my Confession being mutually subscribed: He and Don Francesco besought me earnestly to acknowledge and confesse my guiltinesse in time: if not, he would deliver me in the Alcaldes hands there present: Saying moreover, thou art as yet in my power, and I may spare or pardon thee; providing thou wilt confesse thy selfe a Spie, and a Traytour against our Nation.

But finding mee stand fast to the marke of my spotlesse innocency, he, invective, and malicious hee, after many tremenduous threatnings, com-manded the Scrivan to draw up a Warrant for the chiefe Justice: And done, he set his hand to it, and taking me by the hand, delivered me and the

Warrant in the Alcalde Majors hands, to cause mee bee Tortured, broken, and cruelly Tormented.

Whence being carried along on the Sergeants armes, to the end of a Trance or stone Gallery, where the Pottaro or Racke was placed: The Encarnador or Tormentor, begunne to disburden me of my irons, which beeing very hard inbolted he could not Ram-verse the Wedges for a long time: Whereat the Chiefe Justice being offended, the malicious Villaine with the Hammer which he had in his hand, stroake away above an inch of my left heele with the Bolt. Whereupon I grievously groaning, beeing exceeding faint, and without my three ounces of bread, and a little Water for three dayes together: The Alcalde sayd, O Traytor all this is nothing, but the earnest of a greater bargaine you have in hand.

A mercilesse hurt, before they begun to Racke mee.

Now the irons being dissolved, and my Torments approaching, I fell prostrate on my knees, crying to the Heavens:

O Great and Gracious GOD, it is truely knowne to thy all-seeing Eye, that I am innocent of these false and fearefull accusations, and since therefore it is thy Good will and pleasure, that I must suffer now by the scelerate hands of mercilesse men: Lord furnish mee, with Courage, Strength, and Patience least by an impatient Minde, and feebling Spirit, I become my owne Murtherer, in Confessing my selfe guilty of Death, to shunne present punishment. And according to the Multitude of thy Mercies, O Lord, bee mercifull to my sinfull soule, and that for Jesus thy Sonne and my Redeemer his sake.

After this, the Alcalde, and Scrivan, being both chaire-set, the one to examine, the other to write downe my Confession and Tortures: I was by the Executioner stripped to the skin, brought to the Racke, and then mounted by him on the top of it: Where eftsoones I was hung by the bare shoulders, with two small Cords, which went under both mine armes, running on two Rings of iron that were fixed in the Wall above my head.

Thus being hoysed, to the appoynted height, the Tormentor discended below, and drawing downe my Legs, through the two sides of the three-planked Racke, hee tyed a Cord about each of my ancles: And then ascending upon the Racke, hee drew the Cords upward, and bending forward with maine force, my two knees, against the two plankes; the sinewes of my hammes burst a sunder, and the lids of my knees beeing crushed, and the Cords made fast, I hung so demayned, for a large houre.

The hammes and lids of my knees were both broken.

At last the Encarnador, informing the Governor, that I had the marke of Jerusalem on my right arme, joyned with the name and Crowne of King

James, and done upon the Holy Grave. The Corrigidor came out of his adjoyning stance, and gave direction, to teare a sunder, the name, and Crowne (as hee sayd) of that Hereticke King, and arch-enemy to the Holy Catholicke Church: Then the Tormentor, laying the right arme above the left, and the Crowne upmost, did cast a Cord over both armes, seaven distant times: And then lying downe upon his backe, and setting both his feete on my hollow-pinched belly, he charged; and drew violently with his hands, making my Wombe support the force of his feete, till the seaven severall Cords combined in one place of my arme, (and cutting the Crowne, sinewes, and flesh to the bare bones) did pull in my fingers close to the palme of my hands: the left hand of which is Lame so still, and will be for ever.

Now mine eyes begun to startle, my mouth to foame and froath, and my *O cruell and* teeth to chatter like to the doubling of Drummers stickes. O strange *inhumane* inhumanity of Men-monster Manglers! surpassing the limits of their *murder.* nationall Law; three score Tortures beeing the tryall of Treason, which I had, and was to indure: yet thus to inflict a seaven-fold surplussage of more intollerable cruelties: And notwithstanding of my shivering lippes, in this fiery passion, my vehement groaning, and blood-springing fonts, from armes, broake sinewes, hammes, and knees; yea, and my depending weight on flesh-cutting Cords; yet they stroke mee on the face with Cudgels, to abate and cease the thundring noyse of my wrestling voyce.

At last being loosed from these Pinnacles of paine, I was hand-fast set on the floore, with this their incessant imploration: Confesse, confesse, confesse in time, for thine inevitable torments ensue: where finding nothing from me, but still innocent, O I am innocent, O Jesus! the Lambe of God have mercy upon mee, and strengthen mee with patience, to undergoe this barbarous murder.

Here begun my Then by command of the Justice, was my trembling body layd above, and *mayne tortures.* along upon the face of the Racke, with my head downe-ward, inclosed within a circled hole, my belly upmost, and my heeles upward toward the top of the Racke: my legs and armes being drawne a sunder, were fastned with pinnes and Cords, to both sides of the outward plankes; for now was I to receive my maine torments.

Loe here is the Now what a Pottaro or Racke is (for it stood by the wall declining *manner how I* downe-ward) it is made of three plankes of Timber, the upmost end *was mainly* whereof is larger then a ful stride; the lower end being narrow, and the *Racked.* three planks joyning together, are made conformable to a Mans shoulders:

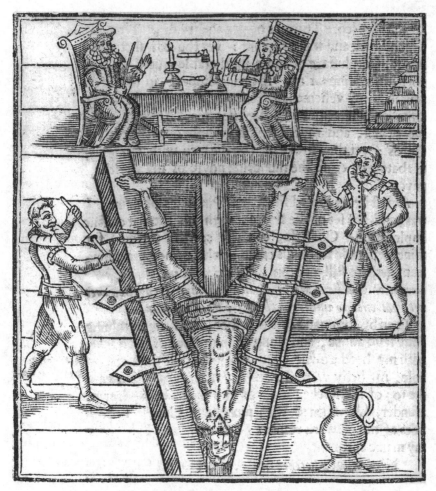

Fig. 5. 'The Author in the Racke at Malaga' (William Lithgow,
Totall Discourse (1632), p. 455)

in the downe-most end of the middle planke there was a hole, wherein my head was layd: in length it is longer than a man, being interlaced with small cords from planke to planke, which divided my supported thighes from the middle plank: Through the sides of which exterious planks there were three distant holes in every one of them; the use wherefore you shall presently heare.

Now the Alcalde giving commission, the executioner layd first a cord over the calfe of my leg, then another on the middle of my thigh, and the

The manner how my body was first fastned to the Racke before my tortures were inflicted.

third cord over the great of my arme; which was severally done, on both sides of my body receaving the ends of the cords, from these sixe severall places through the holes made in the outward planks, which were fastned to pinnes, and the pinnes made fast with a device: for he was to charge on the out side of the planks, with as many pinnes, as there were holes and cords; the cords being first laid meet to my skin: And on every one of these sixe parts of my body, I was to receave seven severall tortures: each torture consisting of three winding throwes, of every pinne; which amounted to twenty one throwes, in every one of these sixe parts.

Then the Tormentor having charged the first passage about my body (making fast by a device each torture as they were multiplied) he went to an earthen Jarre standing full of water, a little beneath my head: from whence carrying a pot full of water; in the bottome whereof, there was an incised hole, which being stopd by his thumb, till it came to my mouth, hee did powre it in my bellie; the measure being a Spanish Sombre, which is an English Potle: The first and second services I gladly receaved, such was the scorching drouth of my tormenting payne, and likewise I had drunke none for three dayes before.

But afterward, at the third charge, perceiving these measures of water to be inflicted upon me as tortures, O strangling tortures! I closed my lips, gaine-standing that eager crudelity.

A cruelty beyond cruelties.

Whereat the Alcalde inraging, set my teeth asunder with a payre of iron cadges, detayning them there, at every severall turne, both mainely and manually; whereupon my hunger-clungd bellie waxing great, grew Drum-like imbolstered: for it being a suffocating payne, in regard of my head hanging downeward, and the water reingorging it selfe in my throat with a strugling force; it strangled and swallowed up my breath from youling and groaning.

And now to prevent my renewing griefe (for presently my heart fayleth and forsaketh me) I will onely briefly avouch, that betweene each one of these seven circular charges, I was aye reexamined, each examination continuing halfe an houre; each halfe houre a hell of infernall paine, and betweene each torment, a long distance of life quelling time.

A hellish and insupportable payne.

Thus lay I sixe houres upon the Racke, betweene foure a clocke after-noone, and ten a clocke at night, having had inflicted upon me three score seven torments: Neverthelesse they continued me a large halfe houre (after all my tortures) at the full bending; where my body being all begored with blood, and cut through in every part, to the crushed and bruised bones,

I pittifully remayned, stil roaring, howling, foaming, bellowing, and gnash-
ing my teeth, with insupportable cryes, before the pinnes were undone, and
my body loosed.

True it is, it passeth the capacity of man, either sensibly to conceave, or I
patiently to expresse the intollerable anxiety of mind, and affliction of body
in that dreadfull time I sustayned.

At last my head being by their armes advanced, and my body taken from
the Rack, the water regushed abundantly from my mouth; then they
recloathing my broken, bloody, and cold trembling body, being all this
time starke naked, I fell twice in a sounding trance: which they againe
refreshed with a little Wine, and two warme Egges, not for charity done,
but that I should be reserved to further punishment; and if it were not too
truely knowne these sufferings to be of trueth, it would almost seeme
incredible to many, that a man being brought so low, with starving hunger,
and extreame cruelties, could have subsisted any longer reserving life.

And now at last they charged my broken legs, with my former eye-
frighting irons, and done, I was lamentably carryed on their armes to the *A lamentable*
Coach, being after mid-night, and secretly transported to my former *remembrance of*
inhumane cruelty.
Dungeon without any knowledge of the Towne, save onely these my
lawlesse, and mercilesse Tormentors: where, when come, I was layd with
my head and my heeles alike high, on my former stones.

Chapter Three

AFRICA AND THE NEAR EAST

THERE had been, of course, extensive contact between Europe and the countries on the far side of the Mediterranean since the early Middle Ages. Pilgrimages were frequently made to Jerusalem and other holy places.[1] The most famous travel book of the later Middle Ages, *The Travels of Sir John Mandeville* (c.1536), was organized around a pilgrimage to Jerusalem.[2] Margery Kempe, author of one of the first women's autobiographies in English, was one of many English men and women who travelled to Jerusalem in the fourteen and fifteenth centuries.[3] Travel beyond the well-established routes, to Russia, the Ottoman Empire, and Africa, was extremely rare.

William Lithgow's pilgrimage to Jerusalem fits into an established pattern of religious travel, albeit one with a distinctly Protestant horror at the Catholic trappings of the most holy sites (see below, pp. 179–87). George Sandys made a similar journey, centred around the Holy City, and he comments extensively and sympathetically on the situation of the Jews living in Palestine.[4] One can see that a discourse of philo-Semitism is already in place in the early modern period, one that was always delicately balanced against a corresponding discourse of anti-Semitism.[5]

---

[1] Norbert Ohler, *The Medieval Traveller*, trans. Caroline Hillier (Woodbridge: The Boydell Press, 1989), 56–9.

[2] *The Travels of Sir John Mandeville*, ed. C. W. R. D. Moseley (Harmondsworth: Penguin, 1983). For a recent examination of the factual and fictional content of the work, see Giles Milton, *The Riddle and the Knight: In Search of Sir John Mandeville* (Bridgend: Allison and Busby, 1996).

[3] *The Book of Margery Kempe*, trans. Barry Windeatt (Harmondsworth: Penguin, 1985), 12.

[4] A stimulating overview of English attitudes is to be found in James Shapiro, *Shakespeare and the Jews* (New York: Columbia Univ. Press, 1996).

[5] David Katz, *Philo-Semitism and the Readmission of the Jews to England, 1603–1655* (Oxford: Clarendon Press, 1982).

There was also considerable contact with the Turks and other peoples of the Ottoman Empire. As Nabil Matar points out 'Renaissance Britons were far more likely to meet or have met a Muslim than ... an [American] Indian.'[6] There were a large number of Muslims and Turks in England, mainly in London; there was extensive trade with the Ottoman Empire; Elizabeth I was especially keen to encourage alliances with the Turks, especially if such a union would help to offset the much greater threat of Catholic Spain; and there was considerable contact through various military expeditions, piracy in the Mediterranean (which involved a number of renegade British sailors), and British captives who remained in Turkey. While there were no plays about the Americas before Shakespeare's *The Tempest* (*c*.1611), there were a large number of plays which featured Muslims and Turks, including Christopher Marlowe's *Tamburlaine the Great* (1587); Thomas Kyd's *The Tragedye of Solyman and Perseda* (1588); George Peele's *The Battle of Alcazar* (1591), which centred around the life and death of the famous English captain, Sir Thomas Stukeley, who perished in the battle; and Philip Massinger's *The Renegado* (1624).[7] Far more fortune hunters ventured East rather than West to try and tap the huge resources of the Ottoman Empire, notably its well-attested reserves of gold.[8] Indeed, there is a great deal of evidence to suggest that the attractions of the Levant in general were such that many Englishmen chose to remain in the area and often converted to Islam, whereas there are no records of the opposite cultural journey being made, whatever English Christian claims were made to the contrary.[9]

The reasons for our often mistaken impressions of the past are twofold. First, assuming that the world as we now know it was prepared by the past. Yet to an observer in *c*.1600, the attractions of Turkey would probably have far outweighed those of the harsh journey to the Americas where five in six died. Colonists to the Americas tended to be from the servant classes, or vagabonds and the unemployed; emigration to the Levant was significantly less class specific.[10] Second has been the assumption that tracts and propaganda can be read at face value. Such readings tend to disguise the

  [6] Nabil Matar, *Turks, Moors and Englishmen in the Age of Discovery* (New York: Columbia Univ. Press, 1999), 3. See also *Islam in Britain, 1558–1685* (Cambridge: Cambridge Univ. Press, 1998).

  [7] Matar, *Islam in Britain*, ch. 2; Jack D'Amico, *The Moor in English Renaissance Drama* (Tampa: Univ. of South Florida Press, 1991).

  [8] Matar, *Turks, Moors and Englishmen*, ch. 3.

  [9] Matar, *Islam in Britain*, ch. 1.

  [10] Matar, *Turks, Moors and Englishmen*, 87–9.

exhortatory and defensive nature of descriptions of the Americas, often specifically designed to counteract negative accounts of those returning from the colonies. The negative descriptions of the Levant were produced to denigrate a powerful and equal—if not superior—culture which threatened the Christian West. There were no attempts to establish colonies on the far shores of the Mediterranean, showing that the relationship between Englishmen and Muslims was simply not the same as that between Englishmen and native Americans.[11]

Hence, we must take some of Fynes Moryson's comments on the Turks with a pinch of salt. Moryson's staunch Protestantism is clearly on display and helps to determine his perception of an alien, hostile culture. He recognizes the power and success of the Turks, notably in his representation of Constantinople, but fears them as he does the Catholic powers within Europe. The obsession of the Turks as sodomites serves a variety of functions. First, it singles them out as a militarized, hyper-masculine culture, perhaps trying to make their lifestyle seem unattractive to potential English converts. Second, it links them to the Catholic monks before the Reformation, who were invariably portrayed as sodomites in Protestant propaganda.[12] Hence, Moryson can link the Turks to Catholic priests and monks as enemies of the true faith. Third, it defines them as unnatural, like the savages of the Americas who were also frequently portrayed as homosexual.[13] Fourth, putting the last two points together, such behaviour indicated that Muslims had no real right to the land they occupied, which could be put to better use by Christians.

English representations of the Turks, based on long-standing contact between the two cultures, shows that careful distinctions between different peoples were made and that it is a serious error to assume that Africans, native Americans, and Muslims were all lumped together as the 'other'. George Sandys's comments on Egypt and the Egyptians (see below, pp. 153–60) shows that English travellers were well aware that different peoples and civilizations inhabited North Africa. To cite Nabil Matar again: 'England's relations with sub-Saharan Africans were relations of power, domination, and slavery, while relations with the Muslims of North Africa and the Levant were of anxious equality and grudging emulation...while one

[11] Matar, *Turks, Moors and Englishmen*, ch. 4.
[12] See, for example, John Bale, *The Actes of the English Votaries* (1546); L. P. Fairfield, *John Bale: Mythmaker for the English Reformation* (Indiana: Purdue Univ. Press, 1976).
[13] Matar, *Turks, Moors and Englishmen*, 110–11.

group served as a model, the other served as a commodity'.[14] John Hawkins's treatment of the slaves he transported from the West Coast to the West Indies (see below, pp. 121–6) bears out the truth of this observation. The natives of Guinea are certainly seen in terms of the most abject inhabitants of the New World. Later, when less obviously confrontational contact was made between the English and West Africans, more interest was shown in sub-Saharan African society, especially by Richard Jobson, the first Englishman to provide a detailed account of West Africa based on first-hand experience.[15] Probably the main source of information on Africa for English readers was Leo Africanus's *The History and Description of Africa* (see below, pp. 139–51), which concentrates on the peoples of North Africa. The account of the peoples of Russia by Giles Fletcher (see below, pp. 127–38), suggests that despite the substantial volume of trade with Russia in Elizabethan times, Russians and Tartars were much less well known than North Africans and Turks in Elizabethan and Jacobean England.[16]

[14] Matar, *Turks, Moors and Englishmen*, 7–8. See also Eldred Jones, *Othello's Countrymen: Africans in English Renaissance Drama* (Oxford: Oxford Univ. Press, 1965); Kim F. Hall, *Things of Darkness: Economies of Race and Gender in Early Modern England* (Ithaca: Cornell Univ. Press, 1995).

[15] *The Discovery of River Gambia by Richard Jobson, 1623*, ed. David P. Gamble and P. E. H. Hair (London: Hakluyt Society, 1999).

[16] K. R. Andrews points out that other accounts of Russia showed less hostility towards Russia, except in terms of religion; *Trade, Plunder and Settlement: Maritime Enterprise and the Genesis of the British Empire, 1480–1630* (Cambridge: Cambridge Univ. Press, 1984), 78.

'The Voyage Made by M. John Hawkins Esquire, and afterward knight, Captaine of the Jesus of Lubek, one of her Majesties shippes, and Generall of the Salomon, and other two barkes going in his companie, to the coast of Guinea, and the Indies of Nova Hispania, begun in An. Dom. 1564'

SIR JOHN HAWKINS (1532–95), was a navigator, privateer, and early slave trader, shipping Negroes from the West Coast of Africa to the Spanish possessions in the West Indies. Hawkins made three such voyages in the 1560s. The first (1562) was a relatively small-scale profit-making experiment financed by a syndicate; the second (1564–5) and third (1567–8) were much more significant enterprises with the additional objective of forming an alliance with the Spanish against the French, who had just established a colony in Florida. Hawkins later played a prominent role in reforming the navy and distinguished himself against the Armada. He died at sea in 1595 after a disastrous privateering enterprise with Sir Francis Drake.[1]

In England, Hawkins was a pioneer in trading in slaves and so has attracted especially hostile condemnation. It is clear from the accounts of his voyage that he was trying to gain access to an already well-established market between Spain and the West Indies and, perhaps more significantly, that he regarded those he captured and sold as fair game.[2] Debates on 'race' in the sixteenth century are complex, but it seems clear that Hawkins would not have treated his fellow countrymen and women in the way that he was prepared to treat Africans.[3] Nevertheless, the anonymous author of this treatise provides a vivid account of the life and society of the peoples they encountered. Extracts provided here are from Hawkins's second voyage.[4]

---

[1] For details of Hawkins's life see C. R. N. Routh, *Who's Who in Tudor England*, rev. Peter Holmes (London: Shepheard-Walwyn, 1990), 389–403.

[2] Angus Calder, *Revolutionary Empire: The Rise of the English-Speaking Empires from the Fifteenth Century to the 1780s* (London: Cape, 1981), 69–71, *passim*.

[3] On the concept of 'race' in the 16th cent., see Margo Hendricks and Patricia Parker (eds.), *Women, 'Race', and Writing in the Early Modern Period* (London: Routledge, 1994); James Shapiro, *Shakespeare and the Jews* (New York: Columbia Univ. Press, 1996).

[4] Text from Richard Hakluyt, *The Principall Navigations*, 12 vols. (Glasgow: MacLehose, 1903), x. 17–21, 24–5.

See also:

'A true Relation of Master Richard Jobsons Voyage', in Samuel Purchas, *Hakluytus Posthumous or Purchas His Pilgrimes*, 20 vols. (Glasgow: MacLehose, 1905–7), vi. 234–353.

The Discovery of River Gambia by Richard Jobson, 1623, ed. David P. Gamble and P. E. H. Hair (London: Hakluyt Society, 1999).

A.D. 1564.

The Island called Sambula.

The Samboses.

Sapies.

The Samboses man-eaters.

The 10 of December, we had a Northeast winde, with raine and storme, which weather continuing two dayes together, was the occasion that the Salomon, and Tygre loste our companie: for whereas the Jesus, and pinnesse ankered at one of the Islands called Sambula, the twelfth day, the Salomon and Tygre came not thither till the 14. In this Island we stayed certaine daies, going every day on shore to take the Inhabitants, with burning and spoiling their townes, who before were Sapies, and were conquered by the Samboses, Inhabitants beyond Sierra Leona. These Samboses had inhabited there three yeres before our comming thither, and in so short space have so planted the ground, that they had great plentie of Mil, Rise, Rootes, Pompions, Pullin, goates, of small frye dried, every house full of the Countrey fruite planted by Gods providence, as Palmito[1] trees, fruites like dates, and sundry other in no place in all that Countrey so aboundantly, whereby they lived more deliciously then other. These inhabitants have diverse of the Sapies, which they tooke in the warres as their slaves, whome onely they kept to till the ground, in that they neither have the knowledge thereof, nor yet will worke themselves, of whome wee tooke many in that place, but of the Samboses none at all, for they fled into the maine. All the Samboses have white teeth as we have, farre unlike to the Sapies which doe inhabite about Rio grande, for their teeth are all filed, which they doe for a braverie, to set out themselves, and doe jagge their flesh, both legges, armes, and bodies, as workemanlike, as a Jerkin-maker with us pinketh a jerkin. These Sapies be more civil then the Samboses: for whereas the Samboses live most by the spoile of their enemies, both in taking their victuals, and eating them also. The Sapies doe not eate mans flesh, unlesse in the warre they be driven by necessitie thereunto, which they have not used but by the example of the Samboses,

---

[1] Pompion: a pumpkin. Pullin: chickens. Palmito: a dwarf palm tree.

but live only with fruites, and cattell, whereof they have great store. This plentie is the occasion that the Sapies desire not warre, except they be therunto provoked by the invasions of the Samboses, whereas the Samboses for want of foode are inforced thereunto, and therefore are not woont onely to take them that they kill, but also keepe those that they take, untill such time as they want meate, and then they kill them. There is also another occasion that provoketh the Samboses to warre against the Sapies which is for covetousnes of their riches. For whereas the Sapies have an order to burie their dead in certaine places appointed for that purpose, with their golde about them, the Samboses digge up the ground, to have the same treasure: for the Samboses have not the like store of golde, that the Sapies have. In this Island of Sambula we found about 50 boates called Almadyes, or Canoas, which are made of one peece of wood, digged out like a trough but of a good proportion, being about 8 yards long, and one in breadth, having a beakhead and a sterne very proportionably made, and on the out side artifically carved, and painted red and blewe: they are able to cary twenty or thirty men, but they are about the coast able to cary threescore and upward. In these canoas they rowe standing upright, with an oare somewhat longer then a man, the ende whereof is made about the breadth and length of a mans hand, of the largest sort. They row very swift, and in some of them foure rowers and one to steere make as much way, as a paire of oares in the Thames of London.

The Sapies burie their dead with golde.

The Canoas of Affrica.

Their Townes are pretily divided with a maine streete at the entring in, that goeth thorough their Towne, and another overthwart street, which maketh their townes crosse wayes: their houses are built in a ranke very orderly in the face of the street, and they are made round, like a dovecote, with stakes set full of Palmito leaves, in stead of a wall: they are not much more then a fathome large, and two of height, & thatched with Palmito leaves very close, other some with reede, and over the roofe thereof, for the better garnishing of the same, there is a round bundle of reede, pretily contrived like a louer: in the inner part they make a loft of stickes, whereupon they lay all their provision of victuals: a place they reserve at their enterance for the kitchin, and the place they lie in is devided with certaine mattes artificially made with the rine of Palmito trees: their bedsteades are of small staves layd along, and raysed a foote from the ground, upon which is layde a matte, and another upon them when they list: for other covering they have none. In the middle of the towne there is a house larger and higher then the other, but in forme alike, adjoyning unto the which there is

The forme of their townes.

a place made of foure good stancions of woode, and a round roofe over it, the grounde also raised round with claye a foote high, upon the which floore were strawed many fine mats: this is the Consultation-house, the like whereof is in all Townes, as the Portugals affirme: in which place, when they sitte in Counsell the King or Captaine sitteth in the midst, and the Elders upon the floore by him: (for they give reverence to their Elders) and the common sorte sitte round about them. There they sitte to examine matters of theft, which if a man be taken with, to steale but a Portugal cloth from another, hee is sold to the Portugals for a slave. They consult also, and take order what time they shall goe to warres: and as it is certainely reported by the Portugals, they take order in gathering of the fruites in the season of the yeere, and also of Palmito wine, which is gathered by a hole cut in the top of a tree, and a gourde set for the receiving thereof, which falleth in by droppes, and yeeldeth fresh wine againe within a moneth, and this devided part and portion-like to every man, by the judgement of the Captaine and Elders, every man holdeth himselfe contented: and this surely I judge to be a very good order: for otherwise, whereas scarsitie of Palmito is, every man would have the same, which might breed great strife: but of such things, as every man doeth plant for himselfe, the sower thereof reapeth it to his owne use, so that nothing is common, but that which is unset by mans hands. In their houses there is more common passage of Lizardes like Evats, and other greater, of blacke and blew colour, of neere a foote long, besides their tailes, then there is with us of Mise in great houses. The Sapies and Samboses also use in their warres bowes, and arrowes made of reedes, with heads of yron poysoned with the juyce of a Cucumber, whereof I had many in my handes. In their battels they have target-men, with broad wicker targets, and darts with heades at both endes, of yron, the one in forme of a two edged sworde, a foote and an halfe long, and at the other ende, the yron long of the same length made to counterpease it, that in casting it might flie level, rather then for any other purpose as I can judge. And when they espie the enemie, the Captaine to cheere his men, cryeth Hungry, and they answere Heygre, and with that every man placeth himselfe in order, for about every target man three bowemen will cover themselves, and shoote as they see advantage: and when they give the onset, they make such terrible cryes, that they may bee heard two miles off. For their beliefe, I can heare of none that they have, but in such as they themselves imagine to see in their dreames, and so worshippe the pictures, whereof wee sawe some like unto devils. In this Island aforesayde wee

The Consultation house or towne-howse.

Palmito is a wilde date.

A venemous Cucumber.

Idoles like devils.

sojourned unto the one and twentieth of December, where having taken
certaine Negros, and asmuch of their fruites, rise, and mill, as we could well
cary away, (whereof there was such store, that wee might have laden one of
our Barkes therewith) wee departed, and at our departure divers of our men
being desirous to goe on shore, to fetch Pompions, which having prooved,
they found to bee very good, certaine of the Tygres men went also, amongst
the which there was a Carpenter, a young man, who with his fellowes
having fet many, and caryed them downe to their boates, as they were ready
to depart, desired his fellow to tary while he might goe up to fetch a few
which he had layed by for him selfe, who being more licorous then *The extreme*
circumspect, went up without weapon, and as he went up alone, possibly *negligence of one*
being marked of the Negros that were upon the trees, espying him what hee *of the companie.*
did, perceaving him to be alone, and without weapon, dogged him, and
finding him occupyed in binding his Pompions together, came behinde
him, overthrowing him and straight cutte his throate, as hee afterwardes
was found by his fellowes, who came to the place for him, and there found
him naked.

The two and twentieth the Captaine went into the River, called Cal- *The river*
lowsa, with the two Barkes, and the Johns Pinnesse, and the Salomons *Calowsa.*
boate, leaving at anker in the Rivers mouth the two shippes, the River being
twenty leagues in, where the Portugals roade: hee came thither the five and
twentieth, and dispatched his businesse, and so returned with two Car-
avels, loaden with Negros.

The 29 of this same moneth[2] we departed with all our shippes from Sierra A.D. 1565
Leona, towards the West Indies, and for the space of eighteene dayes, we
were becalmed, having nowe and then contrary windes, and some Terna-
dos, amongst the same calme, which happened to us very ill, beeing but
reasonably watered, for so great a companie of Negros, and our selves,
which pinched us all, and that which was worst, put us in such feare that
many never thought to have reached to the Indies, without great death of
Negros, and of themselves: but the Almightie God, who never suffereth his
elect to perish, sent us the sixteenth of Februarie, the ordinary Brise, which
is the Northwest winde, which never left us, till wee came to an Island of
the Canybals, called Dominica, where wee arrived the ninth of March, *Dominica Island.*
upon a Saturday: and because it was the most desolate place in all the

[2] January 1565.

Island, we could see no Canybals, but some of their houses where they dwelled, and as it should seeme forsooke the place for want of fresh water, for wee could finde none there but raine water, and such as fell from the hilles, and remained as a puddle in the dale, whereof wee filled for our Negros.

Giles Fletcher, 'The description of the countrey of Russia, with the bredth, length, and names of the Shires' (1588)

GILES FLETCHER the elder (1549?–1611) was an ambassador, Member of Parliament, and a poet. He was sent to Scotland and Germany before travelling to Russia in 1588. Despite being unhappy with his treatment there he managed to secure a number of concessions for English merchants and establish trading contacts. The queen felt moved to make a formal complaint to the emperor.

Fletcher's account of Russia appeared in 1591, but was suppressed when anxious merchants pointed out potentially troubling passages to William Cecil, Lord Burghley. The abridged version appeared in the second edition of Hakluyt's *Principall Navigations* (1598).[1] Fletcher was extremely aware of the variety of peoples under the suzerainty of the Russian emperor. He gives full and detailed accounts of the Russians and the Tartars, whom he regards as a far more savage people, descended from the ancient Scythians (which makes the Tartars related to the Irish in contemporary English anthropological accounts).[2] Fletcher's analysis was the most substantial by an Elizabethan traveller and so undoubtedly became the standard account of the Russian peoples. It should be noted that there was a significant volume of trade with Russia and that Fletcher was following in the footsteps of other pioneers such as Anthony Jenkinson, who met the emperor in 1566 with the queen's blessing and helped establish the Muscovy Company.[3]

See also:

Richard Hakluyt, *The Principall Navigations*, 12 vols. (Glasgow: MacLehose, 1903), *passim*.

Samuel Purchas, *Hakluytus Posthumous or Purchas His Pilgrimes*, 20 vols. (Glasgow: MacLehose, 1905–7), xiv. 108–305.

---

[1] For details of Fletcher's life see *DNB* entry; William B. Hunter (ed.), *The English Spenserians: The Poetry of Giles Fletcher, George Wither, Michael Drayton, Phineas Fletcher and Henry More* (Salt Lake City: Univ. of Utah Press, 1977), 9–13.

[2] See Andrew Hadfield, *Spenser's Irish Experience: Wilde Fruit and Salvage Soyl* (Oxford: Clarendon Press, 1997), ch. 2.

[3] Text from Richard Hakluyt, *Principall Navigations*, 12 vols. (Glasgow: MacLehose, 1903), iii. 389–401, 415–19.

OF THE TARTARS, AND OTHER BORDERERS TO THE COUNTRY OF RUSSIA, WITH WHOM THEY HAVE MOST TO DOE IN WARRE, AND PEACE

Their neighbors with whom they[1] have greatest dealings & intercourse, both in peace & war, are first the Tartar. [...]

The Chrim Tartar.

The greatest and mightiest of them is the Chrim Tartar, (whom some call the Great Can) that lieth South, & Southeastward from Russia, and doth most annoy the country by often invasions, commonly once every yere,

The firing of Mosco by the Chrim Tartar, in the yeare 1571.

sometimes entring very farre within the inland parts. In the yere 1571 he came as farre as the citie of Mosco, with an armie of 200000 men, without any battel, or resistance at al, for that the Russe Emperor (then Ivan Vasiliwich) leading forth his armie to encounter with him, marched a wrong way. The citie he tooke not, but fired the suburbs, which by reason of the buildings (which are all of wood without any stone, brick, or lime, save certeine out roomes) kindled so quickly, and went on with such rage, as that it consumed the greatest part of the citie almost within the space of foure houres, being of 30 miles or more of compasse. Then might you have seene a lamentable spectacle: besides the huge & mighty flame of the citie all on light fire, the people burning in their houses and streetes, but most of all of such as laboured to passe out of the gates farthest from the enemie, where meeting together in a mighty throng, & so pressing every man to prevent another, wedged themselves so fast within the gate, and streetes neere unto it, as that three rankes walked one upon the others head, the uppermost treading downe those that were lower: so that there perished at that time (as was said) by the fire & the presse, the number of 800000 people or more. [...]

The maner of the Tartars fight, and armour.

Their common practise (being very populous) is to make divers armies, and so drawing the Russe to one or two places of the frontiers, to invade at some other place, that is left without defence. Their maner of fight, or ordering of their forces is much after the Russe maner (spoken of before) save that they are all horsemen, and carie nothing els but a bowe, a sheafe of arrowes, and a falcon sword after the Turkish fashion. They are very expert horsemen, and use to shoote as readily backward, as forward. Some wil have a horsmans staffe like to a bore speare, besides their other weapons.

---

[1] The Russians.

The common souldier hath no other armour then his ordinary apparell, viz. a blacke sheeps skin with the wool side outward in the day time, and inwarde in the night time, with a cap of the same. But their Morseys or noblemen imitate the Turk both in apparel and armour. When they are to passe over a river with their armie, they tie three or foure horses together, and taking long poles or pieces of wood, bind them fast to the tailes of their horse: so sitting on the poles they drive their horse over. At handie strokes (when they joyne battell) they are accounted farre better men then the Russe people, fierce by nature, but more hardy and bloody by continuall practise of warre: as men knowing no artes of peace, nor any civil practise.

Yet their subtilty is more then may seeme to agree with their barbarous condition. By reason they are practised to invade continually, and to robbe their neighbours that border about them, they are very pregnant, and ready witted to devise stratagems upon the sudden for their better advantage. As in their warre against Beala the fourth, king of Hungarie, whome they invaded with 500000. men, and obtained against him a great victorie. Where, among other, having slaine his Chancelor called Nicholas Schinick, they found about him the kings privy seale. Whereupon they devised presently to counterfeit letters in the kings name, to the cities and townes next about the place, where the field was fought: with charge that in no case they should convey themselves, and their goods out of their dwellings, where they might abide safely without all feare of danger, and not leave the countrey desolate to the possession of so vile and barbarous an enemie, as was the Tartar nation, terming themselves in all reprochful maner. For notwithstanding he had lost his carriages, with some few straglers that had marched disorderly, yet he doubted not but to recover that losse, with the accesse of a notable victorie, if the savage Tartar durst abide him in the field. To this purpose having written their letters in the Polish character, by certaine young men whom they tooke in the field, and signed them with the Kings seale, they dispatched them forth to all the quarters of Hungaria, that lay neere about the place. Whereupon the Ungarians that were now flying away with their goods, wives, and children, upon the rumour of the kings overthrow, taking comfort of these counterfeit letters, staied at home. And so were made a pray, being surprised on the sudden by this huge number of these Tartars, that had compassed them about before they were aware.

When they besiege a towne or fort, they offer much parle, and send many flattering messages to perswade a surrendry: promising all things that the

The subtiltie of the Tartar.

inhabitants will require: but being once possessed of the place, they use all maner of hostilitie, and crueltie. This they doe upon a rule they have, vz. that justice is to bee practised but towards their owne. They encounter not lightly, but they have some ambush, whereunto (having once shewed themselves, and made some short conflict) they retire as repulsed for feare, and so draw the enemie into it if they can. But the Russe beeing well acquainted with their practise is more warie of them. When they come a roving with some small number, they set on horsebacke counterfaite shapes of men, that their number may seeme greater.

When they make any onset, their maner is to make a great shoute, crying all out together Olla Billa, Olla Billa, God helpe us, God help us. They contemne death so much, as that they chuse rather to die, then to yeeld to their enemie, and are seene when they are slain to bite the very weapon, when they are past striking or helping of themselves. Wherein appeareth how different the Tartar is in his desperate courage from the Russe and Turke. For the Russe souldier, if he begin once to retire, putteth all his safetie in his speedy flight. And if once he be taken by his enemy, he neither defendeth himselfe, nor intreateth for his life, as reckoning straight to die. The Turk commonly, when he is past hope of escaping, falleth to intreatie, and casteth away his weapon, offereth both his hands, and holdeth them, as it were to be tied: hoping to save his life, by offering himselfe bondslave.

The chiefe bootie the Tartars seeke for in all their warres is to get store of captives, specially young boyes, and girles, whome they sell to the Turkes, or other their neighbours. To this purpose they take with them great baskets made like bakers panniers to carry them tenderly, and if any of them happen to tire, or to be sicke by the way, they dash him against the ground, or some tree, and so leave him dead. The Souldiers are not troubled with keeping the captives and the other bootie, for hindering the execution of their warres, but they have certaine bandes that intend nothing else, appoynted of purpose to receive and keepe the captives and the other praye.

The Russe borderers (being used to their invasions lightly every yere in the Sommer) keepe fewe other cattell on the border partes, save swine onely which the Tartar will not touch, nor drive away with him: for that he

The Tartar religion. is of the Turkish religion, and will eate no swines flesh. Of Christ our Saviour they confesse as much as doeth the Turke in his Alkaron, viz. that he came of the Angel Gabriel and the Virgin Marie, that he was a great Prophet, and shall be the Judge of the worlde at the last day. In other matter likewise, they are much ordered after the manner and direction of the

Turke: having felt the Turkish forces when hee wonne from them Azov and Caffa, with some other townes about the Euxine or blacke Sea, that were before tributaries to the Crim Tartar. So that now the Emperor of the Crims for the most part is chosen one of the Nobility whom the Turke doeth commend: whereby it is brought nowe to passe, that the Crim Tartar giveth to the Turke the tenth part of the spoyle which hee getteth in his warres against the Christians.

Herein they differ from the Turkish religion, for that they have certaine idole puppets made of silke, or like stuffe, of the fashion of a man, which they fasten to the doore of their walking houses, to be as Janusses or keepers of their house. And these idoles are made not by all, but by certaine religious women which they have among them for that and like uses. They have besides the image of their King or great Can, of an huge bignesse, which they erect at every stage when the army marcheth: and this every one must bend and bowe unto as he passeth by it, be he Tartar or stranger. They are much given to witchcraft, and ominous conjectures upon every accident which they heare or see.

In making of mariages they have no regard of alliance or consanguinitie. Onely with his mother, sister, and daughter a man may not marrie, and though he take the woman into his house, and accompany with her, yet he accounteth her not for his wife till he have a childe by her. Then hee beginneth to take a dowry of her friends of horse, sheepe, kine, &c. If she be barren after a certaine time, he turneth her home againe.

Under the Emperour they have certaine Dukes, whome they call Mor- *The Tartar nobilitie.* seis or Divoymorseis, that rule over a certaine number of 10000. 20000. or 40000. a piece, which they call Horrds. When the Emperour hath any use of them to serve in his warres, they are bound to come, and to bring with them their Souldiers to a certain number, every man with his two horse at the least, the one to ride on, the other to kill, when it commeth to his turne to have his horse eaten. For their chiefe vitaile is horse flesh, which they *The Tartar diet.* eate without bread, or any other thing with it. So that if a Tartar be taken by a Russe, he shall be sure lightly to finde a horse-legge, or some other part of him at his saddle bowe. [...]

They keepe great heards of kine, & flocks of blacke sheepe, rather for the skins and milke (which they carie with them in great bottels) then for the use of the flesh, though sometimes they eate of it. Some use they have of ryse, figs, and other fruits. They drinke milke or warme blood, and for the most part card them both together. They use sometime as they travel by the way, to let their horse blood in a vaine, and to drinke it warme, as it commeth from his bodie.

The Tartars dwelling.

Townes they plant none, nor other standing buildings, but have walking houses, which the latines call Veii, built upon wheeles like a shepheards cottage. These they drawe with them whithersoever they goe, driving their cattell with them. And when they come to their stage, or standing place, they plant their carte houses verie orderly in a ranke: and so make the forme of streetes, and of a large towne. And this is the manner of the Emperor himselfe, who hath no other seat of Empire but an Agora, or towne of wood, that moveth with him whithersoever hee goeth. As for the fixed and standing building used in other countreyes, they say they are unwholesome and unpleasant.

They begin to moove their houses and cattell in the Spring time from the South part of their Countrey towards the North partes. And so driving on till they have grased all up to the farthest part Northward, they returne backe againe towards their South countrey (where they continue all the Winter) by 10. or 12. miles a stage: in the meane while the grasse being sprung up againe, to serve for their cattell as they returne. From the border of the Shalcan towards the Caspian sea, to the Russe frontiers, they have a goodly Countrey, specially on the South and Southeast parts, but lost for lacke of tillage.

Of money they have no use at all, and therefore prefer brasse and steele before other mettals, specially bullate, which they use for swordes, knives, and other necessaries. As for golde and silver they neglect it of very purpose, (as they doe all tillage of their ground) to bee more free for their wandring kinde of life, and to keepe their Countrey lesse subject to invasions. Which giveth them great advantage against all their neighbors, ever invading and never beeing invaded. Such as have taken upon them to invade their Countrey (as of oldetime Cyrus and Darius Hystaspis, on the East and Southeast side) have done it with very ill successe: as wee finde in the stories written of those times. For their manner is when any will invade them, to allure and drawe them on by flying and reculing (as if they were afraide) till they have drawen them some good way within their countrey. Then when they begin to want victuall and other necessaries (as needes they must where nothing is to be had) to stoppe up the passages, and inclose them with multitudes. By which stratagem (as wee reade in Laonicus Chalcacondylas in his Turkish storie) they had welnigh surprised the great and huge armie of Tamerlan, but that hee retired with all speede hee could towardes the river Tanais or Don, not without great losse of his men, and cariages.

In the storie of Pachymerius the Greeke (which hee wrote of the Emperors of Constantinople from the beginning of the reigne of Michael Palaeologus to the time of Andronicus the elder) I remember he telleth to the same purpose of one Nogas a Tartarian captaine under Cazan the Emperor of the East Tartars (of whom the citie and kingdome of Cazan may seeme to have taken the denomination) who refused a present of Pearle and other jewels sent unto him from Michael Palaeologus: asking withall, for what use they served, and whether they were good to keepe away sicknesse, death, or other misfortunes of this life, or no. So that it seemeth they have ever, or long time bene of that minde to value things no further, then by the use and necessitie for which they serve. *Pachymerius.*

For person and complexion they have broade and flatte visages, of a tanned colour into yellowe and blacke, fierce and cruell lookes, thinne haired upon the upper lippe, and pitte of the chinne, light and nimble bodied, with short legges, as if they were made naturally for horsemen: whereto they practise themselves from their childhood, seldome going afoot about anie businesse. Their speech is verie sudden and loude, speaking as it were out of a deepe hollowe throate. When they sing you would thinke a kowe lowed, or some great bandogge howled. Their greatest exercise is shooting, wherein they traine up their children from their verie infancie, not suffering them to eate till they have shot neere the marke within a certaine scantling. They are the very same that sometimes were called Scythae Nomades, or the Scythian shepheards, by the Greekes and Latines. Some thinke that the Turks took their beginning from the nation of the Crim Tartars. [. . .]

There are divers other Tartars that border upon Russia, as the Nagayes, the Cheremissens, the Mordwites, the Chircasses, and the Shalcans, which all differ in name more then in regiment, or other condition, from the Crim Tartar, except the Chircasses that border Southwest, towardes Lituania, and are farre more civill than the rest of the Tartars, of a comely person, and of a stately behaviour, as applying themselves to the fashion of the Polonian. Some of them have subjected themselves to the Kings of Poland, and professe Christianitie. The Nagay lieth Eastwarde, and is reckoned for the best man of warre among all the Tartars, but verie savage, and cruell above all the rest. The Cheremessen Tartar, that lieth betwixt the Russe and the *The Nagay Tartar the cruellest. The Chircasce the civillest Tartar.*

The Cheremissen Tartar of two sorts: the Lugavoy and the Nagornay.

Nagay, are of two sorts, the Lugavoy (that is of the valley) and the Nagornay, or of the hilly countrey. These have much troubled the Emperours of Russia. And therefore they are content now to buy peace of them, under pretence of giving a yeerely pension of Russe commodities to their Morseys, or Divoymorseis, that are chiefe of their tribes. For which also they are bound to serve them in their wars, under certaine conditions. They are said to be just and true in their dealings: and for that cause they hate the Russe people, whom they account to be double, and false in al their dealing. And therefore the common sort are very unwilling to keepe agreement with them, but that they are kept in by their Morseis, or Dukes for their pensions sake.

The Mordwit Tartar ye most barbarous of the rest.

The most rude & barbarous is counted the Mordwit Tartar, that hath many selfe-fashions and strange kinds of behaviour, differing from the rest. For his religion, though he acknowledge one God, yet his maner is to worship for God, that living thing y^t he first meeteth in the morning, & to sweare by it all that whole day, whether it be horse, dog, cat, or whatsoever els it bee. When his friend dieth, he killeth his best horse, and having flayed off the skinne hee carieth it on high upon a long pole before the corpes to the place of buriall. This hee doeth (as the Russe saieth) that his friend may have a good horse to carie him to heaven: but it is likelier to declare his love towards his dead friend, in that he will have to die with him the best thing that he hath.

Next to the kingdome of Astracan, that is the farthest part Southeastward of the Russe dominion, lyeth the Shalcan, and the countrey of Media: whither the Russe marchants trade for rawe silkes, syndon, saphion, skinnes, and other commodities. The chiefe Townes of Media where the Russe tradeth, are Derbent (built by Alexander the great, as the inhabitants say) and Zamachi where the staple is kept for rawe silkes. Their maner is in

The reviving of silkwormes.

the Spring time to revive the silke-wormes (that lie dead all the Winter) by laying them in the warme sunne, and (to hasten their quickening that they may sooner goe to worke) to put them into bags, and so to hang them under

Chrinisin a kind of silk-worme.

their childrens armes. As for the woorme called Chrinisin (as wee call it Chrymson) that maketh coloured silke, it is bred not in Media, but in Assyria. This trade to Derbent and Samachi for rawe silkes, and other commodities of that Countrey, as also into Persia, and Bougharia downe

Liberty to trade downe the Caspian sea.

the river of Volga, and through the Caspian sea, is permitted aswell to the English as to the Russe merchants, by the Emperours last grant at my being there. Which he accounteth for a very speciall favour, and might prove indeede very beneficial to our English merchants, if the trade were wel and orderly used.

The whole nation of the Tartars are utterly voide of all learning, and without written Law: yet certaine rules they have which they hold by tradition, common to all the Hoords for the practise of their life. Which are of this sort. First, To obey their Emperour and other Magistrates, 1 whatsoever they commaund about the publike service. 2 Except for the 2 publike behoofe, every man to be free and out of controlment. 3 No private 3 man to possesse any lands, but the whole countrey to be as common. 4 To 4 neglect all daintinesse and varietie of meates, and to content themselves with that which commeth next to hand, for more hardnesse, and readines in the executing of their affaires. 5 To weare any base attire, and to patch 5 their clothes whether there be any neede or not: that when there is neede, it be no shame to weare a patcht coate. 6 To take or steale from any stranger 6 whatsoever they can get, as beeing enemies to all men, save to such as will subject themselves to them. 7 Towards their owne hoorde and nation to be 7 true in worde and deede. 8 To suffer no stranger to come within the 8 Realme. If any doe, the same to be bondslave to him that first taketh *No stranger* him, except such merchants and other as have the Tartar Bull, or passport *without pasport* about them. *admitted.*

OF THE PRIVATE BEHAVIOUR, OR QUALITIE
OF THE RUSSE PEOPLE

The private behaviour and qualitie of the Russe people, may partly be understood by that which hath beene sayd concerning the publique state and usage of the Countrey. As touching the naturall habite of their bodies, *Constitution of* they are for the most part of a large size, and of very fleshly bodies: *their bodies.* accounting it a grace to be somewhat grosse and burley, and therefore they nourish and spread their beards, to have them long and broad. But for the most part they are very unwieldy and unactive withall. Which may be thought to come partly of the climate, and the numbnesse which they get by the cold in winter, and partly of their diet that standeth most of rootes, onions, garlike, cabbage, and such like things that breede grosse humors, which they use to eate alone, and with their other meates.

Their diet is rather much then curious. At their meales they beginne *Their diet.* commonly with a Charke or small cuppe of Aqua vitae, (which they call

Russe wine) and then drinke not till towardes the end of their meales, taking it in largely, and all together, with kissing one another at every pledge. And therefore after dinner there is no talking with them, but every man goeth to his bench to take his afternoones sleepe, which is as ordinary with them as their nights rest. When they exceede, and have varietie of dishes, the first are their baked meates (for roste meates they use litle) and then their broathes or pottage. Their common drinke is Mead, the poorer sort use water, and a third drinke called Quasse, which is nothing else (as we say) but water turned out of his wits, with a little branne meashed with it.

This diet would breede in them many diseases, but that they use bath-stoves, or hote houses in steade of all Phisicke, commonly twise or thrise every weeke. All the winter time, and almost the whole Sommer, they heat their Peaches, which are made like the Germane bathstoves, and their Poclads like ovens, that so warme the house that a stranger at the first shall hardly like of it. These two extremities, specially in the winter of heat within their houses, and of extreame colde without, together with their diet, make them of a darke, and sallow complexion, their skinnes being tanned and parched both with cold and with heate: specially the women, that for the greater part are of farre worse complexions, then the men. Whereof the cause I take to be their keeping within the hote houses, and busying themselves about the heating, and using of their bathstoves, and peaches.

An admirable induring of extreme heat, and colde at one and the same time. The Russe because that he is used to both these extremities of heat and of cold, can beare them both a great deale more patiently, then strangers can doe. You shall see them sometimes (to season their bodies) come out of their bathstoves all on a froth, and fuming as hoat almost as a pigge at a spit, and presently to leape into the river starke naked, or to powre cold water all over their bodies, and that in the coldest of all the winter time. The women to mende the bad hue of their skinnes, use to paint their faces with white and red colours, so visibly, that every man may perceive it. Which is made no matter, because it is common and liked well by their husbands: who make their wives and daughters an ordinarie allowance to buy them colours to paint their faces withall, and delight themselves much to see them of fowle women to become such faire images. This parcheth the skinne, and helpeth to deforme them when their painting is of.

The Noble mans attire. They apparell themselves after the Greeke manner. The Noblemans attire is on this fashion. First a Taffia, or little night cappe on his head, that covereth litle more then his crowne, commonly verie rich wrought of silke and golde threede, and set with pearle and precious stone. His head he keepeth shaven close to the very skinne, except he be in some displeasure with the Emperour. Then hee suffereth his haire to growe and hang downe upon his shoulders, covering his face as ugly and deformedly as he can. Over the Taffia hee weareth a wide cappe of blacke Foxe (which they account for the best furre) with a Tiara or long bonnet put within it, standing up like a Persian or Babilonian hatte. About his necke (which is seene all bare) is a coller set with pearle and precious stone, about three or foure fingers broad. Next over his shirt, (which is curiously wrought, because he strippeth himselfe into it in the Sommer time, while he is within the house) is a Shepon, or light garment of silke, made downe to the knees, buttoned before: and then a Caftan or a close coat buttoned, and girt to him with a Persian girdle, whereat he hangs his knives and spoone. This commonly is of cloth of gold, and hangeth downe as low as his ancles. Over that hee weareth a lose garment of some rich silke, furred and faced about with some golde lace, called a Ferris. Another over that of chamlet, or like stuffe called an Alkaben, sleeved and hanging lowe, and the cape commonly brooched, and set all with pearle. When hee goeth abroad, he casteth over all these (which are but sleight, though they seeme to be many) an other garment called an Honoratkey, like to the Alkaben, save that it is made without a coller for the necke. And this is commonly of fine cloth, or Camels haire. His buskins (which he weareth in stead of hose, with linnen folles under them in stead of boot hose) are made of a Persian leather called Saphian, embrodered with pearle. His upper stockes commonly are of cloth of golde. When he goeth abroad, hee mounteth on horsebacke, though it be but to the next doore: which is the maner also of the Boiarskey, or Gentlemen.

The Boiarskey or Gentlemans attire is of the same fashion, but differeth in stuffe: and yet he will have his Caftan or undercoat sometimes of cloth of golde, the rest of cloth, or silke. *The Gentlemans apparel.*

The Noble woman (called Chyna Boiarshena) weareth on her head, first a caull of some soft silke (which is commonly redde) and over it a fruntlet called Obrosa, of white colour. Over that her cappe (made after the coife fashion of cloth of gold) called Shapka Zempska, edged with some rich furre, and set with pearle and stone. Though they have of late begunne to disdaine embrodering with pearle above their cappes, because the Diacks, and some Marchants wives have taken up the fashion. In their eares they weare earerings (which they call Sargee) of two inches or more compasse, *The Noble womans attire.*

the matter of gold set with Rubies, or Saphires, or some like precious stone. In Sommer they goe often with kerchieffes of fine white lawne, or cambricke, fastned under the chinne, with two long tassels pendent. The kerchiefe spotted and set thicke with rich pearle. When they ride or goe abroad in raynie weather, they weare white hattes with coloured bandes, called Stapa Zemskoy. About their neckes they weare collers of three or foure fingers broad, set with rich pearle and precious stone. Their upper garment is a loose gowne called Oposhen commonly of scarlet, with wide loose sleeves, hanging downe to the ground buttened before with great golde buttons, or at least silver and guilt nigh as bigge as a walnut. Which hath hanging over it fastned under the cappe, a large broad cape of some rich furre, that hangeth downe almost to the middles of their backes. Next under the Oposken or upper garment, they weare another called a Leitnick that is made close before with great wide sleeves, the cuffe or halfe sleeve up to the elbowes, commonly of cloth of golde: and under that a Ferris Zemskoy, which hangeth loose buttoned throughout to the very foote. On the hande wrests they weare very faire braselets, about two fingers broad of pearle and precious stone. They goe all in buskins of white, yellow, blew, or some other coloured leather, embrodered with pearle. This is the attire of the Noblewoman of Russia, when she maketh the best shewe of her selfe. The Gentlewomans apparell may differ in the stuffe, but is all one for the making or fashion.

The Mousick or common mans attire.

As for the poore Mousick and his wife they goe poorely cladde. The man with his Honoratkey, or loose gowne to the small of the legge, tyed together with a lace before, of course white or blew cloth, with some Shube or long wastcoate of furre, or of sheepe-skinne under it, and his furred cappe, and buskins. The poorer sort of them have their Honoratkey, or upper garment, made of Kowes haire. This is their winter habite. In the sommer time, commonly they weare nothing but their shirts on their backes, and buskins on their legges. The woman goeth in a red or blewe gowne, when she maketh the best shewe, and with some warme Shube of furre under it in the winter time. But in the sommer, nothing but her two shirts (for so they call them) one over the other, whether they be within doores, or without. On their heads, they weare caps of some coloured stuffe, many of velvet, or of cloth of gold: but for the most part kerchiefs. Without earings of silver or some other mettall, and her crosse about her necke, you shall see no Russe woman, be she wife, or maide.

John Leo (Africanus), *The History and Description of Africa*, trans. John Pory (1600), Comments on North Africans

JOHN LEO (AFRICANUS) (*c.*1495/6–1552) was a scholarly North African Arab, probably from Morocco, who travelled widely before he was captured by Venetian corsairs in the Mediterranean. He was given as a present to Pope Leo X, and subsequently lived in Rome until his death. His lengthy *The History and Description of Africa* was completed in 1526 and became the most comprehensive account of the continent for Europeans in the sixteenth and early seventeenth centuries.[1] John Pory (1579?–1635), a traveller, geographer, and translator connected with Richard Hakluyt, translated the work into English in 1600.[2] It is possible that Shakespeare used Pory's translation for his characterization of *Othello* (1603–4).[3]

Included here are Leo Africanus's comments on the peoples of North Africa, the area he knew best and which occupies most of the narrative of his work.[4]

See also:

Richard Hakluyt, *The Principall Navigations*, 12 vols. (Glasgow: MacLehose, 1903), ii. 164–81; vi. 138–284.

Sandys, George, *A Relation of a Journey Begun An: Dom: 1610* (1615).

Samuel Purchas, *Hakluytus Posthumous or Purchas His Pilgrimes*, 20 vols. (Glasgow: MacLehose, 1905–7), v. 307–529.

---

[1] For John Leo's biography, see Leo Africanus, *The History and Description of Africa*, trans. John Pory, ed. Robert Brown, 3 vols. (London: Hakluyt Society, 1896), vol. i, introd., pp. i–lii.

[2] On Pory, see *DNB* entry.

[3] See L. Whitney, 'Did Shakespeare know Leo Africanus?', *PMLA* 37 (1922), 470–88; Andrew Hadfield, *Literature, Travel, and Colonial Writing in the English Renaissance, 1545–1625* (Oxford: Clarendon Press, 1998), 238–9.

[4] Text from Leo Africanus, *History and Description of Africa*, i. 151–60, 162–4, 182–7.

THE MANNERS AND CUSTOMES OF THE AFRICAN
PEOPLE, WHICH INHABIT THE DESERT OF LIBYA

Those five kindes of people before rehearsed, to wit, the people of Zenega, of Gansiga, of Terga, of Leuta, and of Bardeoa, are called of the Latins *Numidae*: and they live all after one manner, that is to say, without all lawe and civilitie. Their garment is a narrow and base peece of cloth, wherewith scarce halfe their bodie is covered. Some of them wrap their heads in a kinde of blacke cloth, as it were with a scarfe, such as the Turks use, which is commonly called a Turbant. Such as will be discerned from the common sort for gentlemen, weare a jacket made of blew cotton with wide sleeves. And cotton-cloth is brought unto them by certaine merchants from the land of Negros. They have no beastes fit to ride upon except their camels; unto whom nature, betweene the bunch standing upon the hinder part of their backes and their neckes, hath allotted a place, which may fitly serve to ride upon, in stead of a saddle. Their manner of riding is most ridiculous. For sometimes they lay their legs acrosse upon the camels neck; and sometimes againe (having no knowledge nor regard of stirrops) they rest their feete upon a rope, which is cast over his shoulders. In stead of spurres they use a truncheon of a cubites length, having at the one end thereof a goad, wherewith they pricke onely the shoulders of their camels. Those camels which they use to ride upon have a hole bored through the gristles of their nose, in the which a ring of leather is fastened, whereby as with a bit, they are more easily curbed and mastred; after which manner I have seene buffles used in Italie. For beds, they lie upon mats made of sedge and bulrushes. Their tents are covered for the most part with course chamlet, or with a harsh kinde of wooll which commonly groweth upon the boughes of their date-trees. As for their manner of living, it would seeme to any man incredible what hunger and scarcitie this nation will indure. Bread they have none at all, neither use they any seething or rosting; their foode is camels milke onely, and they desire no other dainties. For their breakefast they drinke off a great cup of camels milke: for supper they have certaine dried flesh stieped in butter and milke, whereof each man taking his share, eateth it out of his fist. And that this their meate may not stay long undigested in their stomackes, they sup off the foresaid broth wherein their flesh was steeped: for which purpose they use the palmes of their hands as a most fit instrument framed by nature to the same end. After that, each one drinks his cup of milk, & so their supper hath an ende. These Numidians, while they have any store of milke, regard water nothing at all, which for the most part happeneth in the spring of the yeere, all which time you shall finde some among them that will neither wash their hands nor their faces. Which seemeth not altogether to be unlikely; for (as we said before) while their milke lasteth, they frequent not those places where water is common: yea, and their camels, so long as they may feede upon grasse, will drinke no water at all. They spende their whole daies in hunting and theeving: for all their indevour and exercise is to drive away the camels of their enemies; neither will they remaine above three daies in one place, by reason that they have not pasture any longer for the sustenance of their camels. And albeit (as is aforesaid) they have no civilitie at all, nor any lawes prescribed unto them; yet have they a certaine governour or prince placed over them, unto whom they render obedience and due honour, as unto their king. They are not onely ignorant of all good learning and liberall sciences; but are likewise altogether careles and destitute of vertue: insomuch that you shall finde scarce one amongst them all which is a man of judgement or counsell. And if any injured partie will goe to the lawe with his adversarie, he must ride continually five or sixe daies before he can come to the speech of any judge. This nation hath all learning and good disciplines in such contempt, that they will not once vouchsafe to goe out of their deserts for the studie and attaining thereof: neither, if any learned man shall chance to come among them, can they love his companie and conversation, in regarde of their most rude and detestable behaviour. Howbeit, if they can finde any judge, which can frame himselfe to live and continue among them, to him they give most large yeerely allowance. Some allow their judge a thousand ducats yeerely, some more, and some lesse, according as themselves thinke good. They that will seeme to be accounted of the better sort, cover their heads (as I said before) with a peece of blacke cloth, part whereof, like a vizard or maske, reacheth downe over their faces, covering all their coun-tenance except their eies; and this is their daily kinde of attire. And so often as they put meate into their mouthes they remoove the said maske, which being done, they foorthwith cover their mouths again; alleging this fond reason: for (say they) as it is unseemely for a man, after he hath received meate into his stomack, to vomite it out of his mouth againe and to cast it upon the earth; even so it is an undecent part to eate meate with a mans mouth uncovered. The women of this nation be grosse, corpulent, and of a swart complexion. They are fattest upon their breast and paps, but slender about the girdle-stead. Very civill they are, after their manner, both in speech and gestures: sometimes they will accept of a kisse; but whoso tempteth them farther, putteth his owne life in hazard. For by reason of jealousie you may see them daily one to be the death and destruction of another, and that in such savage and brutish manner, that in this case they will shew no compassion at all. And they seeme to be more wise in this behalfe then divers of our people, for they will by no meanes match themselves unto an harlot. The liberalitie of this people hath at all times beene exceeding great. And when any travellers may passe through their drie and desert territories, they will never repaire unto their tents, neither will they themselves travell upon the common highway. And if any carovan or multitude of merchants will passe those deserts, they are bound to pay certaine custome unto the prince of the said people, namely, for every camels load a peece of cloth woorth a ducate. Upon a time I remember that travelling in the companie of certaine merchants over the desert called by them Araoan, it was our chaunce there to meete with the prince of Zanaga; who, after he had received his due custome, invited the said companie of merchants, for their recreation, to goe and abide with him in his tents fower or five daies. Howbeit, because his tents were too farre out of our way, and for that we should have wandered farther then we thought good, esteeming it more convenient for us to hold on our direct course, we refused his gentle offer, and for his courtesie gave him great thanks. But not being satisfied therewith, he commanded that our camels should proceede on forward, but the merchants he carried along with him, and gave them very sumptuous entertainment at his place of aboad. Where wee were no sooner arrived, but this good prince caused camels of all kindes and ostriches, which he had hunted and taken by the way, to bee killed for his household provision. Howbeit we requested him not to make such daily slaughters of his camels; affirming moreover, that we never used to eate the flesh of a gelt camell, but when all other victuals failed us. Whereunto hee answered, that he should deale uncivilly, if he welcommed so woorthie and so seldome-seene guests with the killing of small cattell onely. Wherefore he wished us to fall to such provision as was set before us. Here might you have seene great plentie of rosted and sodden flesh: their roasted ostriches were brought to the table in wicker platters, being seasoned with sundrie kindes of herbes and spices. Their bread made of Mill and panicke was of a most savorie and pleasante taste: and alwaies at the end of dinner or supper we had plentie of dates and great store of milke served in. Yea, this bountifull and noble prince, that he might sufficiently shew how welcome we were unto him, would together with his nobilitie alwaies beare us companie: howbeit we ever dined and supped apart by our selves. Moreover he caused certaine religious and most learned men to come unto our banquet; who, all the time we remained with the said prince, used not to eate any bread at all, but fed onely upon flesh and milke. Whereat we being somewhat amazed, the good prince gently told us, that they all were borne in such places whereas no kinde of graine would grow: howbeit that himselfe, for the entertainment of strangers, had great plentie of corne laid up in store. Wherefore he bad us to be of good cheere, saying that he would eate onely of such things as his owne native soile affoorded: affirming moreover, that bread was yet in use among them at their feast of passover, and at other feasts also, whereupon they used to offer sacrifice. And thus we remained with him for the space of two daies; all which time, what woonderfull and magnificent cheere we had made us, would seeme incredible to report. But the third day, being desirous to take our leave, the prince accompanied us to that place where we overtooke our camels and companie sent before. And this I dare most deepely take mine oath on, that we spent the saide prince ten times more, then our custome which he recieved came to. Wee thought it not amisse here to set downe this historie, to declare in some sort the courtesie and liberalitie of the said nation. Neither could the prince aforesaid understand our language nor we his; but all our speech to and fro was made by an interpreter. And this which we have here recorded as touching this nation, is likewise to be understood of the other fower nations above mentioned, which are dispersed over the residue of the Numidian deserts.

THE MANNERS AND CUSTOMES OF THE ARABIANS WHICH INHABITE AFRICA

The Arabians, as they have sundrie mansions and places of aboad, so doe they live after a divers and sundry maner. Those which inhabite betweene Numidia and Libya leade a most miserable and distressed life, differing much in this regard from those Africans, whom wee affirmed to dwell in Libya. Howbeit they are farre more valiant than the said Africans; and use commonly to exchange camels in the lande of Negros: they have likewise great store of horses, which in Europe they cal horses of Barbarie. They

take woonderfull delight in hunting and pursuing of deere, of wilde asses,
of ostriches, and such like. Neither is it here to be omitted, that the greater
part of Arabians which inhabite Numidia, are very wittie and conceited in
penning of verses; wherein each man will decipher his love, his hunting, his
combates, and other his woorthie actes: and this is done for the most part in
ryme, after the Italians manner. And albeit they are most liberally minded,
yet dare they not by bountiful giving make any shew of wealth; for they are
daily oppressed with manifold inconveniences. They are apparelled after
the Numidians fashion, saving that their women differ somewhat from the
women of Numidia. [...]

The Arabians which dwell betweene mount Atlas and the Mediterran
sea are far wealthier then these which we now speake of, both for costlines
of apparell, for good horse-meate, and for the statelines and beautie of their
tents. Their horses also are of better shape and more corpulent, but not so
swift as the horses of the Numidian desert. They exercise husbandrie and
have great increase of corne. Their droves and flockes of cattell be innumerable, insomuch that they cannot inhabite one by another for want of
pasture. They are somewhat more vile and barbarous then those which
inhabite the deserts, and yet they are not altogether destitute of liberalitie:
part of them, which dwell in the territorie of Fez are subject unto the king
of Fez. Those which remaine in Marocco and Duccala have continued this
long time free from all exaction and tribute: but so soone as the king of
Portugall began to beare rule over Azafi and Azamor, there began also
among them strife and civill warre. Wherefore being assailed by the king of
Portugall on the one side, and by the king of Fez on the other, and being
oppressed also with the extreme famine and scarcitie of that yeere, they
were brought unto such miserie, that they freely offered themselves as
slaves unto the Portugals, submitting themselves to any man, that was
willing to releeve their intolerable hunger: and by this meanes scarce one of
them was left in all Duccala. Moreover those which possesse the deserts
bordering upon the kingdomes of Tremizen and Tunis may all of them, in
regard of the rest, be called noblemen and gentlemen. For their governours
receiving every yeere great revenues from the king of Tunis, divide the same
afterward among their people, to the end they may avoid all discord: and by
this meanes all dissension is eschewed, and peace is kept firme and inviolable among them. They have notable dexteritie and cunning, both in
making of tents, and in bringing up and keeping of horses. In summer
time they usually come neere unto Tunis, to the end that each man may

provide himselfe of bread, armour, and other necessaries: all which they carrie with them into the deserts, remaining there the whole winter. In the spring of the yeere they applie themselves to hunting, insomuch that no beast can escape their pursuit. My selfe, I remember, was once at their tents, to my no little danger and inconvenience; where I sawe greater quantitie of cloth, brasse, yron, and copper, then a man shall oftentimes finde in the most rich warehouses of some cities. Howbeit no trust is to be given unto them; for if occasion serve, they will play the theeves most slyly and cunningly; not withstanding they seeme to carrie some shewe of civilitie. They take great delight in poetrie, and will pen most excellent verses, their language being very pure and elegant. If any woorthie poet be found among them, he is accepted by their governours with great honour and liberalitie; neither would any man easily beleeve what wit and decencie is in their verses. Their women (according to the guise of that countrie) goe very gorgeously attired: they weare linnen gownes died black, with exceeding wide sleeves, over which sometimes they cast a mantle of the same colour or of blew, the corners of which mantle are very artificially fastened about their shoulders with a fine silver claspe. Likewise they have rings hanging at their eares, which for the most part are made of silver: they weare many rings also upon their fingers. Moreover they usually weare about their thighes and ankles certaine scarfes and rings, after the fashion of the Africans. They cover their faces with certaine maskes having onely two holes for their eies to peepe out at. If any man chance to meete with them, they presently hide their faces, passing by him with silence, except it be some of their allies or kinsfolks; for unto them they alwaies discover their faces, neither is there any use of the said maske so long as they be in presence. These Arabians when they travell any journey (as they oftentimes doe) they set their women upon certaine saddles made handsomely of wicker for the same purpose, and fastened to their camels backes, neither be they anything too wide, but fit onely for a woman to sit in. When they goe to the warres each man carries his wife with him, to the end that she may cheere up her good man, and give him encouragement. Their damsels which are unmarried doe usually paint their faces, brests, armes, hands, and fingers with a kinde of counterfeit colour which is accounted a most decent custome among them. But this fashion was first brought in by those Arabians, which before we called Africans, what time they began first of all to inhabite that region; for before then, they never used any false or glozing colours. The women of Barbarie use not this fond kind of painting, but contenting themselves only with their naturall hiew, they regarde not such fained ornaments: howbeit sometimes they will temper a certaine colour with hens-dung and safron, wherewithall they paint a little round spot on the bals of their cheeks, about the bredth of a French crowne. Like wise betweene their eie-browes they make a triangle; and paint upon their chinnes a patch like unto an olive leafe. Some of them also doe paint their eie-browes: and this custome is very highly esteemed of by the Arabian poets and by the gentlemen of that countrie. Howbeit they will not use these fantasticall ornaments above two or three daies together: all which time they will not be seene to any of their friends, except it be to their husbands and children: for these paintings seeme to bee great allurements unto lust, whereby the said women thinke themselves more trim and beautifull.

OF THE FAITH AND RELIGION OF THE ANCIENT AFRICANS OR MOORES

The ancient Africans were much addicted to idolatrie, even as certain of the Persians are at this day, some of whom worship the sunne, and others the fire, for their gods. For the saide Africans had in times past magnificent and most stately temples built and dedicated, as well to the honour of the sunne as of the fire. In these temples day and night they kept fire kindled, giving diligent heed that it might not at any time be extinguished, even as we read of the Romane Vestall virgines: All which you may read more fully and at large in the Persian and African Chronicles. Those Africans which inhabited Libya and Numidia, would each of them worship some certaine planet, unto whom likewise they offered sacrifices and praiers. Some others of the land of Negros worship *Guighimo*, that is to say, *The Lord of Heaven*. And this sound point of religion was not delivered unto them by any Prophet or teacher, but was inspired, as it were, from God himselfe. After that, they embraced the Jewish law, wherein they are said to have continued many yeeres. Afterward they professed the Christian religion, and continued Christians, until such time as the *Mahumetan* superstition prevailed; which came to passe in the yeere of the Hegeira 208. About which time certaine of *Mahomets* disciples so bewitched them with eloquent and deceiveable speeches, that they allured their weake minds to consent unto their opinion; insomuch that all the kingdomes of the Negros adjoyning unto Libya received the *Mahumetan* lawe. Neither is there any region in all the Negros land, which hath in it at this day any Christians at all. At the same time such as were found to be Jewes, Christians, or of the African religion, were slaine everie man of them. Howbeit those which dwell neere unto the Ocean sea, are all of them verie grosse idolaters. Betweene whom and the Portugals there hath beene from time to time and even at this present is, great traffique and familiaritie. The inhabitants of Barbarie continued for many yeeres idolaters; but before the comming of *Mahomet* above 250. yeeres, they are saide to have embraced the Christian faith: which some thinke came to passe upon this occasion; namely, because that part of Barbarie which containeth the kingdome of Tripolis and Tunis, was in times past governed by *Apulian & Sicilian* Captaines, and the countries of Caesaria[1] and of Mauritania[2] are supposed to have beene subject unto the Gothes. At what time also many Christians fleeing from the furie and madnes of the Gothes left their sweet native soyle of Italy, and at length arrived in Africa neere unto Tunis: where having setled their aboad for some certaine space, they began at length to have the dominion over all that region. Howbeit the Christians which inhabited Barbaria, not respecting the rites and ceremonies of the Church of Rome, followed the Arrians religion and forme of living: and one of the African Christians was that most godly and learned father Saint *Augustine*. When the Arabians therefore came to conquer that part of Africa they found Christians to be Lords over the regions adjacent; of whom, after sundry hot conflicts, the saide Arabians got the victorie. Whereupon the Arrians being deprived of all their dominions and goods went part of them into Italy and part into Spaine. And so about two hundred yeeres after the death of *Mahumet*, almost all Barbarie was infected with his law. Howbeit afterward, civile dissensions arising among them, neglecting the law of *Mahumet*, they slue all the priests and governours of that region. Which tumult when it came to the eares of the Mahumetan Caliphas, they sent an huge armie against the saide rebels of Barbarie, to wit, those which were revolted from the Calipha of Bagdet, and severely punished their misdemeanor. And even at the same time was layd the most pernitious foundation of the Mahumetan law; notwithstanding there have remained many heresies among them even until this verie day. [. . .]

---

[1] Numidia, Telensin [part of modern Algeria].
[2] Morocco and Fez [modern Morocco].

THE COMMENDABLE ACTIONS AND VERTUES
OF THE AFRICANS

Those Arabians which inhabite in Barbarie or upon the coast of the Mediterran sea, are greatly addicted unto the studie of good artes and sciences: and those things which concerne their law and religion are esteemed by them in the first place. Moreover they have beene heretofore most studious of the Mathematiques, of Philosophie, and of Astrologie: but these artes (as it is aforesaid) were fower hundred yeeres agoe, utterly destroyed and taken away by the chiefe professours of their lawe. The inhabitants of cities doe most religiously observe and reverence those things which appertaine unto their religion: yea they honour those doctours and priests, of whom they learne their law, as if they were petie-gods. Their Churches they frequent verie diligently, to the ende they may repeat certaine prescript and formal prayers; most superstitiously perswading themselves that the same day wherein they make their praiers, it is not lawfull for them to wash certaine of their members, when as at other times they will wash their whole bodies. [...] Moreover those which inhabite Barbarie are of great cunning & dexteritie for building & for mathematicall inventions, which a man may easily conjecture by their artificiall workes. Most honest people they are, and destitute of all fraud and guile; not onely imbracing all simplicitie and truth, but also practising the same throughout the whole course of their lives: albeit certaine Latine authors, which have written of the same regions, are farre otherwise of opinion. Likewise they are most strong and valiant people, especially those which dwell upon the mountaines. They keepe their covenant most faithfully; insomuch that they had rather die than breake promise. No nation in the world is so subject unto jealousie; for they will rather leese their lives, then put up any disgrace in the behalfe of their women. So desirous they are of riches and honour, that therein no other people can goe beyonde them. They travell in a manner over the whole world to exercise traffique. For they are continually to bee seene in Aegypt, in Aethiopia, in Arabia, Persia, India, and Turkie: and whithersoever they goe, they are most honorably esteemed of: for none of them will possesse any arte, unlesse hee hath attained unto great exactness and perfection therein. They have alwaies beene much delighted with all kinde of civilitie and modest behaviour: and it is accounted heinous among them for any man to utter in companie, any bawdie or unseemely worde. They have alwaies in minde this sentence of a grave author; Give place to thy superiour. If any youth in presence of his father, his uncle, or any other of his kinred, doth sing or talke ought of love matters, he is deemed to bee woorthie of grievous punishment. Whatsoever lad or youth there lighteth by chaunce into any company which discourseth of love, no sooner heareth nor understandeth what their talke tendeth unto, but immediately he withdraweth himselfe from among them. These are the things which we thought most woorthie of relation as concerning the civilitie, humanitie, and upright dealing of the Barbarians: let us now proceede unto the residue. Those Arabians which dwell in tents, that is to say, which bring up cattell, are of a more liberall and civill disposition: to wit, they are in their kinde as devout, valiant, patient, courteous, hospitall, and as honest in life and conversation as any other people. They be most faithfull observers of their word and promise; insomuch that the people, which before we said to dwell in the mountaines, are greatly stirred up with emulation of their vertues. Howbeit the said mountainers, both for learn-ing, for vertue, and for religion, are thought much inferiour to the Numi-dians, albeit they have little or no knowledge at all in naturall philosophie. They are reported likewise to be most skilfull warriours, to be valiant, and exceeding lovers and practisers of all humanitie. Also, the Moores and Arabians inhabiting Libya are somewhat civill of behaviour, being plaine dealers, voide of dissimulation, favourable to strangers, and lovers of simplicite. Those which we before named white, or tawney Moores, are stedfast in friendship: as likewise they indifferently and favourably esteeme of other nations: and wholy indevour themselves in this one thing, namely, that they may leade a most pleasant and jocund life. Moreover they main-taine most learned professours of liberall artes, and such men are most devout in their religion. Neither is there any people in all Africa that lead a more happie and honorable life.

WHAT VICES THE FORESAID AFRICANS ARE SUBJECT UNTO

Never was there any people or nation so perfectly endued with vertue, but that they had their contrarie faults and blemishes: now therefore let us consider, whether the vices of the Africans do surpasse their vertues & good parts. Those which we named the inhabitants of the cities of Barbarie are somewhat needie and covetous, being also very proud and high-minded, and woonderfully addicted unto wrath; insomuch that (according to the proverbe) they will deeply engrave in marble any injurie be it never so small, & will in no wise blot it out of their remembrance. So rusticall they are & void of good manners, that scarcely can any stranger obtaine their familiaritie and friendship. Their wits are but meane, and they are so credulous, that they will beleeve matters impossible, which are told them. So ignorant are they of naturall philosophie, that they imagine all the effects and operations of nature to be extraordinarie and divine. They observe no certaine order of living nor of lawes. Abounding exceedingly with choler, they speake alwaies with an angrie and lowd voice. Neither shall you walke in the day-time in any of their streetes, but you shall see commonly two or three of them together by the eares. By nature they are a vile and base people, being no better accounted of by their governours then if they were dogs. They have neither judges nor lawyers, by whose wisdome and counsell they ought to be directed. They are utterly unskilfull in trades of merchandize, being destitute of bankers and money-changers: where-fore a merchant can doe nothing among them in his absence, but is himselfe constrained to goe in person, whithersoever his wares are carried. No people under heaven are more addicted unto covetise then this nation: neither is there (I thinke) to bee found among them one of an hundred, who for courtesie, humanitie, or devotions sake will vouchsafe any enter-tainment upon a stranger. Mindfull they have alwaies beene of injuries, but most forgetfull of benefites. Their mindes are perpetually possessed with vexation and strife, so that they will seldome or never shew themselves tractable to any man; the cause whereof is supposed to be; for that they are so greedily addicted unto their filthie lucre, that they never could attaine unto any kinde of civilitie or good behaviour. The shepherds of that region live a miserable, toilsome, wretched and beggerly life: they are a rude people, and (as a man may say) borne and bred to theft, deceit, and brutish manners. Their yoong men may goe a wooing to divers maides, till such time as they have sped of a wife. Yea, the father of the maide most friendly welcommeth her suiter: so that I thinke scarce any noble or gentleman among them can chuse a virgine for his spouse: albeit, so soone as any woman is married, she is quite forsaken of all her suiters; who then seeke out other new paramours for their liking. Concerning their religion, the greater part of these people are neither Mahumetans, Jewes, nor Chris-tians; and hardly shall you finde so much as a sparke of pietie in any of them. They have no churches at all, nor any kinde of prayers, but being utterly estranged from all godly devotion, they leade a savage and beastly life: and if any man chanceth to be of a better disposition (because they have no law-givers nor teachers among them) he is constrained to follow the example of other mens lives & maners. All the Numidians being most ignorant of naturall, domesticall, & commonwealth-matters, are principally addicted unto treason, trecherie, murther, theft, and robberie. This nation, because it is most slavish, will right gladly accept of any service among the Barbarians, be it never so vile or contemptible. For some will take upon them to be dung-farmers, others to be scullians, some others to bee ostlers, and such like servile occupations. Likewise the inhabitants of Libya live a brutish kinde of life; who neglecting all kindes of good artes and sciences, doe wholy apply their mindes unto theft and violence. Never as yet had they any religion, any lawes, or any good forme of living; but alwaies had, and ever will have a most miserable and distressed life. There cannot any trechery or villanie be invented so damnable, which for lucres sake they dare not attempt. They spend all their daies either in most lewd practises, or in hunting, or else in warfare: neither weare they any shooes nor garments. The Negros likewise leade a beastly kinde of life, being utterly destitute of the use of reason, of dexteritie of wit, and of all artes. Yea they so behave themselves, as if they had continually lived in a forrest among wilde beasts. They have great swarmes of harlots among them; whereupon a man may easily conjecture their manner of living: except their conversation perhaps be somewhat more tolerable, who dwell in the principall townes and cities: for it is like that they are somewhat more addicted to civilitie. [...]

George Sandys, *A Relation of a Journey Begun Anno Dom. 1610. Foure Bookes Contayning a description of the Turkish Empire, of Aegypt, of the Holy Land, of the Remote parts of Italy, and Ilands adioyning* (1615), Observations of the Egyptians and the Jews

GEORGE SANDYS (1578–1644), was a poet and travel writer. He left England after graduating from Oxford and went on a tour through France and Italy, then sailed from Venice to Turkey, Egypt, and Palestine, returning to England through Italy and stopping off in Rome. Sandys later published an extensive account of his travels, dedicated to Prince Charles, which was popular and frequently reprinted throughout the seventeenth century. Sandys, like his brother Edwin, became interested in colonial enterprises, specifically the Virginia Company, becoming treasurer in 1621. He sailed to Virginia in that year and became a planter and member of the colonial council and translated Ovid's *Metamorphoses* (published 1621). On returning to England he became part of Prince Charles's entourage, dedicating poems and plays to Charles after he became king.[1]

Included here are Sandys's accounts of the Egyptians and the Jews. Sandys was a perceptive observer of other peoples and cultures, noting details from everyday life as well as those of more obvious importance, and he was able to move easily from one to the other in his writing. He comments on the significance of the crocodile in Egyptian cultural and religious life, as well as recognizing the achievements of Egypian civilization. Sandys's account of the Jews is notably sympathetic to their plight and the anti-Semitic prejudice they have suffered, and he includes comments on Jewish women (again, sympathetic in the main).[2]

See also:

Samuel Purchas, *Hakluytus Posthumous or Purchas His Pilgrimes*, 20 vols. Glasgow: MacLehose, 1905–7), i. 324–37; vii. 523–93.

---

[1] On Sandys's life, see Richard Beale Davis, *George Sandys, Poet–Adventurer: A Study in Anglo-American Culture in the Seventeenth Century* (London: Bodley Head, 1955).

[2] Text from George Sandys, *A Relation of a Journey Begun Anno Dom. 1610. Foure Bookes Contayning a description of the Turkish Empire, of Aegypt, of the Holy Land, of the Remote parts of Italy, and Ilands adioyning* (1615), 100–4, 146–9.

The Crocodile [is] in shape not unlike a Lizard, and some of them of an uncredible greatnesse. So great from so small a beginning is more then wonderfull, some of them being above thirty foot long; hatched of egges no bigger then those that are laid by a Turkie. His taile is equall to his body in length, wherewith he infoldeth his prey, and drawes it into the river. His feete are armed with clawes, and his backe and sides with scales scarce penetrable; his belly tender, soft, and is easily pierced: his teeth indented within one another: having no tongue, and mooving of his upper jaw onely; his mouth so wide when extended, as some of them are able to swallow an entire heiffer. Foure moneths of the yeare he eateth nothing, and those bee during the winter: on the land thicke-sighted; not so in the water, to whom both elements are equally usefull. The female laies an hundred egs; as many dayes they are in hatching; and as many yeares they live that do live the longest, continually growing. Where she layeth, there is (as they write) the uttermost limit of the succeeding over-flow: Nature having endued them with that wonderfull prescience, to avoide the inconveniences, and yet to enjoy the benefit of the river. By the figure therefore of a Crocodile, Providence was by the *Aegyptians* hieroglyphically expressed. Between the Dolphins & these there is a deadly antipathy. *Babillus*, a man highly commended by *Seneca*, obtaining the government of *Aegypt*, reported that he saw at the mouth of *Nilus*, then called *Heraclioticum*, a scole of Dolphins rushing up the river, and encountred by a sort of Crocodiles, fighting as it were for soveraignty; vanquished at length by those milde and harmlesse creatures, who swimming under did cut their bellies with their spiny fins: and destroying many, made the rest to flie, as overthrowne in battell. A creature fearefull of the bold, and bold upon the fearfull. Neither did the *Tenterites* master them in regard of their bloud, or savour, (as some have conjectured) but by being fierce and couragious. A people dwelling farre above, in an Iland environed by *Nilus*; onely hardy against those, and the onely men that durst assaile them before: out of an innate hatred greedily pursuing the encounter. But now few keepe so low as *Cairo* by three dayes journy. They will devoure whom they catch in the river: which makes the countrey people to fence in those places where they fetch their water: By day for the most part he lieth on the land; when between sleeping and waking they write that a little bird called *Troculus*, doth feed her self by the picking of his teeth, wherewith delighted, and gaping wider, the *Icnumon* his mortall enemy spying his advantage, whips into his mouth, and gliding down his throate like an arrow, gnaweth a way thorow his belly,

The Dolphin and our Porpus alone called Sus marinus, of his similitude to a Swine.

and destroyes him. This though now little spoken of, in times past was delivered for a truth, even by the *Aegyptians* themselves: who gave divine honour unto the *Icnumon* for the benefit he did them in the destroying of that serpent. And true perhaps it is, though not observed by the barbarous. The bird is at this day knowne: described to be about the bignesse of a Thrush, of colour white, the points of his feathers sharpe, which he sets up on end like bristles when he lists, and so pricketh the mouth of the Crocodile if he but offer to close it. As for the *Icnumon*, he hath but onely changed his name; now called the Rat of *Nilus*. A beast particular to *Aegypt*, about the bignesse of a Cat, and as cleanly: snowted like a Ferret, but that blacke and without long haire; sharpe tooth, round eard, short legd, long taild (being thicke where it joynes to the body, and spinie at the end) his haire sharpe, hard and branded; bristling it up when angry, and then will flye upon a mastiffe. They are thought (for they have an appearance of both) to be of both genders. Their young ones are brought to markets by the country people, and greedily bought by the townes-men for the destroying of mice and rats, which they will notably hunt after, strongly nimble, and subtill withall. They will rest themselves upon their hinder feete, and rising from the earth, jumpe upon their prey with a violent celerity. They prey also upon Frogs, Lizards, Camelions, & all sorts of lesser serpents: being a deadly enemy to the Aspe, and do destroy the egs of the Crocodile wheresoever they can find them. They will strangle all the cats they meet with: for their mouthes are so little, that they can bite nothing that is thicke. They love nothing better then poultry, and hate nothing more then the wind. But to returne to the Crocodiles, the countrey people do often take them in pitfals, & grappling their chaps together with an iron, bring them alive unto *Cairo*. They take them also with hookes, baited with sheep or goates, and tyed with a rope to the truncke of a tree. The flesh of them they eate, all saving the head and taile, and sell their skins unto Merchants, who convey them into Christendome for the rarity. It is written in the *Arabian* records, how *Humeth Aben Thaulon* (being governour of *Aegypt* for *Gisar Matanichi Caliph* of *Babylon*) in the 270 yeare of their *Hegir*, caused the leaden image of a Crocodile, found amongst the ruines of an ancient Temple, to be molten; since when the inhabitants have complained that those serpents have been more noysome unto them then before; affirming that it was made, and there buried by the ancient Magicians to restraine their indamagings.

Throughout this countrey there are no wines: yet want they none, in that they desire them not. Neither are here any trees to speake of, but such as are

Fig. 6. 'The Pyramids' (George Sandys, *Relation of a Journey* (1615), p. 128)

planted, and those in orchards onely: excepting Palmes, which delight in desarts: & being naturally theirs, do grow without limits. Of these they have plenty: pleasing the eye with their goodly formes, and with diversitie of benefits enriching their owners. Of body straight, high, round, and slender, (yet unfit for buildings) crested about, and by means thereof with facilitie ascended. The branches like sedges, slit on the neather side, and ever greene; growing onely on the uppermost height, resemble faire plumes of feathers which they yearly prune, by lopping off the lowest, & at the top of all by baring a little of the bole. Of these there be male and female: both thrust forth cods (which are full of seeds like knotted strings) at the roote of their branches, but the female is onely fruitfull: and not so, unlesse growing by the male, (towards whose upright growth she inclines her crowne) and have of his seeds commixed with hers; which in the beginning of March they no more faile to do, then to sow the earth at accustomed seasons. Their Dates do grow like fingers, and are thereof named: not ripe untill the fine of December; which begin to cod about the beginning of February. They open the tops of such as are fruitlesse, or otherwise perisht; and take from thence the white pith, of old called the braine, which they sell up and downe: an excellent sallad, not much unlike in taste, but far better then an Artichoke. Of the branches they make bedsteeds, lattices, &c. of the web of the leaves, baskets, mats, fans, &c. of the outward huske of the cod, good cordage; of the inward, brushes, &c. such and such like affoord they yeerely without empaire to themselves. This tree they held to be the perfect image of a man; and by the same represented him. First, for that it doth not fructifie, but by coiture: next, as having a braine, as it were in the uppermost part; which once corrupted, as man, even so it perisheth: and lastly, in regard that on the top thereof grow certaine strings which resemble the haire; the great end of the branches appearing like hands stretch forth, and the Dates as fingers. And because the Palme is never to be suppressed, but shooteth up against all opposition, the boughs thereof have been proposed as rewards for such as were either victorious in armes or exercises,

> —*And noble Palmes advance*
> *Earths Potentates to Gods*—

> —Palmaque nobilis
> Terrarum dominos evehit ad Deos.
> [Horace, *Odes* 1.1. 5–6].

which they bare in their hands at their return from victory. A custome first instituted by *Theseus* in the Iland of *Delos*. Wood then is here but scarce in regard of the quantity; and yet enough, if their uses for the same be considered. For they eate but little flesh, (fresh cheese, sowre milke made solid, roots, fruits, and herbes, especially *Colocasia*, anciently called the *Aegyptian* Beane, though bearing no beane, but like the leafe of a Colewort, being their principall sustenance, baking their bread in cakes on the harth, and mingling therewith the seeds of Coriander.) As for cold they know it not, having sufficient of the refuse of Palmes, sugar canes, and the like, to furnish them with fuell answerable to their necessities. But forreiners that feed as in colder countries, do buy their wood by weight, which is brought in hither by shipping. The Gallions also of *Constantinople*, always goe into the Blacke sea for timber, before they take their voyage for *Cairo*. Omit I must not the sedgie reeds which grow in the marishes of *Aegypt*, called formerly *Papyri*, of which they made paper; and where of ours made of rags, assumeth that name. They divided it into thin flakes, whereinto it naturally parteth: then laying them on a table, and moistning them with the glutinous water of the River, they prest them together, and so dried them in the Sun. By this meanes *Philadelphus* erected his Library. But *Eumenes* King of *Pergamus* striving to exceed him in that kind, *Philadelphus* commanded that no paper should be transported out of his kingdome: whereupon *Eumenes* invented the making and writing upon parchment, so called of *Pergamust*.

The *Aegyptians* were said to have esteemed themselves the prime nation of the world, in regard of their unknowne beginning, the nature of the soile, and excellent faculties attained unto through a long continuance. But certain it is, that most of, or al *Aegypt* was a sea when other parts of the world were inhabited: made manifest by the shels and bones of fishes found in the intralls of the earth, and wells which yeeld but salt and bitter waters: amongst so many, one onely (and that reported to have sprung by a miracle) to be drunke of. So that by the operation of the River, this country hath his being (properly called *The gift of Nilus*) bringing downe earth with his deluges, and extruding the sea by little and little. Insomuch as the Ile of *Pharos* thus described by *Homer*,

> *An Ile there is by surging seas embrac't*
> *Which men call Pharus, before Aegypt plac't;*
> *So farre removed, as a swift ship may*
> *Before the whistling winds saile in a day:*

Insula deinde quondam est vald: un. doso in ponto,
Aegyptum ante (Pharum vero ipsam vocant)
Tantum semota quantum tota die cava navis
Confecit, cui suidulus ventus spirat à puppi.

Odys. l. 4.

doth now adjoyne unto the haven of *Alexandria*.

Busiris, as the fairest seate of the earth, made choise of this country to reigne in: selecting the people unto severall callings, and caused them to intend those only; whereby they became most excellent in their particular faculties. He possessed them first with the adoration of the Gods, emboldening and awing their minds with a being after death, happy or unhappy, according to the good or bad committed in the present: and instituted the honouring of contemptible things; or for some benefit they did, or to appease them for such hurt as they had the power to inflict. Of these thus *Juvenal*, who then lived amongst them:

> What honour brain-sicke Aegypt to things vile
> Affoordeth, who not knowes? a Crocodile
> This part adores: that Ibis, serpent fed.
> Monkie of gold they there divinely dread,
> Where Memnons halfe forme yeelds a magicke sound;
> And old Thebes stood, for hundred gates renownd,
> Her fishes of the Sea, there of the River:
> Whole townes a dog; none her that beares the quiver.
> Onions and leekes to eate, height of impieties.
> O sacred Nation sure, who have these Deities
> Grow in your gardens! all from sheepe abstaine:
> Tis sinne to kill a Kid: yet humanes slaine,
> Inhumanely they feed on.—

Quis nescit Volusi Bithynice, qualia demens,
Aegyptus portenta colat? Crocodilon adorat
Pars haec: illa pavet saturam serpentibus Ibin.
Effigies sacri niter aurea Cereopitheci,
Dimidio magicae resonant ubi Memnone chordae,
Atque vetus Thebe centum iacet obruta portis,
Illic caeruleas, hic piscem fluminis: lillic
Oppida tota canem venerantur: nemo Dianam.

Portum & saepe nefas violares ac frangere morsu.
O sanctas gentes quibus haec nascuntur in hortis
Numina avatis animalibus abstinet omnis
Mensa: nefas illic faetum jugulare capellae,
Carnibus humanis vesci licet.

Juven. Sat. 15.

For the *Tenterites* bearing an inveterate hatred to the *Combos* their neighbours, for adoring the Crocodile which they hated, fell upon them unawares
in their civill janglings at the celebration of their festivall; and putting them
to flight, cut the hindermost in pieces: whom reeking hote, with heart yet
panting, they greedily devoured; the Poet himselfe an eye-witnesse of the
fact. Such jarres proceeded from their fertility of Gods, differing in each
several jurisdiction: and instituted by their politike crafty Kings, that busied
with particular malice, they should not concurre in a generall insurrection.
Above all they honoured *Isis* and *Osiris*, which fable (too tedious for our
professed brevity) contained sundry allegories. Amongst others, by *Osiris*
they prefigured *Nilus*, by *Isis* the Earth made pregnant by the river; and by
Typhon the Sea. They said, that *Typhon* was vanquished by *Osiris*, in that the
River had so repulsed the Sea: and by *Typhon* afterward murdered, because
at length the sea doth as it were devoure it. Their priests were next in dignity
to the King; and of his Councell in all businesses of importance. From
amongst them he was chosen: or if of the souldiery, he forthwith was
invested in the High-priesthood, & instructed by them in the mysteries
of their Philosophy; delivered under fables, and aenigmaticall expressions.
They dranke no wine, until the time of *Psameticus* the last of the *Pharoes*;
esteeming it to have sprung from the blood of the Giants; in that it
provoked the mind to lust, impatiencie, crueltie, and all the disordered
affections that those contemners of the gods were endued with. Of all the
Heathen, they were the first that taught the immortalitie of the soule, & the
transmigration thereof into another body, either of man or beast, clean or
uncleane, as it had behaved it selfe in the former. From whom *Pythagoras*
received that opinion, and divulged it to the *Grecians*: who, the better to
perswade, affirmed himselfe to have bene once *Aethalides* the sonne of
Mercurie: and commanded by his father to aske what he would, immortality
excepted; did desire after death to know what had passed in his life, and to
have his memory entirely preserved: which by not drinking of *Lethe* befell
him accordingly. After the death of *Aethalides*, he became *Euphorbus*:

I (remember) at the warres of Troy,
Euphorbus was, Pantheus sonne, and fell
By Menelaus lance. I knew right well
The shield which our left arme usde to sustaine,
At Argos lately seene in Juno's Fane:

Ipse ego (nam memini) Trojani tempore belli,
Panthonides Euphorbus eram, cui pectore quondam
Haesit in adverso gravis hasta minoris Atridae.
Cognovi clypeum lenae gestamina nostrae,
Nuper Abanteis templo Junonis in Argis.

Ovid. Met. l. 15.

and then *Hemotymus*, then *Delius*, then *Pyrrbus* a fisherman; and last of all *Pythagoras*. By meanes whereof he withdrew the *Grecians* from luxury, and possest their minds with the terror of ill-doing.

The *Aegyptians* first invented Arithmeticke, Musicke, and Geometry; and by reason of the perpetuall serenitie of the aire, found out the course of the Sunne and the starres, their constellations, risings, aspects, and influences; dividing by the same the yeere into moneths, and grounding their divinations upon their hidden properties. Moreover from the *Aegyptians, Orpheus, Museus,* and *Homer,* have fetcht their hymnes and fables of the Gods: *Pythagoras, Eudoxus,* and *Democritus,* their Philosophie: *Lycurgus, Solon,* and *Plato,* the forme of their governments: by which they all in their severall kinds have eternized their memories. Their letters were invented by *Mercury,* who writ from the right hand to the left; as do all the *Africans.* But in holy things especially they expressed their conceits by Hieroglyphicks; which consist of significant figures: whereof there yet are many to be seen though hardly to be interpreted.

[Palestine] is for the most part now inhabited by *Moores,* and *Arabians:* those possessing the vallies, and these the mountaines. *Turkes* there be few: but many *Greeks,* with other Christians, of all sects and nations, such as impute to the place an adherent holinesse. Here be also some *Jewes,* yet inherit they no part of the land, but in their owne country do live as aliens; a people scattered throughout the whole world, and hated by those amongst whom they live; yet suffered, as a necessary mischiefe: subject to all wrongs and contumelies, which they support with an invincible patience. Many of them have I seene abused; some of them beaten: yet never saw I *Jew* with an

angry countenance. They can subject themselves unto times, and to whatsoever may advance their profit. In generall they are worldly wise, and
thrive wheresoever they set footing. The *Turke* imployes them in receipt of
customes, which they by their policies have inhaunced, and in buying and
selling with the Christian: being him selfe in that kind a foole and easily
cousened. They are men of indifferent statures, and the best complexions.
These as well in Christendome, as in *Turky*, are the remaines onely of the
Tribes of *Juda* and *Benjamin*, with some *Levites*, which returned from
Babylon with *Zerubabel*. Some say that the other ten are utterly lost: but
they themselves, that they are in *India*, a mighty Nation incompassed with
rivers of stone; which onely ceasse to runne on their Sabboth, when
prohibited to travell. From whence they expect their Messias: who with
fire and sword shall subdue the world, and restore their temporall kingdome: and therefore whatsoever befalls them they record it in their Annals.
Amongst them there are three sects. One onely allow of the bookes of
Moses. These be *Samaritan Jewes* (not *Jewes* by descent as before said) that
dwell in *Damasco*: who yearely repaire to *Sichem* (now *Neapolis*) and there
do at this day worship a Calfe, as I was informed by a Merchant dwelling in
that countrey. Another allow of all the bookes of the old Testament. The
third sort mingle the same with traditions, and fantasticall fables devised by
their *Rabbins*, and inserted into their *Talmud*. Throughout the *Turks*
dominions they are allowed their Synagogues: so are they at *Rome* and
elsewhere in *Italy*; whose receipt they justifie as a retained testimony of the
verity of Scriptures; and as being a meanes of their more speedy conversions: whereas the offence that they receive from images, and the losse of
goods upon their conversions, oppugne all perswasions whatsoever. Their
Synagogues (for as many as I have seene) are neither faire without, nor
adorned within more then with a curtaine at the upper end, and certaine
lampes (so farre as I could perceive) not lightned by day-light. In the midst
stands a scaffold, like those belonging to Queresters, in some of our
Cathedrall Churches: wherein he stands that reades their law & sings
their Liturgy: an office not belonging unto any in particular; but unto
him (so he be free from deformities) that shall at that time purchase it
with most mony; which redounds to their publicke treasury. They reade in
savage tones; and sing in tunes that have no affinity with musicke: joyning
voyces at the severall closes. But their fantasticall gestures exceede all
barbarisme, continually weaving with their bodies, and often jumping
up-right (as is the manner in daunces) by them esteemed an action of

zeale, and figure of spirituall elevation. They pray silently with ridiculous and continuall noddings of their heads, not to be seene & not laught at. During the time of Service their heads are veiled in linnen, fringed with knots; in number answerable to the number of their lawes: which they carry about with them in procession; and rather boast of then observe. They have it stucke in the jambs of their doores, & covered with glasse: written by their Cacams, and signed with the names of God; which they kisse next their hearts in their goings forth, and in their returnes. They may not print it, but it is to be written on parchment, prepared of purpose (the ink of a prescribed composition) not with a quill, but a cane. They do great reverence to all the names of God, but especially to *Jehovah*; in somuch that they never use it in their speech. And whereas they handle with great respect the other bookes of the old Testament, the booke of *Hester* (that part that is canonicall, for the other they allow not of) writ in a long scrole, they let fall on the ground as they read it, because the name of God is not once mentioned therein; which they attribute to the wisedom of the writer, in that it might be perused by the Heathen. Their other bookes are in the *Spanish* tongue & Hebrew character. They confesse our Saviour to have bin the most learned of their nation, and have this fable dispersed amongst them, concerning him: How that yet a boy, attending upon a great Cacam at such a time as the heavens accustomed to open, and whatsoever he prayed for was granted; the Cacam oppressed with sleepe, charged the boy when the time was come, to awaken him. But he provoked with a franticke desire of peculiar glory, (such is their divelish invention) made for himselfe this ambitious request; that like a God he might be adored amongst men. Which the Cacam over-hearing, added thereunto (since what was craved could not be revoked) that it might not be till after his death. Whereupon he lived contemptibly: but dead, was, is, and shall be honoured unto all posterity. They say withall, that he got into the *Sanctum sanctorum*: and taking from thence the powerfull names of God, did sew them in his thigh. By vertue whereof he went invisible, rid on the Sunbeames, raised the dead to life, and effected like wonders. That being often amongst them, they could never lay hands on him; untill he voluntarily tendered himselfe to their furie: not willing to defer his future glory any longer. That being dead, they buried him privately in a dung-hil, least his body should have bin found and worshiped by his followers: when a woman of great nobility, seduced by his doctrine, so prevailed with the *Roman* governor, that he threatned to put them forthwith to the sword, unlesse they produced the body. Which they digging up, found uncorrupted, and retaining that selfe-same amiable favour which he had when he lived: onely the haire was falne from his crowne; imitated as they say, by the *Romish* Fryers. Such, and more horrible blasphemies invent they; which I feare to utter. But they be generally notorious liars. Although they agree with the *Turke* in circumcision, detestation of Images, abstinency from swines-flesh, and divers other ceremonies: neverthelesse the *Turkes* will not suffer a *Jew* to turne *Mahometan*, unlesse he first turne a kind of Christian. As in religion they differ from others, so do they in habite, in Christendome enforcedly, here in *Turkie* voluntarily. Their under-garments differing little from the *Turkes* in fashon, are of purple cloth; over that they weare gownes of the same colour, with large wide sleeves, and clasped beneath the chin, without band: or collar on their heads high brim-lesse caps of purple, which they move at no time in their salutations. They shave their heads all over; not in imitation of the *Turke*: it being their ancient fashion, before the other were a Nation, as appeareth by *Cherillus* (together with their language & bonnets then used) relating of the sundry people which followed *Xerxes* in his *Grecian* expedition.

> *These warres a people rarely featured, follow;*
> *Who unknowne, the Phoenician language Spake.*
> *On hils of Solymus by a vast lake*
> *Have they their seate. Their heads they shave, and guard*
> *With helmes of horse-skin in the fire made hard.*

> Huius miranda specie gens castra locuta
> Phoenissam ignoto linguam mittebat ab ore,
> Sedes huic Solymi montes stagnum prope vastum.
> Tonsa caput circum; squallenti vertice equini,
> Exuvias capitis duratas igne gerebat.

Their familiar speech is Spanish: yet few of them are ignorant in the *Hebrew, Turkish, Moresco*, vulgar *Greeke*, and *Italian* languages. Their only studies are Divinitie and Physick: their occupations brocage and usury; yet take they no interest of one another, nor lend but upon pawnes; which once forfeited, are unredeemable. The poorer sort have beene noted for fortune-tellers, and by that deceit to have purchased their sustenance.

> *What dreame soever you will buy,*
> *The Jew will sell you readily.*

Qualiacunque voles Judaei somnia vendunt.
Juven. Sat.

They marry their daughters at the age of twelve: not affecting the single life, as repugnant to societie, and the law of creation. The Sabbath (their devotions ended) they chiefly imploy in nuptiall benevolencies: as an act of charity, befitting well the sanctity of that day. Although no City is without them thoroughout the *Grand Signtors* dominions; yet live they with the greatest liberty in *Salonica*, which is almost altogether inhabited by them. Every male above a certaine age, doth pay for his head an annual tribute. Although they be governed by the *Turkish* Justice; neverthelesse if a Jew deserve to die by their law, they will either privatly make him a way, or falsly accuse him of a crime that is answerable to the fact in qualitie, and deserving like punishment. It is no ill turne for the Franks that they will not feede at their tables. For they eate no flesh, but of their owne killing; in regard of the intrails, which being dislocated or corrupted, is an abomination unto them. When so it fals out, though exceeding good (for they kill of the best) they will sell it for a trifle. And as for their wines, being for the most part planted and gathered by *Grecians*, they dare not drinke of them for feare they be baptized: a ceremony whereof we have spoken already. They sit at their meat as the *Turkes* do. They bury in the fields by themselves, having onely a stone set upright on their graves: which once a yeere they frequent, burning of incense, and tearing of their garments, for certaine dayes they fast and mourne for the dead, yet even for such as have beene executed for offences. As did the whole Nation at our being at *Constantinople*, for two of good account that were impaled upon stakes; being taken with a *Turkish* woman, and that on their Sabbath. It was credibly reported, that a *Jew*, not long before, did poyson his sonne, whom he knew to be unrestrainably lascivious, to prevent the ignominie of a publike punishment, or losse by a chargeable redemption. The flesh consumed, they dig up the bones of those that are of their families; whereof whole bark-fulls not seldome do arrive at *Joppa*, to be conveyed, and againe interred at *Jerusalem*: imagining that it doth adde delight unto the soules that did owe them, & that they shall have a quicker dispatch in the generall Judgement. To speake a word or two of their women: The elder mabble their heads in linnen, with the knots hanging downe behind. Others do weare high caps of plate; whereof some I have seene of beaten gold. They weare long quilted wastcoates, with breeches underneath; in winter of cloth, in summer of linnen and over all when they stirre abroad, loose gownes of purple flowing from the shoulders. They are generally fat, and rank of the savours which attend upon sluttish corpulency. For the most part they are goggle-eyd. They neither shun conversation, nor are too watchfully guarded by their husbands. They are good work-women; and can & will do any thing for profit, that is to be done by the art of a woman, and which sutes with the fashion of these countries. Upon injuries received, or violence done to any of their Nation, they will cry out mainly at their windowes, beating their cheeks, and tearing of their garments. Of late they have bene blest with another *Hester*, who by her favour with the *Sultan*, prevented their intended massacre, & turned his fury upon their accusers. They are so well skilled in lamentations, that the *Greeks* do hire them to cry at their funerals,

> *Fruitfull in teares: teares that still ready stand*
> *To sally forth; and but expect command.*

>   —plorat
> Uberibus semper lachrymis, semperque paratis
> In statione sua, atque expectantibus illam
> Quo iubeat manare modo—
>   *Juvenal, Sat.* 6.

Fynes Moryson, *An Itinerary* (1617), Observations of the Ottoman Empire

ON Moryson's life and work, see above, pp. 81–2.

Moryson represents the Ottoman Empire as an absolute tyranny. Preferment is achieved through favouritism and corruption. People are over-taxed and Christians are treated especially badly. Inheritance laws demand that the emperor takes a large slice of the property of the deceased, so people tend to bury and hide their wealth. The Turks are brave and tough but intensely cruel. They are taught that death in defence of one's country is admirable. They are also idle and addicted to sexual pleasure, particularly sodomy.

In some ways Moryson clearly admires the Ottoman Empire and its military prowess in the same way that commentators admired the martial culture of the Spartan, while tempering their respect with fear.[1] He is as much in awe of their wealth and success as he is in many Italian cities (see above, pp. 83–90). Overall, however, the Turks pose as much a threat to European Christianity as they represent respected trading partners.[2] The extracts here represent Moryson's cultural analysis of the Ottoman Empire—sections which were not printed until the twentieth century—and his impressions of Constantinople.[3]

See also:

George Sandys, *A Relation of a Journey Begun An: Dom: 1610. Foure Bookes Contayning a description of the Turkish Empire, of Aegypt [etc.]* (1615).
Samuel Purchas, *Hakluytus Posthumous or Purchas His Pilgrimes,* 20 vols. (Glasgow: MacLehose, 1905–7), viii. 110–71.

[1] See, for example, Herodotus, *The Histories*, trans. Aubrey De Selincourt and A. R. Burn (Harmondsworth: Penguin, 1972), 32–6, *passim*.

[2] See Lisa Jardine, *Wordly Goods: A New History of the Renaissance* (Basingstoke: Macmillan, 1995), 374–6; Nabil Matar, *Islam in Britain, 1558–1685* (Cambridge: Cambridge Univ. Press, 1998), 3–18.

[3] Text from *Shakespeare's Europe*, ed. Charles Hughes (London: Sherratt and Hughes, 1903), 10–13, 38–9, 67–70; *An Itinerary*, 4 vols. (Glasgow: MacLehose, 1907), ii. 90–7.

THE TURKISH STATE

The Turkish Empire in our tyme is more vast and ample then ever it was formerly contayning most large provinces. In Africk it beginnes from the straight of Gibralter and so contains Mauritania, Barbaria, Egipt, and all the Coasts of the Mediterranean sea. The cheife Citty of Egipt Al-caiero hath rich traffick, and yeildes exceeding great Revenues to the Emperor though no doubt much lesse since the Portugalls sailing by the South coast of Affrick and planting themselves in the East, brought all the Commodityes thereof into Portugall, from thence distributing them through Europe, which voyage in our dayes, is yearely made by the English and Flemings. From Egipt it contaynes in Asia the three Provinces of Arabia, all Palestina, Syria, Mesopotamia, the many and large Provinces of Natolia or Asia the lesser, and both the Provinces of Armenia to the very confines of Persia (in these tymes much more straightned then in former ages) herein the famous Citty of Haleppo,[1] whether all the precious wares of the East are brought by great Rivers and uppon the backs of Camells, yeildeth huge Revenues to the Emperor. In Europe it containes all Greece and the innumerable Ilands of the Mediterranean sea, some few excepted, (as Malta fortifyed by an order of Christian knights, Sicilye and Sardinia subject to the king of Spaine, and Corsica subject to the Citty of Genoa, and the two Ilands of Cephalonia, that of Corfu, of Zante and of Candia with some few other small Ilands, subject to the Venetians). Also it contaynes Thracia, Bulgaria, Valachia, almost all Hungary, Albania, Slavonia, part of Dalmatia and other large Provinces to the Confines of the Germane Emperor, and king of Poland.

The forme of the Ottoman Empire is meerely absolute, and in the highest degree Tyrannicall using all his Subjects as borne-slaves.

No man hath any free Inheritance from his father, but mangled if any at all, since all unmovable goods belong to the Emperor, and for moveable goods, they either have litle, or dare not freely use them in life, or otherwise dispose them at death then by a secrett guift, as I shall shew in his place. Yea the Children of the very Bashawes and cheife Subjects, though equall to their fathers in military vertues (since there is no way to avoide contempt or live in estimation but the profession of Armes), yet seldome rise to any place of government. For this Tyrant indeed useth to preferr no borne

---

[1] Aleppo.

Turke to any high place, but they who sitt at the Sterne of the State, or have any great Commaund either in the Army, or in Civill government are for the most part Christians of ripe yeares, either taken Captives or voluntarily subjecting themselves, and so leaving the profession of Christianity to become Mahometans, or els they be the Tributory Children of Christian Subjects gathered every fifth yeare or oftner if occasion requires, and carried farr from their parents while they are young to be brought upp in the Turkish religion and military exercises; So as when they come to age, they neither know their Country nor parents, nor kinsmen so much as by name. [...]

All that live under this Tyrant, are used like spunges to be squeased when they are full. All the Turkes, yea the basest sort, spoile and make a pray of the Frankes (so they call Christians that are straungers, uppon the old league they have with the French) and in like sort they spoile Christian Subjects. The soldiers and officers seeking all occasions of oppression, spoile the Common Turkes, and all Christians. The Governors and greatest Commaunders make a pray of the very souldiers, and of the Common Turkes, and of all Christians, and the superiors among them use like extortion uppon the Inferiors, and when these great men are growne rich, the Emperor strangles them to have their treasure. So as the Turkes hide their riches and many tymes bury them under ground, and because nothing is so dangerous as to be reputed rich, they dare neither fare well, not build faire houses, nor have any rich household stuffe. The Emperor seldome speakes or writes to any, no not to his cheife Visers but by the name of slaves, and so miserable is their servitude, so base their obedience, as if he send a poore Chiaass or messenger to take the head of the greatest Subject, he though riding in the head of his troopes, yet presently submitts himselfe to the execution. Neither indeed hath he any hope in resistance, since his equalls are his enemyes in hope to rise by his fall, his felow soldiers forsake him as inured to absolute obedience, and he not knowing his parents, kinsmen or any freindes, is left alone to stand or fall by himselfe. [...]

This Tyrant seldome speakes to any of his subjects, but will be understood by his lookes, having many dumb men about his person, who will speake by signes among themselves as fast as we doe by wordes, and these men together with some boyes prostituted to his lust, and some of his dearest Concubines, are only admitted to be continually nere his person. The cheife Visere only receives his Commaundements and his mouth gives lawe to all under him, being of incredible power and authority by reason of this pride and retyrednes of the Tyrant, were not this high estate of his very slipperye, and subject to sodaine destruction. They who are admitted to the Tyrants presence, must not looke him in the face, and having kist the hemm of his garment, when they rise from adoring him, must retorne with their eyes cast on the ground, and their faces towards him, not turning their backs till they be out of his sight.

WARFARE IN GENERALL

Certaine positions of religion and the due conferring of rewards and punishments make the Turkes bold adventure their persons and carefully performe all duties in Warr. By blinde religion they are taught, that they mount to heaven without any impediment, who dye fighting for their Country and the Law of Mahomet. And that a Stoicall Fate or destiny governes all humane affaires, so as if the tyme of death be not come, a man is no lesse safe in the Campe then in a Castle, if it be come, he can be preserved in neither of them, and this makes them like beasts to rush uppon all daungers even without Armes to defend or offend, and to fill the ditches with their dead Carkases, thinckeing to overcome by number alone, without military art. Againe all rewards as the highest dignityes, and the like given continually by the Emperor to the most valiant and best deserving, make them apt to dare any thing. And in like sort severe punishments never failing to be inflicted on all offendors, more specially on such as brawle and fight among themselves, who are punished according to the quality of the offence, sometymes with death, and also such as breake martiall discipline, sometymes punishing him with death that pulls but a bunch of grapes in a Vineyard. I say these punishments never failing to be inflicted uppon offendors, make the soldiers formerly incouraged by rewards no lesse to feare base Cowardise, brawling, fighting or any breach of discipline, and keepe them in awe, as they keepe all other Subjects and enemyes under feare of their sword hanging over them. And the forme of this State being absolute tyranny, since all things must be kept by the same meanes they are gotten, the State gotten and mantayned by the sword, must needs give exorbitant Priviledges or rather meanes of oppression to all the Soldiers who (as I formerly have shewed) are not themselves free from the yoke of the same Tyranny which they exercise over others, while the superiors oppressing their inferiors are themselves grinded to dust by greater men, and the greatest of all hold life and goods at the Emperors pleasure, uppon an howers warning, among whome happy are the leane, for the fatt are still drawne to the shambles. The poorest man may aspire to the highest dignityes, if his mynde and fortune will serve him, but uppon those high pinnacles, there is no firme abiding, and the same Vertue and Starr, that made him rise, cannot preserve him long from falling. The great men most ravenously gape for treasure, and by rapine gett aboundance, but when they have it, all that cannot be made portable, must be hidden or buryed, for to build a fairer house, to have rich household stuff, or to keepe a good table, doth but make the Puttock[2] a prey to the Eagle. [...]

JUDGMENTS CORPORALL AND CAPITALL

Touching their Corporall and Capitall Judgments. For small offences they are beaten with Cudgles on the soles of the feete, the bellyes and backs, the strokes being many and paynefull according to the offence, or the anger of him that inflicts them. Myselfe did see some hanging and rotting in Chaynes uppon the Gallowes.

Also I did see one that had bene impaled (vulgarly Casuckde) an horrible kinde of death. The malefactor carryes the woodden stake uppon which he is to dye, being eight foot long and sharpe towards one end, and when he comes into the place of execution, he is stripped into his shirt, and laid uppon the ground with his face downeward, then the sharpe end of the stake is thrust into his fundament, and beaten with beetles upp into his body, till it come out, at or about his Wast, then the blunt end is fastened in the ground, and so he setts at litle ease, till he dye, which may be soone if the stake be driven with favour, otherwise, he may languish two or three dayes in payne and hunger; if torment will permitt him in that tyme to feele hunger, for no man dares give him meat.

They have an other terrible kinde of death vulgarly called Gaucher. The malefactor hath a rope or Chaine fastned about his body, whereof the other end is made fast to the topp of a Tower or of a Gibbett made high of purpose, and so this rope or chaine being of fitt length, his body is cast downe to pitch uppon a hooke of Iron, where he hangs till he dyes, with horror of the hight of payne, and of hunger. For howsoever he may dye

---

[2] A buzzard or kite, which are largely scavengers; in falconry terms, an ignoble bird, despite its size.

presently if any vitall part pitch uppon the hooke, yet hanging by the shoulder or thigh he may live long. And if any men give these executed men, meat, or helpe to prolong their miserable life, he shall dye the same death; Mores and christians and they that are not of the Army, are often putt to this death, yea the Beglerbegs sometymes putt Governors to this death for extortions or Cruelties committed by them, or rather to gett their wealth. They have an other terrible kinde of death to flea the skinn of from the living body, and thus they cruelly putt to death Bragadino a Venetian Governor of Famagosta in Cyprus, after he had yeilded the Citty uppon Composition for life to him and his soldiers.

A Turke forsaking his fayth and a christian doing or speaking any thing against the law of Mahomett are burned with fyer. Traytors or those whome the Emperor so calles, are tortured under the nayles and with diverse torments, but the great men of the Army are only strangled.

A murtherer is putt to some of the former cruell deathes. A theefe is hanged, and I have read of a soldier that had stollen milke and denyed the fact, who was hanged upp by the heeles, till he vomitted the milke, and after was strangled. The Adulterer is imprisoned for some Moneths, and after redeemed with mony, but the Adultresse is sett naked uppon an Asse with the bowells of an oxe about her neck, and so she is whipped about the streetes having stones and durt cast at her. If a Christian man committ fornication with a Turkish woman both are putt to death, and this Common danger to both, makes them more wary of others, and more confident to trust one an other, but the sinne is Common, and at Constantinople the houses of Ambassadors being free from the search of magistrates very Turkes, yea the Janizaries guarding the persons and howses of these Ambassadors, will not stick to play the bawdes for a small reward. In case of this offence nothing frees a Christian from death, but his turning Mahometan. Yet I remember that I saw a Tower at Tripoli called the tower of Love, built by a rich Christian to redeeme his life being condemned for this Crime. But if a Turke lye with a Christian woman, he is not putt to death, but sett uppon an Asse with his face towards the tayle, which he holds in his hand, and hath the bowells of an oxe cast about his neck, and so is ledd through the streetes in scorne. If a Christian lye with a Christian woman, the fault is punished with paying of mony. All harlotts write their names in the booke of the Cady or the Sobbassa, and not only the Turkes but even the Janizaries are permitted to have acquaintance with them so it be not in the two lents, wherein they yearely fast, For in that Case, while I was in Turkye many women were sewed in sacks, and so drowned in the Sea at Constantinople. Generally for greater Crymes, the Judge of the Turkes deviseth and imposeth a death with greater torment especially for reproching their law or Prophett, which a Christian cannot redeeme, but by turning Turke.

OF DEGREES IN THE COMMON WEALTH
AND FAMILY

[...] For the private Family each man may have as many Wives as he is able to feede so he take a letter of permission from the Cady, and some of them keepe their wives in diverse Cittyes to avoyd the strife of women; yet if they live both in one house with him, they seldome disagree, being not preferred one above another. The Turkes use not to take a dowrye but as they buy captive women, (whome they may sell againe or keepe for Concubines or for any other service); so they also buy Free women to be their wives, so as the father is inriched by having many and fayre Daughters. Divorce is permitted for perverse manners, for barrennes or like faults allowed by the Cady. As they buy Captive Women, so may they buy any other for Concubines so they write their names in the booke of the Cady. For as Christians are maryed by Preists in the Church; so Turkes are maryed by taking a letter, or bill from the Cady (who is their spirituall Judge) and writing the mariage in his booke at his private house. But at the day of mariage, they also use to bathe, and to pray in their Moschees.

Lastly it is no disgrace to be borne of a Captive Woman, or out of mariage, for that is the Condition, of the very Emperors, Whose mothers are Captives, and before the birth of their first sonne, never have a letter of dowry to make them free women and wives, which after they have a sonne was of old wont to be graunted them, but the Emperors of late tymes seldome give that letter to them, for jelousy lest they should practice their deathes to have power in the raigne of their succeeding sonne. [...]

Constantinople. Having cast anchor (as I said) in the Port of Constantinople, behold, as soone as day began to breake, many companies of Turkes rushing into our Barke, who like so many starved flies fell to sucke the sweete Wines, each rascall among them beating with cudgels and ropes the best of our Marriners, if he durst but repine against it, till within short space the Candian

Merchant having advertised the Venetian Ambassadour of their arrivall, he sent a Janizare to protect the Barke, and the goods; and assoone as he came, it seemed to me no lesse strange, that this one man should beate all those Turkes, and drive them out of the Barke like so many dogs, the common Turkes daring no more resist a souldier, or especially a Janizare, then Christians dare resist them. And the Serjant of the Magistrate having taken some of our Greeke Marriners (though subject to the State of Venice) to worke for their Ottoman in gathering stones, and like base imployments, this Janizary caused them presently to be released, and to be sent againe into their Barke, such is the tyranny of the Turkes against all Christians aswel their subjects as others, so as no man sayleth into these parts, but under the Banner of England, France, or Venice, who being in league with the great Turke, have their Ambassadours in this Citie, and their Consuls in other Havens, to protect those that come under their Banner, in this sort sending them a Janizare to keepe them from wrongs, so soone as they are advertised of their arrivall. [. . .]

THE DESCRIPTION OF THE CITY OF CONSTANTINOPLE, AND THE ADJACENT TERRITORIES AND SEAS

The great lines or walles shew the forme of the City, and the single small lines describe the Teritory adjoyning.

A.D. 1597 *The description of Constantinople.*

(A) In this Tower they hang out a light of pitch and like burning matter, to direct the Saylers by night, comming to the City, or sayling along the coast out of the Sea Euxinus (which they say is called the Black Sea of many shipwracks therein happening.) And this Tower is sixteene miles distant from the Citie.

(B) Here is a marble pillar erected upon a Rocke compassed with the sea, which they call the pillar of Pompey, and therein many passengers (for their memory) use to ingrave their names. And here are innumerable flocks of Sea foule and of many kindes, wherewith hee that is skilfull to shoote in his Peece, may abundantly furnish himselfe.

(C) Here is the Euxine or black Sea.

(D E) Here lie two strong Castles, one in Europe, the other in Asia, some eight miles distant from the Citie, built to defend the Haven from the assault of the enemies by Sea on that side, and the Garrison there kept,

Two strong Castles.

searcheth the ships comming from the Citie, that no slaves or prohibited goods be carried therein, neither can any ship passe unsearched, except they will hazard to be sunck. Finally, the great Turke sends his chiefe prisoners to be kept in these strong Castles.

(F) Here great ships use to cast anchor at their first arrivall, till they bee unloaded, and here againe they ride at anchor to expect windes, when they are loaded and ready to depart.

(G) All along this banke and the opposite side for a large circuit, the greatest ships use to lie when they are unloaded, and they lie most safely and close by the shore, fastaned by cables on land.

Gallata and Perah.

(H) Here lyes the old Citie built by the Genoesi of Italy, called Gallata by the Turks, and Perah by the Greekes (of the situation beyond the Channell.) It is now accounted a Suburbe of Constantinople, and is seated upon a most pleasant hill, wherein for the most part live Christians, as well subjects as others, and the Ambassadours of England, France, and Venice, only the Emperours Ambassadour must lye within the Citie, more like a pledge of peace, then a free Ambassadour, and very few Turkes live here mingled with the Christians. The situation of Gallata (as I said) is most pleasant. Formerly the Ambassadours of England were wont to dwell upon the Sea-shore in the Plaine, and their Pallace is not farre distant from this note (K); but Master Edward Barton the English Ambassadour at this time dwelt upon the top of the hill, in a faire house within a large field, and pleasant gardens compassed with a wall. And all Gallata is full of very pleasant gardens, and compassed with pleasant fields, whereof some towards the land furthest from the Sea, are used for the buriall of Turkes.

Master Edward Barton's house.

(I) Here a little Creeke of the Sea is compassed with walles and buildings, within which the Gallies of the great Turke lie in safety, and there be fit places to build Gallies, and store-houses for all things thereunto belonging.

(K) Here is the chiefe passage over the water called Tapano, where a man may passe for two aspers. All along this Sea banke lye very many great Gunnes (as upon the Tower Wharfe at London), and here the fishers land, and sell their fish.

Chalcedon.

(L) Here the Megarenses of old built Chalcedon, a Citie of Bethinia, famous for a Councell held there, by the ruine of which Citie, Constantinople increased. At this day there is onely a Village, or rather some scattered houses, and it is commonly called Scuteri, or Scudretta.

(M) Here the Great Turks mother then living, had her private Garden.

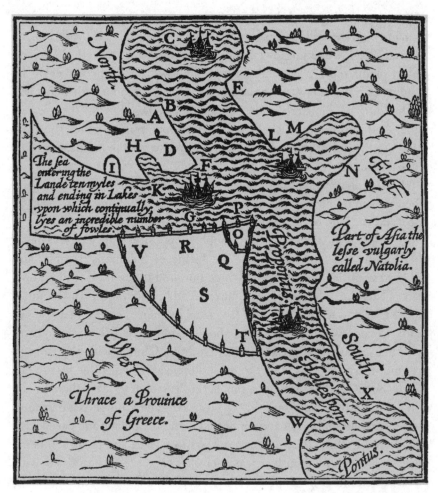

The sea entering the Lande ten myles and ending in Lakes vpon which continually lyes an incredible number of fowles.

Part of Afia the leſse vulgarly called Natolia.

Propontis.

Hellespont.

Pontus.

Thrace a Prouince of Greece.

North.

East.

West.

South.

Fig. 7. 'The Description of the City of Constantinople' (Fynes Moryson, *Itinerary*, I, iii, p. 260)

(N) Hither the Heyre of the Empire is sent, as it were into banishment, under pretence to governe the Province Bursia, assoone as he is circumcised, and so being made a Musulman (that is, a circumcised Turke) first begins to draw the eyes of the Army and Janizares towards him.

(O) Here is the Pallace or Court of the great Turke, called by the Italians *The Pallace of the* Seraglio, and vulgarly Saray, and it was of old the Monastery of Saint *great Turke.* Sophia. Mahomet the second first compassed it with walls, and the buildings together with the large and pleasant gardens are some three or foure miles in circuit. I entered the outward Court thereof by a stately Gate kept by many Janizares called Capigi of that office. The court yard was large, all compassed with building of free stone two stories high, with a low and almost plaine roofe tyled, and without windowes, after the maner of the building of Italy, and round about the inside, it was cast out with arches like the building of Cloisters, under which they walked drie in the greatest raine. And in this Court is a large pulpit or open roome, where the great Turke useth to shew himselfe to the Janizares to satisfie them when they make any mutiny.

(P) Here is a banqueting house, vulgarly called Chuske, the prospect whereof is more pleasant then can be expressed, beholding foure Seats at once, and the land on all sides beyond them.

The Church of
Saint Sophia.

(Q) Here is the Church of Saint Sophia, opposite to the Court Gate, of old built by the Christians after the forme of Salomons Temple, and indowed with the annuall rent of three hundred thousand Zechines, now made a Mosche or Mahometan Church. And howsoever the Turks cannot indure that unwashed Christians (so called by them, because they use not Baths so continually as they doe) should enter their Mosches, or passe over their Sepulchers, yet my self entered this Church with the Janizare my guid, trusting to his power to defend me, yet he willed me first to put of my shooes, and according to the Turkes custome to leave them in the porch, where they were safe till we returned. The Church is of a round forme, and built of bricke, and supported with faire pillars, and paved with Marble (over which the Turks layed Mats to kneele, and prostrate them-selves more commodiously upon them.) The roofe is beautified with

Alla Mosaica.

pictures of that rich painting, which the Italians call alla Mosaica, shining like enameled work, which now by antiquity were much decaied, and in some parts defaced. Round about the Church hung many Lampes, which they use to burne in the time of their Lent (called Beyram); and every weeke upon Thursday in the evening, and Friday all day, which they keepe holy after their fashion for their Sabbath day. Round about the upper part of the Church are large and most faire Galleries. And here I did see two Nuts of Marble of huge bignesse and great beauty. Moreover I did see the great Turke when he entered this Church, and howsoever it lie close to the Gate of his Pallace, Yet he came riding upon a horse richly trapped, with many troopes of his chiefe horsemen, standing in ranke within the Courts of his Pallace, and from the Court Gate to the Church dore, betweene which troopes on both sides, he passed as betweene walles of brasse, with great pompe. And when a Chaus (or Pensioner) being on horseback did see mee close by the Emperours side, hee rushed upon me to strike me with his mace, saying, What doth this Christian dog so neere the person of our great Lord? But the Janizare, whom our Ambassadour had given me for a Guide and Protector, repelled him from doing mee any wrong, and many Janizares (according to their manner) comming to helpe him, the Chaus was glad to let mee alone, and they bade me be bold to stand still, though I were the second or third person from the Emperour. Neere this Church is the stately Sepulcher of Selymus the second, and another Sepulcher no lesse stately, and newly built for Amurath lately deceased, where he lay with those male children round about him, who according to the manner were strangled by his Successour after hee was dead. Not farre thence is the Market place having some one hundred marble pillars about it, and adorned with a Pyramis or pinacle, erected upon foure Globes, and with a pleasant Fountaine of water, together with other ornaments left (as it seemes) by Christian Emperours.

The Sepulcher of Selymus the second.

(R) The wonderfull Mosche and Sepulcher of Solyman, numbred among the miracles of the World.

(S) Two houses for the same use, as the Exchange of London, where the Merchants meete, namely, for the selling of fine wares, but no way to be compared to the same for the building. They are called the great and the lesse Bezestan, and use to bee opened onely certaine daies of the weeke, and for some sixe howers, at which times small and more pretious wares are there to be sold, as Jewels, Semiters (or Swords), set with Jewels, but commonly counterfet, pieces of Velvet, Satten, and Damaske, and the like. And the Market place is not farre distant, where Captives of both sexes are weekely sold, and the buyers if they will, may take them into a house, and there see them naked, and handle them (as wee handle beasts to know their fatnesse and strength.)

Two houses for Exchange.

(T) Here is a Fort that is fortified with seven Towers, called by the Turkes Jadicule, and by Christians the seven Towers, where a garrison of Souldiers is kept, because the Emperors treasure is there laied up, and cheefe Prisoners use to be kept there. The treasure is vulgarly said to bee laied up there, but the great Turke seldome goes thither; and since it is true, that where the treasure is, there is the mind, I thinke it probable (which I have heard of experienced men) that most of the treasure lies in the Seraglio, where the great Turke holds his Court.

Fort Jadicule.

Description of a Giraffa.

(V) Here be the ruines of a Pallace upon the very wals of the City, called the Pallace of Constantine, wherein I did see an Elephant, called Philo by the Turkes, and another beast newly brought out of Affricke, (the Mother of Monsters) which beast is altogether unknowne in our parts, and is called Surnapa by the people of Asia, Astanapa by others, and Giraffa by the Italians, the picture whereof I remember to have seene in the Mappes of Mercator; and because the beast is very rare, I will describe his forme as well as I can. His haire is red coloured, with many blacke and white spots; I could scarce reach with the points of my fingers to the hinder part of his backe, which grew higher and higher towards his foreshoulder, and his necke was thinne and some three els long, so as hee easily turned his head in a moment to any part or corner of the roome wherein he stood, putting it over the beames thereof, being built like a Barne, and high (for the Turkish building, not unlike the building of Italy, both which I have formerly described) by reason whereof he many times put his nose in my necke, when I thought my selfe furthest distant from him, which familiarity of his I liked not; and howsoever the Keepers assured me he would not hurt me, yet I avoided these his familiar kisses as much as I could. His body was slender, not greater, but much higher then the body of a stagge or Hart, and his head and face was like to that of a stagge, but the head was lesse and the face more beautifull: He had two hornes, but short and scarce halfe a foote long; and in the forehead he had two bunches of flesh, his eares and feete like an Oxe, and his legges like a stagge. The Janizare my guide did in my name and for me give twenty Aspers to the Keeper of this Beast. [...]

William Lithgow, *The Totall Discourse of The Rare Adventures* (1632), 'Comments upon Jerusalem'

LITHGOW'S epic journey culminated in a visit to the holy city of Jerusalem as the centre of the Christian universe. It is likely that Lithgow is deliberately imitating Mandeville's *Travels*, one of the central medieval texts behind Renaissance conceptions of the world and the purpose of travel (see above, pp. 5, 117). Lithgow is keen to capture the startling impression of the city and the sense of wonder it inspires in travellers.[1] What becomes clear from the account is how well organized travel to Jerusalem was and how closely pilgrimages tended to resemble tourism.[2] Equally apparent is Lithgow's pugnacious temperament and his constant desire to defend his Protestantism against all-comers whatever the situation and whatever the danger to himself. Lithgow is keen to decry the superstitious Catholicism which he felt had been established in the most sacred of places, a sense of sacrilege that can be compared to the anger English visitors often felt in Rome (see above, pp. 85–9).

See also:

George Sandys, *A Relation of a Journey Begun An: Dom: 1610* (1615), bk. 3.

[1] *The Travels of Sir John Mandeville*, ed. C. W. R. D. Moseley (Harmondsworth: Penguin, 1983), 76–88. See Stephen Greenblatt, *Marvelous Possessions: The Wonder of the New World* (Oxford: Oxford Univ. Press, 1991), ch. 1.

[2] A point made more than two hundred years earlier by Geoffrey Chaucer in *The Canterbury Tales*. See also Margery Kempe's account of her pilgrimage; *The Book of Margery Kempe*, ed. B. A. Windeatt (Harmondsworth: Penguin, 1985), 103–13. Text from William Lithgow, *The Totall Discourse of the Rare Adventures and Painefull Peregrinations* (1632) (Glasgow: MacLehose, 1906), 208–11, 220–5, 234–7.

[...] At last wee beheld the prospect of Jerusalem, which was not onely a   A.D. 1612.
contentment to my weary body, but also beeing ravished with a kinde of
unwonted rejoycing, the teares gushed from my eyes for too much joy. In   *A joyfull harmony.*
this time the Armenians began to sing in their owne fashion, Psalmes to
praise the Lord: and I also sung the 103 Psalme all the way, till we arrived
neere the wals of the Citty, where we ceased from our singing, for feare of
the Turkes. [...]

Anno 1612. upon Palme-Sunday in the morning, wee entred into Jerusalem, and at the Gate wee were particularly searched, to the effect wee carried in no Furniture of Armes, nor Powder with us, and the poore Armenians (notwithstanding they are slaves to Turkes,) behoved to render their weapons to the Keepers, such is the feare they have of Christians. And my name was written up in the Clarkes Booke at the Port, that my tribute for the Gate, and my seeing of the Sepulcher, might bee payed at one time together, before my finall departure thence.

The Gates of the City are of iron outwardly, and above each Gate are brazen Ordonance planted, for their defence.

A foolish ceremony.

Having taken my leave of the Caravan, and the Company, who went to lodge with their owne Patriarke, I was met and received with the Guardian, and twelve Friers upon the streetes, each of them carrying in their hands a burning waxe Candle, and one for mee also: who received mee joyfully, and singing all the way to their Monastery Te Deum Laudamus, they mightily rejoyced, that a Christian had come from such a far Countrey as Scotia, to visite Jerusalem.

Where being arrived, they forthwith brought me to a Roome, and there the Guardian washed my right foote with water, and his Viccar my left: and done, they kissed my feete, so did also all the twelve Friers that stood by: But when they knew afterward that I was no Popish Catholicke, it sore repented them of their Labour. I found here ten Frankes newly come the neerest way from Venice hither, sixe of them were Germanes, noble Gentlemen, and they also good Protestants, who were wonderfull glad to heare me tell the Guardian flatly in his face, I was no Romane Catholicke, nor never thought to be: The other foure Frankes were Frenchmen, two of them Parisians old men, the other two of Provance, all foure being Papists: with nine other Commercing Frankes, also that dwelt in Syria and Cyprus, most of them beeing Venetians, who were all glad of me, shewing themselves so kinde, so carefull, so loving, and so honourable in all respects, that they were as kind Gentle-men, as ever I met withall, especially the Germaines: Such is the love of strangers, when they meete in Forraine and remote places. They had also in high respect the adventures of my halfe yeares travaile, East, and beyond Jerusalem: troubling me all the while wee were together, to show them the rare Discourses of my long two yeares survey of Turkey, but especially of my furthest sights in the East of Asia: And were alwayes in admiration that I had no fellow Pilgrime, in my long Peregrination.

Monday earely, we Pilgrimes went foorth to view the monuments within the Citty, being accompanied with the Padre Viccario, and a French

Predicatore: the places of any note wee saw were these: first they shewed us the place where Christ appeared to Mary Magdalen, who sayd: Touch me not, for I am not yet ascended to my Father, John 20. 15. and this place by them is supposed to be the Center or middle part of the World.[1] Next, where Saint James the first Bishop of the Primitive Church was beheaded: then the House of Saint Thomas, but that is doubtful (say they) because it is not yet confirmed by the Papall Authority: From thence they brought us to the place where Annas one of the High Priests dwelt, and also the Tree to the which our Saviour was bound, whiles Annas was making himselfe ready to leade him to Caiphas; but that I wil not beleeve, for that Tree groweth yet, being an Olive Tree. They shewed us also the house where Saint Peter was imprisoned, when his fetters were shaken off his legges, and the Prison doores cast open, and hee relieved: And where Zebedeus the Father of James and John dwelt, which are nothing but a lumpe of Ruines.

Thence wee came to the decayed lodging of Caiphas, without the Citty, *Caiphas Lodging.* uppon the mount Syon, whereupon there is a Chappell builded, and at the entry of that little Domo, we saw the stone, on which the Cocke crew, when Peter denied Christ. Within the same place is the stone that was rolled to the Sepulcher doore of our Saviour, being now made an Altar to the Abasines. These Abasines, are naturally borne blacke, and of them silly Religious men, who stay at Jerusalem, in two places, to wit, heere at Caiphas House, on mount Syon, and the other Convent on mount Moriah, where Abraham would have sacrificed Isaac: They weare on their heads flat round Caps of a blackish colour, and on their bodies long gownes of white Dimmety, or linnen cloath, representing Ephods: the condition of themselves being more devoute, than understanding the true grounds of their devotion, blind zeale and ignorance overswaying their best light of knowledge. They being a kinde of people, which came from Prester Jehans dominions.[2]

And within that Chappel they shewed us a narrow pit, wherein (say they) Christ was incarcerat, the night before he was brought to the Judgement Hall. Upon the same side of Syon, we saw the place, where Christ did institute the Sacraments: and not far hence, a decayed House, where (say they) the Holy-Ghost discended upon the Apostles, and also the

[1] On Jerusalem as the centre of the world, see Mandeville, *Travels*, 76–80; Greenblatt, *Marvelous Possessions*, 38–44.
[2] On the legendary kingdom of Prester John, see Mandeville, *Travels*, 167–72. This is evidence that Lithgow, like many Renaissance travellers had Mandeville in mind when composing his work.

Sepultures of David, and his sonne Salomon: Over the which, there is a Moskie, wherein no Christian may enter, to see these monuments. For the Turkes doe great Reverence, to most of all the ancient Prophets of the old Testament.

From thence we returned, and entred in via dolorosa, the dolorous way, by which our Lord and Savior passed, when he went to be crucified, carrying the Crosse upon his Backe: And at the end of the same streete (say they) the Souldiers met Simon of Cyrene, and compelled him to helpe *Pilats judgement* Christ, to beare his Crosse when hee fainted. Pilats Judgment Hall, is *Hall.* altogether ruinated, having but onely betweene the two sides of the Lane, an olde Arch of stone, under the which I passed, standing ful in the high Way: Here they shewed us the place, where Christ first tooke up his Crosse, and on the top of that Arche, wee saw that place called Gabbatha, where Jesus stood, when Pilat sayd to the Jewes, Ecce homo.

A little below this, they brought us to the Church of Saint Anna, where (say they) the Virgin Mary was borne. And going downe another narrow Lane, they poynted in to a House, and sayd, heere Dives the rich Glutton dwelt, who would not give to Lazarus the Crummes of Bread that fel from his Table: this I suspend, amongst many other things, for all hold it to bee a Parable, and not a History: And although it were a History, who can demonstrate the particular place, Jerusalem having beene so often transformed by alterations.

This I must needes say, with such leying wonders, these flattering Friers, bring Strangers into a wonderful admiration, and although I rehearse all I saw there, yet I will not beleeve all, onely publishing them as things indifferent, some whereof are frivolous, and others somewhat more credible: But as I sayd before, I will make no (or very small) distinction in the Relation.

From thence we came without the Easterne gate, (standing on a low Banke, called the daughter of Syon, that over-toppeth the valley of Jehosophat,) unto an immoveable stone, upon the which they sayd St. Stephen was stoned to death, the first Martyr of the Christian faith; and the faithfull fore-runner of many noble followers. As we returned to our owne Convent, *Abrahams faith.* they brought us to mount Moriah, and shewed us the place where Abraham offered up Isaac, which is in the custody of Nigroes of Aethiopians: to whom each of us payed ten Madins of Brasse, the common coine of Jerusalem, for our in going to that place. And the other monastery that these Abasines detaine, is on mount Sinay in the Desarts, where the body of S. Katherine lyeth buried, which is richly maintained, and strongly kept by the Aethiopian Emperor: There are 200. Religious Abasines in it, and 100. souldiers to guard them from the incursions of Arabs, who continually molest them, because mount Sinay standeth in midst of that desolate *Mount Sinay.* Arabian wildernesse, and far from any civill or inhabited place; being distant from Jerusalem about 70. English miles. Next they shewed us the place where Jesus sayd, Daughters of Jerusalem, mourne not for me, &c. And neere unto this, where the virgin Mary fell into an agony, when Jesus passed by carrying his Crosse: Also, not farre hence, we beheld the place, where (as they say) Jesus said to his mother, woman, behold thy Sonne, and to S. John behold thy mother.

Ascending more upward, they shewed us the house of Veronica Sancta, and said, that our Saviour going by her doore, all in a sweat to Mount Calvary, she brought him a napkin to wipe his face; which he received, and gave it to her againe: in which (say they) the print of his face remaineth to this day, and is to be seene at Rome. It is also sayd to be in a Towne in Spaine, and another of them at Palermo in Sicilia: wherefore I beleeve the one, as well as the rest.

> So out of one, if Papists can make three
> By it, they would denote heavens Deitie:
> But O! not so, these three revolv'd in one,
> Points forth the Pope, from him his tripled Crowne
> He weav'd these Napkins, leying reard his seat,
> For which this number, makes his number great.

As concerning the Temple of the most high, built by Salomon [...] [t]his present Temple hath two incircling Courts invironed with high wals, having two enteries: In the inner Court standeth the Temple, that is composed of five circling and large Rotundoes, rising high and incorporate from the ground with round tops: The outward fabrick whereof we cannot see, save on Mount Olivet, which is over against the Citie, and twice as high as Mount Sion.

These are all the monuments which in one day, I saw within Jerusalem; but as for Mount Calvary, and the Holy Grave, I saw them afterward, which in their owne place shall be orderly touched. As we were spending that day in these sights, the Guardian had prepared one hundred souldiers, sixty horse-men, and forty foot-men, to take with him the day following, for his conduction to Jordan, and the mountaine in the Wildernesse where

Christ fasted; which is his usuall custome once every yeare betweene
Palme-sunday and Easter, returning againe before Good-friday. These
places cannot be viewed, save onely at that time; neither may a Pilgrime
goe along with the souldiers, unlesse he give the value of seven Crownes or
Piasters (as a propyne) unto the Lieutenant, being forty two shillings
starling: and if the Traveller will not goe to that charge, he may stay
there till their returne, which I would not wish him to doe, if possibly he
may spare the money, for the sight of Sodome, and Jordans sake. That same
night after supper, the Guardian demanded of us Travellers, if we would
goe with him to see these memorable, & singular things, upon the former
condition: To whom we answered, in a generall consent, we would, and so
payed our moneyes.

A voyage to Jordan.

Earely upon Tuesday morning all the Friers and Pilgrimes being
mounted on Mules save onely pedestriall I, and two Mules loaden with
our provision of victuals; we departed from the City, about our nine of
the clocke in the forenoone, keeping our faces South-east, and leaving
Bethphage and Bithania on our left hand, wee had pleasant travelling for
seaven miles; but in the afternoone wee entred in a barren and desart
Countrey till Sun-setting: where at last wee arrived at a standing Well,
and there refreshing our selves and the beasts, wee reposed till two houres
within night. After that the Captaine had cried Catethlanga, that is, march
away: we set forward, being well guarded round about with our keepers,
because we entred into a dangerous way, and a most desolate and fabulous
soile.

At last towards the afternoone, wee safely arrived at the foote of the
Mountayne, and having saluted the Guardian, and all the Rest, who then
were ready to take journey, the Frier told his Reverence how I had saved his
life: Whereupon the Guardian, and the other Friers, did imbrace me kindly
in their Armes, giving me many earnest and loving thankes.

S. Jeromes Abbey.

And now the Souldiers and wee being advanced in our Way, as wee
returned to Jerusalem, wee marched by an olde Ruinous Abbey, where (say
they) Saint Jerome dwelt, and was fed there by wilde Lyons: Having
travailed sore and hard that afternoone, wee arrived at Jerusalem an
houre within night, for the Gate was kept open a purpose for us and our
Guard: and entring our Monastery, wee supped, and rested our selves till
midnight; having marched that halfe Day, more as 34. miles. A little before
midnight, the Guardian and the Friers, were making themselves ready to

goe with us to the Church of the Holy Sepulcher, called Sancto Salvatore; where wee were to stay Good-friday and Satturday, and Easter-Sunday till mid-night: They tooke their Cooke with them also to dresse our Dyet, carrying Wine, Bread, Fishes, and Fruites hither in abundance. Meane while, a Jew, the Trench-man of the Turkies Sanzacke, came to the Monastery, and received from every one of us Pilgrimes, first two chickens of Gold, for our severall heads, and entrey at Jerusalem: and then nine Chickens a peece for our in going to the Holy Grave; and a Chicken of golde a man, to himselfe the Jew, as beeing due to his place.

Thus was there twelve Chickens from each of us dispatched for the Turke: And last one, and all of us, behoved to give to the Guardian two Chickens also for the Waxe Candles and fooleries hee was to spend, in their idle and superstitious Ceremonies, these three aforesayd nights, which amounted in all to every one of us, to foureteene Chickens of gold, sixe pounds sixe shillings starling. So that in the whole from the sixe Germanes, foure French men, and nine Commercing Franks in Cyprus and Syria, Venetians, and Ragusans, and from my selfe, the summe arose for this nights labour to a hundred and twenty sixe pounds starling. *Our tributs for the Holy Grave.*

This done, and at full mid-night wee came to the Church where wee found twelve Venerable like Turkes, ready to receive us, sitting in the Porch without the Doore; who foorthwith opened at randone the two great Brazen halfes of the Doore, and received us very respectively: We being within the doore made fast, and the Turkes returned to the Castle, the first place of any note we saw, was the place of Unction, which is a foure squared stone; inclosed about with an yron Revele,[1] on which (say they) the dead body of our Saviour lay, and was imbalmed; after hee was taken from the Crosse, whiles Joseph of Arimathea, was preparing that new Sepulcher for him wherein never man lay: from thence we came to the holy Grave. Leaving Mount Calvary on our right hand toward the East end of the Church; for they are both contained within this glorious edifice.

The Holy Grave is covered with a little Chappell, standing within a round Quiere, in the west ende of the Church: It hath two low and narrow entries: As we entred the first doore, three after three, and our shoes cast off, for these two roomes are wondrous little, the Guardiano fell downe, ingenochiato, and kissed a stone, whereupon (he sayd) the Angell stood, when Mary Magdalen came to the Sepulchre, to know if Christ was risen, *The Holy Grave.*

---

[1] Railing.

on the third day as he promised: And within the entry of the second doore, we saw the place where Christ our Messias was buried, and prostrating our selves in great humility, every man according to his Religion, offered up his prayers to God.

The Sepulchre it selfe, is eight foote and a halfe in length, and advanced about three foote in height from the ground, and three foote five inches broad, being covered with a faire Marble stone of white colour.

In this Chappell, and about it, I meane without the utter sides of it, and the inward incirclings of the compassing Quiere, there are alwayes burning above fifty Lampes of oyle, maintained by Christian Princes, who stand most of them within incircling bandes of pure Gold, which is exceeding sumptuous, having the names of those, who sent or gave them, ingraven upon the upper edges of the round circles: each of them having three degrees, and each degree depending upon another, with supporters of pure Gold, rich and glorious. The fairest whereof was sent thither by King John of England, whereon I saw his Name, his Title, and crowne curiously indented, I demanded of the Guardiano if any part of the Tombe was here yet extant, who replied, there was; but because (said he) Christians resorting thither, being devoutly moved with affection to the place, carried away a good part thereof, which caused S. Helen inclose it under this stone; whereby some relicts of it should alwaies remaine. I make no doubt but that same place is Golgotha, where the holy Grave was, as may appeare by the distance, betweene Mount Calvary and this sacred Monument; which

The glorious Chappell of the Holy Grave. extendeth to forty of my pases: This Chappell is outwardly decored, with 15. couple of Marble Pillars, and of 22. foote high; and above the upper coverture of the same Chappell, there is a little sixe-angled Turret made of Cedar wood, covered with Lead, and beautified with six small Columnes of the same tree. The Chappell it selfe standeth in a demicircle or halfe Moone, having the little doore or entry looking East: to the great body of the Church, and to Mount Calvary, being opposite to many other venerable monuments of memorable majesties.

The forme of the Quiere wherein it standeth, is like unto that auncient Rotundo in Rome, but a great deale higher and larger, having two gorgeous Galleries; one above another, and adorned with magnificent Columnes being open at the top, with a large round; which yeeldeth to the heavens the prospect of that most sacred place.

In which second Gallery we strangers reposed all these three nights we remained there: whence we had the full prospect of all the spacious Church, and all the Orientall people were there at this great feast of Easter day, being about 6000. persons: from this curious carved Chappell we returned through the Church to Mount Calvary; To which we ascended by twenty one steps, eighteene of them were of Marble, and three of Cedar-wood: where, when we came I saw a most glorious & magnifick roome, whose covert was supported all about with rich columnes of the Porphyre stone, and the oversilings loaden with Mosaick worke, & overgilded with gold, the floore being curiously indented with intermingled Alabaster and black shining Parangone: On my left hand I saw a platformd rocke, all covered with thicke and ingraven boords of silver; and in it a hole of a cubits deepe, in which (say they) the Crosse stood whereon our Saviour was crucified: And on every side thereof a hole for the good & bad theeves, were then put to death with him. [...]

The beauty of Mount Calvary.

Chapter Four

THE FAR EAST AND THE
SOUTH SEA ISLANDS

THE work which overshadowed all subsequent European contact with the East was Marco Polo's *Travels*, probably written in the late twelfth century while the author was in prison in Genoa.[1] Marco Polo's account of his stay at the court of the Great Khan influenced Christopher Columbus's attempt to reach the Indies which led to the discovery of America, although Columbus himself appears not to have realized that he had reached a new continent.[2] As with the Ottoman Empire (see above, pp. 166–78), Europeans were conscious that they were dealing with peoples whose cultural sophistication matched their own, even if they were infidels and pagans. Trade and profit were the principal goals of travellers to the region, not colonization or conquest.[3] After all, it should not be forgotten that the aim of many explorers who reached the Americas—Martin Frobisher, John Davis, and Humphrey Gilbert in the 1560s—was to find a route through to the riches of the Far East.[4]

Trade with the Indonesian islands became increasingly important for the British economy after 1600 when the East India Company was formed.[5]

[1] Marco Polo, *The Travels*, trans. R. E. Latham (Harmondsworth: Penguin, 1958).

[2] Marco Polo, *Travels*, ch. 3; Peter Hulme, *Colonial Encounters: Europe and the Native Caribbean, 1492–1797* (London: Methuen, 1986), ch. 1; Gianni Granzotto, *Christopher Columbus: The Dream and the Obsession: A Biography*, trans. Stephen Sartarelli (London: Collins, 1986), ch. 1.

[3] Angus Calder, *Revolutionary Empire: The Rise of the English-Speaking Empires from the Fifteenth Century to the 1780s* (London: Cape, 1981), 3.

[4] Gerald S. Graham, *A Concise History of the British Empire* (London: Thames and Hudson, 1970), 16.

[5] Calder, *Revolutionary Empire*, 101.

The British had to compete with the Portuguese who had established a trading base in the region when they took possession of Goa in 1511, which became the capital of their Eastern empire.[6] They also had to deal with the aggressive rivalry of the Dutch, another rising European power keen to acquire wealth and colonies.[7] A good account of such trade rivalry is given in the two accounts of Sir Henry Middleton's voyage to the Moluccan islands (1604–6), in which he has to compete with armed Dutch and Portuguese traders (see below, pp. 208–18). Middleton's voyages were pioneering and helped to establish the success of British trade later in the century. The British presence in this region was still negligible, except for the Moluccas and parts of Java, until the middle of the seventeenth century. European traders were liable to lose out to Arab, Persian, Indian, and Chinese traders when fair competition held sway.[8]

English presence in China and Japan was limited, principally because of the isolationist policies of the rulers of those countries (although the Dutch had rather more success in the later seventeenth century).[9] Richard Willes, writing in support of Humphrey Gilbert's ventures to discover the North-West passage, was aware of 'a law denying all Aliens to enter into China, and forbidding all the inhabiters under a great penaltie to let in any stranger into those countryes'.[10] Nevertheless, Thomas Cavendish brought back a map with some notes after his circumnavigation of the globe (see below, pp. 192–7).[11] In 1596 Elizabeth wrote a letter to the Emperor asking if two merchants, Richard Allot and Thomas Bromefield, might be permitted to trade with the Chinese.[12] Unfortunately, their fleet perished at sea.[13]

Descriptions of European contact with the Chinese were far more extensive in Purchas's collection of voyages than in Hakluyt's—although Hakluyt had included a translation of a Portuguese treatise on China in Latin and a collection of reports of China translated by Richard Willes.[14] The obvious reason was that Purchas was not limited to English voyages as

---

[6] Graham, *British Empire*, 12.

[7] Fernand Braudel, *Civilisation and Capitalism, 15th to 18th Century*, iii: *The Perspective of the World*, trans. Sian Reynolds (London: Collins, 1984), pt. 3.

[8] Calder, *Revolutionary Empire*, 156–63.

[9] Braudel, *Perspective of the World*, 218–22.

[10] Richard Hakluyt, *Principall Navigations of the English Nation*, 12 vols. (Glasgow: MacLehose, 1903), vii. 195.

[11] Hakluyt, *Principall Navigations*, xi. 376–81.

[12] Hakluyt, *Principall Navigations*, xi. 417–21.

[13] Samuel Purchas, *Purchas His Pilgrimes*, 20 vols. (Glasgow: MacLehose, 1905), ii. 288–9.

[14] Hakluyt, *Principall Navigations*, vi. 348–77, 295–327.

Hakluyt had been, but was able to include accounts of the Spanish Jesuits who had made a concerted effort to convert the Chinese in late sixteenth and early seventeenth centuries. I have included one of these here (see below, pp. 198–207). The relationship between England and Japan was similar, despite Hakluyt's best efforts to stimulate interest in the region by including all the information that was available to him at the time.[15] Rather more contact was made in the second decade of the seventeenth century when the East India Company took a serious interest in the trading possibilities of the region, and Purchas was able to include much more material from English voyages in his collection. I have reproduced two relevant extracts here (see below, pp. 219–24).

British trade with India was slightly more extensive but gave no hint of the significance the subcontinent was to have later on for the development of the British Empire.[16] John Newbery and Ralph Fitch's account on their experience at the court of the 'Great Mogul' (1580s) was reprinted by Hakluyt.[17] More substantial contact was made in the early 1600s when the East India Company started to spread its net wider. William Hawkins arrived in Surat on the north-west coast in 1608 and Sir Henry Middleton in 1612. In 1615 James I was persuaded to send an ambassador to the Mogul court, but he failed to secure a proper trading agreement because 'eastern potentates were not interested in haggling over the details of trade with a man from a faraway nation which had so little to offer'.[18] Trade continued on an ad hoc basis between individual merchants. I have included extracts from the unpublished diaries of the Cornish traveller, Peter Mundy (see below, pp. 225–34). These were not published until the early 1900s, but were clearly intended to reach a wider audience. I have selected them for their wide-ranging analysis of Indian life and customs which goes beyond any of the contemporary printed sources.

The first extract included contains observations of the South Sea islanders encountered on Thomas Cavendish's circumnavigation of the globe (see below, pp. 192–7).

[15] Hakluyt, *Principall Navigations*, vi. 327–47.
[16] Graham, *British Empire*, 80–5; Calder, *Revolutionary Empire*, 589–617.
[17] Hakluyt, *Principall Navigations*, v. 450–505.
[18] Calder, *Revolutionary Empire*, 159–60.

Francis Petty, 'The admirable and prosperous voyage of... Thomas Cavendish... into the South Sea, and from thence round about the circumference of the whole earth' (1586–8), Observations of the South Sea Islanders

THOMAS CAVENDISH (1560–92) was one of a number of remarkable Elizabethan seamen and explorers. He is chiefly famous for his circumnavigation of the globe (1586–8), but was also a notable privateer in the West Indies and Americas, and had been involved in the Virginian colonies, earning a reputation for aggression towards the indigenous peoples. Cavendish died at sea attempting to relive the glories of his earlier exploit.[1] Francis Petty was one of his crew on his circumnavigatory voyage.

Petty represents the South Sea islanders within a discourse of 'savagism', noting their nakedness, sporadic friendship and hostility, ignorance, and uncontrollable lust.[2] Clearly, most Europeans could not and did not want to distinguish between the various types of people they discovered in the lands of the New World. Equally significant is the last paragraph reproduced here which shows how keen English sailors were to continue and use their rivalry with the Spanish outside Europe.[3]

See also:

Samuel Purchas, *Hakluytus Posthumous or Purchas His Pilgrimes*, 20 vols. (Glasgow: MacLehose, 1905–7), xvii. 57–199.

---

[1] For details, see *DNB* entry.

[2] See H. C. Porter, *The Inconstant Savage: England and the North American Indian, 1500–1660* (London: Duckworth, 1979); Bernard W. Sheehan, *Savagism and Civility: Indians and Englishmen in Colonial Virginia* (Cambridge: Cambridge Univ. Press, 1980).

[3] Text from Richard Hakluyt, *Principall Navigations*, 12 vols. (Glasgow: MacLehose, 1903), xi. 328–33.

A.D.1588.

The island of Guana one of the Ladrones in 13 degrees and two thirds.

The 3 day of January by sixe of the clocke in the morning wee had sight of one of the islands of Ladrones[1] called the island of Guana, standing in 13 degrees ⅔ toward the North, and sayling with a gentle gale before the winde, by 1 or 2 of the clocke in the afternoone, wee were come up within 2 leagues

---

[1] The Marianas.

of the island, where we met with 60 or 70 sailes of canoas full of Savages, who came off to sea unto us, and brought with them in their boates plantans, cocos, potato rootes, and fresh fish, which they had caught at sea, and helde them up unto us for to truck or exchange with us; which when we perceived, we made fast little pieces of old iron upon small cords and fishing lines, and so vered the iron unto their canoas, and they caught hold of them and tooke off the iron, and in exchange of it they would make fast unto the same line either a potato roote, or a bundle of plantans, which we haled in: and thus our company exchanged with them until they had satisfied themselves with as much as did content them: yet we could not be rid of them. For afterward they were so thicke about the ship, that it stemmed & brake 1 or 2 of their canoas: but the men saved themselves being in every canoa 4, 6, or 8 persons all naked & excellent swimmers and divers. They are of a tawny colour & marveilous fat, & bigger ordinarily of stature then the most part of our men in England, wearing their haire marveilous long; yet some of them have it made up and tyed with a knot on the crowne, & some with 2 knots, much like unto their images which wee saw them have carved in wood, and standing in the head of their boates like unto the images of the devill. Their canoas were as artificially made as any that ever wee had seene: considering they were made and contrived without any edge-toole. They are not above halfe a yard in bredth and in length some seven or eight yardes, and their heades and sternes are both alike, they are made out with raftes of canes and reedes on the starrebordside, with maste and sayle: their sayle is made of mattes of sedges, square or triangle wise: and they saile as well right against the winde, as before the winde: These Savages followed us so long, that we could not be ridde of them: untill in the end our General commanded some halfe dozen harquebuzes to be made ready; and himselfe strooke one of them and the rest shot at them: but they were so yare and nimble, that we could not discerne whether they were killed or no, because they could fall backward into the sea and prevent us by diving. [...]

Commodities of the isles of Ladrones.

The colour and stature of the people of the isles of Ladrones.

Their images.

Artificial canoas.

Canoas sayling right against the winde.

The nimblenes of the people of the Ladrones.

The fifteenth of January wee fell with an island called Capul, and had betwixt the sayd island and another island but an narrowe passage, and a marveilous rippling of a very great tyde with a ledge of rockes lying off the poynt of the island of Capul: and no danger but water ynough a fayre bredth off: and within the point a fayre bay and a very good harborough in foure fathomes water hard aboord the shore within a cables length. About 10 of the clocke in the morning wee came to an anker.

The island of Capul at which our men stayed 9 dayes.

FIG. 8. 'Chart of the World showing the circumnavigation of Drake and Cavendish'
(Judocus Hondius, *Vera Totius Expenditionis Nauticae* (1595))

Our shippe was no sooner come to an anker, but presently there came a
canoa rowing aboord us, wherein was one of the chief Casiques[2] of the
island whereof there be seven, who supposing that we were Spaniardes,
brought us potato rootes, which they call camotas, and greene cocos, in
exchange whereof we gave his company pieces of linnen to the quantitie of
a yard for foure Cocos, and as much linnen for a basket of potato rootes of a
quart in quantitie; which rootes are very good meat, and excellent sweete
either rosted or boyled.

This Casiques skinne was carved and cut with sundry and many strakes
and devises all over his body. We kept him still aboord and caused him to
send those men which brought him aboord backe to the island to cause the
rest of the principals to come aboord: who were no sooner gone on shore,
but presently the people of the island came downe with their cocos and
potato rootes, and the rest of the principals likewise came aboord and
brought with them hennes and hogges: and they used the same order
with us which they doe with the Spaniardes. For they tooke for every hog
(which they cal Balboye) eight rials of plate, and for every henne or cocke
one riall of plate. Thus we rode at anker all that day, doing nothing but
buying rootes, cocos, hennes, hogges, and such things as they brought,
refreshing our selves marveilously well. [...]

*Hennes and
hogges.*

We roade for the space of nine dayes about this island of Capul, where we
had diverse kindes of fresh victuals, with excellent fresh water in every bay,
and great store of wood. The people of this island go almost all naked and are
tawny of colour. The men weare onely a stroope about their wastes, of some
kinde of linnen of their owne weaving, which is made of plantan leaves, and
another stroope comming from their backe under their twistes, which
covereth their privie parts, and is made fast to their girdles at their navels.

*The maner of the
people of Capul.*

These people use a strange kinde of order among them, which is this.
Every man and man-childe among them hath a nayle of Tynne thrust quite
through the head of his privie part, being split in the lower ende and
rivetted, and on the head of the nayle is as it were a crowne: which is driven
through their privities when they be yong, and the place groweth up againe,
without any great paine to the child: and they take this nayle out and in, as
occasion serveth: and for the truth thereof we our selves have taken one of
these nailes from a sonne of one of the kings which was of the age of 10
yeeres, who did weare the same in his privie member.

A strange thing.

---

[2] Nobles or leaders.

This custome was granted at the request of the women of the countrey, who finding their men to be given to the fowle sinne of Sodomie, desired some remedie against that mischiefe, and obteined this before named of the magistrates. Moreover all the males are circumcised, having the foreskinne Circumcision. of their flesh cut away. These people wholly worship the devill, and often times have conference with him, which appeareth unto them in most ugly and monstrous shape.

On the 23 day of January, our Generall M. Thomas Candish caused al the principals of this island, and of an hundred islands more, which he had made to pay tribute unto him (which tribute was in hogges, hennes, potatoes and cocos,) to appeare before him, and made himselfe and his company knowne unto them, that they were English men, and enemies to the Spaniardes: and thereupon spredde his Ensigne and sounded up the drummes, which they much marvelled at: to conclude, they promised both The inhabitants of Capul with all the islands themselves and all the islands thereabout to ayde him, whensoever hee adjoyning, shoulde come againe to overcome the Spaniardes. Also our Generall gave promise to ayde them, in token that wee were enemies to the Spaniardes, money backe the English againe for all their tribute which they had payed: which they tooke mar- against the Spaniards. veilous friendly, and rowed about our shippe to shewe us pleasure marveil-ous swiftly: at the last our generall caused a saker to be shot off, whereat they wondered, and with great contentment took their leaves of us.

'A Letter of Father Diego De Pantoia ... to Father Luys De Guzman ... written [from] the Court of the King of China' (9 March 1602)

THE following account is taken from a translation printed in *Purchas His Pilgrimes*. Purchas collected extensive material on China and Japan, reflecting an increased trade interest in the area after the establishment of the East India Company in 1600.[1] He included several accounts from Spanish sources, as Spanish Jesuits had been assiduous in establishing missions in China in the late sixteenth century, including this one from a priest who entered China in 1599.[2] Not Surprisingly, numerous descriptions of China emphasized the fabulous wealth to be found there—a constant feature of descriptions since Marco Polo's visit—and pagan superstition.[3]

See also:

Richard Hakluyt, *The Principall Navigations*, 12 vols. (Glasgow: MacLehose, 1903), vi. 295–327, 348–77.
Samuel Purchas, *Hakluytus Posthumous or Purchas His Pilgrimes*, 20 vols. (Glasgow: MacLehose, 1905–7), xi. 408–43, 474–565; xii. 59–221.

[1] Purchas printed the details of the Company's charter; *Purchas His Pilgrimes*, 20 vols. (Glasgow: MacLehose, 1905–7), ii. 366–91.
[2] Purchas includes a History of the Jesuits in the Far East; *Purchas His Pilgrimes*, xii. 239–331.
[3] Text from Purchas, *Purchas His Pilgrimes*, xii. 374–83. I have omitted some marginal notes.

THEIR MONEYS, APPARELL, PERSONS, TRADES, WEALTH, LEARNING, MARRIAGES, SUPERSTITIONS, RITES, AND OPINIONS

Timber plenty. There is in this Kingdome great store of Timber; for proofe whereof wee need no more but to see the multitude of Barges laden therewith so good cheape as it is. And therefore I thinke a man may build a ship with all things necessary thereunto, three parts of foure better cheape then in our Countrey. *Much Gold to be bought in China.* They use not Gold, though there be much to be bought, but all is Silver, which they doe not coyne in Money, but cast it in Barres, and when they would buy any thing, they cut it and weigh it in certayne fine Weights

like the Romane Weights in our Countrey: and therefore every body that
will buy or sell, carryeth one of those Weights with them. Great store of
Silver commeth out of forreine Countreys. But the chiefe Masse of it is out
of the Mynes of the Kingdome it selfe, as also the Gold. When they buy or
sell, they try the Silver of how many Kiliates it is: and one is worth more,
another lesse, according to the goodnesse thereof. It was very necessary for
the Chinois to weigh and try their Silver, and not to coyne it into money:
for otherwise there would have beene a thousand deceits, wherein the
Chinois are very cunning. They use Brasse Money, wherein also they try   *Brasse money used*
that which is true or false: for in all sorts there is deceit and mixture. They   *in China.*
have the best Porcelane that hitherto hath beene found, which is exceeding
good cheape, and in such plentie, that besides all the Kingdome of China
doth furnish it selfe thereof, they send forth as many ships ladings as they
will.

For their Apparell, though they have great abundance and cheapnesse,
yet in goodnesse they may not compare with out Countrey. There is much
Silke and that very good, but they know not how to dresse it. They make
good Damaskes, razed Velvets, Taffataes, and other sorts: but the colours,
though at the first sight they seeme reasonable, are quickly lost and fade
away. The ordinary apparell of the common people is of blacke cloth made
of Cotton, or of certayne shags of Silke, which are very great, farre greater
then a flocke, which only serve for this purpose, and are very warme.
Persons of Honour weare commonly an outward Garment of Silke which
they use in Visitations, and other like Actions: And there are many which
always goe abroad apparelled in Silke, but not in such great number as that
Booke setteth downe, whereof I made mention before. All men, even to the
very Souldiers, weare their apparell long downe to the in-step of the foot,
with very broad sleeves, open before, and fastened to the sides beneath the
arme. They be so well contented and pleased with their manner of apparell,
that they think there is none in the World comparable to theirs. And in very
truth they bee grave and modest, and especially those of the Mandarins,
which differeth from all others, saving the Bonzi, which shave their Beards
and Heads. All the men and women let their Hayre grow long, and the men
trusse it up, and wind it on a knot on the top of their crowne. They weare
certayne Nets on their heads like Coyfes, made very cunningly of Horse-
hayre: and in the Summer time many weare Caps and Hats of the same.
There are many sorts of Caps or Hats (for I know not what their severall
names are) according to the state of every one. The basest sort which the

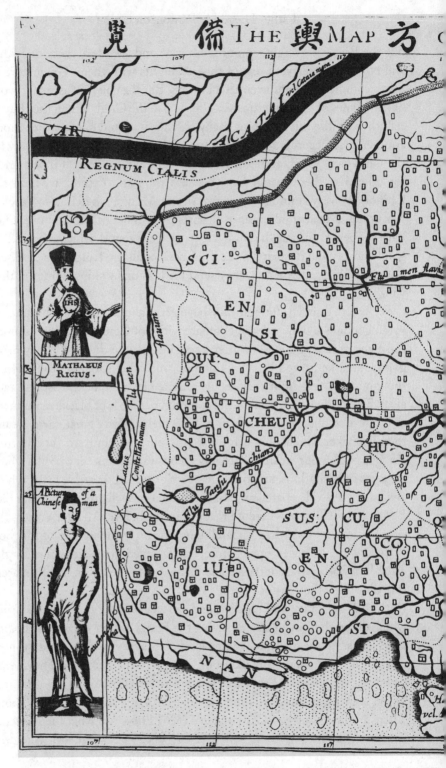

FIG. 9. 'Map of China' (Samuel Purchas, *Hakluytus Posthumus or Purchase His Pilgrimes* (1625), III, pp. 400–1)

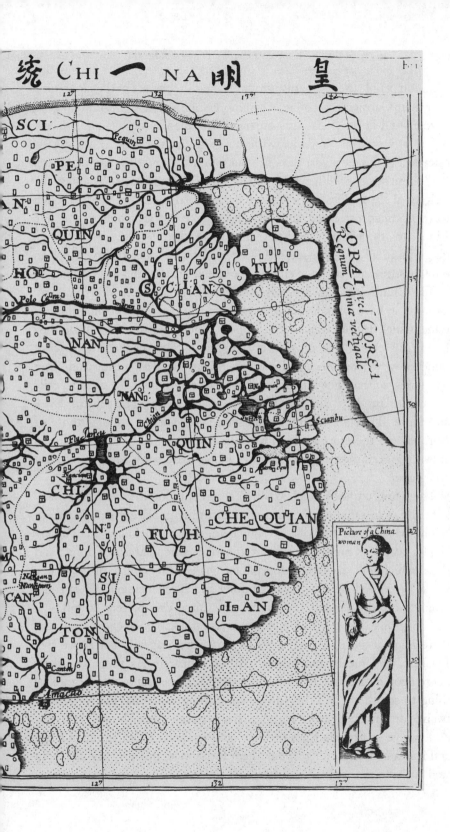

繞 CHI 一 NA 明 皇

SCI

PE

QUIN

HO

AN

Pequm

POLE Colm

NAN

NAN

Chiu

Flue Infou

Blancieu

CHI

AN

FU CH

SI

Nchgan

Ninghuu

CAN

TON

Canth

Amacto

S CI AN

TUM

Na Anquur

Suhoci

Chiu

QUIN

Icug cyu

CHE QU'IAN

I AN

Scuanbu

CORAI vel COREA
Regnum China vectigale

Picture of a China woman

127   132   137

127   132   137

common people use ordinarily is round. Their shooes, are of the same stuffe that their Garments are of, very commonly of Silke made with many faire borders and knots. It is a discourtesie for a man to be seene (especially before any man of Worship) without a Cap on his head. They greatly esteeme for the most part things of our Countrey, and they are very deare. And some pieces of Silke which the Portugall Merchants brings, especially Velvets of three Piles, are far more dearer then their owne. All woollen cloth is much esteemed and very deare, likewise Chamblets, and fine Linnen-cloth, which they bring from India are very deare. Looking-glasses, and all things made of Glasse, and many other things, which in our Countrey are very good cheape, are here deare, and in great estimation.

The Chineses have commonly little Beards, small Eyes, and Noses, and all of them have black Eyes, so that they much marvelled at the colour of mine, which are of Gray or Iron colour (which they never saw) and they find many secrets in them, and very commonly they say, that these eyes of mine know where stones and precious things are, with a thousand other Mysteries, so that they thinke they have Letters in them. To paint an evil-favoured man, they paint him in short apparell, with a great Beard, Eyes, and Nose. They are commonly all white, yet not so white as those of Europe: and therefore to them we seeme very white. The Learned men are very grave, of very good capacitie, and appeare outwardly very modest and grave.

Trades.

There are Artificers of all Arts that are in our Countrey, and very many with the selfe-same manner forme of Instruments. Every man is free to follow what Trade he will, without being bound to follow his Fathers Trades, as divers times I have heard it spoken when I was in Europe: and those which will may study, forsake, or change that course of life. They worke very good cheape: but in cunning and excellencie ours most commonly excell them much, though in some things they be very skilfull.

Servants cheape.

The service of young men and maydes is easie and good cheape, because there is great store of people, so that a yeares wages is not above two Duckets, and meate and drinke, without apparell. As there are many poore people that have many Sonnes and Daughters, it is a very ordinary thing to sell them, and this the cheapest thing in China. For a youth of twelve or fifteene yeares without any naturall blemish will cost not past twelve or fifteene Rials of Plate, and in time of Dearth much lesse, and it is a common thing to buy them for service; though they use them well, and marry them at their time.

Sale of children vile.

Although the abundance and riches of this Kingdome be very great, as the people also is: yet there is no body that is very rich, neyther in any state *None very rich.* of people may they compare in this point with our Countrey. You shall not find in China, which is able to spend twenty thousand Duckets of Rent, how neere of Kinne soever he be to the King, and very few, and those easie to bee numbred that can spend ten thousand Duckets, and the ordinary is no more which they possesse then that which their Lands and Offices yeeld them, which is not great. But though it bee true that those of our Countrey possesse much more Silver, considering the cheapnesse of things in their *Yet as rich as ours* Countrey, all commeth to one account. *very rich.*

There are very few of the poore people idle, because all of them com- *Few idle.* monly take paines, and earne their living. Though the multitude of the Nation be so many, and the Kingdome so great, yet the surnames of all the *Surnames.* Kingdome are not above three hundred, and all of one syllable.

There are some, though very few, which may be called Knights, which *Knights.* for service to the Kings in some necessities have given them Offices in succession: but the common use is not to have any Nobilitie by Descent in China; neyther can any man say, I am of a better House then you. But the honour and Nobilitie dependeth wholly upon Learning, and to obtayne *Nobilitie only in* degrees and Offices of Mandarins. And therefore an House which now is in *Learning.* Office, and his Father bee one, if he have a Sonne a Doctor, which is made a Mandarin, he is honourable, and the honour continueth as long as the Learned men and Mandarins doe live. There is no man, neyther Kinsman *No Lord but the* nor not Kinsman of the King which hath ever a Village of his owne that *King.* payeth him Tribute: but all men pay it to the King; and hee giveth stipends and wages to the Mandarins, so that they receive nothing of particular men by right, though they extort much continually by oppression. *Extortion.*

Commonly the Chinois doe marry from fifteene to eighteene and *Marriage.* twentie yeares, and all of them doe marrie one Wife that is chiefe; and this is their lawfull Marriage. On the day of their Marriage, when the Bride doth passe to the House of her Husband, shee carrieth openly before her through the streets all the things which she bringeth with her, and all her house-hold stuffe: But besides her they may marrie (I say they may keepe and doe keepe as many as they are able) as many Wives as they will, which *Polygamie.* for the most part they buy: and afterward when they will, sell them away againe. They may not only not marrie with any Kinswomen of their Wives, but with none of that surname, though they have no shew of Alliance. The sonnes of the Concubines doe likewise inherit, and there is little or no *Inheritance.*

difference in their state and honour, to be the Sonne of the lawfull Wife or of the other, neyther make they any question of it.

Funerals and mournings.
The thing wherein the Chinois are most observant, Ceremonious and Superstitious, is in their Burials, Funerals, and Mournings: for herein they shew their obedience and love to their Parents, whereof their bookes are full. It is a very ordinary thing to have great respect to their Father and Mother, and the disobedient are grievously punished. Many grave men and Mandarins begge leave of the King to leave their Offices which they have, and to goe home to keepe their Father and Mother company, yeelding for a reason that they be old, and that they would goe to serve them. And it is a Petition in the sight of all men so just, that they grant it very usually. When the Father or the Mother dieth, all the Sonnes and Daughters (from the King to the meanest Peasant) doe mourne for three yeares. The mourning colour, which among us is blacke Bayes, among them is white Linnen, whereof they make all their apparell even to the Cap. The first monethes they weare a very rough Sack-cloth, girded with a Coard, like the bare-footed Friers. And though he be never so great a Mandarin, without any exception (save only the Mandarins of the Warre) assoone as hee heareth newes of the death of any of his Parents, he is to leave his Office and Dignitie, and all other Employment whatso-ever of Government and Examinations of obtayning his degree, and is to goe home for three yeares to burie his Father or Mother (and to mourne and bewaile them). The grave men which have an house for this purpose, doe not straitway burie their dead, but keepe them two or three yeares in the house, in a Chamber which they keepe for this Office, and it is not the worst in the house: and very usually or every day they go thither to make them a thousand Ceremonies and Reverences, and to burne Incense, and other sweet savours, and to set over the place where they be laid, meate to eate; and at severall times, many of those Bonzi doe meet, and with great Ceremonies begin their Service and Prayers, and their Sonnes, Kinsefolkes and Wives make lamentation. The Mandarins do not only leave their Offices, and change their Weeds, but also all the things which they did use. Many sit not in Chaires, but upon low Stooles: they visit, or suffer themselves to be seene very seldome: they change even the very Paper wherein they write, wherein they have a piece of another colour, in token of mourning: when they name themselves in their Letters, they use not the name which they did at other times, but others proper to the partie, as when he nameth himselfe, hee calleth himselfe disobedient,

Three yeares mourning in white Linnen.

Keeping the dead at home.

Other Funerall Rites.

signifying, that by his disobedience to his Parents he did not preserve them alive.

They use no kind of Musicke, and many change their ordinarie Diet into courser food. Upon the Funerall day they provide great company: many *Funerall day.* Kinsfolkes and Friends meete together, all clad in white, with many Bonzi, (according to every mans abilitie) which sing with dolefull Instruments. And by their apparell which they weare, and their time in singing, hee that knew them not, would take them for Clerkes revested, singing plaine Song; for they much resemble them. They make many Beeres with men of Paper or of white Silke, many Banners and other Ensignes. The place whither the Corps goeth is adorned with many figures: the Corps is put into a very great *Funerall Figures.* Coffin. This Nation holdeth a great part of their felicitie, for them and their Successours to consist in these things of their Funerals, especially in two, the Coffin or Chist wherein the Corps is to be layed, and the place of *Coffin.* their buriall. The stuffe to make the Coffin of, wherein themselves are to bee buried, and the making of the Coffin, they leave not to others to doe after their deathes, neither then may the body looke for much cost to make one of these Coffins, neither in this (as a thing of great importance) will they trust, no not their owne Sons: but they themselves at leisure seeke some kind of Wood that is least corruptible, and Plankes which are commonly foure, sixe, or eight fingers thicke: which because they bee so thicke, and the Chists or Coffins very closely shut they can keepe their Corps in their Houses without any evill smell. Some spend in making their Coffin seventy, eighty, and an hundred Duckets. They hold it for a felicity to be able to get one of these that is good; on the contrary for a great disgrace, not to have a Coffin to burie himselfe in, and they are very few which faile in that one point.

The Sepulchre and place thereof is the thing for choosing whereof they *Buriall place.* use great Sorcerie or casting of Lots, and doe it with great heedfulnesse, and with the helpe of some that are skilfull in this Art. For they hold opinion, that in making a good choice of the place dependeth a great part of their owne good fortune and of their Posteritie. And oftentimes they are a yeare in resolving whether it shall looke toward the North, or to any other part. And therefore the greatest and most contentious Sutes which are in China, are about places of Burials. These places of Burials are alwayes without the wals in the fields, or Mountaynes wherein they build Vaults very well made and strong of Bricke, stone, or other matter, wherein they lay the Coffin, and then close it up very surely: And afterward now and then they come thither to performe certain Ceremonies, & to bring things to

Unluckie to burie in the Citie.
eat. They hold it very unluckie to burie a dead man in the Citie: and if they know it, though he were the greatest man that is in China, they will not suffer him to bewaile his dead Friends much, especially those which are women. There are many which beleeve the passing of the soules from

Transition of soules. Metempsuchicall Superstition.
one bodie into another: and therefore after the death of their Father and Mother, they will never kill any living beast, yeelding for a reason why they will not doe so, lest some of them should bee their Mother or Father, or some other person. And likewise many of them fast, because, that whereas some of them bee poore; they desire afterward to be borne againe in a rich and honourable Family.

Although it bee true that the most part of them beleeve not in Idols, and it offendeth them not to speake evill of them, yet commonly all of

Idolatrie.
them at a certaine time of the yeare doe them some reverence, because it is the custome, though in no sort they worship them as Gods: and those which put most confidence in them, burne Paper, Incense, and sweet smels unto them, and kill beasts before them. Their Bookes of these Idols speake of Hell, and in many places, or in a manner in all the Cities there is set up a portraiture of Hell made with bodily shapes, and many Devils, as uglie as wee paint them. It is very well set foorth, but badly beleeved: for it serveth only there for a bugbeare. And if any beleeve that

Of Hell.
which the Idols say of Hell, that it is a place of torments, they say, that after so many yeeres be passed, all men come out againe, and are transformed into some beast. Those which beleeve in the Idols, come before them to

Lots.
cast lots to know what things shall come to passe: howbeit I have not heard in all China, that there was any answer of a Divell in an Idoll, as is in other parts, in regard of the small beliefe that they have in them, and the

Wicked Bonzi.
lewdnesse of the Bonzi that serve them. Their houses wherein they set them, whereof as yet I never saw any good one, are commonly verie filthy and stinking.

And besides this consulting of Idols, the Chinois are much given to

Diviners and divinations.
Divinations to know things to come, and whether they shall have good or bad fortune; whether they shall have that which they desire or no: and there bee an infinite number of these South-sayers, and all of them pratlers, mumblers, and cooseners, whereby they deceive many. And though the Chinois be of good understanding, and know that these fellowes know nothing, and every foot doe take them in lyes: yet for all this, there are verie few that when any occasion is offered, doe not consult with them. And

though they seeme to bee but few, yet some of them are in league with the Devill, as oftentimes wee gather by certaine things.

Many of these grave men of China, have commonly two follies, wherein they doe erre more then in other things. The first is, that they perswade themselves that they can much prolong their Lives; and for this purpose *Studies to prolong* they use a thousand inventions, and take many medicines, which indeed *life.* rather doe shorten their dayes. There are many Masters and Bookes of this follie, which usuallie are grave and rich men. There are many that make themselves very old folks, whom the people follow like Saints to learne some rule of life of them, wherein they put all their felicitie. Many doe not beleeve that we are so old, as we say we be, and that we doe dissemble: but that in deed we bee an hundred yeeres old, and that we know this rule to live for ever, and that we doe not Marrie because wee would live long. The other follie is, that they perswade themselves that they are able, and goe about to make Silver, whereof likewise there are many Bookes. They use for this *Bookes of* purpose many Hearbs, and Quick-silver, wherein they spend that little *Alchimie.* Silver which they have, and remaine beggers, but not perswaded but that it is fecible, but that it was not their good lucke, and good fortune: and to obtaine this, many of them fast many yeeres.

Sir Henry Middleton, *Two Accounts of his Voyage to the Moluccas* (1604–6)

AFTER the East India Company was founded in 1600, English merchants made significant efforts to exploit the trade routes to India and East Asia. However, they found themselves in direct competition with the equally bullish Dutch and Portuguese, who were considerably more successful in establishing contact with the inhabitants of the wealthy islands of the Malay Archipelago.[1] In 1604 Sir Henry Middleton, an experienced sailor who had been involved in previous expeditions to the area, was dispatched on a mission to re-establish contact with British merchants left on the Moluccan islands of Ternate and Tidore and so attempt to place trade on an equal footing with England's European rivals for Asian trade.

On his arrival at the islands, Middleton was involved in complex negotiations with the Moluccans, who—according to the English accounts at least—hinted that if Middleton could protect the Moluccas from the Dutch and Portuguese then they could have sole rights to trade with the islanders. Middleton, however, had neither the power nor the authority to make such promises and left for home with his ships laden with enough cloves, pepper, and other spices to give the investors in the company a return on their initial outlay. Although the company's records have not survived, it is likely that Middleton's efforts were deemed satisfactory.[2]

The first extract included here is from Anon., *The Last East-Indian Voyage containing much varietie of the state of the severall kingdomes where they have traded* (1606), written by one of the crew members as a defence of the worth of the expedition and the actions of the company. It gives a fascinating account of the complex negotiations between the English and the Moluccans, precipitated by the intense European rivalries for trade and profit. The second is taken from Edmund Scott's *An Exact Discourse of the Subtilties, Fashions, Pollicies, Religion, and Ceremonies of the* East Indians, *as well* Chyneses *and* Javans, *there abyding and dweling* (1606). Scott was a merchant who was resident in Bantam, Java, from February 1603 until he returned to London with Middleton in October 1605. His observations of the Javanese and Chinese are clearly based on some first-hand experience,

---

[1] For details see Angus Calder, *Revolutionary Empire: The Rise of the English-Speaking Empires from the Fifteenth Century to the 1780s* (London: Cape, 1981), 100–1, 160–2, *passim*.

[2] The account given here is dependent on Sir William Foster's introduction to his *The Voyage of Sir Henry Middleton to the Moluccas, 1604–1606* (London: Hakluyt Society, 1943).

although how closely he was acquainted with either people is a matter for conjecture.[3]

See also:

Samuel Purchas, *Hakluytus Posthumous or Purchas His Pilgrimes*, 20 vols. (Glasgow: MacLehose, 1905–7), vol. xiv.

[3] Texts for both extracts are taken from Foster, *Voyage of Sir Henry Middleton*, 50–1, 56–7, 169–76.

This 13 day [May 1605] our Generall and the maister went to the King of Tarnata, to know whether hee would let him leave a factory in his iland of Tarnata. He answered he should, but willed him to returne the next day, for that he would call a counsell concerning the matter and then would give them an answer. From thence the Generall went aboard the Dutch Admirall, and there told him how the King of Tarnata had promised he should have a factory there; yet nevertthelesse, if he would buy such wares as we had left, and make paiment at Bantam, he should have them. Who answered he thought the King of Tarnata would not forget himselfe so much as to graunt us a factory, considering he had written to His Excellency,[1] and likewise promised him, that they would trade with no nation but with them. And as touching our commodityes, he would not deale withall, for that they had two ships which were sent, one to Bengalla[2] and the other to Cambaia,[3] to buy such commodities; which they dayly expected. Our Generall said he had no reason to crosse him for leaving a factory there, for that Sir Francis Drake had trade in Tarnata before the names of the Hollanders were knowne in those parts of the world. So for that time they parted, either part to take their best advantage for their adventures.

The 14 day, the Generall went againe to the King, to know his answer concerning his factory. He found him aboard a carricole, and one of the Dutch captaines in his company. The Generall told him his comming was according to his appointment. The King made present [i.e. immediate] answer he could grant him no factory, for that he had made promise, by writing and word, to the Hollanders that no nation should have trade with him or his people but onely they. The Generall demanded why he had not

[1] Prince Maurice of Orange, son of William the Silent, was Stadtholder of the United Provinces.
[2] Probably Masulipatam is intended.   [3] Cambay, in western India.

told him so when he saved him from the Tydorians, and then he could have told what to have done. He said both he and his subjects were willing we should tarry there, but the Hollanders did still urge his promise. The Generall, seeing he could not leave a factory, desired him to send such order to Tarnata that hee might have leave to carry those small quantity of cloves as his factors had bought and payed for aboard, and he would trouble neither him nor the Hollanders. The King answered that within seaven dayes he would be there himselfe; desiring the Generall to ride still. He made answer he lived at too great charges to lye still and doe nothing, and therefore could stay no longer, but wold be gone the next morning; and so departed from him. [...]

The 7 day [June 1605], the Generall waited to be sent for to the King; but seeing nobody came, he sent to know the reason. He sent word he was very busie that day and could not intend it till the morrow. The Dutch Admiral had conference with the King twise this day; where belike he had what he desired, for as soone as night came hee departed for Tydore.

The 8 day, the King sent his secretary and one of the Dutch marchants unto him, with a letter sealed with hard waxe; which seale had two letters, an H and a B, which stood for Hance Beerepot,[4] with a marchants marke betweene the letters. This letter they delivered, and told him it was the Kings letter to the King of England. The Generall would not beleeve the King would send so great a prince as the King of England a letter with so little state and a marchants seale upon it. They answered: and if he doubted thereof, they would cause the King to come and justifie it. The Generall said he would not otherwise beleeve it. So they left the letter and departed. Halfe an houre after, came the King and a great traine to our Generals chamber; where, saluting him kindely, they sat downe upon a trunck togither. The King said: I sent you a letter sealed by my secretary; which you have received, making doubt it is not sent by mee, to so great a king, and delivered with so little state and sealed with a marchants seale; now you heard me say thus much, I hope you are satisfied the letter is sent by me and none other; therefore prepare yourselfe tomorrow to bee gone. The General neither would, nor durst, deliver it to the King of England; willing him to take it againe. He would not, but departed.

The 9 [day], Chichell Gegogoe, the Kings uncle, hearing how the Generall had bin used by the King and the Hollanders, came to visit him

---

[4] A popular nickname for a Dutchman.

at his chamber; where there passed much talke betweene them concerning the foresaid counterfeit letter intended to have bin sent (to the disgrace of the Generall) to the King of England; Chichell Gegogoe assuring the Generall that, if it lay in his power, he wold procure of the King that they might leave a factory there; moreover, that, at his next returne to him, he should know the contents of that base and slanderous letter, invented by the Hollanders. And so he departed, with promise to returne the next day.

The people of the country, understanding the Hollanders had procured our banishment, were much offended that the petty prince of Holland and his [people?] (whom they esteemed but debaushed drunkards) should be esteemed before the mighty King of England and his subjects; and knowing we were commanded to depart, brought all their commodities to us, and none to the Hollanders. Whereat they, finding themselves agreeved, caused our beame, that we weighed cloves with, to be taken away; but it was restored againe, by the meanes of Chichell Gegogoe. Which the Hollanders perceiving, they sent to their Admiral at Tydore to returne to Tarnata; which he did, threatning the King that he would leave him and establish a factory at Tydore. Whereupon the King, with the unwilling consent of his councell, gave order for our banishment; sending the Sabendor to our Generall to will him to lingar no longer, but to depart aboard.

THE DESCRIPTION OF JAVA MAJOR, WITH THE MANNER AND FASHIONS OF THE PEOPLE, BOTH JAVANS AND CHINESES, WHICH DOE THERE INHABITE

[...] The Javans houses are altogether built of great canes and some few small timbers, being sleight buildings. In many of the principall mens houses is good workemanship shewed, as carvings, &c. And some of the chiefest have a square brick rowme, being built in no better forme than a bricke-kill[n]; which is onely to put in all their houshold stuffe when fier commeth; but they seldome or never lodge nor eat in them.

There are many small rivers running thorough the towne. Also there is a good rhode for ships; whereby, if they were people of any reasonable capacitie, it would be made a verie goodly citie. Also it is walled round with a bricke wall, being verie warlike built, with flankers and turrets scowring everie way. I have been told by some that it was first built by the

Chineses, and by others that it was first built by the Portingales; wherefore I cannot say certainely by which of them it was first built; but it is most likelye by the Chineses, by reason of the oldnesse of it, for in many places it is fallen to decay for want of repayring.

At the verie west end of this towne is the China towne; a narrow river parting them, which runneth crosse the end of the China towne up to the Kings court, and so thorough the middle of the great towne, and doth ebb and flowe, so that at a high water both galleys and junckes of great burthen may goe up to the middle of the great towne. This China towne is for the most part built of bricke; everie house square and flat overhead, having bordes and smale timbers or split canes layd over crosse, on which is layd bricks and sand, to defend them from fire. Over these bricke warehouses is set a shed, being built up with great canes and thatched; and some are built up with small timbers, but the greatest number with canes onely. Of late yeares, since wee came thether, many men of wealth have built their houses to the top all fire-free; of the which sort of houses, at our first comming, there was no more but the Sabindars house and the rich China marchants house; which, neverthelesse, by meanes of their windowes and sheds round about them, have been consumed with fire.

In this [China] towne stand the English and Dutch houses; which are built in the same manner, onely they are verie much bigger and higher than the ordinarie houses. And the Dutchmen of late, though with great cost and trouble, have built one of their houses up to the top all of bricke, fire-free, as they suppose.

The King of this place is absolute, and since the deposing and death of the late Emperour of Damacke is held the principall king of that island. He useth alway marshall law uppon any offender whome hee is disposed to punish. More, if any private mans wife, or wives, bee taken with dishonestie (so that they have good proofe of it), they have power in their owne hands to cause them presently to be put to death, both man and woman. And for their slaves, they may execute them for any small fault. If the King send for any subject or stranger dwelling or being in his dominions, if he send a man, the partie may refuse to come; but if once he send a woman, hee may not refuse nor make no excuse. Moreover, if any inferiour bodie have a suit to a man of authoritie, if they come not themselves, they alwayes send a woman; neither doe they ever come or send but they present the party they sue too with some present, be their suite never so small. To everie wife that a Javan (being a free man) marrieth, he must keep 10 women slaves, which they as ordinarie use as their wives; and some of them keepe for every wife 40 slaves, for, so they keepe 10, they may have as many more as they will; but they may have but 3 wives onely.

The Javans are generally exceeding proud; although extreame poore, by reason that not one amongst a hundreth of them will worke. The gentlemen of this land are brought to be poore by the number of slaves that they keepe, which eat faster than their pepper or rise groweth. The Chineses do both plant, dresse and gather the pepper, and also sowe their rise; living as slaves under them, but they sucke away all the wealth of the land, by reason that the Javans are so idle. And a Javan is so proude that he will not endure one to sit an inch higher in height above him, if hee bee but of the like calling. They are a people that do very much thirst after blood. If any Javan have committed a fact worthy of death and that he be pursued by any, whereby he thinketh hee shall die, he will presently draw his weapon and cry *Amucke*, which is as much [as] to say: I am resolved;[5] not sparing to murther either man, woman, or childe which they can possibly come at; and he that killeth most dieth with greatest honor and credit. They will seldom fight face to face with one another, or with any other nation, but do altogether seek revenge of their enemie cowardly, albeit they are, for the most part, men of a goodlie stature. Their law for murther is to pay a fine to the King, and that but a small summe; but evermore the friends of the partie murthered will be revenged on the murtherer or his kindred. So that the more they kill one another, the more fines or profite hath their King.

Their ordinarie weapon which they weare is called a crise. It is about two foote in length; the blade beeing waved and crooked too and fro, indenture[6] like, and withall exceeding sharpe; most of them having the temper of their mettall poysoned, so that not one amongst five hundred that is wounded with them in the bodie escapeth with his life. The handles of these weapons are either of horne or wood, curiously carved in the likenesse of a divell, the which many of them do worship. In their warres their fight is altogether with pikes, dartes, and targets. Of late some few of them have learned to use their peeces [i.e. muskets], but verie untowardly.

The gentilitie, both men and women, never goe abroad but they have a pike borne before them. The apparrell of the better sort is a tucke on their heads, and about their loynes a faire pintado; all the rest of their bodies

---

[5] This is wrong. *Amok* means 'a furious attack'.
[6] The wavy line along which a document was separated from its counterfoil as a ready means of identification.

naked. Sometimes they will weare a loose coate, somewhat like a mandil-lion,[7] of velvet, chamlet[8] cloth, or some other kind of silke; but it is but seldome, and uppon some extraordinarie ocasion. The common sort weare on their heads a flat cap of velvet, taffata, or callico cloth, the which is cut in many peeces and seamed with a faire stitch, to make them sit flatte and compasse. About they loynes they weare a kinde of callico cloth, which is made at Clyn, in manner of a silke girdle,[9] but at the least two yards broad, beeing of two cullours.

Also there commeth from thence many sorts of white callicoes, which they themselves doe both die, paint, and guild, according to the fashions of that countrey. Likewise they can weave a kind of striped stuffe, both of cotten and rinds of trees; but by meanes of their laysinesse there is very little of that worne.

The men, for the most part, have verie thicke curled haire on their heads; in which they take great pride, and often will goe bareheaded to shew it. The women goe all bareheaded; some of them having their haire tucked up like a carthorse tayle, but the better sort doe tucke it up like our riding geldings tayles. About their loynes they weare of the same stuffes which I have before mentioned; always having a faire girdle or pintado of their countrey fashion throwne over one of their shoulders, which hangeth downe loose behinde them.

The principallest of them are most religious; but they very seldome goe to church. They doe acknowledge Christ to be a great prophet, whom they call *Naby Isat*; and some of them do keepe of Mahomets priestes in their houses. But the common people have very little knowledge in any religion; onely they say there is a God which made heaven and earth and them also. Hee is good (they say) and will not hurt them; but the Divell is naught and will doe them hurt; wherefore many of them, for want of knowledge, doe pray to him onely, for feare least he should hurt them. And surely, if there were men of learning (which were perfect in their language) to instruct them, a number of them would be drawne to the true fayth of Christ, and also would be brought to civilitie. For many which I have reasoned with concerning the lawes of Christians have liked all well, excepting onely their pluralitie of women, for they are all very lasciviously given, both men and women.

---

[7] A loose overcoat, worn by soldiers and men-servants.
[8] Camlet. The stuff so called was supposed to be made of camel's hair and silk, but other materials were often used.
[9] The skirt commonly worn by both sexes.

The better sort which are in authoritie are great takers of bribes; and all the Javans in generall are badd paymasters when they are trusted. Notwithstanding, their lawes for debts are so strict that the creditour may take his debtour, his wives, children, and slaves, and all that hee hath, and sell them for his debt.

Likewise they are all much given to stealing, from the highest to the lowest. And surely in times past they have been no better then maneaters,[10] before trafficke was had with them by the Chyneses; which, as I have heard some of them say, is not above one hundred yeares since.

They delight much in ease and musicke. And for the most part they spend the day sitting crosse-legged like a taylor, whitling of stickes; whereby many of them become very good carvers to carve their cryse handles; and that is all the worke the most of them indevour to doe.

They are very great eaters; but the gentlemen allow their slaves nothing but rice, sodden in water, with some rootes and hearbes. And they have a certaine hearbe called *bettaile*, which they usually have carryed with them wheresoever they goe, in boxes or wrapped up in cloath, like a sugerloafe; and also a nutt called *pinange*;[11] which are both in operation very hott, and they eate them continually, to warme them within and keepe them from the fluxe. They doe likwise take much tobacco and opium.

The Javans themselves are very dull and blockish to mannage any affaires of a commonwealth; whereby all strangers goe beyond them that come into their land. And many of the countrey of Clyn, which commeth thither to dwell, doe grow very rich and rise to great offices and dignitie amongst them, as their Sabendar, their Caytomongon, and others.[12] But especially the Chyneses, who, like Jewes, live crooching under them, but robb them of their wealth and send it for Chyna.

The Chyneses are very craftie people in trading, using all kind of cosoning and deceit which may possible be devised. They have no pride in them, nor will refuse any labour; except they turne Javans (as many of them doe when they have done a murther or some other villanie). Then they are every whit as proud and as loftie as the Javans.

For their religion, they are of divers sectes, but the most of them are atheists. And many of them hold opinion that, when they die, if they be

---

[10] Accusations of cannibalism against the inhabitants of the Malayan Archipelago are common.
[11] *Pinang* is the Malay name of the areca nut. The chewing of this with a betel leaf was a widespread practice in the East.
[12] Names of high-ranking positions in Javanese Society.

good men, they shal be borne againe to great riches and be made governours; and if they be wicked men, then they should be turned into some uglie
beast, as a frogge or a toad.

They burne sacrifice every new moone, mumbling prayers over them,
with a kinde of singing voyce; and as they sing, they ting a litle bell, which
at the end of every prayer they ring out as fast as ever they can. This
ceremonie they also use when any amongst them of acount lyeth a dying.
The maner of their sacrifice is this. They furnish their altars with goates,
hennes, duckes, and divers sortes of fruites; the which are sometimes
dressed to eate and sometimes raw, and then are dressed afterwardes and
eaten. All that they burne is onely papers, painted and cut out in curious
workes, and valued by them at a certaine price. I have many times asked
them to whom they burne their sacrifice, and they have answered mee: to
God. But the Goserats and Turkes which are there say they burne it to the
Divell. If they doe so, they are ashamed to confesse it.

They are many of them well seene [i.e. skilled] in astronomie, and keepe
a good account of their months and yeares.

They observe no Sabboth, nor one day better then other; except they lay
the foundation of a house, or begin some other great worke; which day they
ever after observe as a holiday.

When any of them that are wealthie die in Bantam, their bodyes are
burnt to ashes; which ashes they put up close in jarres and carrie it to China
to their friends.

I have seene, when some of them have lien a dying, they have set up 7
odowres burning; 4 of them being great and burning light, and they were
set upon a cane, which lay crosse upon two crotches, about sixe foote from
the ground; and three set on the ground right under them, beeing verie
small and burning dimme. I have demaunded the meaning of it many
times, but I could never have other answere but that it was the fashion of
China. And surelie many suchlike thinges they doe, not knowing why or
wherefore, but onely that it hath been a fashion amongst them.

They delight verie much in playes and singing; but they have the worst
voyces that one shall heare any people have. The which playes or interludes
they holde as service to their god; in the beginning of which they often use
to burne a sacrifice, the priestes many times kneeling downe and kissing the
ground three times, one presently after another. These playes are made
commonly when they thinke their junckes or shipping are set foorth from
China; likewise when they are arived at Bantam, and also when they set out

from Bantam towardes China. Sometimes they begin at noone and ende not till the next day morning; beeing most commonly in the open streete, having staiges set up for the purpose.

Moreover, they have amongst them some southsayers, which sometimes rage and run up and downe the streetes like madd-men, having swordes drawne in their handes, tearing their haire and throwing themselves against the ground. When they are in this franticke taking, they affirme (and other Chineses beleeve) that they can tell what shall come to passe aforehand. Whether they bee possest with the Divell or no, which revealeth something to them, I know not; but manie Chineses use them when they sende a juncke of any voyage, to know whether they shall speede well or no; and (by their report) it hath fallen out according as those southsayers have tolde them.

The Javans use playes too; but they have no more but some historie painted on a carde or mappe, the which one maketh relation of, with such jesture as befitteth the matter. Likewise, there be puppet playes, made by certaine people of Clyn which dwell there; the which puppets are apparrelled like unto the Christian manner; and they have lions and divers kinde[s] of beasts, artificially made, with which they performe their sport verie pretilie. But these hold the playes no poynt of religion or service to their gods, as the people of China doe.

The Chineses are apparrelled in long gownes, wearing kirtles under them hanging something lower then their gownes. They are surely the most effeminate and cowardliest people that live. On their heades they weare a caull;[13] some of them beeing made of silke, and some of haire. The haire of their heades is verie long; which they bind up on a knot right on the crowne of their heads. The nobilitie and governours weare hoodes of sundry fashions; some beeing one halfe like a hatte and the other like a French hood; others beeing of netwarke, with a high crowne and no brimmes.

Those people are tall and strong of bodie; having all verie small blacke eyes, and verie few have any haire on their faces. They will steale and doe any kind of villanie to get wealth.

Their manner at Bantam is to buy women slaves (for they bring no women out of China), by whom they have manie children. And when they returne to their owne countrey, not minding to come to Bantam againe,

---

[13] Net-work for the hair.

they sell their women, but their children they carrie with them. As for their goodes, they take an order to send some at everie shipping; for if they die in Bantam, all the goods they have there is the Kinges. And if once they cut their haire, they may never returne to their countrie againe; but their children may, always provided that they never cut their haire.

Two Accounts of Japan: Arthur Hatch (1623) and John Saris (1613)

JAPAN had been known to educated Western readers since it had been depicted in Marco Polo's *Travels* written at the start of the thirteenth century.[1] Once Polo had represented the 'island' as a land of untold wealth with 'gold in great abundance', it had figured in the imagination of travellers as a desirable goal.[2] John Cabot, the Venetian explorer employed by Henry VII, after his success in landing at Newfoundland (1497), boasted that he would sail to 'Cipango [Japan], where he thought all the spices and jewels in the world had their origin, and set up a "factory" there'.[3] English contact was minimal until William Adams sailed to Japan in 1598 and subsequently lived there until his death in 1621, confirming reports of the abundance of riches in a letter to Purchas in 1611.[4] The East India Company sponsored some early voyages to Japan and there was a small amount of trade, which was conducted in terms of a fierce rivalry with the Dutch and the Portuguese.

The following two accounts are taken from a letter dated 25 November 1623, to Samuel Purchas from Arthur Hatch, evidently a merchant who had spent some time in Japan, and a longer account of the eighth voyage sponsored by the East India Company undertaken by Captain John Saris (1611–13). The latter provides an interesting observation on Japanese theatre, comparing women actors to their English male counterparts. Both accounts were collected by Purchas.[5]

See also:

Richard Hakluyt, *The Principall Navigations*, 12 vols. (Glasgow: Mac-Lehose, 1903), vi. 327–47.
Samuel Purchas, *Hakluytus Posthumous or Purchas His Pilgrimes*, 20 vols. (Glasgow: MacLehose, 1905–7), ii. 326–46.

---

[1] Marco Polo, *The Travels*, trans. R. E. Latham (Harmondsworth: Penguin, 1958), 243–8.

[2] Polo, *Travels*, 244.

[3] Angus Calder, *Revolutionary Empire: The Rise of the English-Speaking Empires from the Fifteenth Century to the 1780s* (London: Cape, 1981), 16.

[4] Samuel Purchas, *Hakluytus Posthumous or Purchas His Pilgrimes*, 20 vols. (Glasgow: MacLehose, 1905–7), ii. 326–46.

[5] Text from Purchas, *Purchas His Pilgrimes*, x. 83–8; ii. 355–519, at pp. 447–8.

ARTHUR HATCH

A LETTER TOUCHING JAPON WITH THE GOVERNMENT, AFFAIRES AND LATER OCCURRENTS THERE, WRITTEN TO ME BY MASTER ARTHUR HATCH MINISTER, LATELY RETURNED THENCE

Salutem in authore salutis.

Description of Japon.

[...] The Countrey of Japan is very large and spacious, consisting of severall Ilands and pettie Provinces; it is Mountainous and craggie, full of Rockes and stonie places, so that the third part of this Empire is not inhabited or manured; neither indeed doth it affoord that accommodation for Inhabitants which is needfull, or that fatnesse and conveniencie for the growth of Corne, Fruit, and small grayne as is requisite; which causeth the people to select the choysest and plainest parts and places of the land both to till and dwell in. The Climate is temperate and healthie not much pestred with infectious or obnoxious ayres, but very subject to fierce windes, tempestuous stormes, and terrible Earthquakes, insomuch that both Ships in the harbour have beene over-set, and driven a shore by the furie of the one, and Houses on the land disjoynted and shaken to pieces by the fearefull trembling of the other.

Soyle.

Climate.

Stormes. Earthquakes.

Emperour and Government. 65. Vassals.

It is governed by an Emperour who hath threescore and five Kings under his command; they have but small and pettie Kingdomes, yet all of them challenge and assume to themselves that Royall state and dignitie, which may well become the persons of farre more famous Princes. There are but five of the Emperours privie Counsell, who commonly are such, that for Wisdome, Policie, and carefull vigilancie in managing the State affaires, in preventing of Treasons and Rebellions, in executing of Justice and continuing of peace and quietnesse may bee compared with many, nay most in Christendome. No man may make knowne any cause unto the Emperour himselfe, either by word of mouth or petition, but every one must acquaint the Counsell with his cause, and if they approve it, the Emperour shall know of it, if not, you must be content to have it drowned in oblivion. The Emperour lives in great Royaltie and seldome goes abroad either to Hawke or Hunt without a thousand followers at least to attend him: he hath but one Wife, and it is generally reported that hee keepes companie with no

Councell.

Magnificence.

Chastitie.

other, but her onely; and if it bee true as it is thought, hee may in that respect be tearmed the Phoenix of all those parts of the world: as for those within his owne Dominions they are so farre either from imitating or following him, that one is scarcely contented with a hundred women, and they are so shamelesse in that kinde, that they will boast of it, and account it a glory unto them to make relation of the multitude of women which they have had the use of. Consuetudo peccandi tollit sensum peccati.[1] This Emperour hath abundance of Silver and Gold, and not onely his Coffers but whole Store-houses are cramm'd with coyne; hee hath some balls of Gold which were brought to his Court from Ozechya Castle of that waight and magnitude, that fifteene or sixteene men are scarcely able to beare one of them.

Riches.

All Rivers doe in a kinde of thankfull renumeration returne their waters to the Sea, because they tooke them from thence, but the Princes of Japon doe cleane contrarie, for they receive nothing from the Emperour, and yet they give all to the Emperour, for they doe even impoverish themselves, by enriching him by presents; nay, they strive and contend who may give the greatest and chiefest Present. And each of those severall Princes must alwayes bee either himselfe in person, or his Brother, eldest Sonne, or the chiefe Nobleman within his Realme at the Emperours Court; the reason of it is not well knowne, but it is pretended, that it is done to keepe the severall Kingdomes in quiet, and free from tumults, treasons and rebellions. The Emperour doth ordinarily requite his Princes presents after this manner: hee gives them a Feather for a Goose, some few Kerrimoones or Coates, for Gold, Silver or other precious and rare commodities; and that they may not grow rich, and of sufficient abilitie to make head against him, he suffers not their Fleeces to grow, but sheares them off, by raising Taxes on them for the building of Castles, and the repairing of Fortifications, and yet they are not suffered to repaire their owne, or any way to fortifie themselves.

Presents. Jealousie.

Policie to impoverish Subjects.

Ozechya is the most famous Castle that the Emperour hath, or that is within the Empire; it is of an extraordinarie bignesse and compassed round with three severall walls; the Castle of Edo is likewise walled and moated, having some few Ordnance on it; at Crates and Falkata there are likewise Castles both walled and moated, the circumference of each of them is neere about two mile. The chiefe Noble-men of those Kingdomes have Houses within the Castle walls to come and live there, either at the Kings

Osaca or Ozechia.

Edo and other Castles.

---

[1] 'The habit of transgressing takes away the sense of sin.' (I owe this translation to Diane Watt.)

or their owne pleasures, within each of those Castles there is a Storehouse kept ordinarily full of Rice, which may serve for their provision at all occasions and needs. At Falkata there is a Wood of Pine trees neere about three mile square, which is all the Summer time swept and kept so cleane, that you shall hardly see any small twig bough, or leafe under the Trees, and the trees stand so close together, that you may solace and recreate your selfe there at all houres of the day without any hurt or heat of the Sunne. In the midst of it there is a great Pagod or Church very richly adorned with gilded Images, and all sorts of curious carved workes.

Falcata neatnesse & Temple.

The people are generally Courteous, affable and full of Complements, they are very punctuall in the entertayning of Strangers, and they will assoone lose a limbe as omit one Ceremonie in welcomming their friend; they use to give and receive the emptie Cup at one the others hands, and before the Master of the house begins to drinke, hee will proffer the Cup to every one of his Guests, making shew to have them to begin though it bee farre from his intention; they feed not much upon varietie; for Fish, Rootes and Rice are their common junkates, and if they chance to kill a Hen, Ducke or Pigge, which is but seldome, they will not like Churles eate it alone, but their friends shall be surely partakers of it. Their ordinary drinke is Water, and that is made most times hot, in the same pot where they seeth their Rice, that so it may receive some thicknesse and substance from the Rice. They have strong Wine and Rack distill'd of Rice, of which they will sometimes drinke largely, especially at their Feasts and meetings, and being moved to anger or wrath in the heate of their Drinke, you may assoone perswade Tygres to patience and quietnesse as them, so obstinate and wilfull they are in the furie of their impatience. Their Lawes are very strict and full of severitie, affoording no other kinde of punishment but either Death or Banishment: Murther, Theft, Treason, or the violation of any of the Emperours Proclamations or Edicts, are punished with death; so is Adulterie also if it bee knowne and the parties pursued, but the Devill their master in those actions hath taught them such cleanly conveyances, that seldome or never are they apprehended; they proceed both in Controversies and criminall causes according to the verdict of the produced witnesses, and the Sentence being once past, they will not revoake or mittigate the severitie of it, but if the parties attached have deserved death they shall surely have it, and for the manner, they are either Beheaded or Crucified; hee kneeles downe on his knees and then comes the Executioner behind him and cuts off his head with a Catan or their Countrie-sword, and his

Customes of the people.

head being off, the young Cavalleers trie their weapons on his limbes, and prove whether they can cut off an Arme or Leg at a blow; the other have their armes and legges spread abroad on a Crosse, which done, they set the Crosse upright in the ground, and then comes one either with a Lance or Speare and runnes the partie through the bodie, where hee hangs untill he rots off, no man being suffered to take him downe.

Every one may change his Name three times, when he is a childe, when he is a young-man, and when he is old; some change their names more often, every one as hee pleaseth may make choyse of his owne name, and they are commonly named either by the King, or else by some Noble or Great man with whom they are chiefely in favour.

They have the use of Writing and Printing, and have had the space of many yeeres, no man knowes certainly how long. They have seven sorts of Letters, each single letter serving for a word, and many of them in their placing serve for sixe or seven; and each Alphabet hath eight and fortie Letters, and yet with all these letters they are not able to write our Christian names; they have not the true pronounciation of H. B. T. and some other letter, and a Chinesse if his life lay on it, cannot truely pronounce D.

They observe no Sabbath, but certaine Feast dayes according to the Moone, as the first of the Moone, the 15. or 28.; on these dayes they goe to the Church, visit the Sepulchers of the dead, and use many foolish and apish Ceremonies, which time will not permit me now to relate.

The ninth day of the Moone throughout the yeere they hold for accursed, and therefore in that day they will not begin or undertake any worke of consequence and importance.

They strictly observe a Fast on that day of the moneth, in which their Father or Mother dyed, which they doe so precisely keepe, that they will not touch or eate any thing that hath blood. [...]

JOHN SARIS

The one and twentieth, the old king came aboord againe, and brought with him divers women to be frollicke. These women were Actors of Comedies, which passe there from Iland to Iland to play, as our Players doe here from Towne to Towne, having severall shifts of apparrell for the better grace of the matter acted; which for the most part are of Warre, Love, and such like. These Women are as the slaves of one man, who putteth a price what every man shall pay that hath to doe with any of them; more then which he is not

Women Actors of Comedies in Japan, being also common women, and their price rated.

Bawdes in Japan.

to take upon paine of death, in case the partie injured shall complaine. It is left to his owne discretion to prize her at the first, but rise he cannot afterwards, fall he may. Neither doth the partie bargaine with the Wench, but with her Master, whose command she is to obey. The greatest of their Nobilitie travelling, hold it no disgrace to send for these Panders to their Inne, & do compound with them for the Wenches, either to fill their drinke at Table (for all men of any ranke have their drinke filled to them by Women) or otherwise to have the use of them. When any of these Panders die (though in their life time they were received into Company of the best, yet now as unworthy to rest amongst the worst) they are bridled with a bridle made of straw, as you would bridle an Horse, and in the cloathes they died in, are dragged through the streetes into the fields, and there cast upon a dunghill, for dogges and fowles to devoure.

Their abhominable esteeme after death.

The Travels of Peter Mundy in Asia (1628–34), Observations of India

MUNDY (*c.*1596–*c.*1667), was a traveller whose diary records in detail and with a variety of illustrations, his extensive travels throughout Europe and Asia. He had already travelled to Spain, France, and Turkey when he set off for India in 1628, where he remained at various destinations for the next six years. In 1635–8 he returned to India, and also visited Japan and China. Mundy divided the rest of his life between further expeditions—to Russia, Poland, Holland, and another voyage to India—and expanding his diary. This remained in manuscript until the early years of last century, but was obviously designed to be read by others. Whether Mundy tried to get his work published and failed, or whether the diary did reach an audience of close acquaintances, is not known.[1]

Included here are some of Munday's observations of India.[2]

See also:

Richard Hakluyt, *The Principall Navigations*, 12 vols. (Glasgow: Mac-Lehose, 1903), v. 365–449.
Samuel Purchas, *Hakluytus Posthumous or Purchas His Pilgrimes*, 20 vols. (Glasgow: MacLehose, 1905–7), ix. 503–70; xi. 291–306.

[1] On Mundy's life see *The Travels of Peter Mundy, in Europe and Asia, 1608–1667*, ed. Richard Carnac Temple, 2 vols. (London: Hakluyt Society, 1907), vol. i, introd., pp. xiii–lvii.
[2] Text from *Travels of Peter Mundy*, ii. 29–36, 157–62.

Suratt its Description

Suratt it selfe lyeth Eastward from Port Swallye, distant about 12 miles on the River Tapee [Tāpti], and may bee neere 2 miles in Compasse, environ'd with a badd ditch, excepting towards the River side. There are 7 Gates belonging to it, *vizt.* Baroche Gate, out of which goe many a Englishman that never returne, it being the way to our place of Buriall. This Gate leadeth to Ahmudavad and soe to Agra that way; Brampore [Burhānpur] Gate leadinge to Brampore, Decan and to the English garden without the Towne; Nunsaree [Nausāri] Gate to Nunsaree etts. [and other] Sea townes to the Southward, and the way to the great Tancke, with others which I omitt.

Heere are some reasonable long straight streetes, as that goeing to Nunsaree gate etts., some faire buildings scattered heere and there, a strong Castle furnished with good ordinance. By it is a very faire spacious greene, called Castle Greene, alsoe the Bunder [*bandar*] or wharffe, where Goods are embarqued to be transported unto shipps or Juncks rideinge att Swally or the Rivers mouth.

Junckes

Juncks are theis Country vessels, soe called by us, of which many belong to this place, among the rest some of 1000 or 1200 Tunn each, and but one Deck. Theis put to Sea with Easterly Monsoon, and before the wynde out goe our Shipps, by reason of the monstrous breadth of their maine sayles,[1] soe fitted of purpose, as being confident of the continuance of faire and moderate winds and weather duringe that Monsoon.

What a Monsoon is

Monsoon is a tyme of the yeare when the wyndes blowe continually one way, of which there are twoe, *Vizt.* the Easterly Monsoon and the Westerly. The Easterly begins about the end of September, and continues untill the Midle of Aprill followinge, with perpetuall faire weather, except per- chaunce some 2 or 3 dayes of rayne happeninge in that Tyme. The Westerly Monsoon beginneth from the middle of April and continueth untill the end of September againe, in the latter 3 monethes whereof fall the raynes accompanied with great Stormes and violent Currants etts, soe that in this Monsoon there is noe putting to Sea, their vessels beinge either hailed [hauled] on Shoare or drawne up into secure places.

The Great Tancke

The Great Tancke[2] is a Fabricke of as great Coste, labour and tyme, admirable for its workemanshipp and bignes. Tancks in generall are 2 sorts, *vizt.* naturall and artificiall. The first are some lower ground, where- unto the waters runne from the upper part in tyme of Rayne. Of this sort there bee many, both great and small, which wee may terme Lakes, Ponds or Pooles, according to their bignesse. The other sort are artificiall, made by

---

[1] The term junk is here used to indicate a native vessel.   [2] A reservoir, well, or cistern.

hands (as this of Suratt), by takeing away the earth, makeing it to what depth they please, which is afterwards built of stone to what forme they thinck best. Theis sorts are in or neere to Citties and great Townes for Common use; Also great men and others have them in their Gardens and dwellings of a lesser sort. Theis Tancks being places of much use and delight, by reason of the want of rayne most part of the yeare in theis Countries. Suratt Tanck is neere half a mile about, made into 16 squares, built of great hard hewen stone, haveing from the upper Superficies stepps descending downewards about 20 in number, which goe round about. Between every 5 or 6 is one much wider then the rest to walke on. It hath 8 entrances for people and Cattle, which goe downe wards; with walls, turretts and very faire pavement of great Stones. In the middle of all stands a howse. The passage where the water cometh in deserveth also notice, walled on each side, vaulted and supported with pillars. In the Midle of this Entrey lyes a very prettie small Tanck, hard by the greater. This I conceive is that the troubled water might settle there before it runne into th' other, beinge that the litle one must be first filled, which is done, in tymes of Rayne, as well litle as greate; and then in the greatest may bee about 3 Fathom water att the deepest, and before the rayne Come againe very litle, or none att all, makeinge use of the bottome or floore for the soweing of muske and Water Millions [melons], which growe up verie sodainely there.[3] Round about stand many faire Tombes, gardens and trees, which make a pleasant prospect, the Tancke beinge full, whether wee resort manie tymes for recreation, and sometymes to the Toddy gardens, which in [tyme of] Rayne are very faire and green, yeilding forth a most fragrant smell.

Tarree trees

Of these Tarree trees are a verie great number round about Suratt, out of which they drawe a Liquor wee call Toddy, or rather Tarree [*tārī*]. The best sort thereof may bee compaired to new white wyne, both in Coulor and Taste, pleasant and wholesome, which distilleth from severall sorts of trees, as the Coco tree, the date tree and another called   ,[4] in forme all alike, differinge a litle in the spriggs or leaves on the Topp, having noe branches

[3] All the 17th-cent. travellers appear to have been much impressed by the celebrated Gopi Talão or tank at Surat.
[4] There is a blank here in all the copies. Mundy probably intended to add the palmyra palm or *tār* tree, which gave its name to the liquor.

but the maine Stemm. The Governour hath yerely for the rent of the said Tree 12000 Ms. [*mahmūdīs*]. Above the rest the Coco tree is most wonderfull and necessarye, as in many places elsewhere is described. [...]

Townes about Surratt

Places adjoyninge are Raneile on the other side of the River, a pleasant Scituation, Also Ragem, Battee, etts. on that side. On Suratt side are Ckhaturgam [Katargām] Pulparre, where the Banians burne theire dead, Cankei Carro, a curious Sollitarie place with a litle Brooke makeing many deepe and learge pooles, fine shadye bancks and trees on the Margent, frequented with fowle, and stored with fish.

The Banian Tree

The Banian Tree is a litle beyond the Great Tanck and not to bee forgotten, being of those the Portugalls call Arbore de Rais [*raiz*, Port., 'tree of roots'], because the roots descend from alofte. This is of an exceedinge bredth, much honoured by the Banians.

Townes neere the Port

Neere Porte Swally lyes Swally [Suwālī] Towne, Damkee [Damkin], Mora, etts., much frequented by English in tyme of Shippinge, whether they resort for recreation.

The burning of a Banian woman with her dead husband

Now before I take leave of Suratt I will relate one accident that happened att my beinge there, whereof I was Eye witnesse, *vizt.* a Banian Woman that voluntarilye burned her selfe alive with the body of here dead husband. The manner of it was as followeth:

A Certaine Banian dieing att Suratt, his wife resolved to burne herselfe alive with the body of her husband, It beinge an ancient Custome used in India, but now not soe much by farr as in former tymes. The Mogull haveinge Conquered their Countrie hath almost abollished that Custome, soe that it may not bee done without speciall lycense from the kinge or Governour of the place where they dwell. This Woman through much importunitie gott leave of the Governour of Suratt to effect her desire.

The Body of her husband was carried to Palparre [Phūlpārā], which lyes on the River Tapee [Tāpti], where are many of their Pagodes or Churches, and great resort thither att severall of their Feastivalls. There was it layd att the brinck of the river, with his feete and part of his body in the Water. His wife by him, with other weomen in the said river, stood upp to the midle performinge on themselves certaine washinge Ceremonies, for they attribute much holynesse to great Rivers (especiallie to Ganges), and much of their religion consists in Washinges. In the meane tyme there was readye made the pile or place for the funerall fire, layeinge a good quantitie of wood on the floore round about, which were stakes driven in, on which are put a great quantitie of a small kinde of drye Thornes and other Combustable stuffe, fashioned like a little lowe house with a doore of the same to it. First the dead body was brought and layed on the said pile, on whome they sett more wood and drye Oxe dunge (a great fuell in this Countrie). Then came his wife from the River accompanied with Bramanes [Brāhmans], (whoe are their Preists). Then Compassinge the Cottage three tymes, shee taketh leave of her Kindred, freinds and acquaintance very Cheirefullie, without any shewe of feare or alteration att all, and entreth into it, where sittinge downe, shee taketh her husbands head on her Lapp. The doore is presentlie [immediately] shutt upon her, one of her kindred holding a greate pole against it, and others with longe poles in their hands to Right the fire if neede bee (or rather I thinck to knock her downe if shee should chance to gett out). Then shee herselfe with a litle torche she carried with her (made of Oyled Lynnen) kindleth it first within, when her freindes without with the like Torches sett it on fire round aboute, which on the suddaine burneth with greate violence, The Spectators in the meane tyme makeinge all the noyse they can, some with drumms and Countrie Instruments, beateing of brasse platters, Cryeinge or hollowinge, Clapping their hands, all in a Confused manner, while the furie of the flame lasteth. This I conceive is to drowne her voyce if shee should chance to Crye. The sides and upper part of the place was quicklye consumed; yett satt shee upp with life in her, holding upp both her Armes, which might bee occasioned through the scorchinge and shrinckinge of the Sinnewes, for shee held her handes under his head until the fire was kindled; soe att last not able to sett upp anie Longer, shee fell downe upon her husbands body, when by their freinds they were covered with more fuell untill they were both burned to ashes, which presentlie [immediately] is throwne into the river. Hereunder I have set it downe in figure, as neere as I can (see Fig. 10).

FIG. 10. Peter Mundy, 'A Case of *Satī* at Surat in 1630' (*Travels* (1628–34))

RELATION XI

OF PUTTANA (PATNA) AND OF ABDULLA CKAUN
(ABDU'LLAH KHĀN) GOVERNOUR THEREOF

The Cittie lyes alongst on the river Ganges, which, with the suburbs, may conteyne in length about 3 miles; a very longe Bazare with trees on each side (which is much used in theis parts). It hath above 200 of Grocers or Druggists, and of severall druggs a world. It is the greatest Mart of all this Countrie, from whence they repaire from Bengala that way to the Sea side, and from Indostan and other Inland Countries round about, plentifull in provisions, abounding with sundrie Commodities as before mentioned.

Great Mens Pleasure Boates

Heere are certaine pleasure boats used by Great Men, which (because of their strange Shape) I will describe in few words, as also by figure (see Fig. 11). Theis boats I cannot resemble to any thinge better then a Gaefish [garfish], extraordinarie lowe, longe and slender,[5] with 20, 25 or 30 oares of a side, all severally painted, some greene, some redd and blew, etts. The place where the great man Sitts is either fore or in the middle, in a Curious Chowtree[6] made of purpose. When they rowe to any place, they are stuck full of Flaggs There, hanginge downe on the prow, which shoots forward a mightie way, as doth the Sterne afterward on, both ends sharpe alike[7] I say, on both sides of the prowe, hang downe many of those Cowe Tailes[8] so much esteemed. They use a Cheere to their Guing [? going], as wee doe in our Barges, one giveinge the word first and then all the rest answere.

From our hired howse, which lay on the bancks of the river, wee might oftentimes see, hard by the shoare, many great fishes, as bigg as Boneitoes or Albacores, which did leape in the same manner as they doe att Sea. They are here called Soa, their perticuler forme I knowe not.[9]

The Hindowes of this place ferrie all their dead over the river and there burne them, being as I heere not permitted to doe it on this side.

---

[5] The garfish or garefish (*belone vulgaris*) has a long, slender body.

[6] Elaborately constructed platform or covered seat.

[7] Mundy apparently means a *bajrā* or pleasure boat, the budgerow of Europeans. But the description applies equally to the *mayūr pankhī* (peacock's wing) or native pleasure boat.

[8] The bushy tail of the Tibetan yak (*chaunrī*, chowry) used for horse trappings in Mundy's time.

[9] *Sūā*, the garfish of the Indian rivers: *belone cancila*.

Fig. 11. Peter Mundy, 'Drawings of a *Bajrā* or *Mayūr Pankhī*, a native pleasure boat' (*Travels* (1628–34))

Zeffe Ckauns Sarae

Heere is also the fairest Sarae (*sarāi*) that I have yett seene, or I thinck is in India, not yett finished. It hath two faire Courts, each haveinge ware-howses round about beneath, and roomes with galleries to lodge in alofte, a very Stately entrance, lyeing by the river. This place is cheifely for Mer-chants of straunge Countries, as Mogolls, Persians, Armenians, where they may lodge and keepe their goods the tyme of their stay heere, payeinge so much by the moneth. Theis are usuallie in great Citties, but the other sort of Saraes are in all places, servinge for all sorts of Travellers that come att night and away in the morninge. This was built by Zeffe Ckaun [Saif Khān] late Governour of this place, and now of Ellahabaz [Allahābād], with a faire Messitt (*masjid*) adjoyninge to it. Hee also began a faire garden on the other side the river. Hee is generallie Commended and his returne wished for by all, as much as this now Governour, Abdulla Ckaun ['Abdu'llah Khān], is hated, feared, and his expulsion by them desired.

Abdulla Ckaun

This Governour, Abdulla Ckaun, is said to bee [have been] the death of above 200000 persons,[10] a Cruell natured and Covetuous Tirant, and therefore more fitter to bee alwaies imployed againste Theeves and Rebells then to reside in a peaceable Governement. Beinge sent by Jehangueere against Sultan Ckorum [Khurram], when hee was out in rebellion, hee revolted from the father to the Sonne. On a tyme his brother shewed him a poore woman almost dead, and a litle childe cryeinge and pulling att the mothers Dugg for milke. Hee tooke his Launce and runn them both through, sayeing hee would remedie them both. Annother tyme there was a great buildinge filled with poore Captived Weomen and Children, when word was brought him that they would quickly perrish with hunger and cold if they were not releived. Hee cawsed the said building to bee sett on Fire and soe burnt them all upp together. And nowe, since my arrivall hither, hee caused Chowdree Pertabb [Chaudhari Pratāp], an auntient man of great place and respect, to be Chawbackt,[11] beaten with Staves and shoes, which all the Cittie greived att, knoweing him to bee a good man, and

---

[10] While under surveillance, in Jahāngīr's reign, 'Abdu'llah Khān boasted that he had caused 200,000 infidels' heads to be cut off, so that there might be two rows of minarets of heads from Agra to Patna.

[11] Flogged with a *chābak*, whip.

guiltlesse of any Cryme, except to gett out of him some thousands of Rupees. Alsoe, since my beinge heere, hee cawsed divers Mogolls of respect to ride in open shame on Asses backes, being first beaten and their faces blackt all over with soote, whereof one of them for verie greife poysoned himselfe the next daye. A Raja comeinge to him in peaceable manner was received with a Serepawe [*saropā*, dress of honour], but two dayes after hee was layd hold of and made prisoner, his goods made spoile or pillage, whereupon they saie his wife and freinds have risen upp against him ['Abdu'llah Khān], and have putt Bababeag [Bābā Beg] to the worst, whoe was sent Fouzdare [*faujdār*, military officer] to Callianpore [Kālyān-pur], the Raias [Rājā's] residence. This Bababeag was Customer [revenue officer] att my comeinge, whoe advised mee to looke to myselfe, for that his Master was a badd man and cared for noebody, noe not for the King himselfe. Hee ['Abdu'llah Khān] hath imposed new Customes both Inwards and outwards, that never were, Soe much, as poore weomen that sell milke upp and downe streets hee makes them pay custome for it. I was twice before him, but never neerer then a Stones cast. Some part of the reason was because I brought him noe present. From the Broker that sold our Quicksilver etts, hee extorted rupees 250, alleadginge that hee had sold Jewells that I brought (which were none att all), and that hee was not made acquainted with it. Hee sleepes but litle, rises att Midnight, findes fault with one, beats another. The cheifest Merchants of the Cittie resolve to leave the place untill hee bee removed hence, fearinge howrely that hee will pick some quarrell with them. In fine, hee plaies the Tirant.[12] One of his daughters (att my being there) was burned to death, for a Candle catchinge hold of her Clothes, they all suddenlie tooke fire, being of most fine linnen, with much sweete Oyle, Chua (a kind of perfume), etts., which soe scorched and frighted her, that shee fell into a feaver and in fewe dayes dyed.

Chua is a rich perfume, made liquid, of Colour black, which comonly they put under their Armepitts and thereabouts, and many tymes over bosome and backe.

---

[12] 'Abdu'llah Khān was Governor of Bihār (Patna) from 1632 till 1643, when he was transferred to Allahābād. He died in Dec. 1644.

Chapter Five

THE AMERICAS

MORE has been written about England's colonization of the Americas than any of the other areas represented in this volume.[1] Perhaps, in line with the explosion of interest in 'post-colonialism' in recent years, and the hegemony of the United State of America in economic—and academic—world affairs, the perceived colonial relationship between England and the Americas has come to dominate and distort the field of 'travel writing'.[2] This is a clear case of teleological reading as the current state of affairs comes to represent the past, when the correlation between the two is by no means so obvious.

The simple fact is that there was really relatively little interest in colonial expansion to the Americas until the early decades of the seventeenth century. Henry VII was keen enough to grant the Venetian John Cabot letters patent which gave him leave to take possession of whatever lands he could discover and govern them as the king's lieutenant. Cabot sailed to Newfoundland in the summer of 1497, was scantly rewarded by the king, and promptly disappeared in one of the four ships lost on his second

---

[1] Recent studies include Walter S. H. Lim, *The Arts of Empire: The Poetics of Colonisation from Ralegh to Milton* (Newark: Univ. of Delaware Press, 1998); Joan Pong Linton, *The Romance of the New World Gender and the Literary Formation of English Colonialism* (Cambridge: Cambridge Univ. Press, 1998); Mary Fuller, *Voyages in Print: English Travel to America, 1576–1624* (Cambridge: Cambridge Univ. Press, 1995).

[2] For example, Howard Marchitello's otherwise useful and perceptive descriptive analysis of 'Recent Studies in Tudor and Early Stuart Travel Writing' (*ELR* 29 (1999), 326–47), concentrates solely on 'trans-oceanic voyages by English travellers'. Marchitello confesses that 'a number of works surveyed here discuss travel to the East', but 'the majority focus on New World travel and exploration' (p. 326). It is not clear why the essay makes this choice, one which can only serve to reinforce the innocent reader's notion that travel to the Americas was more important than any other travel.

voyage.[3] A few other voyages were partially sponsored by the crown, and one of these, led by João Fernandes, brought back some exotic birds, wildcats, and three natives of Newfoundland.[4] More spectacular, albeit in a disastrous sense, was Richard Hore's voyage to the same region in 1536. Hore took thirty tourists in two ships. One was lost at sea and the other became trapped in ice in Newfoundland where the starving passengers and crew began to eat each other, before the capture of a passing French ship secured a passage home.[5]

The contrast to Spanish and Portuguese exploits is striking. Ferdinand Magellan's ships had already circumnavigated the globe (1519–22); Hernán Cortés had conquered Mexico (1519–22); and Francisco de Pizarro was just finishing off his conquest of Peru (1530–5).[6] Even the French were more active and successful at colonizing the Americas in the sixteenth century than the English, establishing a colony in Florida in 1562 (which was destroyed by the Spanish in 1565).[7] England's main experience of the Americas until half-way through Elizabeth's reign was through a series of translations of Spanish works, most notably Richard Eden's translation of Peter Martyr d'Anghera's *Decades of the Newe Worlde* (1555), published as part of Mary's attempt to encourage the English to follow the Spanish during their brief union in the 1550s (see below, pp. 240–9).[8] Important later were accounts of Spanish cruelty in the Americas, designed to emphasize the dangers of Spanish dominance in Europe and the Americas, and promote the benefits of rival English efforts. The most significant account of Spanish brutality in the New World published in English was M.M.S.'s translation of Las Casas's *Brevisima relación* (see below, pp. 250–5).

---

[3] Angus Calder, *Revolutionary Empire: The Rise of the English-Speaking Empires from the Fifteenth Century to the 1780s* (London: Cape, 1981), 15–16. See also Patrick McGrath, 'Bristol and America, 1480–1631', in K. R. Andrews, Nicholas Canny, and P. E. H. Hair (eds.), *The Westward Enterprise: English Activities in Ireland, the Atlantic and America, 1480–1650* (Liverpool, 1978), 81–102.

[4] Calder, *Revolutionary Empire*, 16.

[5] Calder, *Revolutionary Empire*, 16. The voyage is recounted in Richard Hakluyt, *The Principall Navigations, Voyages, Traffiques & Discoveries of the English Nation*, 12 vols. (Glasgow: MacLehose, 1903), viii. 3–7. See also Andrew Hadfield, 'Writing the New World: More "Invisible Bullets"', *Literature and History*, 2: 2, 2nd ser. (1991), 3–19.

[6] One commentator has argued that English writings in the 16th cent. were in fact anti-colonial and demanded a concentration on internal affairs rather than external expansion; see Jeffrey Knapp, *An Empire Nowhere: England, America, and Literature from* Utopia *to* The Tempest (Berkeley: Univ. of California Press, 1992).

[7] A. L. Rowse, *The Expansion of Elizabethan England* (Basingstoke: Macmillan, 1955), 225.

[8] David Gwyn, 'Richard Eden: Cosmographer and Alchemist', *Sixteenth-Century Journal*, 15 (1984), 13–34; Andrew Hadfield, *Literature, Travel and Colonial Writing in the English Renaissance, 1545–1625* (Oxford: Clarendon Press, 1998), 71–91.

The next English voyages to the Americas were Martin Frobisher's three expeditions to discover the North-West passage through to the Spice Islands of the Indies (1576–8). Frobisher reached Baffin Island and returned with an Inuit (Frobisher seems to have thought that he was a Tartar), and a hold full of iron pyrites ('fool's gold').[9] At the same time, Sir Francis Drake became the first Englishman to circumnavigate the globe (1577–80). The first serious English colonist of the Americas was Humphrey Gilbert, one of a number of soldiers who had been active in Ireland.[10] Gilbert wrote a treatise in 1566 entitled *Discourse of a Discoverie for a New Passage to Cataia*, arguing that the North-West Passage to the Indies would require a trading base and a series of colonies in the Americas. These could be populated by various criminals and dissidents who would be put to use instead of being a burden upon the state (a common theme in subsequent colonial literature).[11]

Gilbert's more serious colonial exploits took place in the wake of Frobisher's achievements. In June 1578 he was granted letters patent to establish colonies anywhere on the North American coast, which England claimed after Cabot's voyage. Gilbert may have been more interested in piracy and harassing the Spanish—many of the early English colonies had precisely this goal—but he did have the legal means and crown support to establish colonies. Gilbert's small fleet reached Newfoundland in August 1583 and, as the passage included here reveals, made plans to establish a colony on the island. Unfortunately Gilbert was drowned near the Azores on the return voyage. He was last seen holding a book in his hand shouting 'We are as neere to heaven by sea as by land' (a quotation from More's *Utopia*), before the ship finally disappeared.[12]

In 1584 Gilbert's colonial patent was taken up by his half-brother, Sir Walter Raleigh, the major figure in Elizabethan colonization of the Americas.[13] By now, Richard Hakluyt and others had realized the importance of establishing colonies in the Americas to rival and control the spread

---

[9] Calder, *Revolutionary Empire*, 79–80; Stephen Greenblatt, *Marvelous Possessions: The Wonder of the New World* (Oxford: Oxford Univ. Press, 1991), 109–18. Accounts of the voyages in Hakluyt, *Principall Navigations*, vii. 204–42.

[10] Nicholas Canny, 'The Ideology of English Colonisation: From Ireland to America', *WMQ* 30 (1973), 575–98.

[11] Calder, *Revolutionary Empire*, 79; William Gilbert Gosling, *The Life of Sir Humphrey Gilbert: England's First Empire Builder* (London: Constable, 1911), ch. 4. Text is in Hakluyt, *Principall Navigations*, vii. 158–203.

[12] Gosling, *Life of Sir Humphrey Gilbert*, ch. 13.

[13] David Beers Quinn, *Raleigh and the British Empire* (London: Hodder and Stoughton, 1947).

of the Spanish Empire (see above, pp. 24–7). Raleigh took no part in the Virginian voyages he sponsored and encouraged, making expeditions to Guiana instead (see below, pp. 279–85). He left his cousin, the aggressive Sir Richard Grenville (1541?–91), in charge and the first fleet sailed on 9 April 1585, eventually establishing a colony on the unsuitable site of Roanoke Island.[14] There was some early success, when Grenville captured a Spanish galleon, which satisfied the queen's constant fears about money. John White and Thomas Harriot were sent over to record native society and the natural world, a combined effort which led to *A Briefe and True Report of the New Found Land of Virginia*, one of the best records of the native Virginians in existence (see below, pp. 266–78).

Ralph Lane, a brutal soldier who had extensive experience in Ireland, became virtual dictator of the colony, and clearly caused considerable friction with the natives, as Harriot notes (see below, p. 272). The colonists found it hard to grow their own food and had to rely on their reluctant hosts, who eventually turned against them and refused to supply them with any food at all. The colony was evacuated in 1586, but was started again in May 1587, with more colonists willing to take a chance in the New World under the leadership of John White, the artist. But by November, the colony was again in trouble and White returned to England to procure help and supplies. He did not return to Roanoke until 1590, where he found the colony destroyed and no trace of the colonists apart from the word 'CROATOAN' scored in the bark of a tree. What this means is unclear as is the fate of the colonists, although it is likely that they met their end at the hands of the local chief, Powhatan.[15]

The simple truth was that the queen and those she chose to sponsor, such as Sir Walter Raleigh and Sir Francis Drake, were clearly far more interested in privateering and profiteering than establishing colonial settlements.[16] Raleigh, a perceptive and intelligent observer of other peoples, poured his energies into an attempt to discover the mythical city of El Dorado in the South American country, Guiana. The treatise he wrote after his first voyage there (1595), was designed to foster future interest in

[14] Karen O. Kupperman, *Roanoke: The Abandoned Colony* (Savage, Md.: Rowman and Littlefield, 1984).

[15] David Beers Quinn, *England and the Discovery of America, 1481–1620* (London: Allen and Unwin, 1974), 432–81.

[16] K. R. Andrews, *Elizabethan Privateering during the Spanish War, 1585–1603* (Cambridge: Cambridge Univ. Press, 1964).

the expedition, but is at least as interesting for its account of the peoples in the region and Anglo-Spanish rivalry.

Colonies were not securely established until the reign of James I. In 1606 the chaotic sponsorship of voyages was finally ended with the establishment of the Virginia Company, a joint-stock company which spread the risk of ventures between a number of wealthy sponsors, the whole enterprise overseen by a Royal Council.[17] In 1607 Jamestown was established in Chesapeake Bay, a better site than Roanoke Island in terms of its positioning and strategic defences, but marshy and malarial. The colony was now established on a secure footing, even though much was still to be done (see the comments of William Strachey below, pp. 296–302). Relations with the natives were complex, problematic, and often confusing, as the famous story of John Smith's rescue at the hands of Pocahontas indicates (although viewers of the Disney film (1995) are provided with a more straightforward account) (see below, pp. 303–8). Hopes of a rapprochement with the local tribes had to be reassessed in 1622, when an uprising in the Virginia colonies destroyed much of the settlement and left 300 dead.[18] Nevertheless, the pattern of colonial settlement in the Americas had been established. The Virginia colonies recovered and new colonies were established in Plymouth, Massachusetts (1620), Massachusetts Bay (1629), and Connecticut (1634).[19]

As these accounts indicate, attempts to establish colonies in the Americas were not always greeted with enthusiasm and one can reconstruct many of the debates from a careful reading of published material. There were fears that the enterprise would fail; that it was too dangerous to be worth while; that it was actually a bloody and cruel exercise, as the Spanish experience demonstrated. A critical perspective on the European presence in the Americas is provided in Michel de Montaigne's well-known essay, 'Of the Canniballes', translated into English in 1603 by John Florio (see below, pp. 286–95).

---

[17] Calder, *Revolutionary Empire*, 130.

[18] Two very different approaches to the question of Anglo-Indian relations in the early 17th cent. are provided in Karen Ordhal Kupperman, *Settling with the Indians: The Meeting of English and Indian Cultures in America, 1580–1640* (New Jersey: Rowman and Allanheld, 1980); Bernard W. Sheehan, *Savagism and Civility: Indians and Englishmen in Colonial Virginia* (Cambridge: Cambridge Univ. Press, 1980).

[19] A stimulating account of later colonial rivalry is provided in Thomas Scanlan, *Colonial Writing and the New World, 1583–1671* (Cambridge: Cambridge Univ. Press, 1999), chs. 4–6. See also Calder, *Revolutionary Empire*, 166–247.

Richard Eden, *The Decades of the Newe Worlde, or West India* (1555), Three Descriptions of American Natives

PETER MARTYR D'ANGHERA's extensive documentation of the progress of the Spanish in the immediate aftermath of Columbus's landing in the Americas in 1492 became one of the standard accounts of the New World and was used extensively throughout Europe.[1] The first translation in English was by Richard Eden (see above, pp. 16–19), containing Martyr's account of the first three decades (*c.*1492–*c.*1522), as well as material from Gondola Oviedo's *Natural History of the West Indies*, Antonio Pigafetta's account of Ferdinand Magellan's circumnavigation of the globe, and other material.

The Decades of the Newe Worlde are full of descriptions of savage and compliant natives, cannibals, earthly paradises, delight and suffering, Spanish heroism and greed. Included here are some representative selections. First, the oration of the son of King Comogrus who attacks Spanish greed for gold, but then shows that his people are really no different themselves. Second, a description of the gentle and compliant people and their pleasant lands that Columbus encounters on his fourth voyage. Third, a brief comment on the threat of the ubiquitous cannibals, even in otherwise desirable locations; and fourth, a general description of the peoples of the West Indies in Oviedo's *Natural History of the West Indies.*[2]

See also:

Christopher Columbus, *The Four Voyages of Christopher Columbus*, ed. and trans. J. M. Cohen (London: Hutchinson, 1969).

Bernal Díaz, *The Conquest of New Spain*, trans. J. M. Cohen (Harmondsworth: Penguin, 1963).

Richard Hakluyt, *Divers Voyages touching the discoverie of America, and the islands adjacent* (1582).

---

[1] See the translation by Francis Augustus McNutt, *De Orbe Novo: The Eight Decades of Peter Martyr D'Anghera* (New York: B. Franklin, 1970 repr. of 1912), which also contains an account of Peter Martyr's life.

[2] Text from Anglerius, Petrus Martyr, *The decades of the newe worlde or west India. Written in Latine and tr. By R. Eden [w. additions from other sources]* (1555), 65–6, 105–6, 138–9, 208–10.

Here as brabblynge and contention arose emonge owr men abowt the dividinge of gold, this eldeste soonne of Kynge *Comogrus* beinge presente, whome we praysed for his wysedome, commynge sume what wyth an angery countenaunce towarde hym whiche helde the balences, he strooke theym wyth his fyste, and scatered all the golde that was therein, abowte the porche, sharpely rebukynge theym with woordes in this effecte. What is the matter yowe Christian men, that yow soo greatly esteme soo litle a portion of golde more then yowr owne quietnes, whiche neverthelesse yow entend to deface from these fayre ouches[1] and to melte the same into a rude masse. If yowre hunger of goulde bee soo insatiable that onely for the desyre yowe have therto, yowe disquiete soo many nations, and yow yowre selves also susteyne soo many calamit[i]es and incommodities, lyving like banished men owte of yowre owne countrey, I wyll shewe yowe a Region floweinge with goulde, where yowe may satisfie yowr raveninge appetites. But yowe muste attempte the thynge with a greater poure: For it standeth yow in hande by force of armes to overcome kynges of greate puissaunce, and rigorous defenders of theyr dominions. For besyde other, the greate kinge *Tumanama* will coome foorthe ageynste yowe, whose kengdome is moste ryche with golde, and distante from hense onely syx soonnes: that is, syx dayes: for they number the dayes by the sonne. Furthermore, or ever yowe canne coome thether, yow must passe over the mountaynes inhabited of the cruell Canybales a fierce kynde of men, devourers of mans flesshe, lyving withowte lawes, wanderinge, and withowte empire. For they also, beinge desyrous of golde, have subdewed them under theyr dominion whiche before inhabited the golde mynes of the mountaynes, and use them lyke bondemen, usyng their laboure in dygginge and workynge theyr golde in plates and sundry Images lyke unto these whiche yowe see here. For we doo no more esteeme rude golde unwrought, then we doo cloddes of earthe, before it bee formed by the hande of the workeman to the similitude eyther of sume vessell necessarie for owre use, or sume ouche bewetifull to be worne. These thynges doo wee receave of theim for exchaunge of other of owre thynges, as of prisoners taken in warre, whiche they bye to eate, or for sheetes and other thynges perteynynge to the furnyture of householde, suche as they lacke which inhabite the moun-taynes: And especially for vitayles whereof they stande in greate neede by reason of the barrennes of the mountaynes. This jorney therfore, must bee

Young Comogrus his oration.

The hunger of golde.

A region flowinge wyth golde.

Kynge Tumanama.

Canibales.

The golde mynes of the mountaynes.

Unwrought golde not estemed.

Exchaunge.

---

[1] Necklaces, bracelets, jewels.

made open by force of men. And when yowe are passinge over these mountaynes (poyntinge with his fynger towarde the southe mountaynes) yowe shal see an other sea, where they sayle with shyppes as bygge as yowres (meanynge the caraveles) usinge both sayles and ores as yowe doo, althowghe the men bee naked as wee are. All the waye that the water runnethe frome the mountaynes, and all that syde lyinge towarde the
Abundance of golde.
Southe, bryngeth foorth golde abundantly. As he sayde these woordes, he poynted to the vesselles in whiche they use to serve theyr meate, affirmynge that kynge *Tumanama*, and all the other kynges beyonde the mountaynes,
Householde stuffe of gold.
had suche and al their other householde stuffe of golde: And that there was noo lesse plentie of golde amonge those people of the Southe, then of Iren with us. For he knewe by relation of owre men, wherof owre swoordes and other weapons were made. Owre capitaynes marveylyng at the oration of the naked younge man (for they had for interpretours those three men whiche had byn before a yere and a halfe conversant in the court of kynge *Careta*) pondered in theyr myndes, and ernestly considered his sayinges. Soo that his rasshenes in scatteringe the golde owte of the balances, they turned to myrth and urbanitie, commendynge his dooinge and sayinge therin. Then they asked hym frendely, uppon what certeyne knoweleage he spake those thynges: Or what he thowght beste herein to bee doone yf they shulde brynge a greater supplye of men. To this, younge *Comogrus*, stayinge a whyle with hym selfe as it were an oratour preparinge him selfe to speake of sume grave matter, and disposynge his bodye to a giesture meete to persuade, spake thus in his mother tonge. Gyve eare unto me o yowe Chrystians. Albeit that the gredie hunger of golde hathe not yet vexed us
Naked people tormented with ambition.
naked men, yet doo we destroy one an other by reason of ambition and desyre to rule. Hereof springeth mortall hatred amonge us, and hereof commethe owre destruction. Owre predicessours kepte warres, and soo dyd *Comogrus* my father with princes beinge bortherers abowte hym. In the which warres, as wee have overcoome, so have wee byn overcoome, as dothe appere by the number of bondemen amonge us, which we tooke by the overthrowe of owre enemyes, of the whiche I have gyven yowe fiftie. Lykewyse at an other tyme, owre adversaries havinge th[e]upper hande agenste us, ledde away manye of us captive. For suche is the chaunce of warre. Also, amonge owre familiers (wherof a great number have byn captives with them) beholde here is one whiche of longe tyme ledde a paynefull lyfe in bondage under the yoke of that kynge beyonde the mountaynes, in whose kyngdome is suche abundance of golde. Of hym,

and suche other innumerable, and lykewyse by the resort of free men on theyr syde comminge to us, and ageyne of owre men resortinge to theim by safe conduct, these thynges have byn ever as well knowen unto us, as owre owne possessions. But that yowe maye bee the better assured hereof, and bee owte of all suspicion that yowe shal not bee deceaved, make me the guyde of this viage, byndynge me fast and keepyng me in safe custodie to bee hanged on the next tree, yf yowe fynde my sayinges in any point untrewe. Folowe my counsayle therfore, and send for a thousande Christian men apte for the warres, by whose power we may with also the men of warre of *Comogrus* my father armed after owre maner, invade the dominions of owre enemyes: where, bothe yowe may bee satisfyed with golde, and we for owre conductinge and aydynge yowe in this enterpryse, shall thynke owre selves abundantly rewarded, in that yowe shall helpe to delyver us from the injuries and perpetuall feare of owre enemies. After these woordes, this prudente younge *Comogrus* helde his peace. And owre men moved with greate hope and hunger of golde, beganne ageine to swalowe downe theyr spettle.

A vehement persuasion.

A token of hunger.

Directing therfore his vyage from thense towarde the weste, leavyng the Ilandes of *Cuba* and *Jamaica* on his ryght hande towarde the northe, he wryteth that he chaunsed uppon an Ilande more southewarde then *Jamaica*, whiche th[e]inhabitantes caule *Guanassa*, so florysshinge and frutefull that it myghte seeme an earthlye Paradyse. Coastynge alonge by the shores of this Ilande, he mette two of the Canoas or boates of those provinces, whiche were drawne with two naked slaves ageynst the streame. In these boates, was caryed a ruler of the Ilande with his wyfe and chyldren, all naked. The slaves seeynge owre men a lande, made signes to them with proude countenaunce in their maisters name, to stande owte of the waye, and threatned them if they woolde not gyve place. Their sympelnes is suche that they nother feared the multitude or poure of owre men, or the greatnes and straungenes of owre shippes. They thought that owre men woolde have honoured their maister with like reverence as they did. Owre men had intelligence at the length that this ruler was a greate marchaunte whiche came to the marte from other coastes of the Ilande. For they exceryse byinge and sellynge by exchaunge with their confinies. He had also with him good stoore of suche ware as they stande in neede of or take pleasure in: as laton belles, rasers, knyves, and hatchettes made of a certeyne sharpe yelowe bryght stone, with handles of a stronge kynd of woodde. Also many

The florysshing Ilande of Guanassa.

Simple people.

A greate marchaunt.

other necessary instrumentes with kychen stuffe and vesselles for all necessary uses. Lykewise sheetes of gossampine cotton wrought of sundrye
colours. Owre men tooke hym prysoner with all his famely. But *Colonus*
commaunded hym to bee losed shortely after, and the greatest parte of his
goodes to bee restored to wynne his fryndeshippe. Beinge here instructed
of a lande lyinge further towarde the southe, he tooke his vyage thether.
Therfore lytle more then tenne myles distant from hense, he founde a large

The regyon of
Quiriquetana or
Ciamba.
lande whiche th[e]inhabitantes cauled *Quiriquetana*: But he named it
Ciamba. When he wente a lande and commaunded his chaplaine to saye
masse on the sea bankes, a great confluence of the naked inhabitantes

Gentle people.
flocked thither symplye and without feare, bringynge with them plenty
of meate and freshe water, marveylynge at owre men as they had byn
summe straunge miracle. When they had presented their giftes, they
went sumwhat backewarde and made lowe curtesy after their maner
bowinge their heades and bodyes reverently. He recompensed their gen-
tylnes rewardinge them with other of owre thynges, as counters, braslettes
and garlandes of glasse and counterfecte stoones, lookyng glasses, nedelles,
and pynnes, with suche other trashe, whiche seemed unto them precious
marchaundies. In this great tracte there are two regions wherof the one is

The regyons of
Taia and Maia.
cauled *Taia* and the other *Maia*. He writeth that all that lande is very fayre
and holsome by reason of the excellent temperatnesse of the ayer: And that
it is inferiour to no lande in frutefull ground beinge partly full of mon-
taines, and partly large playnes: Also replenyshed with many goodly trees,
holsome herbes, and frutes, continuynge greene and floryshynge all the
hole yeare. It beareth also verye many holy trees and pyne aple trees. Also.

Seuen kyndes of
date trees.
Wylde vines.
vii. kyndes of date trees wherof summe are frutefull and summe baren. It
bringeth furth lykewyse of it selfe *Pelgoras* and wilde vynes laden with
grapes even in the wooddes emonge other trees. He saythe furthermore
that there is suche abundaunce of other pleasaunte and profitable frutes,
that they passe not of vynes. Of one of those kyndes of date trees, they make
certeyne longe and brode swoordes and dartes. These regyons beare also
gossampyne trees here and there commonly in the wooddes. Lykewise

Mirobalanes.
Mirobalanes of sundry kyndes, as those which the phisitians caule *Emblicos*
and *Chebulos*, *Maizium* also, *Iucca*, *Ages*, and *Battatas*, lyke unto those
whiche we have sayde before to bee founde in other regions in these coastes.
The same nooryssheth also lyons, Tygers, Hartes, Roes, Goates, and dyvers

Byrdes and
foules.
other beastes. Lykewyse sundry kyndes of byrdes and foules: Emonge the
whiche they keepe only them to franke and feede, whiche are in colour,

bygnes, and taste, muche lyke unto owre pehennes. He saith that th[e]in-
habitantes are of high and goodly stature, well lymmed and proportioned People of goodly stature.
both men and women: Coverynge their privye partes with fyne breeches of
gossampine cotton wrought with dyvers colours. And that they may seeme
the more cumlye and bewtifull (as they take it) they paynte their bodyes They paynt theyr bodyes.
redde and blacke with the juce of certeyne apples whiche they plante in
their gardens for the same purpose. Summe of them paynte their hole
bodies: summe but parte: and other summe drawe the portitures, of herbes,
floures, and knottes, every one as seemeth beste to his owne phantasye.
Their language differeth utterlye from theirs of the Ilandes nere aboute
them.

The Ilande of *Guadalupea* (fyrste named *Caraqueira*) lyinge on the Southe The Iland of Guadalupea.
syde of *Hispaniola*, is foure degrees nearer the Equinoctiall. It is eaten and
indented with two goulfes (as wee reade of great Britanye nowe cauled
Englande, and Caledonia nowe cauled Scotlande) beinge in maner two England and Scotlande.
Ilandes. It hath famous portes. In this they founde that gumme whiche the The gumme cauled Anime album.
Apothecaries caule *Animæ Album*, whose fume is holsome ageynst reumes
and heavynesse of the heade. The tree whiche engendereth this gumme,
beareth a fruite muche lyke to a date, beinge a spanne in length. When it is Dates.
opened, it seemeth to conteyne a certayne sweete meale. As owre husbande
men are accustomed to reserve chestenuttes and suche other harde fruites
all the wynter, soo do they the dates of this tree, beynge muche lyke unto a
fygge tree. They founde also in this Ilande, Pyne trees of the beste kynde, Pine trees.
and suche other deyntie dysshes of nature, wherof wee have spoken largely
before. Ye, they thyncke that th[e]inhabitauntes of other Ilandes, had their
seedes of soo many pleasaunt frutes from hense. For the Canibales beinge a The Canibales.
wylde and wanderynge people, and over runnynge all the countreys aboute
them to hunte for mannes fleshe, were accustomed to brynge home with
them what so ever they founde straunge or profytable in any place. They are
intractable, and wyll admytte no straungiers. It shall therfore bee needefull
to overcoome them with great poure. For as well the women as men, are
experte archiers, and use to inveneme their arrowes. When the men go
foorthe of the lande a man huntynge, the women manfully defende their
coastes ageynst suche as attempte to invade the same. And hereby I suppose
it was thought that there were Ilandes in the Ocean, inhabited onely with Whereby it was thought that there were Ilandes of women.
women, as *Colonus* the admirall hym selfe perswaded me, as I have sayde in
the fyrste decade. This Ilande hath also frutefull mountaynes and playnes,

and notable ryvers. It nouryssheth honye in trees, and in the caves of rockes, as in *Palma* one of the Ilandes of *Canarie*, honye is gathered emong the briers and bramble busshes.

OF THE MANERS AND CUSTOMES OF THE
INDIANS OF THE FIRME LANDE, AND OF
THEYR WOMEN

The maners and customes of these Indians, are dyvers in divers provinces. Sum of them take as many wyves as them lyste, and other lyve with one wyfe whome they forsake not without consent of both parties, which chauncethe especially when they have no chyldren. The nobilitie aswel men as women, repute it infamous to joyne with any of base parentage or strangers, except Christians, whom they count noble men by reason of theyr valientnes, although they put a difference betwene the common sorte and the other to whom they shewe obedience, countynge it for a great matter and an honorable thyng yf they bee beloved of any of them. In so much that yf they knowe any Christian man carnally, they keepe theyr fayth to hym, so that he bee not longe absent farre from them. For theyr intent is not to bee widowes or to lyve chast lyke religious women. Many of theym have this custome, that when they perceave that they are with chylde, they take an herbe wherwith they destroy that is conceaved. For they say that only wel aged women shulde beare chyldren, and that they wyl not forbeare theyr pleasures and deforme theyr boddies with bearynge of chyldren, wherby theyr teates becoome loose and hangynge which thynge they greatly dysprayse. When they are delyvered of theyr chyldren they go to the ryver and washe them. Whiche doone, theyr bludde and purgation ceaseth immediatly. And when after this they have a few days absteyned from the company of men, they becomme so strayght as they say which have had carnall familiaritie with them, that such as use them, can not without much difficultie satisfie theyr appetite. They also whiche never had chyldren, are ever as vyrgins. In sum partes they weare certeyne lyttle apernes rounde about them before and behynde as lowe as to theyr knees and hammes, wherwith they cover theyr privie partes, and are naked all

theyr boddie bysyde. The principal men beare theyr privities in a holowe pype of golde: but the common sorte have theym inclosed in the shelles of certeyne great welkes, and are bysyde utterly naked. For they thynke it no more shame to have theyr coddes seene then any other parte of theyr boddies. And in many provinces bothe the men and women go utterly naked without any such coverture at al. In the province of *Cueua* they caul a man *Chuy*, and a woman *Ira*: which name is not greately disagreeable to many both of theyr women and of owres.

These Indians gyve great honour and reverence to theyr *Cacique* (that is) theyr kynges and rulers. The principall *Cacique*, hath twelve of his most stronge Indians appoynted to beare hym when he removeth to any place, or gothe abrod for his pleasure. Two of them cary hym syttyng uppon a longe piece of woodde which is naturally as lyght as they can fynd The other tenne folowe nexte unto hym as foote men. They keepe continually a trottynge pase with hym on theyr shulders. When the twoo that cary hym are wery, other twoo coomme in theyr places without any disturbance or stey. And thus if the way bee playne, they cary hym in this maner for the space of. xv. or. xx. leaques in one day. The Indians that are assigned to this office, are for the moste parte slaves or *Naboriti*, that is, such as are bounde to continuall service. *(margin: The kynge is borne on mens backes.)*

I have also noted that when the Indians perceave them selves to bee troubled with to much bludde, they lette theym selves blud in the calfes of theyr legges and brawnes of theyr armes. This doo they with a very sharpe stone, and sumtymes with the smaule toothe of a vyper, or with a sharpe reede or thorne. *(margin: Lettinge of bludde.)*

All the Indians are commonly without beardes: In so much that it is in maner a marvayle to see any of them eyther men or women to have any downe or heare on theyr faces or other partes of theyr boddies. Albeit, I sawe the *Cacique* of the province of *Catarapa* who had heare on his face and other partes of his boddie, as had also his wyfe in suche places as women are accustomed to have. This *Cacique* had a great part of his body paynted with a blacke colour which never fadeth: And is much lyke unto that wherwith the Mores paynt them selves in Barberie in token of nobilitie. But the Moores are paynted specially on theyr vysage and throte and certeyne other partes. Likewyse the principall Indians use these payntynges on theyr armes and brestes, but not on theyr vysages, bycause amonge them the slaves are so marked. When the Indians of certeyne provinces go to the battayle (especially the Caniball archers) they cary certeyne shelles of greate welkes of the sea which they blowe and make therwith great sounde muche lyke the noyse of hornes. They carye also certeyne tymbrels which they use in the steade of drummes. Also very fayre plumes of fethers, and *(margin: They have no beardes.)* *(margin: They paynte theyr bodies.)* *(margin: The Canibales.)*

Armure of golde. certeyne armure of golde: especially great and rounde pieces on theyr brestes, and splintes on there armes. Lykewyse other pieces whiche they put on theyr heades and other partes of theyr bodyes. For they esteeme Their galantnes in the warres. nothynge so much as to appeare galante in the war[re]s, and to go in most coomely order that they can devyse, glysterynge with precious stones, jewelles, golde, and fethers. Of the leaste of these welkes or perewincles, Their Juells they make certeyne lyttle beades of divers sortes and colours. They make also little brasselets whiche they mengle with gaudies of golde. These they rowle about there armes frome the elbowe to the wreste of the hande. The lyke also doo they on theyr legges from the knee to the soles of theyr feete in token of nobilitie. Especially theyr noble women in dyvers provinces are accustomed to weare such Jewelles, and have theyr neckes in maner laden therwith. These beades and Jewels and such other trynkettes, they caule *Caquiras*. Bisyde these also, they weare certeyne rynges of golde at theyr eares and nostrelles which they bore ful of holes on both sides, so that the ringes hange uppon theyr lyppes. Sum of these Indians, are poulde and rounded. Albeit, commonly both the men and women take it for a decent thynge to weare longe heare, which the women weare to the myddest of theyr shulders and cut it equally, especially above theyr browes. This doo they with certeyne harde stones which they keepe for the same purpose. The principall women when theyr teates faule or becoome loose, beare them Howe the women beare up their teates, wyth barres of golde. up with barres of golde of the length of a spanne and a halfe, wel wrought, and of such byggenesse that sum of them way more then two hundreth Castilians or ducades of golde. These barres have holes at both th[e]endes, whereat they tye two smaul cordes made of cotton at every ende of the barres. One of these cordes go[e]th over the shulder, and the other under the arme holes where they tye togyther, so that by this meanes the barre beareth up theyr teates. Sum of these chiefe women go to the battayle with theyr husbandes, or when they them selves are regentes in any provinces, in the which they have all thynges at commaundement and execute th[e]office of generall capitaynes, and cause them selves to bee caryed on mens backes in lyke maner as doo the Caciques of whom I have spoken before.

The stature and col
coloure of the Indians. These Indians of the firme lande are muche of the same stature and coloure as are they of the Ilandes. They are for the most part of the colour of an olyve. If there bee any other difference, it is more in byggenesse then The Indians cauled Coronati. otherwyse. And especially they that are cauled *Coronati*, are stronger and bygger then any other that I have seene in these parties, except those of the The Ilande of giantes. Ilande of giantes whiche are on the south syde of the Ilande of *Hispaniola*

nere unto the coastes of the firme lande: And lykewyse certeyne other
which they caule *Yucatos* which are on the north syde. All which chiefely, *Iucatos.*
although they bee no giantes, yet are they doubtelesse the byggeste of the
Indyans that are knowen to this day, and commonly bygger then the
Flemynges: and especially many of them aswell women as men, are of
very hyghe stature, and are all archiers bothe men and women. These
Coronati inhabite thirtie leaques in length by these coastes from the
poynt of *Canoa* to the greate ryver which they caule *Guadalchibir* nere
unto *Sancta Maria de gratia*. As I traversed by those coastes, I fylled a butte
of freshe water of that ryver syxe leaques in the sea frome the mouthe therof
where it fauleth into the sea. They are cauled *Coronati* (that is crowned)
bycause theyr heare is cutte round by theyr eares, and poulde lower a great
compase abowte the crowne much lyke the fryers of saynt Augustines
order. And bycause I have spoken of theyr maner of wearynge theyr
heare, here commeth to my rememberaunce a thynge which I have often-
tymes noted in these Indians. And this is, that they have the bones of the
sculles of theyr heades foure tymes thycker and much stronger then owres. The sculles of
So that in commyng to hand strokes with them, it shalbe requisite not to the Indians
strike them on the heades with swoordes. For so have many swoordes heades.
bynne broken on theyr heades with lyttle hurt doone. [...]

Bartolomé de Las Casas, *A briefe narration of the destruction of the Indies by the Spaniards,* trans. M.M.S. (1583)

ONE of the most significant strands in English perceptions of the Americas was an envy of the Spanish, whose imperial success was in marked contrast to the failure of the English to follow up their early voyages to the Americas in the sixteenth century.[1] While writers like Richard Eden (see above, pp. 16–19) urged the need to learn from the Spanish success in the New World, when the ad hoc wars were fought with Spain towards the end of Elizabeth's reign writers more frequently sought to assert a moral superiority over the Spanish. They claimed that the Spanish had been spectacularly cruel in the Americas and sought to contrast their viciousness to the civilized behaviour of the English, an opposition clearly at work in the extract from Raleigh's *Discoverie of Guiana* (see below, pp. 279–85). 'The Black Legend', as tales of Spanish atrocities was known, was also an extension of Europe's religious wars.[2]

The most frequently cited work which represented Spanish cruelties was the Dominican friar, Bartolomé de Las Casas's, *Brevisima relación de la Destruycion de las Indias occidentales* (1552), first translated into English in 1582 by the unknown M.M.S. Las Casas, who became Bishop of Chiapas in Mexico, was known throughout Europe as the champion of the indigenous peoples of the New World.[3] In England his works had a more propagandist use and it is notable that Las Casas's descriptions of Spanish barbarity were translated not his elaborate defence of the rights of the Amerindians. The passage excerpted here is typical of Las Casas's examples of Spanish brutality. Las Casas provides the reader with a survey of the nations and islands of the Americas which the Spanish occupied and lists the atrocities committed in each one.[4]

---

[1] See Jeffrey Knapp, *An Empire Nowhere: England, America, and Literature from Utopia to The Tempest* (Berkeley: Univ. of California Press, 1992), introd.

[2] William Maltby, *The Black Legend in England: The Development of Anti-Spanish Sentiment* (Durham, NC: Duke Univ. Press, 1971); Andrew Hadfield, *Literature, Travel and Colonial Writing in the English Renaissance, 1545–1625* (Oxford: Clarendon Press, 1998), ch. 2.

[3] See Anthony Pagden, *The Fall of Natural Man: The American Indian and the Origins of Comparative Ethnology* (Cambridge: Cambridge Univ. Press, 1982) for details.

[4] Text taken from Samuel Purchas, *Hakluytus Posthumous or Purchas His Pilgrimes*, 20 vols. (Glasgow: MacLehose, 1905–7), xviii. 85–8, 120–2.

A BRIEFE NARRATION OF THE DESTRUCTION OF THE INDIES BY THE SPANIARDS: WRITTEN BY A FRIER BART. DE LAS CASAS A SPANIARD, AND BISHOP OF CHIAPA IN AMERICA

The Indies were discovered the yeere 1492. and inhabited by the Spanish A.D. 1542 the yeere next after ensuing: so as it is about fortie nine yeeres sithence that the Spaniards some of them went into those parts. And the first Land that they entred to inhabite, was the great and most fertile Ile of Hispaniola, which containeth six hundred leagues in compasse.[1] There are other great and infinite Iles round about, and in the Confines on all sides: which we have seene the most peopled, and the fullest of their owne native people, as any other Countrie in the World may be. The firme Land lying off from this Iland two hundred and fiftie leagues, and somewhat over at the most, containeth in length on the Sea Coast more then ten thousand leagues: which are alreadie discovered, and daily be discovered more and more, all full of people, as an Emmote hill of Emmots. Insomuch, as by that which since, unto the yeere the fortieth and one hath beene discovered: It seemeth that God hath bestowed in that same Countrie, the gulfe or the greatest portion of Mankind.

God created all these innumerable multitudes in every sort, very simple, without subtletie, or craft, without malice, very obedient, and very faithfull to their naturall Liege Lords, and to the Spaniards whom they serve, very humble, very patient, very desirous of peace making, and peacefull, without brawles and strugglings, without quarrels, without strife, without rancour or hatred, by no meanes desirous of revengement.

They are also people very gentle, and very tender, and of an easie complexion, and which can sustaine no travell, and doe die very soone of any disease whatsoever, in such sort as the very children of Princes and Noblemen brought up amongst us, in all commodities, ease, and delicatenesse, are not more soft then those of that Countrie: yea, although they bee the children of Labourers. They are also very poore folke, which possesse little, neither yet doe so much as desire to have much worldly goods, and therefore neither are they proud, ambitious, nor covetous. Their diet is such (as it seemeth) that of the holy Fathers in the Desert hath not bin

---

[1] Hispaniola is the island that contains Haiti and the Dominican Republic. It is 400 miles from East to West and contains 30,000 square miles.

more scarce, nor more straight nor lesse daintie, nor lesse sumptuous. Their apparelling is commonly to goe naked: all save their shamefast parts alone covered. And when they be clothed, at the most, it is but of a Mantle of Bombacie[2] of an ell and a halfe, or two ells of linnen square. Their lodging is upon a Mat, and those which have the best sleepe as it were upon a Net fastened at the foure corners, which they call in the Language of the Ile of Hispaniola, Hamasas.[3] They have their understanding very pure and quicke, being teachable and capeable of all good Learning, very apt to receive our holy Catholike Faith, and to be instructed in good and vertuous manners, having lesse incumberances and disturbances to the attaining thereunto, then all the folke of the world besides, and are so enflamed, ardent, and importune to know and understand the matters of the faith after they have but begunne once to taste them, as likewise the exercise of the Sacraments of the Church, and the divine Service: that in truth, the religious men have need of a singular patience to support them. And to make an end, I have heard many Spaniards many times hold this as assured, and that which they could not denie, concerning the good nature which they saw in them. Undoubtedly these folkes should bee the happiest in the World, if onely they knew God.

Upon these Lambes so meeke, so qualified and endued of their Maker and Creator, as hath bin said, entred the Spanish incontinent as they knew them, as, Wolves, as Lions, and as Tigres most cruell of long time famished: and have not done in those quarters these fortie yeeres past, neither yet doe at this present, ought else save teare them in pieces, kill them, martyr them, afflict them, torment them, and destroy them by strange sorts of cruelties never neither seene, nor read, nor heard of the like (of the which some shall be set downe hereafter) so far forth that of above three Millions of soules that were in the Ile of Hispaniola, and that we have seene, there are not now two hundred natives of the Countrey.[4] The Ile of Cuba, the which is in length as farre as from Valladolid untill Rome, is at this day as it were all waste. Saint Johns Ile,[5] and that of Jamayca, both of them very great, very fertill, and very faire, are desolate. Likewise the Iles of Lucayos,[6]

Three Millions perished in Hispaniola, Oviedo hath but 1600000.

---

[2] Cotton material in the Spanish text.

[3] Hammock.

[4] Las Casas's estimate of the devastation of the native population in the Americas is matched by modern historians; see J. H. Elliott, 'The Spanish Conquest and the Settlement of America', in Leslie Bethell (ed.), *The Cambridge History of Latin America*, vol. i (Cambridge: Cambridge Univ. Press, 1984), 149–206.

[5] Puerto Rico.   [6] The Bahamas.

neere to the Ile of Hispaniola, and of the North side unto that of Cuba, in number being above threescore Ilands, together with those which they call the Iles of Geante,[7] one with another, great and little, whereof the very worst is fertiler then the Kings Garden at Sivill,[8] and the Countrie the healthsomest in the World: there were in these same Iles more then five hundred thousand soules, and at this day there is not one only creature. For they have beene all of them slaine, after that they had drawne them out from thence to labour in their Minerals in the Ile of Hispaniola, where there were no more left of the Natives of that Iland. A ship riding for the space of three yeeres betwixt all these Ilands, to the end, after the inning of this kind of Vintage, to gleane and cull the remainder of these folke (for there was a good Christian moved with pittie and compassion, to convert and win unto Christ such as might be found) there were not found but eleven persons which I saw: other Iles more then thirty, neere to the Ile of Saint John have likewise bin dispeopled and marred. All these Iles containe above two thousand leagues of land, and are all dispeopled and laid waste. [...]

500000 lost in the Lucayos.

OF THE REALME OF YUCATAN

The yeare one thousand five hundred twenty and six, was deputed over the Realme of Yucatan another caitiffe Governour, and that through the lies and false reports which himselfe had made unto the King: in like manner as the other tyrants untill this present, to the end there might be committed unto them offices and charges, by meanes whereof they might rob at their pleasures.[9] This Realme of Yucatan was full of inhabitants; for that it was a Countrie in every respect wholesome, and abounding in plentie of victuals, and of fruites more then Mexico; and singularly exceeded for the abundance of Honie and Waxe there to be found, more then in any quarter of the Indies, which hath beene seene unto this present. It containeth about three hundred leagues compasse. The people of that Countrie were the most notable of all the Indies, as well in consideration of their policie and prudencie, as for the uprightnesse of their life, verily worthy the training of the knowledge of God: amongst whom there might have beene builded

---

[7] Isles of Giants (uncertain which islands they correspond to).
[8] The Royal Gardens outside the city walls of Seville.
[9] Francisco de Montejo (1479?–1553), who had been part of Cortés's expedition to Mexico.

great Cities by the Spanish, in which they might have lived as in an earthly
Paradise, if so be they had not made themselves unworthy, because of their
exceeding covetousnesse, hard hartednesse, and heinous offences: as also
unworthy they were of other moe blessings a great many, which God had
set open in these Indies. This tyrant began with three hundred men to
make warre upon these poore innocent people, which were in their houses
without hurting any body: where he slew and ransacked infinite numbers.
And for because the Countrey yeeldeth no Gold, for if it had yeelded any,
he would have consumed those same Indians, in making them to toyle in
the Mines; to the end he might make Gold of the bodies and soules of those
for whom Jesus Christ suffered death, he generally made slaves of all those
whom he slew not, and returned the Ships that were come thither, upon the
blowing abroad and noyse of the selling of slaves, full of people bartered for
Wine, Oyle, Vinegar, powdred Bacons flesh, Garments, Horses, and that
that every man had neede of, according to the Captains estimate and
judgement. He would let choose amongst an hundred or fiftie yong
Damosels, bartering some one of the fairest, and of the best complexion,
for a Caske of Wine, Oyle, Vinegar, or for Porke powdred. And in like
manner he would let choose out a young hansome Stripling amongst two or
three hundred for the foresaid Merchandize. And it hath beene seene, that
a youth seeming to bee the Sonne of some Prince, hath beene bartered for a
Cheese, and a hundred persons for an Horse. Hee continued in these
doings from the yeere twentie sixe, untill the yeere thirtie three.

As these Spaniards, went with their mad Dogges a foraging by the
tracke, and hunting out the Indian men and women: An Indian woman
being sicke, and seeing she could not escape their Dogges, that they should
not rent her as they did others: shee tooke a coard and hanged her selfe at a
beame, having fastened at her foot a child she had of a yeere old, and she
had no sooner done: behold these Curres, which come and dispatch this
infant, howbeit that before it died, a Religious man a Frier baptized it.

When the Spanish parted out of this Realme, one amongst others said,
to a Sonne of a Lord of some Citie or Province, that he should goe with
him: the Boy answered, and said, he would not forsake his Countrie. The
Spaniard replied: Goe with me, or else I will cut off thine eares. The young
Indian persisted in his first saying, that he would not forsake his Countrie.
The Spaniard drawing out his Dagger, cut off first one, and then his other
eare. The young man abiding by it still that he would not leave his
Countrie: he mangled off also his Nose, with the uppermost of his lips:

making no more scrupulositie of the matter, then if he had given him but a philip. This damnable wretch magnified himselfe, and vaunted him of his doings villanously unto a reverend Religious person, saying: that hee tooke as much paines as hee could, to beget the Indian women in great numbers with child, to the end, he might receive the more money for them in selling them great with childe for slaves.

In this Realme, or in one of the Provinces of New Spaine, a certaine Spaniard went one day with his Dogges on hunting of Venison, or else Conies, and not finding game, hee minded his Dogges that they should bee hungrie, and tooke a little sweet Babie which hee bereaved the mother of, and cutting off from him the armes and the legges, chopped them in small gobbets, giving to every Dogge his Liverie or part thereof, by and by after these morsels thus dispatched, he cast also the rest of the bodie or the carkasse to all the kenell together. [...]

Sir George Peckham, 'A true report of the late discoveries, and possession taken in the right of the Crowne of England of the Newfound Lands, By that valiant and worthy Gentleman, Sir Humfrey Gilbert Knight' (1583)

HUMPHREY GILBERT (1539?–83) was a solider who had spent much time in Ireland before undertaking a number of voyages to North America. He finally established a colony at St John's, Newfoundland, in 1583, but was lost at sea in the southern Azores on the voyage home. The patent to establish colonies granted to him was transferred to his half-brother, Sir Walter Raleigh.[1]

Peckham's account of Gilbert's voyage is worthy of note on a number of counts. Apart from its value as the depiction of an encounter between Europeans and native North Americans, it also seems to indicate the sleights of hand performed when establishing and legitimizing colonies.[2] Peckham provides an invaluable account of the ways in which colonies were planned and set up, as well as a wealth of insight into colonial ideology. Peckham's justification of English colonialism concentrates on the need to convert the native Americans to Christianity (specifically, Protestantism) and the universal law of free trade. Historians of colonialism differ considerably in their judgement of the sincerity of such pronouncements, some arguing that treatises like Peckham's form part of a larger outlook that merits examination; others regard them as cynical disguises for base economic motives.[3] The use of Classical examples shows the importance of Greek and Roman writings in the planning of English colonialism in the Renaissance.[4]

---

[1] For details of Gilbert's life, see William Gilbert Gosling, *The Life of Sir Humphrey Gilbert: England's First Empire Builder* (London: Constable, 1911).

[2] For details of other deceptions, see Stephen Greenblatt, *Marvelous Possessions: The Wonder of the New World* (Oxford: Clarendon Press, 1991), 97–8.

[3] For differing interpretations see K. R. Andrews, *Trade, Plunder and Settlement: Maritime Enterprise and the Genesis of the British Empire, 1480–1630* (Cambridge: Cambridge Univ. Press, 1984), introd.; Andrew Hadfield, 'Rethinking the Black Legend: Sixteenth-Century English Identity and the Spanish Colonial Antichrist', *Reformation*, 3 (1998), 303–22.

[4] For one example see Lisa Jardine, 'Encountering Ireland: Gabriel Harvey, Edmund Spenser, and English Colonial Ventures', in Brendan Bradshaw, Andrew Hadfield, and Willy Maley (eds.), *Representing Ireland: Literature and the Origins of Conflict, 1534–1660* (Cambridge: Cambridge Univ. Press, 1993), 60–75. Text from Richard Hakluyt, *Principall Navigations*, 12 vols. (Glasgow: MacLehose, 1903), viii. 90–101.

See also:

'A discourse by Sir Humphrey Gilbert Knight, to prove a passage by the Northwest to Cathaia, and the East Indies', in Richard Hakluyt, *The Principall Navigations*, 12 vols. (Glasgow: MacLehose, 1903), vii. 158–203 (and subsequent material, pp. 204–466).

David Beers Quinn (ed.), *The Voyages and Colonising Enterprises of Sir Humphrey Gilbert* (London: Hakluyt Society, 1940).

On Munday being the fift of August, the Generall[1] caused his tent to be set upon the side of an hill, in the viewe of all the Fleete of English men and strangers, which were in number betweene thirtie and fourtie sayle: then being accompanied with all his Captaines, Masters, Gentlemen and other souldiers, he caused all the Masters, and principall Officers of the ships, aswell Englishmen as Spanyards, Portugales, and of other nations, to repayre unto his tent: And then and there, in the presence of them all, he did cause his Commission under the great Seale of England to bee openly and solemnely read unto them, whereby were granted unto him, his heires, and assignes, by the Queenes most excellent Majestie, many great and large royalties, liberties, and priviledges. The effect whereof being signified unto the strangers by an Interpreter, hee tooke possession of the sayde land in the right of the Crowne of England by digging of a Turffe and receiving the same with an Hasell wand, delivered unto him, after the maner of the law and custome of England.

Sir Humfrey tooke possession of the Newfound land in right of the Crowne of England.

Then he signified unto the company both strangers and others, that from thencefoorth, they were to live in that land, as the Territories appertayning to the Crowne of England, and to be governed by such Lawes as by good advise should be set downe, which in all points (so neere as might be) should be agreeable to the Lawes of England: And for to put the same in execution, presently he ordained and established three Lawes.

First, that Religion publiquely exercised, should be such, and none other, then is used in the Church of England.

Three lawes established there by Sir Humfrey.

The second, that if any person should bee lawfully convicted of any practise against her Majestie, her Crowne and dignitie, to be adjudged as traitors according to the Lawes of England.

[1] Sir Humphrey Gilbert.

The third, if any should speake dishonourably of her Majestie, the partie so offending, to loose his eares, his ship and goods, to be confiscate to the use of the Generall.

All men did very willingly submit themselves to these Lawes. Then he caused the Queenes Majesties Armes to be ingraved, set up, and erected with great solemnitie. After this, divers Englishmen made sute unto Sir Humfrey to have of him by inheritance, their accustomed stages, standings & drying places, in sundry places of that land for their fish, as a thing that they doe make great accompt of, which he granted unto them in fee farme. And by this meanes he hath possession maintained for him, in many parts of that Countrey. To be briefe, he did let, set, give and dispose of many things, as absolute Governor there, by vertue of her Majesties letters patents.

And after their ships were repaired, whereof one he was driven to leave behind, both for want of men sufficient to furnish her, as also to carrie home such sicke persons as were not able to proceede any further: He departed from thence the 20. of August, with the other three, namely, the Delight, wherein was appointed Captaine in M. William Winters place, (that thence returned immediatly for England) M. Maurice Browne: the Golden Hinde, in which was Captaine and owner, M. Edward Hays: and the little Frigat where the Generall himselfe did goe, seeming to him most fit to discover and approch the shore.

The 21. day they came to Cape Race, toward the South partes whereof, lying a while becalmed, they tooke Cod in largenes and quantitie, exceeding the other parts of Newfound land, where any of them had bene. And from thence, trending the coast West, toward the Bay of Placentia, the Generall sent certaine men a shore, to view the Countrey, which to them as they sayled along, seemed pleasant. Whereof his men at their returne gave great commendation, liking so well of the place, as they would willingly have stayed and wintred there. But having the wind faire and good, they proceeded on their course towards the firme of America, which by reason of continuall fogs, at that time of the yeere especially, they could never see, till Cox Master of the Golden Hinde did discerne land, and presently lost sight thereof againe, at what time they were all upon a breach in a great and outragious storme, having under 3. fathome water. But God delivered the Frigat and the Golden Hind, from this great danger. And the Delight in the presence of them all was lost, to their unspeakeable griefe, with all their chiefe victuall, munition, and other necessary provisions, and other things of value not fit here to be named. Whereupon, by reason also that Winter was come upon them, and foule weather increased with fogs and mists that so covered the land, as without danger of perishing they could not approch it: Sir Humfrey Gilbert and M. Hays were compelled much against their willes to retyre homewards: And being 300. leagues on their way, were after by tempestuous weather separated the one from the other, the ninth of September last, since which time M. Hays with his Barke is safely arrived, but of Sir Humfrey as yet they heare no certaine newes.

Upon this report (together with my former intent, to write some briefe discourse in the commendation of this so noble and worthy an enterprise) I did call to my remembrance, the Historie of Themystocles the Grecian,[2] who (being a right noble and valiant Captaine) signified unto his Countreymen the Citizens of Athens, that he had invented a devise for their common wealth very profitable: but it was of such importance and secrecie, that it ought not to be revealed, before private conference had with some particular prudent person of their choyse.

The Athenians knowing Aristides the Philosopher,[3] to be a man indued with singular wisedome and vertue, made choyse of him to have conference with Themystcles, and thereupon to yeelde his opinion to the Citizens concerning the sayd devise: which was, that they might set on fire the Navie of their enemies, with great facilitie, as he had layde the plot: Aristides made relation to the Citizens, that the strategeme devised by Themystocles was a profitable practise for the common wealth but it was dishonest. The Athenians (without further demaund what the same was) did by common consent reject and condemne it, preferring honesty and upright dealing before profite.

By occasion of this Historie, I drewe my selfe into a more deepe consideration of this late undertaken Voyage, whether it were as well pleasing to almightie God, as profitable to men: as lawfull, as it seemed honourable: as well gratefull to the Savages, as gainefull to the Christians. And upon mature deliberation I found the action to be honest and profitable, and therefore allowable by the opinion of Aristides if he were now alive: which being by me herein sufficiently prooved, (as by Gods grace I purpose to doe) I doubt not but that all good mindes will endevour themselves to be assistants to this so commendable an enterprise, by the valiant and worthy Gentlemen our Countrey men already attempted and undertaken.

---

[2] Plutarch (AD c.46–c.120), Greek moral philosopher and biographer. 'The History of Themystocles' was one of his *Lives*, a popular work in Renaissance Europe.

[3] Aristides (d. AD 189), Greek rhetorician.

Now whereas I doe understand that Sir Humfrey Gilbert his adherents, associates and friends doe meane with a convenient supply (with as much speede as may be) to maintaine, pursue and follow this intended voyage already in part perfourmed, and (by the assistance of almightie God) to plant themselves and their people in the continent of the hither part of America, betweene the degrees of 30. and 60. of septentrionall latitude: Within which degrees by computation Astronomicall and Cosmographicall are doubtlesse to bee found all things that be necessarie, profitable, or delectable for mans life: The clymate milde and temperate, neyther too hote nor too colde, so that under the cope of heaven there is not any where to be found a more convenient place to plant and inhabite in: which many notable Gentlemen, both* of our owne nation and strangers, (who have bene travailers) can testifie: and that those Countries are at this day inhabited with Savages (who have no knowledge of God:) Is it not therefore (I say) to be lamented, that these poore Pagans, so long living in ignorance and idolatry, and in sort thirsting after Christianitie, (as may appeare by the relation of such as have travailed in those partes) that our hearts are so hardened, that fewe or none can be found which will put to their helping hands, and apply themselves to the relieving of the miserable and wretched estate of these sillie soules?

Whose Countrey doeth (as it were with armes advanced) above the climates both of Spaine and France, stretch out it selfe towards England only: In maner praying our ayde and helpe, as it is not onely set forth in Mercators generall Mappe, but it is also found to be true by the discoverie of our nation, and other strangers, who have oftentimes travailed upon the same coasts.

Christopher Columbus of famous memorie, the first instrument to manifest the great glory and mercie of Almightie. God in planting the Christian faith, in those so long unknowen regions, having in purpose to acquaint (as he did) that renoumed Prince, the Queenes Majesties grand-father King Henry the seventh, with his intended voyage for the Westerne *God doeth not* discoveries, was not onely derided and mocked generally, even here in *alwayes begin his* England, but afterward became a laughing stocke to the Spaniards them-*greatest workes by* selves, who at this day (of all other people) are most bounden to laude and *the greatest* prayse God, who first stirred up the man to that enterprise. *persons.*

* Englishmen. Master John Hawkins. Sir Francis Drake. M. William Winter. M. John Chester. M. Martin Frobisher. Anthony Parkhurst. William Battes. John Lovel. David Ingram. Strangers. French. John Ribault. Jaques Cartier. Andrew Thevet. Monsieur Gourgues. Monsieur Laudonnicre. Italians. Christopher Columbus. John Verazanus.

And while he was attending there to acquaint the King of Castile (that then was) with his intended purpose, by how many wayes and meanes was he derided? Some scorned the pildnesse of his garments, some tooke occasion to jest at his simple and silly lookes, others asked if this were he that lowts so lowe, which did take upon him to bring men into a Countrey *His custome was* that aboundeth with Golde, Pearle, and Precious stones? If hee were any *to bowe himselfe very lowe in* such man (sayd they) he would cary another maner of countenance with *making of* him, and looke somewhat loftier. Thus some judged him by his garments, *courtesie.* and others by his looke and countenance, but none entred into the consideration of the inward man.

In the ende, what successe his Voyage had, who list to reade the Decades, the Historie of the West Indies, the conquest of Hernando Cortes about *Hernando Cortes.* Mexico, and those of Francisco Pizarro in Peru about Casamalcha and *Francisco* Cusco, may know more particularly.[4] All which their discoveries, travailes *Pizarro.* and conquests are extant to be had in the English tongue. This devise was then accounted a fantasticall imagination, and a drowsie dreame.

But the sequele thereof hath since awaked out of dreames thousands of soules to knowe their Creator, being thereof before that time altogether ignorant: And hath since made sufficient proofe, neither to be fantasticke nor vainely imagined.

Withall, how mightily it hath inlarged the dominions of the Crowne of Spaine, and greatly inriched the subjects of the same, let all men consider. Besides, it is well knowen, that sithence the time of Columbus his first discoverie, through the planting, possessing, and inhabiting those partes, there hath bene transported and brought home into Europe greater store of Golde, Silver, Pearle, and precious stones, then heretofore hath bene in all ages since the creation of the worlde.

I doe therefore heartily wish, that seeing it hath pleased almightie God of his infinite mercy, at the length to awake some of our worthy Countrey men out of that drowsie dreame, wherein we have so long slumbered:

That wee may now not suffer that to quaile for want of maintenance, which by these valiant Gentlemen our Countreymen is so nobly begun & enterprised. For which purpose, I have taken upon me to write this simple short Treatise, hoping that it shall be able to perswade such as have bene,

---

[4] Many of these works were translated in the 1580s, at the same time that Peckham was composing his treatise, all part of a propaganda effort to encourage colonial expansion. For details, see Andrew Hadfield, *Literature, Travel, and Colonial Writing in the English Renaissance, 1545–1625* (Oxford: Clarendon Press, 1998), 97–8.

and yet doe continue detractors and hinderers of this journey, (by reason perhaps that they have not deliberately and advisedly entred into the judgement of the matter) that yet now upon better consideration they will become favourable furtherers of the same. And that such as are already well affected thereunto, will continue their good disposition: And withall,

I most humbly pray all such as are no nigards of their purses in buying of costly and rich apparel, and liberall Contributors in setting forth of games, pastimes, feastings and banquets, (whereof the charge being past, there is no hope of publique profite or commoditie) that henceforth they will bestowe and employ their liberality (heretofore that way expended) to the furtherance of these so commendable purposed proceedings.

And to this ende have I taken pen in hand, as in conscience thereunto mooved, desiring much rather, that of the great multitude which this Realme doeth nourish, farre better able to handle this matter then I my selfe am, it would have pleased some one of them to have undertaken the same. But seeing they are silent, and that it falleth to my lotte to put pen to the paper, I will endevour my selfe, and doe stand in good hope (though my skill and knowledge bee simple, yet through the assistance of almightie

The argument of the booke.

God) to proove that the Voyage lately enterprised for trade, traffique, and planting in America, is an action tending to the lawfull enlargement of her Majesties Dominions, commodious to the whole Realme in generall, profitable to the adventurers in particular, beneficiall to the Savages, and a matter to be atteined without any great danger or difficultie.

And lastly, (which is most of all) A thing likewise tending to the honour and glory of Almightie God. And for that the lawfulnesse to plant in those Countreyes in some mens judgements seemeth very doubtfull, I will beginne the proofe of the lawfulnesse of trade, traffique, and planting.

THE SECOND CHAPTER SHEWETH, THAT IT IS LAWFULL AND NECESSARIE TO TRADE AND TRAFFIQUE WITH THE SAVAGES: AND TO PLANT IN THEIR COUNTRIES: AND DIVIDETH PLANTING INTO TWO SORTS

And first for traffique, I say that the Christians may lawfully travell into those Countries and abide there: whom the Savages may not justly impugne and forbidde in respect of the mutuall societie and fellowshippe betweene man and man prescribed by the Law of Nations.

For from the first beginning of the creation of the world, and from the renewing of the same after Noes flood, all men have agreed, that no violence should be offered to Ambassadours: That the Sea with his Havens should be common: That such as should fortune to be taken in warre, should be servants or slaves: And that strangers should not bee driven away from the place or Countrey whereunto they doe come.

If it were so then, I demaund in what age, and by what Law is the same forbidden or denied since? For who doubteth but that it is lawfull for Christians to use trade and traffique with Infidels or Savages, carrying thither such commodities as they want, and bringing from thence some part of their plentie?

A thing so commonly and generally practised, both in these our dayes, and in times past, beyond the memorie of man, both by Christians and Infidels, that it needeth no further proofe.

And forasmuch as the use of trade and traffique (be it never so profitable) ought not to be preferred before the planting of Christian faith: I will therefore somewhat intreate of planting, (without which, Christian Religion can take no roote, be the Preachers never so carefull and diligent) which I meane to divide into two sortes.

The first, when Christians by the good liking and willing assent of the Savages, are admitted by them to quiet possession. *The principall causes why this voyage is undertaken.*

The second, when Christians being unjustly repulsed, doe seeke to attaine and mainteine the right for which they doe come.

And though in regard of the establishment of Christian Religion, eyther of both may be lawfully and justly exercised: (Whereof many examples may be found, as well in the time of Moyses and Josua, and other rulers before the birth of Christ, as of many vertuous Emperours and Kings sithence his incarnation:) yet doe I wish, that before the second be put in practise, a proofe may be made of the first, saving that for their safetie as well against the Savages, as all other forreigne enemies, they should first well and strongly fortifie themselves: which being done, then by all fayre speeches, and every other good meanes of perswasion to seeke to take away all occasions of offence.

As letting them to understand, how they came not to their hurt, but for their good, and to no other ende, but to dwell peaceably amongst them, and to trade and traffique with them for their owne commoditie, without molesting or grieving them any way: which must not be done by wordes onely but also by deedes.

For albeit, to maintaine right and repell injury, be a just cause of warre: yet must there hereof be heedefull care had, that whereas the Savages be fearefull by nature, and fond otherwise, the Christians should doe their best endevour to take away such feare as may growe unto them by reason of their strange apparell, Armour, and weapon, or such like, by quiet and peaceable conversation, and letting them live in securitie, and keeping a measure of blamelesse defence, with as little discommoditie to the Savages as may bee: for this kinde of warre would be onely defensive and not offensive.

And questionlesse there is great hope and likelyhoode, that by this kinde of meanes we should bring to passe all effects to our desired purposes: Considering that all creatures, by constitution of nature, are rendred more tractable and easier wonne for all assayes, by courtesie and mildnesse, then by crueltie or roughnesse: and therefore being a principle taught us by naturall reason, it is first to be put in ure.

For albeit as yet the Christians are not so throughly furnished with the perfectnesse of their language, eyther to expresse their mindes to them, or againe to conceive the Savages intent: Yet for the present opportunitie, such policie may be used by friendly signes, and courteous tokens towards them, as the Savages may easily perceive (were their sences never so grosse) an assured friendship to be offered them, and that they are encountered with such a nation, as brings them benefite, commoditie, peace, tranquilitie and safetie. To further this, and to accomplish it in deedes, there must bee presented unto them gratis, some kindes of our pettie marchandizes and trifles: As looking glasses, Belles, Beades, Bracelets, Chaines, or collers of Bewgle, Chrystall, Amber, Jet, or Glasse &c. For such be the things, though to us of small value, yet accounted by them of high price and estimation: and soonest will induce their Barbarous natures to a liking and a mutuall societie with us.

Moreover, it shall be requisite eyther by speeche, if it be possible, either by some other certaine meanes, to signifie unto them, that once league of friendship with all loving conversation being admitted betweene the Christians and them: that then the Christians from thenceforth will always be ready with force of Armes to assist and defend them in their just quarrels, from all invasions, spoyles and oppressions offered them by any Tyrants, Adversaries, or their next borderers: and a benefite is so much the more to be esteemed, by how much the person upon whom it is bestowed standeth in neede thereof.

For it appeareth by the relation of a Countryman of ours, namely David Ingram,[5] (who travelled in those countries xi. Moneths and more) That the Savages generally for the most part, are at continuall warres with their next adjoyning neighbours, and especially the Cannibals, being a cruell kinde of people, whose foode is mans flesh, and have teeth like dogges, and doe pursue them with ravenous mindes to eate their flesh, and devoure them.

And it is not to be doubted, but that the Christians may in this case justly and lawfully ayde the Savages against the Cannibals. So that it is very likely, that by this meanes we shall not only mightily stirre and inflame their rude mindes gladly to embrace the loving company of the Christians, proffering unto them both commodities, succour, and kindnesse: But also by their franke consents shall easily enjoy such competent quantity of Land, as every way shall be correspondent to the Christians expectation and contentation, considering the great abundance that they have of Land, and how small account they make thereof, taking no other fruites thereby then such as the ground of it selfe doeth naturally yeelde. And thus much concerning the first sort of planting, which as I assuredly hope, so I most heartily pray may take effect and place.

But if after these good and fayre meanes used, the Savages neverthelesse will not bee herewithall satisfied, but barbarously will goe about to practise violence eyther in repelling the Christians from their Ports & safe-landings, or in withstanding them afterwards to enjoy the rights for which both painfully and lawfully they have adventured themselves thither: *The seconde kinde of planting.*

Then in such a case I holde it no breach of equitie for the Christians to defend themselves, to pursue revenge with force, and to doe whatsoever is necessarie for the atteining of their safetie: For it is allowable by all Lawes in such distresses, to resist violence with violence: And for their more securitie to increase their strength by building of Forts for avoyding the extremitie of injurious dealing. [...]

---

[5] David Ingram's travels are recorded elsewhere in Hakluyt's *Principall Navigations*, ix. 412–13. See also Samuel Purchas, *Purchas His Pilgrimes*, 20 vols. (Glasgow: MacLehose, 1905–7), xvi. 109.

Thomas Harriot, *A Briefe and True Report of the New Found Land of Virginia* (1588, 1590)

THOMAS HARRIOT (1560–1621), was a scientist, mathematician, and New World colonist. Sir Walter Raleigh employed him as an 'excellent fellow' to teach him cosmography and navigation when Raleigh was starting to become interested in colonizing the Americas in the early 1580s.[1] Raleigh was keen to take over Sir Humphrey Gilbert's rights to explore and colonize eastern North America (see above, p. 256), although he never set foot in the Virginian colonies he promoted himself.[2] Harriot probably first sailed to Virginia in 1584 and started his fruitful collaboration with the artist John White, who recorded visual images of the Algonkian natives. Harriot had learnt Algonkian by July 1585 and was 'sent out . . . to take special note of everything concerning the Indians which was relevant to the English plans for settlement'.[3] The result of his labours was the *Brief and True Report*, first published in an unremarkable quarto in 1588, detailing the advantages to be gained from colonization. Harriot's short text was clearly designed to scotch rumours of the futility of the enterprise and dissension among the colonists. The preface darkly refers to some of the company being 'worthily punished' for 'their misdemeanour and ill dealing in the countrey' and 'some slanderous and shamefull speeches bruited abroad by many that returned from thence'. Harriot divides his treatise into three sections, the first two dealing with the vast list of commodities that were to be found in the Americas, and the third principally with the 'nature and manners of the people'. Harriot is at pains to represent the Algonkians as docile, friendly, and accommodating to their new guests.

Harriot's published report was only a summary of his complete record of the colony, which, sadly, has not survived. It was reprinted in a spectacularly handsome folio edition as the first part of the Belgian printer Theodor De Bry's massive survey, *America* (1590–1634). Twenty-three plates detailing the behaviour, society, and culture of the Algonkians based on White's drawings were appended with a commentary usually ascribed to Harriot, as were five representing ancient Britons and Picts.

---

[1] David Beers Quinn, 'Thomas Harriot and the New World', in John Shirley (ed.), *Thomas Harriot: Renaissance Scientist* (Oxford: Clarendon Press, 1974), 36–53, at p. 38.

[2] For details see David Beers Quinn, *Raleigh and the British Empire* (London: Hodder and Stoughton, 1947), chs. 2–4.

[3] Quinn, 'Thomas Harriot', 39.

I have included two extracts and four illustrations (Figs. 13, 14, 15, 16). The first extract gives a sense of Harriot's extensive list of the wonderful commodities that could be found in Virginia. Harriot was especially keen on tobacco and was a vigorous defender of the virtues of smoking, as were many keen propagandists for colonial enterprises in the Americas.[4] He died of cancer of the nose.[5] The second details the natives' complex and disturbing response to the new diseases which were brought over by the English.[6] The passage has been variously interpreted but seems to balance an intellectual sympathy for and curiosity at the fate of the native Americans with an awareness that whatever the scope and significance of the disaster, it helps to confirm English power and so encourage more Englishmen to become interested in colonial ventures.[7]

See also:

David Beers Quinn (ed.), *The Roanoke Voyages, 1584–1590: Documents to illustrate the English voyages to north America under the patent granted to Walter Raleigh in 1584*, 2 vols. (London: Hakluyt Society, 1955).

[4] See Jeffrey Knapp, *An Empire Nowhere: England, America, and Literature from* Utopia *to* The Tempest (Berkeley: Univ. of California Press, 1992), ch. 4.

[5] For details see John Shirley, 'Sir Walter Raleigh and Thomas Harriot', in Shirley (ed.), *Thomas Harriot*, 16–35, at p. 31.

[6] The most celebrated discussion of this passage is Stephen Greenblatt, 'Invisible Bullets', in *Shakespearean Negotiations: The Circulation of Social Energy in Renaissance England* (Oxford: Clarendon Press, 1988), 21–65.

[7] Text from Thomas Harriot, *A briefe and true report [rep. with additions]* (1590), 15–16 (corrected against the 1588 edition), 28–30.

Then their setting or sowing is after this maner. First for their corne,[1] beginning in one corner of the plot, with a pecker they make a hole, wherein they put foure graines with that care they touch not one another, (about an inch asunder) and cover them with the moulde againe: and so through out the whole plot, making such holes and using them after such maner: but with this regard that they bee made in rankes, every ranke differing from other halfe a fadome or a yarde, and the holes also in every ranke, as much. By this meanes there is a yarde spare ground betwene every hole: where according to discretion here and there, they set as many Beanes

[1] Growing food, especially corn, was a huge problem for the English colonists. They invariably proved incompetent at New World agriculture and unable to feed themselves. This led to conflict with the natives, who would resent having to supfnply the English with food after initial generosity. See Greenblatt, 'Invisible Bullets', 29.

and Peaze: in divers places also among the seedes of *Macócqwer*, *Melden* and *Planta Solis*. [...]

I thought also good to note this unto you, that you which shall inhabite and plant there, maie know how specially that countrey corne is there to be preferred before ours: Besides the manifold waies in applying it to victuall, the increase is so much that small labour and paines is needful in respect that must be used for ours. For this I can assure you that according to the rate we have made proofe of, one man may prepare and husband so much grounde (having once borne corne before) with lesse then foure and twentie houres labour, as shall yeelde him victuall in a large proportion for a twelve moneth, if hee have nothing else, but that which the same ground will yeelde, and of that kinde onelie which I have before spoken of: the saide ground being also but of five and twentie yards square. And if neede require, but that there is ground enough, there might be raised out of one and the selfsame ground two harvestes or ofcomes; for they sowe or set and may at anie time when they thinke good from the middest of March untill the ende of June: so that they also set when they have eaten of their first croppe. In some places of the countrey notwithstanding they have two harvests, as we have heard, out of one and the same gound.

For English corne nevertheles whether to use or not to use it, you that inhabite maie do as you shall have farther cause to thinke best. Of the grouth you need not to doubt: for barlie, oates and peaze, we have seene proof of, not beeing purposely sowen but fallen casually in the worst sort of ground, and yet to be as faire as any we have ever seene here in England. But of wheat because it was musty and had taken salt water wee could make no triall: and of Rye we had none. Thus much have I digressed and I hope not unnecessarily: nowe will I returne againe to my course and intreate of that which yet remaineth appertaining to this Chapter.

There is an herbe which is sowed a part by itselfe & is called by the inhabitants *Uppówoc*: In the West Indies it hath divers names, according to the severall places & countries where it groweth and is used: The Spaniardes generally call it *Tobacco*. The leaves thereof being dried and brought into powder: they use to take the fume or smoke thereof by sucking it through pipes made of claie into their stomacke and heade; from whence it purgeth superfluous fleame & other grosse humors, openeth all the pores & passages of the body: by which meanes the use thereof, not only preserveth the body from obstructions; but also if any be, so that they have not beene of too long continuance, in short time breaketh them:

wherby their bodies are notably preserved in health, & know not many greevous diseases wherewithall wee in England are oftentimes afflicted.

This *Uppówoc* is of so precious estimation amongest them, that they thinke their gods are marvelously delighted therwith: Wherupon some-time they make hallowed fires & cast some of the pouder therein for a sacrifice: being in a storme uppon the waters, to pacifie their gods, they cast some up into the aire and into the water: so a weare for fish being newly set up, they cast some therein and into the aire: also after an escape of danger, they cast some into the aire likewise: but all done with strange gestures, stamping, somtime dauncing, clapping of hands, holding up of hands, & staring up into the heavens, uttering therewithal and chattering strange words & noises.

We ourselves during the time we were there used to suck it after their maner, as also since our returne, & have found manie rare and wonderful experiments of the vertues thereof; of which the relation woulde require a volume by itselfe: the use of it by so manie of late, men & women of great calling as else, and some learned Phisitions also, is sufficient witnes.

One other rare and strange accident, leaving others, will I mention before I ende, which mooved the whole countrey that either knew or hearde of us, to have us in wonderfull admiration.

There was no towne where we had any subtile devise practised against us, we leaving it unpunished or not revenged (because wee sought by all meanes possible to win them by gentlenesse) but that within a few dayes after our departure from everie such towne, the people began to die very fast, and many in short space; in some townes about twentie, in some fourtie, in some sixtie, & in one six score, which in trueth was very manie in respect of their numbers. This happened in no place that wee coulde learne but where wee had bene, where they used some practise against us, and after such time; The disease also so strange, that they neither knew what it was, nor how to cure it; the like by report of the oldest men in the countrey never happened before, time out of minde. A thing specially observed by us as also by the naturall inhabitants themselves.

Insomuch that when some of the inhabitants which were our friends & especially the *Wiroans Wingina*[2] had observed such effects in foure or five towns to follow their wicked practises, they were perswaded that it was the

---

[2] Harriot defines Wiroan as a 'great lord'. Wingina was the Wiroan of the people 'with whom we dwelt'.

The aged man in his wynter garment.

FIG. 12. John White, Old Indian Man (*c.*1585–6)

worke of our God through our meanes, and that wee by him might kil and slai whom wee would without weapons and not come neere them.

And thereupon when it had happened that they had understanding that any of their enemies had abused us in our journeyes, hearing that wee had wrought no revenge with our weapons, & fearing upon some cause the matter should so rest: did come and intreate us that we woulde bee a meanes to our God that they as others that had dealt ill with us might in like sort die; alleaging howe much it would be for our credite and profite, as also theirs; and hoping furthermore that we would do so much at their requests in respect of the friendship we professe them.

Whose entreaties although wee shewed that they were ungodlie, affirming that our God would not subject him selfe to anie such praiers and requestes of men: that in deede all thinges have beene and were to be done according to his good pleasure as he had ordained: and that we to shew our selves his true servants ought rather to make petition for the contrarie, that they with them might live together with us, bee made partakers of his truth & serve him in righteousnes; but notwithstanding in such sort, that wee referre that as all other thinges, to bee done according to his divine will & pleasure, and as by his wisedome he had ordained to be best.

Yet because the effect fell out so sodainly and shortly after according to their desires, they thought neverthelesse it came to passe by our meanes, and that we in using such speeches unto them did but dissemble the matter, and therefore came unto us to give us thankes in their manner that although wee satisfied them not in promise, yet in deedes and effect we had fulfilled their desires.

This marvelous accident in all the countrie wrought so strange opinions of us, that some people could not tel whether to think us gods or men, and the rather because that all the space of their sicknesse, there was no man of ours knowne to die, or that was specially sicke: they noted also that we had no women amongst us, neither that we did care for any of theirs.

Some therefore were of opinion that wee were not borne of women, and therefore not mortall, but that wee were men of an old generation many yeeres past then risen againe to immortalitie.

Some would likewise seeme to prophesie that there were more of our generation yet to come, to kill theirs and take their places, as some thought the purpose was by that which was already done.

Those that were immediatly to come after us they imagined to be in the aire, yet invisible & without bodies, & that they by our intreaty & for the love of us did make the people to die in that sort as they did by shooting invisible bullets into them.

To confirme this opinion their phisitions to excuse their ignorance in curing the disease, would not be ashemed to say, but earnestly make the simple people beleve, that the strings of blood that they sucked out of the sicke bodies, were the strings wherewithal the invisible bullets were tied and cast.

Some also thought that we shot them our selves out of our pieces from the place where we dwelt, and killed the people in any such towne that had offended us as we listed, how farre distant from us soever it were.

And other some saide that it was the speciall woorke of God for our sakes, as wee ourselves have cause in some sorte to thinke no lesse, whatsoever some doe or maie imagine to the contrarie, specially some Astrologers knowing of the Eclipse of the Sunne which wee saw the same yeere before in our voyage thytherward, which unto them appeared very terrible.[3] And also of a Comet which beganne to appeare but a few daies before the beginning of the said sicknesse.[4] But to exclude them from being the speciall an accident, there are farther reasons then I thinke fit at this present to bee alleadged.

These their opinions I have set downe the more at large that it may appeare unto you that there is good hope they may be brought through discreet dealing and governement to the imbracing of the trueth, and consequently to honour, obey, feare and love us.

And although some of our companie towardes the ende of the yeare, shewed themselves too fierce, in slaying some of the people, in some towns, upon causes that on our part, might easily enough have been borne withall:[5] yet notwithstanding because it was on their part justly deserved, the alteration of their opinions generally & for the most part concerning us is the lesse to bee doubted. And whatsoever els they may be, by carefulnesse of our selves neede nothing at all to be feared. The best neverthelesse in this as in all actions besides is to be endevoured and hoped, & of the worst that may happen notice to bee taken with consideration, and as much as may be eschewed.

[3] There was an eclipse of the sun on 19 Apr. 1585.

[4] A comet appeared in mid-October and was visible until mid-November in 1585.

[5] This is probably a reference to the brutal tactics of the governor, Ralph Lane (d. 1603). Elsewhere Harriot records his disapproval of Lane's militaristic behaviour and harsh treatment of the Indians. See David Beers Quinn (ed.), *The Roanoke Voyages, 1584–1590*, 2 vols. (London: Hakluyt Society, 1955), *passim*.

FIG. 13. 'A weroan or great Lorde of Virginia' (Harriot, *Briefe and True Report of... Virginia* (1590), plate III)

The Princes of Virginia are attyred in suche manner as is expressed in this figure. They weare the haire of their heades long and bynde opp the ende of the same in a knot under thier eares. Yet they cutt the topp of their heades from the forehead to the nape of the necke in manner of a cokscombe, stirkinge a faier longe pecher of some berd att the Begininge of the creste uppun their foreheads, and another short one on bothe seides about their eares. They hange at their eares ether thicke pearles, or somwhat els, as the clawe of some great birde, as cometh in to their fansye. Moreover They ether pownes, or paynt their forehead, cheeks, chynne, bodye, armes, and leggs, yet in another sorte then the inhabitantz of Florida. They weare a chaine about their necks of pearles or beades of copper, wich they muche esteeme, and ther of wear they also braselets ohn their armes. Under their brests about their bellyes appeir certayne spotts, whear they use to lett them selves bloode, when they are sicke. They hange before them the skinne of some beaste verye feinelye dresset in suche sorte, that the tayle hangeth downe behynde. They carye a quiver made of small rushes holding their bowe readie bent in on hand, and an arrowe in the other, radie to defend themselves. In this manner they goe to warr, or tho their solemne feasts and banquetts. They take muche pleasure in huntinge of deer wher of theris great store in the contrye, for yt is fruit full, pleasant, and full of Goodly woods. Yt hathe also store of rivers full of divers sorts of fishe. When they go to battel they paynt their bodyes in the most terible manner that thei can devise.

FIG. 14. 'Their manner of careynge ther Childern and a tyere of the cheiffe Ladyes of the towne of Dasamonquepeuc' (Harriot, *Briefe and True Report*, plate x)

In the towne of Dasemonquepeuc distant from Roanoac 4. or 5. milles, the woemen are attired, and pownced, in suche sorte as the woemen of Roanoac are, yet they weare noe worathes uppon their heads, nether have they their thighes painted with small pricks. They have a strange manner of bearing their children, and quite contrarie to ours. For our woemen carrie their children in their armes before their brests, but they taking their sonne by the right hand, bear him on their backs, holdinge the left thighe in their lefte arme after a strange, and conuesnall fashion, as in the picture is to bee seene.

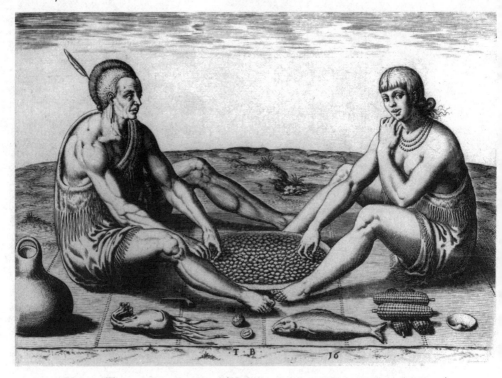

FIG. 15. 'Their sitting at meate' (Harriot, *Briefe and True Report*, plate xvi)

Their manner of feeding is in this wise. They lay a matt made of bents one the grownde and sett their meate on the mids therof, and then sit downe Rownde, the men uppon one side, and the woemen on the other. Their meate is Mayz sodden, in suche sorte as I described yt in the former treatise of verye good taste, deers flesche, or of some other beaste, and fishe. They are verye sober in their eatinge, and trinkinge, and consequentlye verye longe lived because they doe not oppress nature.

XX.   THE TOWNE OF SECOTA

Their townes that are not inclosed with poles aire commonlye fayrer. Then suche as are inclosed, as appereth in this figure which livelye expresseth the towne of Secotam. For the howses are Scattered heer and ther, and they have gardein expressed by the letter E. wherin groweth Tobacco which the

FIG. 16. 'The Towne of Secota' (Harriot, *Briefe and True Report*, plate xx)

inhabitants call Uppowoc. They have also groaves wherin thei take deer, and fields [w]herin they sowe their corne. In their corne fields they builde as yt weare a scaffolde wher on they sett a cottage like to a rownde chaire, signiffied by F. wherin they place one to watche. for there are suche nomber of fowles, and beasts, that unless they keepe the better watche, they would soone devoure all their corne. For which cause the watcheman maketh continual cryes and noyse. They sowe their corne with a certaine distance noted by H. other wise one stalke would choke the growthe of another and the corne would not come unto his rypeurs G. For the leaves therof are large, like unto the leaves of great reedes. They have also a severall broade plotte C. whear they meete with their neighbours, to celebrate their cheefe solemne feastes as the picture doth declare: and a place D. whear after they have ended their feaste they make merrie togither. Over against this place they have a rownd plott B. wher they assemble themselves to make their solemne prayers. Not far from which place ther is a lardge buildinge A. wherin are the tombes of their kings and princes [. . .] likewise they have garden notted bey the letter I. wherin they use to sowe pompions.[6] Also a place marked with K. wherin the make a fyre att their solemne feasts, and hard without the towne a river L. from whence they fetche their water. This people therfore voyde of all covetousnes lyve cherfullye and att their harts ease. Butt they solemnise their feasts in the nigt, and therfore they keepe verye great fyres to avoyde darkenes, ant to testifie their Joye.

[6] Pumpkins.

Sir Walter Raleigh, *The Discoverie of the Large, Rich and Bewtiful Empyre of Guiana* (1596)

THE public career of Sir Walter Raleigh (1554–1618) was nothing if not adventurous and organized around a series of risks, calculated or otherwise. Raleigh was briefly imprisoned in the Tower of London when his secret marriage to Elizabeth Throckmorton, one of Elizabeth's ladies-in-waiting, was discovered when she gave birth to their son in 1592. The Raleighs settled in Sherborne in Dorset but attempted to regain favour with the queen when he led an expedition up the Orinoco River in South America. The carefully crafted work, which he wrote soon after the enterprise, presents a persuasive case for colonization in the Americas. Raleigh argues that unless the English seek to compete with the Spanish in the Americas then they will establish a dominance that will be hard to resist. Raleigh contrasts the brutality of Spanish colonialism with the benign and virtuous behaviour of the English who manage to establish a rapport with the natives. The extravagant claims Raleigh makes for the existence of the fabled city of El Dorado where the streets were paved with gold was to lead to his downfall twenty years later when he was sent on a do-or-die mission by James I.

The text has usually been read in terms of Raleigh's anxieties and desire to flatter the queen in order to win her favour once again. It is no accident that Raleigh is at pains to stress the sexual continence of the English colonists, partly as a means of reasserting his own reformed character after his fall from grace three years earlier. Equally, the apparent discovery of the Amazons, the legendary women warriors, may have been included to flatter Elizabeth and incite her interest in the area.[1] However, as the *Discoverie*'s most recent editor, Neil Whitehead, has observed, such concerns should not blind us to the fact that Raleigh was a good ethnographical observer of the natives and his account should be taken seriously as an accurate record of the lives of a vanished people.[2]

The four extracts included here provide a representative sample of Raleigh's concerns in his work. The first describes the huge wealth which can be gained from Guiana and the legend of El Dorado; the second describes the legendary race of Amazon women whom Raleigh does not

---

[1] Louis A. Montrose, 'The Work of Gender in the Discourse of Discovery', *Representations*, 33 (1991), 1–41; Jeffrey Knapp, *An Empire Nowhere: England, America, and Literature from Utopia to* The Tempest (Berkeley: Univ. of California Press, 1992), 189–204.

[2] Sir Walter Raleigh, *The Discoverie of the Large, Rich and Bewtiful Empyre of Guiana*, ed. Neil L. Whitehead (Manchester: Manchester Univ. Press, 1997), 60–116.

see but hears much about; the third relates a specific encounter with the
native Guianans, illustrating the complexity of relationships between the
indigenous population and the two competing colonial communities; and
the fourth, another description of the natural advantages of Guiana, provides a familiar colonial trope whereby the land is represented as a willing
female ready for the advances of the male colonizers.[3]

[3] Text from Sir Walter Raleigh, *The Discoverie of the Large, Rich and Bewtiful Empire of
Guiana. Performed in the yeere 1595. By Sir W. Ralegh* (1596), pp. 10–13, 22–24, 48–52, 96–7.

The Empyre of *Guiana* is directly east from *Peru* towards the sea, and lieth
under the Equinoctiall line, and it hath more abundance of Golde then any
part of *Peru*, and as many or moe great Cities then ever *Peru* had when it
florished most: it is governed by the same lawes, and the Emperour and
people observe the same religion, and the same forme and pollicies in
government as was used in *Peru*, not differing in any part: and as I have
beene assured by such of the *Spanyardes* as have seene *Manoa* the imperial
Citie of *Gurana*, which the *Spaniards* cal *El Dorado*, that for the greatnes,
for the riches, and for the excellent seate, it farre exceedeth any of the
world, at least of so much of the world as is knowen to the Spanish nation:
it is founded upon a lake of salt water of 200. leagues long like unto *mare
caspium*. And if we compare it to that of *Peru*, & but read the report of
Francisco Lopez & others, it wil seeme more then credible, and because we
may judge of the one by the other, I thought good to insert part of the 120.
chapter of *Lopez* in his generall historie of the *Indies*, wherein he discribeth
the court and magnificence of *Guynacapa*, auncestor to the Emperour of
Guiana, whose very wordes are these. [...]

All the vessels of his house, table and kitchin were of Gould and Silver,
and the meanest of silver & copper for strength and hardness of mettal.
He had in his wardroppe hollow statues of golde which seemed giants, and
the figures in proportion and bignes of all the beastes, birdes, trees and
hearbes, that the earth bringeth forth: and of all the fishes that the sea or
waters of his kingdome breedeth. Hee had also ropes, budgets, chestes and
troughs of golde and silver, heapes of billets of golde that seemed woode,
marked out to burne. Finally there was nothing in his countrey, whereof he
had not the counterfeat in gold: Yea and they say, The *Ingas* had a garden of
pleasure in an Iland neere *Puna*, where they went to recreate themselves,

when they would take the ayre of the sea, which had all kind of garden hearbes, flowers and trees of Gold and Silver, an invention, & magnificence til then never seene. Besides all this, he had an infinite quantitie of silver and gold unwrought in *Cuzco* which was lost by the death of *Guascar*, for the Indians hid it, seeing that the Spaniards tooke it, and sent it into Spaine.

And in the 117. Chapter *Francisco Picarro* caused the Goulde, and Silver of *Atabalipa* to bee weyed, after hee had taken it, which *Lopez* setteth downe in these wordes following. [...]

They found fiftie and two thousand markes of good silver, and one million, and three hundred twentie and six thousand and five hundred pesoes of golde.

Nowe although these reportes may seeme strange, yet if wee consider the many millions which are daily brought out of *Peru* into spaine, wee may easely beleeve the same, for wee finde that by the abundant treasure of that countrey, the Spanish King vexeth all the Princes of Europe, and is become in a fewe yeares from a poore king of *Castile* the greatest monarke of this parte of the worlde, and likelie every day to increase, if other Princes forsloe the good occasions offered, and suffer him to adde this Empire to the rest, which by farre exceedeth all the rest: if his golde now indanger us, hee will then be unresistable.[1]

There was another this yeere in *Helford* that also came from thence, and had been 14. moneths at an ancor in *Amazones*, which were both very rich. Although as I am perswaded; *Guiana* cannot be entred that way, yet no doubt the trade of gold from thence passeth by braunches of rivers into the river of *Amazones* and so it doth on every hand farre from the countrey it selfe, for those Indians of *Trinedado* have plates of gold from *Guiana*, and those *Canibals* of *Dominica* which dwell in the Ilands by which our ships passe yeerly to the *West Indies*, also the Indians of *Paria*, those Indians called *Tucaris, Chochi, Apotomios, Cumanagotos*, and all those other nations inhabiting nere about the mountains that run from *Paria* thorow the Province of *Vensuello*, and in *Maracapana*, and the Canibals of *Guanipa*, the Indians called *Assawai, Coaca, Aiai*, and the rest (all which shall be described in my description as they are situate) have plates of gold of

---

[1] On Spanish bullion from the Americas and its significance, see R. Trevor Davies, *The Golden Century of Spain, 1501–1621* (London: Macmillan, 1967, repr. of 1937), 62–4, 263–7, *et passim*.

Guiana. And upon the river of *Amazones Thevet*[2] writeth that the people weare *Croissants* of gold, for of that form the *Guianinians* most commonly make them: So as from *Dominica* to *Amazones* which is above 250. leagues, al the chiefe Indians in al parts weare of those plates of *Guiana.* Undoubtedly those that trade *Amazones* returne much gold, which (asis aforesaide) commeth by trade from *Guiana,* by some branch of a river that falleth from the countrey into *Amazones,* and either it is by the river which passeth by the nations called *Tisnados,* or by *Carepuna.* I made inquiry amongst the most ancient and best traveled of the *Orenoqueponi,* & I had knowledge of all the rivers between *Orenoque* and *Amazones,* and was very desirous to understand the trueth of those warlike women, bicause of some it is beleeved, of others not: And though I digresse from my purpose, yet I will set downe that hath beene delivered me for truth of those women, and I spake with a *Casique* or Lorde of people that told me he had been in the river, and beyond it also. The nations of these women are on the south side of the river in the Privinces of *Topago,* and their chiefest strengths, and retracts are in the Ilands scituate on the south side of the entrance, some 60, leagues within the mouth of the saide river. The memories of the like women are verie ancient as well in *Africa* as in *Asia*: In *Africa* those that had *Medusa* for *Queene*: others in *Scithia* neere the rivers of *Tanais* and *Thermadon*: we finde also that *Lampedo* and *Marthesia* were *Queens* of the *Amazones*: in many histories they are verified to have been, and in divers ages and Provinces: But they which are not far from *Guiana* do accompanie with men but once in a yeare, and for the time of one moneth, which I gather by their relation to be in Aprill. And that time all Kings of the borders assemble, and Queenes of the *Amazones,* and after the Queenes have chosen, the rest cast lots for their *Valentines.* This one moneth, they feast, dance, & drinke of their wines in abundance, and the Moone being done, they all depart to their owne Provinces. If they conceive, and be delivered of a sonne, they returne him to the father, if of a daughter they nourish it, and retaine it, and as many as have daughters send unto the begetters a Present, all being desirous to increase their owne sex and kind, but that they cut of the right dug of the brest I do not finde to be true. It was farther told me, that if in these wars they tooke any prisoners that they used to accompany with those also at what time soever, but in the end for

---

2 André Thevet (1504–92), French cosmographer and chronicler of the French colony established in Brazil, 1555–65, eventually destroyed by the Spanish.

certaine they put them to death: for they are said to be very cruell and bloodthirsty, especially to such as offer to invade their territories. These *Amazones* have likewise great store of these plates of golde, which they recover by exchange chiefly for a kinde of greene stones, which the Spaniards call *Piedras Hijadas*, and we use for spleene stones, and for the disease of the stone we also esteeme them: of these I saw divers in *Guiana*, and commonly every king or *Casique* hath one, which their wives for the most part weare, and they esteem them as greate jewels.

On both sides of this river, we passed the most beautifull country that ever mine eies beheld. and whereas all that we had seen before was nothing but woods, prickles, bushes, and thornes, heere we beheld plaines of twentie miles in length, the grasse short and greene, and in divers parts groves of trees by themselves, as if they had been by all the art and labour in the world so made of purpose: and stil as we rowed, the Deere came downe feeding by the waters side, as if they had beene used to a keepers cal.[3] Upon this river there were great store of fowle, and of many sorts: we saw in it divers sorts of strange fishes, & of marvelous bignes, but for *Lagartos* it exceeded, for there were thousands of those uglie serpents, and the people call it for the abundance of them the river of *Lagartos*, in their language. I had a *Negro* a very proper yoong fellow, that leaping out of the *Galley* to swim in the mouth of this river, was in all our sights taken and devoured with one of those *Lagartos*. In the mean while our companies in the *Galley* thought we had beene all lost, (for we promised to returne before night) & sent the *Lions Whelps* ships bote with Captaine *Whiddon* to follow us up the river, but the next day after we had rowed up and downe some fower score miles, we returned, and went on our way, up the great river, and when we were even at the last cast for want of victuals, Captaine *Gifford* being before the *Galley*, and the rest of the botes, seeking out some place to land upon the banks to make fire espied fower *Canoas* comming downe the [r]iver, & with no small joy caused his men to trie the uttermost of their strengths, and after a while two of the 4. gave over, and ran themselves ashore, every man betaking himselfe to the fastnes of the woods, the two other lesser got away, while he landed to lay holde on these, and so turned into some by-creeke, we knew not whither: those *Canoas* that were taken were loden with

---

[3] Far from being obviously 'natural', native populations carefully managed the natural ecological system around them. See Raleigh, *Discoverie of Guiana*, ed. Whitehead, p. 93.

bread, & were bound for *Marguerita* in the west Indies, which those Indians (called *Arwacas*) purposed to carrie thither for exchange: But in the lesser, there were three Spaniards, who having heard of the defeat of their governour in *Trinedado*, and that we purposed to enter *Guiana*, came away in those *Canoas*: one of them was a *Cavallero*, as the Captaine of the *Arwacas* after told us, another a souldier, and the third a refiner. [...] but seeking after the Spaniardes, we found the *Arwacas* hidden in the woods which were pilots for the Spaniardes, and rowed their *Canoas*: of which I kept the chiefest for a Pilot, and carried him with me to *Guiana*, by whom I understood, where and in what countries the Spaniards had labored for gold. [...]

This *Arwacan* Pilot with the rest, fearing that we would have eaten them, or otherwise have put them to some cruell death, for the Spaniards to the end that none of the people in the passage towards *Guiana* or in *Guiana* it selfe might come to speech with us, perswaded all the nations, that we were men eaters, and *Canibals*[4] but when the poore men & women had seen us, and that we gave them meate, and to every one somthing or other, which was rare and strange to them, they began to conceive the deceit and purpose of the *Spaniards*, who indeed (as they confessed) tooke from them both their wives, and daughters daily, and used them for the satisfying of their owne lusts, especially such as they tooke in this manner by strength. But I protest before the majestie of the living God, that I neither know nor beleeve, that any of our companie one or other, by violence or otherwise, even knew any of their women, and yet we saw many hundreds, and had many in our power, and of those very yoong, & excellently favoured which came among us without deceit, starke naked.[5]

Nothing got us more love amongst them then this usage, for I suffered not any man to take from any of the nations so much as a *Pina*, or a *Potato* roote, without giving them contentment, nor any man so much as to offer to touch any of their wives or daughters: which course so contrary to the Spaniards (who tyrannixe over them in all things) drew them to admire her Majestie, whose commaundement I told them it was, and also wonderfully to honour our nation.

---

[4] Representations of native Americans frequently divide peoples up into friendly Arawaks and hostile Caribs/Cannibals, after divisions which Columbus made in his writings. See Hulme, *Colonial Encounters*, ch. 2.

[5] Raleigh deliberately contrasts the restraint of the English to the abusive licentiousness of the Spanish in their respective treatments of the natives.

But I confesse it was a very impatient worke to keep the meaner sort from spoile and stealing, when we came to their houses, which by cause in all I could not prevent, I caused my Indian interpreter at every place when we departed, to know of the losse or wrong don, and if ought were stolen or taken by violence, either the same was restored, and the partie punished in their sight, or else was paid for to their uttermost demand.

To conclude, *Guiana* is a Countrey that hath yet her Maydenhead, never sackt, turned, nor wrought, the face of the earth hath not beene torne, nor the vertue and salt of the soyle spent by manurance, the graves have not beene opened for golde, the mines not broken with sledges, nor their Images puld down out of their temples. It hath never been entred by any armie of strength, and never conquered or possessed by anie Christian Prince. It is besides so defensible, that if two fortes be builded in one of the Provinces which I have seen, the flood setteth in so neere the banke, where the channell also lyeth, that no shippe can passe up, but within a Pikes length of the Artillerie, first of the one, and afterwardes of the other: Which two Fortes willbe a sufficient Guard both to the *Empire* of *Inga*, and to an hundred other severall kingdomes, lying within the said River, even to the citie of *Quito in Peru.*[6]

[6] Raleigh's representation of Guiana as a *virgo intacta* may have been designed to appeal to Elizabeth's cult of virginity and her equation of her inviolability with that of England itself, notably before and after the attempted invasion of the Spanish Armada (1588).

Michel Eyquem de Montaigne, 'Of the Canniballes' (1580), trans. John Florio (1603)

MICHEL DE MONTAIGNE'S (1533–92) famous essay is one of the most celebrated pieces of writing about the New World in the early modern period. His apparently liberal and tolerant cultural relativism, the sentiments of a European who has 'abjured the desire to possess the souls of others', has appealed to many commentators appalled by the violence of European colonists in the Americas.[1] Certainly Montaigne's insistence that the barbarity of the wars of religion in Europe exceeds anything that New World cannibals could perform is instructive. However, one should bear in mind that the comparison was not lost on other thinkers, who feared increased destruction and slaughter in Europe if the Spanish advance in the Americas was not halted.[2] It should also not be forgotten that Montaigne was an aristocrat who had explicitly chosen to leave the royal court in Paris and Rouen so that he could devote himself to reading and studying in his tower at Montaigne (1571). Out of this experience he developed the new form of the 'essai' (attempt), a form of writing which wandered wherever and how far the author chose to take his subject.

It is highly unlikely that Montaigne was not aware of this difference between his political and intellectual freedom and the constraints of patronage and action placed upon colonists like Columbus, Bernal Díaz, and the Huguenots who chose to leave France to establish colonies in Brazil (which neatly brings us back to the problem of sectarian conflict in Europe). Indeed, the careful patterning in the essay and the pointed link between the ideal interpreter, 'a man so simple, that he may have no invention to build upon', and the ideal society which is without government, law, or letters, suggests that both are really European fictions invented by Montaigne to challenge the preconceptions of the reader. References to Plato's *Republic* and the enigmatic conclusion to the essay further strengthen such suspicions and suggest that Montaigne is, yet again, meditating on the nature of knowledge.[3]

[1] Stephen Greenblatt, *Marvelous Possessions: The Wonder of the New World* (Oxford: Clarendon Press, 1991), 150.

[2] Andrew Hadfield, *Literature, Travel, and Colonial Writing in the English Renaissance* (Oxford: Clarendon Press, 1998), ch. 2.

[3] Useful perspectives on Montaigne are collected in Keith Cameron (ed.), *Montaigne and his Age* (Exeter: Exeter Univ. Printing Unit, 1981). Text from Michel de Montaigne, *The Essayes or morall, politique and militarie discourses. Done into English by (J. Florio)* (1603), 100–7.

I have had long time dwelling with mee a man, who for the space of ten or twelve yeares had dwelt in that other world, which in our age was lately discovered in those parts where *Villegaignon* first landed, and surnamed *Antartike France*.[1] This discoverie of so infinite and vast a countrie, seemeth worthy great consideration. [...]

This servant I had, was a simple and rough-hewen fellow: a condition fit to yeeld a true testimonie. For, subtile people may indeede marke more curiously, and observe things more exactly, but they amplifie and glose them: and the better to perswade, and make their interpretations of more validitie, they cannot chuse but somewhat alter the storie. They never represent things truely, but fashion and maske them according to the visage they saw them in; and to purchase credit to their judgement, and draw you on to beleeve them, they commonly adorne, enlarge, yea, and Hyperbolise the matter. Wherein is required either a most sincere Reporter, or a man so simple, that he may have no invention to builde-upon, and to give a true likelihood unto false devices, and be not wedded to his owne will. Such a one was my man; who besides his owne report, hath many times shewed me divers Mariners, and Merchants, whom hee had knowne in that voyage. So am I pleased with his information, that I never enquire what Cosmographers say-of-it. [...]

Now (to returne to my purpose) I finde (as farre as I have beene informed) there is nothing in that nation, that is either barbarous or savage, unlesse men call that barbarisme which is not common to them. As indeede, we have no other ayme of truth and reason, than the example and *Idea* of the opinions and customes of the countrie we live-in. Where is ever perfect religion, perfect policie, perfect and compleate use of all things. They are even savage, as we call those fruites wilde, which nature of hir selfe, and of hir ordinarie progresse hath produced: whereas indeede, they are those which our selves have altered by our artificiall devices, and diverted from their common order, we should rather terme savage. [...]

Those nations seeme therefore so barbarous unto me, because they have received very little fashion from humane wit, and are yet neere their originall naturalitie. The lawes of nature doe yet command them, which

---

[1] Durand de Villegaignon landed in Brazil in 1557. An anonymous account of his voyage appeared in 1557. Montaigne had read a number of accounts of the Brazilian Indians, notably Jean de Léry's *Story of a Voyage to Brazil* (1578), which had just appeared. It is also likely that he met, as he says he did, three Brazilians in Rouen in 1562 and talked to them through an interpreter. See Peter Burke, *Montaigne* (Oxford, 1981), 44–7; Dorothy Gabe Coleman, *Montaigne's Essais* (London: Allen and Unwin, 1987), 57.

are but little bastardized by ours, And that with such puritie, as I am sometimes grieved the knowledge of it came no sooner to light, at what time there were men, that better than we could have judged of it. I am sorie, *Lycurgus* and *Plato* had it not: for me seemeth that what in those nations we see by experience, doth not only exceed all the pictures wherewith licentious Poesie hath proudly imbellished the golden age,[2] & all hir quaint inventions to faine a happy condition of man, but also the conception & desire of Philosophie. They could not imagine a genuitie so pure and simple, as we see it by experience; nor ever beleeve our societie might be maintained with so little arte and humane combination. It is a nation, would I answer *Plato*, that hath no kinde of traffike, no knowledge of Letters, no intelligence of numbers, no name of magistrate, nor of politike superioritie; no use of service, of riches or of poverty; no contracts, no successions, no partitions, no occupation but idle; no respect of kinred, but common, no apparell but naturall, no manuring of lands, no use of wine, corne, or mettle. The very words that import lying, falshood, treason, dissimulations, covetousness, envie, detraction, and pardon, were never heard of amongst them. How dissonant would hee finde his imaginarie common-wealth from this perfection?

Hos nature modos primum dedit.

Nature at first uprise,
These manners did devise.[3]

Furthermore, they live in a country of so exceeding pleasant and temperate situation, that as my testimonies have told me, it is verie rare to see a sicke body amongst them; and they have further assured me, they never saw any man there, either shaking with the palsie, toothlesse, with eies dropping, or crooked and stooping through age. They are seated alongst the sea-coast, encompassed toward the land with huge and steepe mountaines, having betweene both, a hundred leagues or thereabout of open and champaine ground. They have great abundance of fish and flesh, that have no resemblance at all with ours, and eat them without any sawces, or skill of Cookerie, but plaine boiled or broiled. The first man that brought a horse thither, although he had in many other voyages conversed with them, bred so great a horror in the land, that before they could take notice of him, they slew him with arrowes. Their buildings are very long, and able

---

[2] See Ovid, *Metamorphoses*, trans. Mary M. Innes (Harmondsworth: Penguin, 1955), 31–2.
[3] Vergil, *Georgics* 2. 208.

to containe two or three hundred soules, covered with barkes of great trees, fastned in the ground at one end, enterlaced and joyned close together by the tops, after the manner of some of our Granges; the covering whereof hangs downe to the ground, and steadeth them as a flancke. They have a kinde of wood so hard, that ryving and cleaving the same, they make blades, swords, and grid-irons to broile their meate with. Their beds are of a kinde of cotton coth, fastned to the house-roofe, as our ship-cabbanes; everie one hath his severall cowch; for the women lie from their husbands. They rise with the Sunne, and feed for all day, as soone as they are up: and make no more meales after that. They drinke not at meat, as *Suidas* reporteth of some other people of the East, which dranke after meales, but drinke many times a day, and are much given to pledge carowses. Their drinke is made of a certraine root, and of the colour of our Claret wines, which lasteth but two or three daies; they drinke it warme: It hath some-what a sharp taste, wholesome for the stomack, nothing heady, but laxative for such as are not used unto it, yet verie pleasing to such as are accustomed unto it. In stead of bread, they use a certaine white composition, like unto Corianders confected. I have eaten some, the taste whereof is somewhat sweet and swallowish. They spend the whole day in dancing. Their young men goe a hunting after wilde beasts with bowes and arrowes. Their women busie themselves therewhil'st with warming of their drinke, which is their chiefest office. Some of their old men, in the morning before they goe to eating, preach in common to all the household, walking from one end of the house to the other, repeating one selfe-same sentence many times, till he have ended his turne (for their buildings are a hundred paces in length) he commends but two things unto his audiotire, *First, valour against their enemies, then lovingnesse unto their wives*. They never misse (for their restraint) to put men in minde of this dutie, that it is their wives which keepe their drinke luke-warme and well-seasoned. The forme of their beds, cords, swords, blades, and wooden bracelets, wherewith they cover their hand wrists, when they fight, and great Canes open at one end, by the sound of which they keepe time and cadence in their dancing, are in many places to be seene, and namely in mine owne house. They are shaven all over, much more close and cleaner than wee are, with no other Razors than of wood or stone. They beleeve their soules to be eternall, and those that have deserved well of their Gods, to be placed in that part of heaven where the Sunne riseth, and the cursed toward the West in opposition. They have certaine Prophets and Priests, which commonly abide in the mountains, and very seldome shew themselves unto the people; but when they come downe, there is a great feast prepared, and a solemne assembly of manie townships together (each Grange as I have described maketh a village, and they are about a French league one form another). The Prophet speakes to the people in publike, exhorting them to embrace vertue, and follow their dutie. All their morall discipline containeth but these two articles; first an undismaied resolution to warre, then an inviolable affection to their wives. Hee doth also Prognosticate of things to come, and what successe they shall hope for in their enterprises: hee either perswadeth or disswadeth them from warre; but if he chance to misse of his divination, and that it succeed otherwise than hee foretetold them, if hee be taken, he is hewen in a thousand peeces, and condemned for a false Prophet. And therefore he that hath once misreckoned himselfe is never seene againe. Divination is the gift of God; the abusing whereof should be a punishable imposture. When the Divines amongst the Scythians had foretold an untruth, they were couched along upon hurdles full of heath or brushwood, drawne by oxen, and so manicled hand and foot, burned to death. Those which manage matters subject to the conduct of mans sufficiencie, are excusable, although they shew the utmost of their skill. But those that gull and conicatch us with the assurance of an extraordinarie facultie, and which is beyond our knowledge, ought to be double punished; first because they performe not the effect of their promise, then for the rashnesse of their imposture and unadvisednesse of their fraud. They warre against the nations, that lie beyond their mountains, to which they go naked, having no other weapons than bowes, or woodden swords, sharpe at one end, as our broaches are. It is an admirable thing to see the constant resolution of their combats, which never end but by effusion of bloud and murther: for they know not what feare or rowts are. Every Victor brings home the head of the enemie he hath slaine as a Trophey of his victorie, and fastneth the same at the entrance of his dwelling place. After they have long time used and entreated their prisoners well, and with all commodities they can devise, he that is the Master of them; sommoning a great assembly of his aquaintance; tieth a corde to one of the prisoners armes, by the end whereof he holds him fast, with some distance from him, for feare he might offend him, and giveth the other arme, bound in like manner, to the dearest friend he hath, and both in the presence of all the assembly kill him, with swords: which done, they roast, and then eat him in common, and send some slices of him to such of their friends as are absent. It is not as some imagine, to nourish themselves with it, (as anciently the Scithians wont to doe,) but to represent an extreme, and inexpiable revenge. Which we prove thus; some of them perceiving the Portugales, who had confederated themselves with their adversaries, to use another kinde of death, when they took them prisoners; which was, to burie them up to the middle, and against the upper part of the body to shoot arrows, and then being almost dead, to hang them up; they supposed, that these people of the other world (as they who had sowed the knowledge of many vices amongst their neighbours, and were much more cunning in all kindes of evils and mischiefe than they) undertooke not this manner of revenge without cause, and that consequently it was more smartfull, and cruell than theirs, and thereupon began to leave their old fashion to follow this. I am not sorie we note the barbarous horror of such an action, but grieved, that prying so narrowly into their faults we are so blinded in ours. I thinke there is more barbarisme in eating men alive, than to feed upon them being dead; to mangle by tortures and torments a body full of lively sense, to roast him in peeces, to make dogges and swine to gnaw and teare him in mammockes (as wee have not only read, but seene very lately, yea and in our owne memorie, not amongst ancient enemies, but our neighbours and fellow-citizens; and which is worse, under pretence of pietie and religion) than to roast and eat him after he is dead. *Chrysippus* and *Zeno*, arch-pillers of the Stoicke sect, have supposed that it was no hurt at all, in time of need, and to what end soever, to make use of our carrion bodies, and to feed upon them, as did our fore-fathers, who being besieged by *Caesar* in the Citie of *Alexia*, resolved to sustaine the famine of the siege, with the bodies of old men, women, and other persons unserviceable & unfit to fight.

> *Vascones (fama est) alimentis talibus usi*
> *Produxere animas*   Juven. *Sat.* 15. 93
>
> *Gascoynes* (as fame reports)
> Liv'd with meats of such sorts.

And Physitians feare not, in all kindes of compositions availefull to our health, to make use of it, be it for outward or inward applications: But there was never any opinion found so unnaturall and immodest, that would excuse treason, treacherie, disloyaltie, tyrannie, crueltie, and such like, which are our ordinarie faults. We may then well call them barbarous, in regard of reasons rules, but not in respect of us that exceed them in all kinde of barbarisme. Their warres are noble and generous, and have as much excuse and beautie, as this humane infirmitie may admit: they ayme at nought so much, and have no other foundation amongst them, but the meere jelousie of vertue. They contend not for the gaining of new lands; for to this day they yet enjoy that naturall ubertie and fruitfulnesse, which without labouring toyle, doth in such plenteous abundance furnish them with all necessary things, that they need not enlarge their limits. They are yet in that happy estate, as they desire no more, than what their naturall necessities direct them: whatsoever is beyond it, is to them superfluous. Those that are much about one age, doe generally enter-call one another brethren, and such as are younger, they call children, and the aged are esteemed as fathers to all the rest. These leave this full possession of goods in common, and without division to their heires, without other claime or title, but that which nature doth plainely impart unto all creatures, even as shee brings them into the world. If their neighbours chance to come over the mountains to assaile or invade them, and that they get the victorie over them, the Victors conquest is glorie, and the advantage to be and remaine superior in valour and vertue: else have they nothing to doe with the goods and spoyles of the vanquished, and so returne into their countrie, where they neither want any necessaire thing, nor lacke this great portion, to know how to enjoy their condition happily, and are contented with what nature affoordeth them. So doe these when their turne commeth. They require no other ransome of their prisoners, but an acknowledgement and confession that they are vanquished. Ane in a whole age, a man shall not finde one, that doth not rather embrace death, than either by word or countenance remissely to yeeld one jot of an invincible courage. There is none seene that would not rather be slaine and devoured than sue for life, or shew any feare: They use their prisoners with all libertie, that they may so much the more hold their lives deare and precious, and commonly enter-taine them with threats of future death, with the torments they shall endure, with the preparations intended for that purpose, with mangling and slicing of their members, and with the feast that shall be kept at their charge. All which is done, to wrest some remisse, and exact some faint-yeelding speech off submission from them, or to possesse them with a desire to escape or run away; that so they may have the advantage to have danted and made them afraid, and to have forced their constancie. For certainly true victorie consisteth in that only point. [...]

These prisoners, howsoever they are dealt withall, are so farre from yeelding, that contrariwise during two or three moneths that they are kept, they ever carry a cheerefull countenance, and urge their keepers to hasten their triall, they outragiously defie, and injure them. They upbraid them with their cowardlinesse, and with the number of battels, they have lost againe theirs. I have a song made by a prisoner, wherein is this clause, Let them boldly come altogether, and flocke in multitudes, to feed on him; for with him they shall feed upon their fathers, and grandfathers, that heretofore have served his body for food and nourishment: These muscles, (saith he) this flesh, and these veines, are your owne; fond men as you are, know you not that the substance of your forefathers limbes is yet tied unto ours? Taste them well, for in them shall you finde the relish of your owne flesh: An invention, that hath no shew of barbarisme. Those that paint them dying, and that represent this action, when they are put to execution, delineate the prisoners spitting in their executioners faces, and making mowes at them. Verily, so long as breath is in their body, they never cease to brace and defie them, both in speech and countenance. Surely, in respect of us these are very savage men: for either they must be so in good sooth, or we must be so indeed: There is a wondrous distance, betweene their forme and ours. Their men have many wives, and by how much more they are reputed valiant, so much the greater is their number. The manner and beautie in their marriages is wondrous strange and remarkable: For, the same jealousie our wives have to keepe us from the love and affection of other women, the same have their to procure it. Being more carefull for their husbands honour and content, than of any thing else: They endeavour and apply all their industrie, to have as many rivals as possibly, they can, forasmuch as it is a testimonie of their husbands vertue. Our women would count it a wonder, but it is not so: It is vertue properly Matrimoniall; but of the highest kinde. And in the Bible, *Lea, Rachell, Sara,* and *Jacobs* wives, brought their fairest maiden servants unto their husbands beds. And *Livia* seconded the lustfull appetites of *Augustus* to her great prejudice. And *Stratonica* the wife of King *Dejotarus* did not only bring a most beauteous chamber-maide, that served her, to her husbands bed, but very carefully brought up the children he begot on her, an by all possible meanes aided and furthered them to succeed in their fathers roialtie. And least a man should thinke, that all this is done by a simple, and servile, or awefull dutie unto their custome, and by the impression of their ancient customes authoritie, without discourse or judgement, and because they are so blockish, and dull spirited, that they can take no other resolution, it is not amisse, wee alleage some evidence of their sufficiencie. Besides what I have said of one of their warlike songs, I have another amorous canzonet, which beginneth in this sense: *Adder stay, stay good adder, that my sister may by the patterne of they partie-coloured coat drawe the fashion and worke of a rich lace, for me to give unto my love; so may thy beautie, thy nimblenesse or disposition be ever preferred before all other serpents.* The first couplet is the burthen of the song. I am so conversant with Poesie, that I may judge, this invention hath no barbarisme at all in it, but is altogether Anacreontike.[4] Their language is a kind of pleasant speech, and hath a pleasing sound, and some affinite with the Greeke terminations. Three of that nation, ignorant how deare the knowledge of our corruptions will one day cost their repose, securitie, and happinesse, and how their ruine shall proceed from this commerce, which I imagine is already well advanced, (miserable as they are to have suffered themselves to be so cosoned by a desire of new-fangled novelties, and to have quit the calmenesse of their climate, to come and see ours) were at *Roane* in the time of our late King *Charles* the ninth, who talked with them a great while. They were shewed our fashions, our pompe, and the forme of a faire Citie; afterward some demanded their advise, and would needs know of them what things of note and admirable they had observed amongst us: they answered three things, the last of which I have forgotten, and am very sorie for it, the other two I yet remember. They said, *First, they found it very strange, that so many tall men with long beards, strong and well armed, as it were about the Kings person (it is very likely they meant the Switzers of his guard) would submit themselves to obey a beardlesse childe, and that we did not rather chuse one amongst them to command the rest.* Secondly (they have a manner of phrase whereby they call men but a moytie one of another). *They had perceived, there were men amongst us full gorged with all sortes of commodities, and others which hunger-starved, and bare with need and povertie, begged at their gates: and found it strange, these moyties so needy could endure such an injustice, and that they tooke not the others by the throte, or set fire on their houses.* I talked a good while with one of them, but I had so bad an interpreter, and who did so ill apprehend my meaning, and who through his foolishnesse was so troubled to conceive my imaginations, that I could draw no great matter from him. Touching that point, wherein I demanded of him, what good he received by the superioritie he had

---

[4] Named after the style of poetry produced by Anacreon (fl. 540 BC).

amongst his countriemen (for he was a Captaine and our Marriners called him King) he told me, it was to march formost in any charge of warre: further, I asked him, how many men did follow him, hee shewed me a distance of place, to signifie they were as many as might be contained in so much ground, which I guessed to be about 4. or 5. thousand men: moreover I demanded, if when warres were ended, all his authoritie expired; he answered, that hee had only this left him, which was, that when he went on progresse, and visited the villages depending of him, the inhabitants prepared paths and high-waies athwart the hedges of their woods, for him to passe through at ease. All that is not verie ill; but what of that? They weare no kinde of breeches nor hosen.

William Strachey, *The Historie of Travell into Virginia Britania* (1612)

ALTHOUGH the English in the Americas were often inclined to see the natives as uncivilized and savage, there is much force in the argument that such views were more prevalent amongst those who stayed at home rather than those who actually travelled to the New World.[1] As the extracts from Thomas Harriot and Walter Raleigh demonstrate (see above, pp. 266–79, 279–85), travellers and colonists acknowledged that native Americans had a stable system of government, a sophisticated sense of religion, as well as established social rituals, and agricultural and economic practices. William Strachey's lucid and informative account of Algonkian society is, as his editor suggests, original and based on eyewitness observation. Even here, however, Strachey relies on previous accounts by Harriot and John Smith.[2]

William Strachey (1572–1621?) was educated at Cambridge and Gray's Inn. He married Frances Forster in 1595 and started to move in literary circles in London. In need of money, he became involved in various voyages and expeditions designed for profit. In 1609 he sailed for Virginia in a fleet commanded by Christopher Newport. On route the admiral's ship, *The Sea Venture* was wrecked in a huge storm off the Bahamas. Strachey, who was on board the ship, wrote an account of the disaster, which was used by Shakespeare in *The Tempest*.[3] When he arrived in Jamestown, Strachey was appalled at the chaotic state of the colony. He was made secretary and obviously took detailed notes for his *Historie*, which he presented to various prominent figures when he returned to England in 1611 in the hope of attracting employment. The manuscript, which remained unpublished until the middle of the nineteenth century, is sketchy and incomplete, probably as a result of Strachey's hopes of writing a more substantial work that may have been beyond his abilities. The manuscript stands as a militant defence of England's right to colonial expansion and a series of acute observations on native society.[4]

---

[1] This is the argument of Karen Ordhal Kupperman's *Settling with the Indians: The Meeting of English and Indian Cultures in America, 1580–1640* (New Jersey: Rowman and Allanheld, 1980).

[2] *The Historie of Travell into Virginia Britania (1612), By William Strachey, gent.*, ed. Louis B. Wright and Virginia Freund (London: Hakluyt Society, 1953), p. xxxi.

[3] For details see William Shakespeare, *The Tempest*, ed. Stephen Orgel (Oxford: Oxford Univ. Press, 1987), appendix B.

[4] This account of Strachey's life and works is based on *Historie of Travell into Virginia Britania*, ed. Wright and Freund, introd. Text reproduced from William Strachey, *The Historie of Travell into Virginia Britania* (1612), 77–87.

See also:

Philip L. Barbour (ed.), *The Jamestown Voyages under the First Charter, 1606–1609* (London: Hakluyt Society, 1969).

THE MANNER OF THE GOVERNMENT OF THE PEOPLE OF VIRGINIA, THEIR TOWNES, HOWSES, DYET, FISHING, FOWLING, HUNTING ETC.

Although the Country people be very barbarous, yet have they amongst them such governement, as that their Magistrates for good Comaunding, and their people for due subjection and obeying excell many places that would be accompted Civile, the forme of their comon wealth by what hath bene alreddy delivered, you may well gather to be a *Monarchall governe-ment*, where one as Emperour ruleth over many kings: their Chief ruler likewise for the present you have heard before how named and from whence; as also you have heard the nomber of his Weroances, their forces, and his owne description, you shall now understand, how his kingdome descendeth not to his sonnes, nor Children, but first to his breathren, whereof he hath (as you have heard) three, and after their deceasse to his sisters; first to the eldest sister, then to the rest, and after them to the heires male and Feemale of the eldest sister, but never to the heires of the male.

He nor any of his people understand howe to expresse their myndes by any kyndes of Letters, or any kind of ingraving which necessity or inven-tion, might have instructed them in, as doe other Barbarians in these new Discoveries; nor have they posetive lawes, only the law whereby he ruleth is custome; yet when he pleaseth his will is lawe, and must be obeyed, not only as a king, but as half a god, his People esteeme him so. His inferiour kings are tyed likewise to rule by like Customes, and have permitted them power of life and death over their people as their Comaund in that nature.

Theire habitations or Townes, are for the most parte by the Rivers; or not far distant from fresh Springes comonly upon the Rice of a hill, that they maie overlooke the River and take every smale thing into view which sturrs upon the same, their howses are not manie in one towne, and those that are stand dissite [apart] and scattered, without forme of a street, far and wyde asunder.

As for their howses, who knoweth one of them knoweth them all, even the Chief kings house yt self, for they be all alike builded one to another, they are like gardein arbours, (at best like our sheppardes Cottages), made yet handsomely enough, though without strength or gaynes;[1] of such young plants as they can pluck up, bow, and make the greene toppes meete togither in fashion of a rownd roofe, which they thatch with mattes, throwne over, the walls are made with barkes of trees, but then those be principall howses, for so many barkes which goe to the making up of a howse, are long tyme of purchasing, in the middst of the howse there is a lover [vent], out of which the smoake yssueth, the fire being kept right under, every howse commonly hath twoo doores, one before and a Posterne, the doores be hung with matts, never locked nor bolted, but only those matts be to turne up, or lett fall at pleasure, and their howses are Comonly so placed under Covert of Trees, that the Violence of fowle weather, snow or rayne cannot assault them, nor the Sun in Somer annoy them, and the roofe being covered, as I say, the wynd is easely kept out, in so much as they are as warme as stoaves albeit very smoakye, wyndoes they have none, but the light comes in at the doare, and at the Lover, for should they have broad open wyndowes in the quarters of their howses, they knew not well, how upon any occasion, to make them close to lett in the light too; for glasse they know not (though the Country wants not Salsodiack[2] enough to make glasse off, and of which we have made some store in a goodlie howse, sett up for the same purpose, with all offices and furnaces thereto belonging, a little without the Island where James towne standes) nor have they lynnen Cloth (albeyt they want not neither naturally the Materialls for that) paper, or such like to dippe in oyle to convey in as a *Diaphanick* body the light, or to keepe out the weather. [...]

It is straunge to see how their bodies alter with their dyett even as the deare and wylde beasts, they seeme fatt and leane, strong and weake, *Powhatan*[3] and some others that are provident roast their fish and flesh upon hurdells and reserve of the same untill the scarse tymes, Commonly their Fish and Flesh they boyle, either very tenderly, or broyle yt long on hurdells over the fire, or ells (after the Spanish Fashion) putting yt on a spitt, they turne first the one syde, then the other till yt be as dry as their Jerkyn-beef,[4] in the West Indies, and so they may keepe yt a moneth or

---

[1] Supports or holes for a girder or beam.   [2] Sodium carbonate.
[3] Algonkian chief (see above, p. 238).
[4] 'Jerked beef', cut into long slices and cured in the sun.

more, without putryfying. The broath of Fish or Flesh they sup up as ordinarily, as they eate the meate. [...]

The men bestowe their tymes in fishing, hunting, wars, and such man-like exercises without the doores, scorning to be seen in any effemynate labour, which is the Cause that the women be very paynefull, and the men often idle. [...]

In the tyme of their huntings, they leave their habitations and gather themselves into Companies as doe the Tartars, and goe to the most desart places with their famelyes, where they passe the tyme with hunting and fowling up towards the mountaynes by the heades of their Rivers, where indeed there is plenty of game, for betwixt the Rivers the land is not so large below, that therein breed sufficient to give them all content, considering especially how at all tymes and seasons they destroy them, yt may seeme a Marvayle how they can so directly passe and wander in those desartes, sometimes three or fower dayes Journyes, meeting with no habitations, and by reason of the woodes not having sight of the Sun, whereby to direct them how to coast yt. [...]

A kynd of Excercise they have often amongest them much like that which boyes call Bandy,[5] in English and may be an auncyent game as yt seemeth in *Virgill*, for when Aeneas came into Italy at his Marriage with Lavinia King Latinus daughter, yt is said the Trojans taught the Latins scipping and frisking at the Ball: likewise they have the excercise of Foote-ball, in which yet they only forceably encounter with the foote to carry the Ball the one from the other, and spurne yt to the goale with a kynd of dexterity and swift footmanshippe, which is the honour of yt, but they never strike up one anothers heeles as we doe, not accompting that praise worthy to purchase a goale by such advantage.

Dice plaie or cardes or lotts they knowe not, howbeit they use a game upon rushes much like Primero,[6] wherein they card and discard and lay a stake too, and so wyn and loose, they will play at this for their bowes and arrowes, their Copper beads, hatchetts, and their leather Coates.

If a great Commaunder arrive at the habitation of a Weroaunce, they spredd a Matt (as the Turks doe a carpett) for him to sitt upon, upon another right opposite they sitt themselves, then doe they all with a tunable voice of showting byd him welcome: after this doe 2. or more of their chief men make severall orations testefying their love, which they doe with such

[5] 'An old form of tennis and a kind of field hockey' (note in Freund and Wright's edition).
[6] A card game.

vehemency and so great earnestnes of passion, that they sweat till they droppe, and are so out of breath, that they can scarse speake, in so much as a Straunger would take them to be exceeding angry or stark mad: after this verbal Entertaynement, they cause such victuall as they have or can provide to be brought forthe with which they feast him fully and freely, and at night they bring him to the lodging appointed for him, whither (upon their departure, they send a young woman fresh paynted redd with *Pochone* and oyle to be his bedfellow [)].

The voyd tyme betweene their sleepe and meat, they commonly bestowe in revelling dauncing and singing, and in their kynd of Musique, and have sondry Instrumentes for the same; they have a kynd of Cane, on which they pipe as on a Recorder and are like the Greeke Pips which they called *Bombices*, being hardly to be sounded without great strayning of the breath, upon which they observe certain rude tunes, but their chief Instruments are Rattles made of smale Gourdes or Pumpeon shells, of these they have Base, Tenor, Countortenor, Meane, and Treble, these mingled with their voices sometymes 20. or 30. togither make such a terrible howling as would rather affright then give pleasure to any man.

They have likewise their *errotica carmina*, or amorous dittyes in their language, some numerous and some not, which they will sing tunable ynough: they have contryved a kynd of angry song against us in their homely rymes, which concludeth with a kynd of Petition unto their *Okeus*, and to all the host of their Idolls, to plague the Tassantasses (for so they call us) and their posterityes, as likewise another scornefull song they made of us the last yeare at the Falls in manner of Tryumph at what tyme they killed Capt. William West our Lord Generalls nephew, and 2. or 3. more, and tooke one Symon Score a saylor and one Cob a boy prisoners, that song goes thus

1. Mattanerew shashashewaw crawango pechecoma
    Whe Tassantassa inoshashaw yehockan pocosack
    Whe, whe, yah, ha, ha, ne, he, wittowa, wittowa.
2. Mattanerew shashashewaw, erawango pechecoma
    Capt. Newport inoshashaw neir in hoc nantion matassan
    Whe, whe, yah, ha, ha, etc.
3. Mattanerew shashashewaw erowango pechecoma
    Thom. Newport inoshashaw neir in hoc nantion monocock
    Whe whe etc.

4. Mattanerew shushashewaw erowango pechecoma
   Pockin Simon moshasha mingon nantian Tamahuck.
   Whe whe, etc.

Which may signife how that they killed us for all our Poccasacks, that is our Guns, and for all Capt Newport brought them Copper and could hurt Thomas Newport (a boy whose name indeed is Thomas Savadge, whome Capt Newport leaving with Powhatan to learne the Language, at what tyme he presented the said Powhatan with a copper Crowne and other guifts from his Majestie, sayd he was his sonne) for all his *Monnacock* that is his bright Sword, and how they could take Symon (for they seldome said our Sirname) Prysoner for all his Tamahauke, that is his Hatchett, adding as for a burden unto their song what lamentation our people made when they kild him, namely saying how they would cry whe whe, etc., which they mock't us for and cryed agayne to us Yah, ha, ha, Tewittaw, Tewittawa, Tewittawa: for yt is true they never bemoane themselves, nor cry out, giving up so much as a groane for any death how cruell soever and full of Torment.

As for their dauncing the sport seemes unto them, and the use almost as frequent and necessary as their meat and drinck in which they consume much tyme, and for which they appoint many and often meetings, and have therefore, as yt were sett Orgies or Festivalls for the same Pastime, as have at this day the merry Greekes within the Arches; at our Colonies first sitting downe amongest them, when any of our people repayred unto their Townes, the Indians would not thinck they had expressed their welcome unto them sufficiently ynough untill they had shewed them a daunce: the manner of which is thus: one of them standeth by with some furre or leather thing in his left hand, upon which he beates with his right, and sings withall, as if he began the Quier, and kept unto the rest their just tyme, when upon a certayne stroke or word (as upon his Cue or tyme to come in) one riseth up and begynns the daunce; after he hath daunced a while steppes forth an other, as if he came in just upon his rest, and in this order all of them so many as there be one after another who then daunce an equall distaunce from each other in a ring, showting, howling and stamping their feet against the grownd with such force and payne, that they sweat againe, and with all variety a straung minick-trickes and distorted faces, making so confused a Yell and noise, as so many frantique and disquieted *Bacchanalls*, and sure they will keepe stroake just one with another, but with the handes, head, face, and body every one hath a severall gesture, as who have seene the Darvises in their holy daunces in the Moschas upon Wednesdayes and Frydayes in Turkey many resemble these unto them, you shall fynd the manner expressed in the figure in the second booke Chapt. [...]

Captain John Smith, *The Generall Historie of Virginia, New-England, and the Summer Isles* (1624), The Story of Pocahontas

CAPTAIN JOHN SMITH (1580–1631) was a colonist and historian, with a colourful past, having been captured by the Turks in Hungary. He went on the first expedition to the Virginia colony in 1606. He became leader of Jamestown in Chesapeake Bay. He was captured by local natives under the command of Powhatan in 1607, was on the point of being executed, but was spared by the pleas of Powhatan's daughter, Pocahontas. Smith returned to England in 1609, going back to America on one more expedition in 1615. His voluminous writings, which are the most detailed account of the Virginia colony, were mainly written to justify his actions and appeared after he had ceased to be an active colonist and adventurer. They include *A Description of New England* (1625); *The True Travels, Adventures and Observations of Captaine John Smith in Europe, Asia, Africa and America* (1630), as well as *The Generall Historie of Virginia* (1624).[1] Pocahontas married Smith's compatriot, John Rolfe, travelled to England and met James I and Queen Anne. She died at Gravesend in 1617, aged about 22.

The story of Smith's rescue by Pocahontas has become the most powerful myth of positive contact between Europeans and natives of the Americas, culminating in the 1995 Disney film.[2] I have included two extracts which represent Smith's version of events, indicating his incomprehension and fear of the peoples who surrounded the English colonies.[3]

[1] Collected in *The Complete Works of Captain John Smith (1580–1631)*, ed. Philip L. Barbour, 3 vols. (Chapel Hill: Univ. of North Carolina Press, 1986).

[2] For commentary see Robert S. Tilton, *Pocahontas: The Evolution of an American Narrative* (Cambridge: Cambridge Univ. Press, 1994); *Colonial Encounters: Europe and the Native Caribbean, 1492–1797* (London: Methuen, 1986), ch. 4.

[3] Useful recent analyses of John Smith are David Read, 'Colonialism and Coherence: The Case of Captain John Smith's *Generall Historie of Virginia*,' *MP* 91 (1994), 428–48; Mary C. Fuller, *Voyages in Print: English Travel to America, 1576–1624* (Cambridge: Cambridge Univ. Press, 1995), ch. 3. Text is from *Complete Works*, ii. 150–1, 258–62.

FIG. 17. 'King Powhatan commands C. Smith to be slayne, his daughter
Pokahontas beggs his life' (John Smith, *Generall Historie of Virginia* (1624),
between pp. 40 and 41)

At last they brought him to Meronocomoco, where was Powhatan their
Emperor. Here more then two hundred of those grim Courtiers stood
wondering at him, as he had beene a monster; till Powhatan and his trayne
had put themselves in their greatest braveries.[1] Before a fire upon a seat like
a bedsted, he sat covered with a great robe, made of Rarowcun[2] skinnes, and
all the tayles hanging by. On either hand did sit a young wench of 16 or 18
yeares, and along on each side the house, two rowes of men, and behind
them as many women, with all their heads and shoulders painted red; many
of their heads bedecked with the white downe of Birds; but every one with
something: and a great chayne of white beads about their necks. At his
entrance before the King, all the people gave a great shout. The Queene of

How Powhatan
entertained him.

---

[1] Finest attire.   [2] Racoon; a frequent early spelling.

Appamatuck was appointed to bring him water to wash his hands, and another brought him a bunch of feathers, in stead of a Towell to dry them: having feasted him after their best barbarous manner they could, a long consultation was held, but the conclusion was, two great stones were brought before Powhatan: then as many as could layd hands on him, dragged him to them, and thereon laid his head, and being ready with their clubs, to beate out his braines, Pocahontas the Kings dearest daughter, when no intreaty could prevaile, got his head in her armes, and laid her owne upon his to save him from death: whereat the Emperour was contented he should live to make him hatchets, and her bells, beads, and copper; for they thought him as well of all occupations as themselves. For the King himselfe will make his owne robes, shooes, bowes, arrowes, pots; plant, hunt, or doe any thing so well as the rest.

To the most high and vertuous Princesse Queene Anne of Great Brittanie.

Most admired Queene,

The love I beare my God, my King and Countrie, hath so oft emboldened mee in the worst of extreme dangers, that now honestie doth constraine mee presume thus farre beyond my selfe, to present your Majestie this short discourse: if ingratitude be a deadly poyson to all honest vertues, I must bee guiltie of that crime if I should omit any meanes to bee thankfull. So it is,

That some ten yeeres agoe being in Virginia, and taken prisoner by the power of Powhatan their chiefe King, I received from this great Salvage exceeding great courtesie, especially from his sonne Nantaquaus, the most manliest, comeliest, boldest spirit, I ever saw in a Salvage, and his sister Pocahontas, the Kings most deare and wel-beloved daughter, being but a childe of twelve or thirteene yeeres of age, whose compassionate pitifull heart, of my desperate estate, gave me much cause to respect her: I being the first Christian this proud King and his grim attendants ever saw: and thus inthralled in their barbarous power, I cannot say I felt the least occasion of want that was in the power of those my mortall foes to prevent, notwithstanding al their threats. After some six weeks fatting amongst those Salvage Courtiers, at the minute of my execution, she hazarded the beating out of her owne braines to save mine, and not onely that, but so prevailed with her father, that I was safely conducted to James towne, where I found about eight and thirtie miserable poore and sicke creatures, to keepe possession of all those large territories of Virginia, such was the weaknesse of this poore Common-wealth, as had the Salvages not fed us, we directly had starved.

And this reliefe, most gracious Queene, was commonly brought us by this Lady Pocahontas, notwithstanding all these passages when inconstant Fortune turned our peace to warre, this tender Virgin would still not spare to dare to visit us, and by her our jarres have beene oft appeased, and our wants still supplyed; were it the policie of her father thus to imploy her, or the ordinance of God thus to make her his instrument, or her extraordin-arie affection to our Nation, I know not: but of this I am sure; when her father with the utmost of his policie and power, sought to surprize mee, having but eighteene with mee, the darke night could not affright her from comming through the irkesome woods, and with watered eies gave me intelligence, with her best advice to escape his furie; which had hee knowne, hee had surely slaine her. James towne with her wild traine she as freely frequented, as her fathers habitation; and during the time of two or three yeeres, she next under God, was still the instrument to preserve this Colonie from death, famine and utter confusion, which if in those times had once beene dissolved, Virginia might have line as it was at our first arrivall to this day. Since then, this businesse having beene turned and varied by many accidents from that I left it at: it is most certaine, after a long and troublesome warre after my departure, betwixt her father and our Colonie, all which time shee was not heard of, about two yeeres after she her selfe was taken prisoner, being so detained neere two yeeres longer, the Colonie by that meanes was relieved, peace concluded, and at last rejecting her barbarous condition, was maried to an English Gentleman, with whom at this present she is in England; the first Christian ever of that Nation, the first Virginian ever spake English, or had a childe in mariage by an Englishman, a matter surely, if my meaning bee truly considered and well understood, worthy a Princes understanding.

Thus most gracious Lady, I have related to your Majestie, what at your best leasure our approved Histories will account you at large, and done in the time of your Majesties life, and however this might bee presented you from a more worthy pen, it cannot from a more honest heart, as yet I never begged any thing of the state, or any, and it is my want of abilitie and her exceeding desert, your birth, meanes and authoritie, hir birth, vertue, want and simplicitie, doth make mee thus bold, humbly to beseech your Majestie to take this knowledge of her, though it be from one so unworthy to be the reporter, as my selfe, her husbands estate not being able to make her fit to attend your Majestie: the most and least I can doe, is to tell you this, because none so oft hath tried it as my selfe, and the rather being of so great a spirit, how ever her stature: if she should not be well received, seeing this Kingdome may rightly have a Kingdome by her meanes; her present love to us and Christianitie, might turne to such scorne and furie, as to divert all this good to the worst of evill, where finding so great a Queene should doe her some honour more than she can imagine, for being so kinde to your servants and subjects, would so ravish her with content, as endeare her dearest bloud to effect that, your Majestie and all the Kings honest subjects most earnestly desire: And so I humbly kisse your gracious hands.

Being about this time preparing to set saile for New-England, I could not stay to doe her that service I desired, and she well deserved; but hearing shee was at Branford[3] with divers of my friends, I went to see her: After a modest salutation, without any word, she turned about, obscured her face, as not seeming well contented; and in that humour her husband, with divers others, we all left her two or three houres, repenting my selfe to have writ she could speake English. But not long after, she began to talke, and remembred mee well what courtesies shee had done: saying, You did promise Powhatan what was yours should bee his, and he the like to you; you called him father being in his land a stranger, and by the same reason so must I doe you: which though I would have excused, I durst not allow of that title, because she was a Kings daughter;[4] with a well set countenance she said, Were you not afraid to come into my fathers Countrie, and caused feare in him and all his people (but mee) and feare you here I should call you father; I tell you then I will, and you shall call mee childe, and so I will bee for ever and ever your Countrieman. They did tell us alwaies you were dead, and I knew no other till I came to Plimoth; yet Powhatan did command Uttamatomakkin to seeke you, and know the truth, because your Countriemen will lie much.

This Salvage, one of Powhatans Councell, being amongst them held an understanding fellow; the King purposely sent him, as they say, to number the people here, and informe him well what wee were and our state. Arriving at Plimoth, according to his directions, he got a long sticke, whereon by notches hee did thinke to have kept the number of all the

3 Brentford, Middlesex.
4 A later story went that King James was angry because Rolfe married a 'royal princess' without his permission.

men hee could see, but he was quickly wearie of that taske: Comming to London, where by chance I met him, having renewed our acquaintance, where many were desirous to heare and see his behaviour, hee told me Powhatan did bid him to finde me out, to shew him our God, the King, Queene, and Prince, I so much had told them of: Concerning God, I told him the best I could, the King I heard he had seene, and the rest hee should see when he would; he denied ever to have seene the King, till by circumstances he was satisfied he had: Then he replyed very sadly, You gave Powhatan a white Dog, which Powhatan fed as himselfe, but your King gave me nothing, and I am better than your white Dog.

Pocahontas her
entertainment
with the
Queene.

The small time I staid in London, divers Courtiers and others, my acquaintances, hath gone with mee to see her, that generally concluded, they did thinke God had a great hand in her conversion, and they have seene many English Ladies worse favoured, proportioned and behavioured, and as since I have heard, it pleased both the King and Queenes Majestie honourably to esteeme her, accompanied with that honourable Lady the Lady De la Ware, and that honourable Lord her husband, and divers other persons of good qualities, both publikely at the maskes and otherwise, to her great satisfaction and content, which doubtlesse she would have deserved[5] had she lived to arrive in Virginia.

[5] Paid back, requited.

GUIDE TO FURTHER READING

PRIMARY SOURCES

ANGLERIUS, PETRUS MARTYR, *The decades of the newe worlde or west India. Written in Latine and tr. By R. Eden [w. additions from other sources]* (1555).
—— *The Decades of the Newe Worlde, or West India*, trans. Richard Eden (1555), in Edward Arber (ed.), *The First Three English Books on America* (Birmingham: privately printed, 1885).
—— *De Orbe Novo: The Eight Decades of Peter Martyr D'Anghera*, trans. Francis Augustus McNutt, 2 vols. (New York: Burt Franklin, 1970, repr. of 1912).
ASCHAM, ROGER, *The Scholemaster or plaine and perfite way of teachyng children, the Latin tong* (1570).
BACON, FRANCIS, *Essayes* (1625).
BARBOUR, PHILIP L. (ed.), *The Jamestown Voyages under the First Charter, 1606–1609* (London: Hakluyt Society, 1969).
COLUMBUS, CHRISTOPHER, *The Four Voyages of Christopher Columbus*, ed. and trans. J. M. Cohen (London: Hutchinson, 1969).
CORYAT, THOMAS, *Coryats Crudities, Hastily gobled up in five monethes travells in France, Savoy [etc. with 2 orations]* (1611).
—— *Coryat's Crudities*, 2 vols. (Glasgow: MacLehose, 1905).
DALLINGTON, Sir ROBERT, *The View of France* (1604).
—— *The View of France (1604)*, ed. W. P. Barrett (London: Oxford University Press, Shakespeare Association Facsimile, 13; 1936).
DÍAZ, BERNAL, *The Conquest of New Spain*, trans. J. M. Cohen (Harmondsworth: Penguin, 1963).
HADFIELD, ANDREW, and McVEAGH, JOHN (eds.), *Strangers to that Land: British Perceptions of Ireland from the Reformation to the Famine* (Gerrards Cross: Colin Smythe, 1994).
HAKLUYT, RICHARD, 'Discourse of Western Planting', in E. G. R. Taylor (ed.), *The Original Writings and Correspondence of the Two Richard Hakluyts* (London: Hakluyt Society, 1935), 211–326.
—— *Divers Voyages touching the discoverie of America, and the islands adjacent* (1582).
—— *The Principall Navigations, Voyages, Traffiques & Discoveries of the English Nation: Made by Sea or Over-land to the Remote and Farthest Distant Quarters of*

the Earth at any time within the compasse of these 1600 Yeeres, 3rd edn., rev. and expanded (1600).

HAKLUYT, RICHARD, *The Principall Navigations of the English Nation*, 12 vols. (Glasgow: MacLehose, 1903).

—— *Voyages and Discoveries*, ed. Jack Beeching (Harmondsworth: Penguin, 1972).

HARRIOT, THOMAS, *A Briefe and True Report of the New Found Land of Virginia. Directed to the adventurers, fauourers, and welwillers for the planting there* (1588).

—— *A briefe and true report [rep. with additions]* (1590).

—— *A Brief and True Report of the New Found Land of Virginia (1590)*, introduced by Paul Hulton (New York: Dover, 1972).

JOBSON, RICHARD, *The Discovery of River Gambia by Richard Jobson, 1623*, ed. David P. Gamble and P. E. H. Hair (London: Hakluyt Society, 1999).

LAS CASAS, BARTOLOMÉ DE, *A Short Account of the Destruction of the Indies*, trans. Nigel Griffin (Harmondsworth: Penguin, 1992).

LEO, JOHN (AFRICANUS), *A geographical historie of Africa, written in Arabicke and Italian. Tr. And [with additions] collected by J. Pory* (1600).

—— *The History and Description of Africa*, trans. John Pory, ed. Robert Brown, 3 vols. (London: Hakluyt Society, 1896).

LITHGOW, WILLIAM, *A most delectable, and true discourse, of an admired and painefull peregrination in Europe, Asia and Affricke* (1614).

—— *The Pilgrimes farewell, to his native countrey of Scotland* (1618).

—— *The Totall Discourse of The Rare Adventures & Painfull Peregrinations of long Nineteene Yeares Travayles from Scotland to the most famous Kingdomes in Europe, Asia and Affrica* (1632).

—— *Totall Discourse* (Glasgow: MacLehose, 1906).

MANDEVILLE, Sir JOHN, *The Travels of Sir John Mandeville*, ed. C. W. R. D. Moseley (Harmondsworth: Penguin, 1983).

MIDDLETON, Sir HENRY, *The Voyage of Sir Henry Middleton to the Moluccas, 1604–1606*, ed. Sir William Foster (London: Hakluyt Society, 1943).

MONTAIGNE, MICHEL DE, *The Essayes or morall, politique and militarie discourses. Done into English by (J. Florio)* (1603).

—— *The Essayes*, trans. John Florio (1603) (London: Everyman, 1910).

MORE, THOMAS, *Utopia*, ed. Edward Surtz and J. H. Hexter (New Haven: Yale University Press, 1965).

MORYSON, FYNES, *An Itinerary Containing His Ten Yeeres Travell through the Twelve Dominions of Germany, Bohmerland, Sweitzerland, Netherland, Denmarke, Poland, Italy, Turky, France, England, Scotland & Ireland* (1617).

—— *An Itinerary*, 4 vols. (Glasgow: MacLehose, 1907).

—— *Shakespeare's Europe: Unpublished Chapters of Fynes Moryson's Itinerary. Being a Survey of the Condition of Europe at the end of the 16th Century*, ed. Charles Hughes (London: Sherratt and Hughes, 1903).

—— *The Irish Sections of Fynes Moryson's Unpublished* Itinerary, ed. Graham Kew (Dublin: Irish Manuscripts Commission, 1998).

MUNDY, PETER, *The Travels of Peter Mundy, in Europe and Asia, 1608–1667*, ed. Richard Carnac Temple, 2 vols. (London: Hakluyt Society, 1907).

PALMER, THOMAS, *An essay of the meanes how to make our travailes more profitable* (1606).

PARR, ANTHONY (ed.), *Three Renaissance Travel Plays* (Manchester: Manchester University Press, 1995).

POLO, MARCO, *The Travels*, trans. Ronald Latham (Harmondsworth: Penguin, 1958).

PURCHAS, SAMUEL, *Hakluytus Posthumus or Purchas His Pilgrimes Contayning a History of the World in Sea Voyages and Lande Travells by Englishmen and others* (1625).

—— *Hakluytus Posthumus or Purchas His Pilgrimes*, 20 vols. (Glasgow: Mac-Lehose, 1905–7).

QUINN, DAVID BEERS (ed.), *The Voyages and Colonising Enterprises of Sir Humphrey Gilbert* (London: Hakluyt Society, 1940).

—— *The Roanoke Voyages, 1584–1590: Documents to illustrate the English voyages to north America under the patent granted to Walter Raleigh in 1584*, 2 vols. (London: Hakluyt Society, 1955).

RALEIGH, Sir WALTER, *The Discoverie of the Large, Rich and Bewtiful Empire of Guiana. Performed in the yeere 1595. By Sir W. Ralegh* (1596).

—— *The Discoverie of the Large, Rich and Bewtiful Empyre of Guiana*, ed. Neil L. Whitehead (Manchester: Manchester University Press, 1997).

SANDYS, GEORGE, *A Relation of a Journey Begun An: Dom: 1610. Foure Bookes Contayning a description of the Turkish Empire, of Aegypt [etc.]* (1615).

SHAKESPEARE, WILLIAM, *The Tempest*, ed. Virginia Mason Vaughan and Alden T. Vaughan (Walton-on-Thames: Nelson, 1999).

SMITH, JOHN, *The Complete Works of Captain John Smith (1580–1631)*, ed. Philip L. Barbour, 3 vols. (Chapel Hill: University of North Carolina Press, 1986).

SOMERSET, Sir CHARLES, *The Travel Diary (1611–1612) of an English Catholic, Sir Charles Somerset*, ed. Michael Brennan (Leeds: Leeds Philosophical and Literary Society, 1993).

STRACHEY, WILLIAM, *The Historie of Travell into Virginia Britania (1612), By William Strachey, gent.*, ed. Louis B. Wright and Virginia Freund (London: Hakluyt Society, 1953).

THOMAS, WILLIAM, *Historie of Italie* (1549).

VITKUS, DANIEL J. (ed.), *Three Turk Plays from Early Modern England* (New York: Columbia University Press, 2000).

WOTTON, Sir HENRY, *Letters and Dispatches from Sir Henry Wotton to James the First and his Ministers, in the years MDCXVII–XX* (London: William Nicols, 1850).

SECONDARY SOURCES

ANDREWS, K. R., *Elizabethan Privateering during the Spanish War, 1585–1603* (Cambridge: Cambridge University Press, 1964).

—— *Trade, Plunder and Settlement: Maritime Enterprise and the Genesis of the British Empire, 1480–1630* (Cambridge: Cambridge University Press, 1984).

—— CANNY, NICHOLAS, and HAIR, P. E. H. (eds.), *The Westward Enterprise: English Activities in Ireland, the Atlantic and America, 1480–1650* (Liverpool, 1978).

AXTELL, JAMES, *After Columbus: Essays in the Ethnohistory of Colonial North America* (New York: Oxford University Press, 1988).

BRAUDEL, FERNAND, *Civilisation and Capitalism, 15ᵗʰ to 18ᵗʰ Century*, iii: *The Perspective of the World*, trans. Sian Reynolds (London: Collins, 1984).

BUCHER, BERNADETTE, *Icon and Conquest: A Structural Analysis of the Illustrations of the New Found Land of Virginia*, trans. Basia Miller Gulati (Chicago: Chicago University Press, 1981).

CALDER, ANGUS, *Revolutionary Empire: The Rise of the English-Speaking Empires from the Fifteenth Century to the 1780s* (London: Cape, 1981).

CANNY, NICHOLAS P., 'The Ideology of English Colonisation: From Ireland to America', *WMQ* 30 (1973), 575–98.

CHANEY, EDWARD, *The Evolution of the Grand Tour: Anglo-Italian Cultural Relations since the Renaissance* (London: Frank Cass, 1998).

CHIAPPELLI, FREDI, *First Images of America: The Impact of the New World on the Old*, 2 vols. (Berkeley: University of California Press, 1976).

D'AMICO, JACK, *The Moor in English Renaissance Drama* (Tampa: University of South Florida Press, 1991).

DAVIS, RICHARD BEALE, *George Sandys, Poet-Adventurer: A Study in Anglo-American Culture in the Seventeenth Century* (London: Bodley Head, 1955).

EDWARDS, PHILIP, *Sea-Mark: The Metaphorical Voyage, Spenser to Milton* (Liverpool: Liverpool University Press, 1997).

FULLER, MARY, *Voyages in Print: English Travel to America, 1576–1624* (Cambridge: Cambridge University Press, 1995).

GILLIES, JOHN, *Shakespeare and the Geography of Difference* (Cambridge: Cambridge University Press, 1994).

GRAHAM, GERALD S., *A Concise History of the British Empire* (London: Thames and Hudson, 1970).

GREENBLATT, STEPHEN, 'Invisible Bullets', in *Shakespearean Negotiations: The Circulation of Social Energy in Renaissance England* (Oxford: Clarendon Press, 1988), 21–65.

—— *Marvelous Possessions: The Wonder of the New World* (Oxford: Clarendon Press, 1991).

—— (ed.), *New World Encounters* (Berkeley: University of California Press, 1993).

GWYN, DAVID, 'Richard Eden: Cosmographer and Alchemist', *Sixteenth- Century Journal*, 15 (1984), 13–34.

HADFIELD, ANDREW, 'Writing the New World: More "Invisible Bullets"', *Literature and History*, 2: 2, 2nd ser. (1991), 3–19.

—— 'Travel Literature', in *ABES*, ch. 4, 'Renaissance and Seventeenth Century' (1994–   ).

—— *Literature, Travel, and Colonial Writing in the English Renaissance, 1545–1625* (Oxford: Clarendon Press, 1998).

HALL, KIM F., *Things of Darkness: Economies of Race and Gender in Early Modern England* (Ithaca: Cornell University Press, 1995).

HELFERS, JAMES P., 'The Explorer or the Pilgrim? Modern Critical Opinion and the Editorial Methods of Richard Hakluyt and Samuel Purchas', *SP* 94 (1997), 160–86.

HELGERSON, RICHARD, *Forms of Nationhood: The Elizabethan Writing of England* (Chicago: Chicago University Press, 1992), ch. 4.

HENDRICKS, MARGO, and PARKER, PATRICIA (eds.), *Women, 'Race', and Writing in the Early Modern Period* (London: Routledge, 1994).

HOGDEN, MARGARET T., *Early Anthropology in the Sixteenth and Seventeenth Centuries* (Philadelphia: University of Pennsylvania Press, 1971).

HÖLTGEN, KARL JOSEPH, 'Sir Robert Dallington (1561–1637): Author, Traveller and Pioneer of Taste', *HLQ* 47 (1984), 147–77.

HOWARD, CLAIRE, *English Travellers of the Renaissance* (London: John Lane, 1914).

HULME, PETER, 'Hurricanes in the Caribbes: The Constitutions of the Discourse of English Colonialism', in Francis Barker *et al.* (eds.), *1642: Literature and Power in the Seventeenth Century* (Colchester; University of Essex, 1981), 55–83.

—— *Colonial Encounters: Europe and the Native Caribbean, 1492–1797* (London: Methuen, 1986).

HULTON, PAUL (ed.), *America 1585: The Complete Drawings of John White* (London: British Museum, 1984).

HUNTER, G. K., '*Othello* and Colour Prejudice', in *Dramatic Identities and Cultural Tradition* (Liverpool: Liverpool University Press, 1978), 31–59.

ISLAM, SYED MANZURUL, *The Ethics of Travel: From Marco Polo to Kafka* (Manchester: Manchester University Press, 1996).

JARDINE, LISA, *Worldly Goods: A New History of the Renaissance* (Basingstoke: Macmillan, 1996).

JONES, ELDRED, *Othello's Countrymen: Africans in English Renaissance Drama* (Oxford: Oxford University Press, 1965).

KIDD, COLIN, *British Identities Before Nationalism: Ethnicity and Nationhood in the Atlantic World, 1600–1800* (Cambridge: Cambridge University Press, 1999).

KNAPP, JEFFREY, *An Empire Nowhere: England, America, and Literature from Utopia to* The Tempest (Berkeley: University of California Press, 1992).

KUPPERMAN, KAREN ORDHAL, *Settling with the Indians: The Meeting of English and Indian Cultures in America, 1580–1640* (New Jersey: Rowman and Allanheld, 1980).

—— *Roanoke: The Abandoned Colony* (Savage, Md.: Rowman and Littlefield, 1984).

LIM, WALTER S. H., *The Arts of Empire: The Poetics of Colonisation from Ralegh to Milton* (Newark: University of Delaware Press, 1998).

LINTON, JOAN PONG, *The Romance of the New World: Gender and the Literary Formation of English Colonialism* (Cambridge: Cambridge University Press, 1998).

LOOMBA, ANIA, *Gender, Race, Renaissance Drama* (Manchester: Manchester University Press, 1989).

McLEOD, BRUCE, *The Geography of Empire in English Literature, 1580–1745* (Cambridge: Cambridge University Press, 1999).

McPHERSON, DAVID, *Shakespeare, Jonson and the Myth of Venice* (Newark: University of Delaware Press, 1990).

MALTBY, WILLIAM, *The Black Legend in England: The Development of Anti-Spanish Sentiment* (Durham, NC: Duke University Press, 1971).

MAQUERLOT, JEAN-PIERRE, and WILLEMS, MICHÈLE (eds.), *Travel and Drama in Shakespeare's Time* (Cambridge: Cambridge University Press, 1996).

MARCHITELLO, HOWARD, 'Recent Studies in Tudor and Early Stuart Travel Writing', *ELR* 29 (1999), 326–47.

MARRAPODI, MICHELE, HOENSELAARS, A. J., CAPPUZZO, MARCELLO, and SANTUCCI, L. FALZON (eds.), *Shakespeare's Italy: Functions of Italian Locations in Renaissance Drama* (Manchester: Manchester University Press, rev. edn., 1997).

MATAR, NABIL, *Islam in Britain, 1558–1685* (Cambridge: Cambridge University Press, 1998).

—— *Turks, Moors and Englishmen in the Age of Discovery* (New York: Columbia University Press, 1999).

MONTROSE, LOUIS A., 'The Work of Gender in the Discourse of Discovery', *Representations*, 33 (1991), 1–41.

MORISON, SAMUEL ELIOT, *The European Discovery of America*, 2 vols. (New York: Oxford University Press, 1971–4).

OHLER, NORBERT, *The Medieval Traveller*, trans. Caroline Hillier (Woodbridge: The Boydell Press, 1989).

PAGDEN, ANTHONY, *The Fall of Natural Man: The American Indian and the Origins of Comparative Ethnology* (Cambridge: Cambridge University Press, 1982).

——— *European Encounters with the New World* (New Haven: Yale University Press, 1993).

PARKER, JOHN, *Books to Build an Empire: A Bibliographical History of English Overseas Interests to 1620* (Amsterdam: New Israel, 1965).

PARKER, KENNETH, 'Telling Tales: Early Modern English Voyages and the Cape of Good Hope', *SCen* 10 (1995), 121–49.

PENROSE, BOIES, *Travel and Discovery in the Renaissance, 1420–1620* (Cambridge, Mass.: Harvard University Press, 1952).

PORTER, H. C., *The Inconstant Savage: England and the North American Indian, 1500–1660* (London: Duckworth, 1979).

QUINN, ALISON, and QUINN, DAVID BEERS (eds.), *The Hakluyt Handbook*, 2 vols. (London: Hakluyt Society, 1974).

QUINN, DAVID BEERS, *Raleigh and the British Empire* (London: Hodder and Stoughton, 1947).

——— *England and the Discovery of America, 1481–1620* (London: Allen and Unwin, 1974).

——— (ed.), *The Roanoke Voyages, 1584–1590: Documents to illustrate the English Voyages to north America under the patent granted to Walter Raleigh in 1584*, 2 vols. (London: Hakluyt Society, 1955).

RAAB, FELIX, *The English Face of Machiavelli: A Changing Interpretation, 1500–1700* (London: Routledge, 1964).

READ, DAVID, 'Colonialism and Coherence: The Case of Captain John Smith's *Generall Historie of Virginia*', *MP* 91 (1994), 428–48.

RENNIE, NEIL, *Far-Fetched Facts: The Literature of Travel and the Idea of the South Seas* (Oxford: Clarendon Press, 1995).

ROWSE, A. L., *The Expansion of Elizabethan England* (Basingstoke: Macmillan, 1955).

SCANLAN, THOMAS, *Colonial Writing and the New World, 1583–1671* (Cambridge: Cambridge University Press, 1999).

SELLS, A. LYTTON, *The Paradise of Travellers: The Italian Influence on Englishmen in the Seventeenth Century* (London: George Allen and Unwin, 1964).

SHAPIRO, JAMES, *Shakespeare and the Jews* (New York: Columbia University Press, 1996).

SHEEHAN, BERNARD W., *Savagism and Civility: Indians and Englishmen in Colonial Virginia* (Cambridge: Cambridge University Press, 1980).

SHIRLEY, JOHN (ed.), *Thomas Harriot: Renaissance Scientist* (Oxford: Clarendon Press, 1974).

STOYE, JOHN, *English Travellers Abroad, 1604–1667: Their Influence in English Society and Politics* (New Haven: Yale University Press, 1989, rev. edn.).

STRACHAN, MICHAEL, *The Life and Adventures of Thomas Coryate* (London: Oxford University Press, 1962).

TAYLOR, E. G. R., *Tudor Geography, 1485–1583* (London: Routledge, 1930).

TAYLOR, E. G. R., *Late Tudor and Early Stuart Geography, 1583–1650* (London: Routledge, 1934).

TILTON, ROBERT S., *Pocahontas: The Evolution of an American Narrative* (Cambridge: Cambridge University Press, 1994).

TODOROV, TZVETAN, *The Conquest of America: The Question of Difference* (New York: Harper/Collins, 1984).

VAUGHAN, ALDEN T., and VAUGHAN, VIRGINIA MASON, *Shakespeare's Caliban: A Cultural History* (Cambridge: Cambridge University Press, 1991).

VAUGHAN, VIRGINIA MASON, *Othello: A Contextual History* (Cambridge: Cambridge University Press, 1994).

WRIGHT, LOUIS B., *Middle-Class Culture in Elizabethan England* (Chapel Hill: North Carolina University Press, 1935).

INDEX

Important references, and extracts by the writer concerned, are given in **bold**.